CAMBRIDGE STUDIES IN
ANGLO-SAXON ENGLAND
I

ANGLO-SAXON CRUCIFIXION
ICONOGRAPHY
AND THE ART OF THE MONASTIC REVIVAL

CAMBRIDGE STUDIES IN ANGLO-SAXON ENGLAND

EDITORS

SIMON KEYNES

MICHAEL LAPIDGE

Editors' preface

Cambridge Studies in Anglo-Saxon England is a series of scholarly texts and monographs intended to advance our knowledge of all aspects of the field of Anglo-Saxon studies. The scope of the series, like that of *Anglo-Saxon England*, its periodical counterpart, embraces original scholarship in various disciplines: literary, historical, archaeological, philological, art-historical, palaeographical, architectural, liturgical and numismatic. It is the intention of the editors to encourage the publication of original scholarship which advances our understanding of the field through interdisciplinary approaches.

Volumes published:

ANGLO-SAXON CRUCIFIXION ICONOGRAPHY

AND THE ART OF THE MONASTIC REVIVAL

BARBARA C. RAW

Reader in English
University of Keele

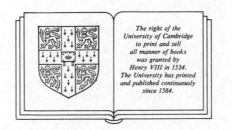

The right of the
University of Cambridge
to print and sell
all manner of books
was granted by
Henry VIII in 1534.
The University has printed
and published continuously
since 1584.

CAMBRIDGE UNIVERSITY PRESS

CAMBRIDGE

NEW YORK   PORT CHESTER

MELBOURNE   SYDNEY

Published by the Press Syndicate of the University of Cambridge
The Pitt Building, Trumpington Street, Cambridge CB2 1RP
40 West 20th Street, New York, NY 10011, USA
10 Stamford Road, Oakleigh, Melbourne 3166, Australia

First published 1990
Printed in Great Britain at
the University Press, Cambridge

British Library cataloguing in publication data
Raw, Barbara C.
Anglo-Saxon crucifixion iconography and the art of the
monastic revival – (Cambridge studies in Anglo-Saxon England; v. 1)
1. Religious visual arts. Anglo-Saxon
1. Title
704.9'48'0942

Library of Congress cataloguing in publication data
Raw, Barbara Catherine.
Anglo-Saxon crucifixion iconography and the art of the
monastic revival/Barbara C. Raw.
p.   cm. – (Cambridge studies in Anglo-Saxon England; v. 1)
Bibliography.
Includes index.
ISBN 0 521 36370 5
1. Jesus Christ – Crucifixion – Art. 2. Art, Anglo-Saxon.
I. Title. II. Series.
N6763.R38 1990
704.9'4853'0942–dc20   89–1044   CIP

ISBN 0 521 36370 5

Contents

Plates

List of plates

Acknowledgements

I am grateful to the University of Newcastle upon Tyne for the award of a Sir James Knott Fellowship, which enabled me to begin the research for this book, to the University of Keele for a research award, which gave me the freedom from teaching necessary to complete it and to the British Academy for a grant towards the expenses of preparing the work for the press.

My more personal thanks are due to Reginald Dodwell of the University of Manchester, James McLaverty of the University of Keele and Andrew Wawn of the University of Leeds who have read parts or the whole of the book in typescript and have helped me with their comments, and to Martin Biddle, Birthe Kjølbye-Biddle, Peter Clemoes, Betty Coatsworth, Malcolm Godden, Carolyn Heighway, Shirley Lloyd, Ruth Murphy, Jennifer O'Reilly, Warwick Rodwell, Richard Wallace and Andrew Watson for help and information of various kinds. Specific debts are noted in the footnotes. My final debt is to Michael Lapidge, one of the general editors of this series, for his help in preparing the manuscript for the press.

The following individuals and institutions have kindly given permission to publish photographs of manuscripts and ivories in their possession: the Biblioteca Apostolica Vaticana, Vatican City (pl. XIIa); the Bibliothèque Municipale, Rouen (pls. vb and XV); the Bibliothèque Nationale, Paris (pl. I); the British Library, London (pls. VIII, IX, XIII and XIV); the Syndics of Cambridge University Library, Cambridge (pl. X); the Master and Fellows of Corpus Christi College, Cambridge (pls. va, XI and XIIb); M. Hubert Descamps and Harvey Miller (publishers of John Beckwith, *Ivory Carvings in Early Medieval England*) (pl. IIIa); the Syndics of the Fitzwilliam Museum, Cambridge (pl. IIIb); the Musée de Cluny, Paris (pl. VII, Cliché des Musées Nationaux); the Musée Sandelin, Saint-Omer (pl. VI, phot. Giraudon); the Nationalmuseet, Copenhagen (pl. IVa); the Pierpont Morgan Library, New York (pls. II and XVI); the Board of Trustees of the Victoria and Albert Museum, London (pl. IVb).

Abbreviations and note on the text

AB	*Analecta Bollandiana*
Ags. Prosa	Bibliothek der angelsächsischen Prosa
AntJ	Antiquaries Journal
Archiv	*Archiv für das Studium der neueren Sprachen und Literaturen*
ArchJ	*Archaeological Journal*
ASC	Anglo-Saxon Chronicle
ASE	*Anglo-Saxon England*
ASPR	The Anglo-Saxon Poetic Records, ed. G. P. Krapp and E. V. K. Dobbie, 6 vols. (New York, 1931–42)
BAR	British Archaeological Reports, British Series (Oxford)
Bibl. Mun.	Bibliothèque Municipale
BL	British Library
BN	Bibliothèque Nationale
CBA	Council for British Archaeology
CCCC	Corpus Christi College, Cambridge
CCCMed	Corpus Christianorum, Continuatio Mediaevalis (Turnhout)
CCM	Corpus Consuetudinum Monasticarum
CCSL	Corpus Christianorum, Series Latina (Turnhout)
CDH	Anselm, *Cur Deus homo*
CH	Ælfric, *Catholic Homilies*
CSEL	Corpus Scriptorum Ecclesiasticorum Latinorum (Vienna)
CUL	Cambridge University Library
DACL	*Dictionnaire d'archéologie chrétienne et de liturgie*
DTR	Bede, *De temporum ratione*
EEMF	Early English Manuscripts in Facsimile (Copenhagen)
EETS	Early English Text Society (London)
	es extra series

os	original series	
ss	supplementary series	
EHR	*English Historical Review*	
EL	*Ephemerides liturgicae*	
ES	English Studies	
HBS	Henry Bradshaw Society Publications (London)	
HE	Bede's *Historia ecclesiastica gentis Anglorum*	
JBAA	*Journal of the British Archaeological Association*	
JWCI	*Journal of the Warburg and Courtauld Institutes*	
L-B	O. Lehmann-Brockhaus, *Lateinische Schriftquellen zur Kunst in England, Wales und Schottland vom Jahre 901 bis zum Jahre 1307*, 5 vols. (Munich, 1955–60)	
LC	*Libri Carolini sive Caroli Magni Capitulare de Imaginibus*, ed. H. Bastgen, MGH, Concilia II, Suppl.	
LS	Ælfric, *Lives of Saints*	
MÆ	*Medium Ævum*	
MGH	Monumenta Germaniae Historica	
	Auct. antiq.	Auctores antiquissimi
	Concilia	Legum Sectio III: Concilia
	Epist.	Epistolae in quarto
	PLAC	Poetae Latini aevi Carolini
	Script. fol.	Scriptores in folio
	Script. Germ.	Scriptores rerum Germanicarum in usum scholarum
MLR	*Modern Language Review*	
N&Q	*Notes and Queries*	
PBA	*Proceedings of the British Academy*	
PG	Patrologia Graeca, ed. J. P. Migne	
PL	Patrologia Latina, ed. J. P. Migne	
RB	*Revue bénédictine*	
RES	*Review of English Studies*	
RS	Rolls Series (London)	

Note on the text

Full details of churches, carvings and manuscripts, together with references to associated bibliographical material, are given in the Catalogue at
the end of the book (pp. 188–252); this information is not normally
repeated in the footnotes to the main text.

Biblical quotations are taken from the Jerusalem Bible unless otherwise
stated, but psalm numbers are taken from the Vulgate. The punctuation of
quotations in Latin and Old English has been modernized.

Introduction

This book is concerned with the different ways in which Christ's death on
the cross was portrayed in the art, literature and theology of tenth- and
eleventh-century England. The main focus of the book is the drawings,
paintings and carvings of the Crucifixion produced in England during the
tenth and eleventh centuries, but these works are considered in relation to
the period at which they were produced, to the society of that period and to
their function within that society rather than as part of an independent
artistic development with a life of its own.

Very little has been published on Anglo-Saxon Crucifixion pictures, and
most of what has been published has been of a strictly art-historical kind.
The large-scale surveys of Crucifixion iconography by Reil,[1] Thoby[2] and
Schiller[3] concentrated on identifying the iconographies favoured in
different regions in the early Christian period and on tracing the development of these iconographies in Carolingian, Ottonian and Byzantine art;
their emphasis was on historical development rather than on the art of any
single period and they paid little attention to Anglo-Saxon England.
The gap left by these works has been filled in part by Elizabeth
Coatsworth's recent survey of stone carvings of the Crucifixion produced in
southern England during the late Anglo-Saxon period[4] and by the detailed
studies of the Bury Psalter and the Arenberg Gospels by Mark Harris[5] and

---

[1] Reil, *Die frühchristlichen Darstellungen der Kreuzigung Christi* and *Christus am Kreuz in der
Bildkunst der Karolingerzeit*.
[2] Thoby, *Le crucifix des origines au Concile de Trente*.
[3] Schiller, *Iconography of Christian Art* II.
[4] Coatsworth, 'Late Pre-Conquest Sculptures with the Crucifixion South of the Humber'.
[5] Harris, 'The Marginal Drawings of the Bury St Edmunds Psalter'.

Jane Rosenthal.[6] We still lack any discussion of Anglo-Saxon Crucifixion iconography as a whole, however. Moreover, research on Anglo-Saxon art is frequently limited to the study of artistic sources and ignores the fact that works of art reflect the interests and preoccupations of the period in which they were produced. In the same way, scholars studying the literature of tenth- and eleventh-century England tend to concentrate on literary sources and to neglect the artistic remains of the period, which could contribute to our understanding of the literature. One or two writers have ranged more widely. Reginald Dodwell's book, *Anglo-Saxon Art: A New Perspective*, draws on the documents of the period to give a vivid picture of the wealth of carvings, paintings and embroideries which once existed in this country, and Robert Deshman and Jennifer O'Reilly have linked artistic and textual material in their studies of the imperialization of biblical imagery in late Anglo-Saxon art and of the theological and liturgical background to pictures of the cross as the tree of life.[7] This work now needs to be extended to include the relationship of works of art to the culture of the late Anglo-Saxon period as a whole.

The representations of the Crucifixion created during the period of the Anglo-Saxon monastic revival are presented in this book as part of a network of relationships between art, literature, theology and liturgy rather than as part of an evolutionary process. Consideration of sources and analogues in earlier works of art, therefore, plays a smaller part than it has done in previous work on Crucifixion iconography. The process of tracing the form of a picture back to its source tells one little about the meaning of the picture in the society which created it. Even when a picture is copied mechanically from a model its meaning is not the same because its context is different: it may, for example, be used to illustrate a different text or be associated with a different cycle of scenes. When details of a scene are modified the situation is more complicated. In tenth- and eleventh-century English art the main type of Crucifixion picture is one in which Mary and John are shown standing beneath the arms of the cross, but this basic scene is given a variety of meanings by varying the position or gestures of the three main figures or by the addition of details such as angels above the cross or a chalice at its foot. No detailed parallels can be found between these scenes and Carolingian, Ottonian or Byzantine representations of the

---

[6] Rosenthal, 'The Historiated Canon Tables of the Arenberg Gospels'.

[7] Deshman, '*Christus rex et magi reges*'; O'Reilly, 'The Rough-Hewn Cross in Anglo-Saxon Art'.

Crucifixion in which the main figures are limited to Christ, Mary and John and it is clear that tenth- and eleventh-century English Crucifixion pictures were not closely dependent on earlier, non-English models even though some of their details belong to a well-established repertoire of motifs. The meaning of these scenes, and the reasons for the new combinations of motifs – some of which have no known artistic parallels – must be looked for outside the art.

The emphasis, then, is on representations of the Crucifixion in relation to context. Meaning, in the sense of something existing within people's minds, is excluded since in most cases it is impossible to recover the intention of the artist or patron of a work of art or the response of someone looking at it. What can be studied is the relationship between manuscript pictures, the texts in which they are found and their position within those texts, or the relationship between carvings, church design and liturgical practices. On a broader scale, works of art can be related to the redemption theology and devotional practices of tenth- and eleventh-century England. It is not suggested that all the interpretations discussed would have been available to any one person; they do, however, indicate the range of options open to those who saw the various works of art. Finally, an attempt is made to draw some conclusions as to what people living in the late Anglo-Saxon period thought art was for. It is sometimes assumed that the main function of art in the medieval period was the instruction of the illiterate. Study of Anglo-Saxon Crucifixion pictures suggests, on the contrary, that the major function of much religious art was to provide a focus for meditation and that, far from explaining Christian belief in simple terms, it reflected many of the most subtle and precocious ideas of the time.

I

The nature and purpose of Anglo-Saxon church art

The meaning of the drawings, paintings and carvings produced in tenth- and eleventh-century England is closely bound up with their function in relation to their context, whether the immediate physical context or the wider social one. Traditionally the function of medieval art has been seen as one of instruction, the key text being a passage in a letter from Pope Gregory the Great to Serenus, bishop of Marseilles. Gregory says: 'Aliud est enim picturam adorare, aliud picturae historia, quid sit adorandum, addiscere. Nam quod legentibus scriptura, hoc idiotis praestat pictura cernentibus, quia in ipsa ignorantes vident, quod sequi debeant, in ipsa legunt qui litteras nesciunt; unde praecipue gentibus pro lectione pictura est.'[1] The passage suggests that Gregory had in mind a translation of biblical narrative into pictorial form. Much early Christian art was not of this kind, however, and the same is true of late Anglo-Saxon religious art.

The earliest Christian pictures were signs: figures like the Good Shepherd which were used to evoke ideas in a metaphorical way instead of representing people or events directly. When historical events were represented they were selected and arranged in order to illustrate non-historical themes. The catacomb paintings of Jonah and Daniel, for instance, are subordinated to the theme of God's deliverance of those who trust in him; they are not examples of story-telling in pictures. During the fourth and fifth centuries two new categories of Christian art developed, both based ultimately on late Greco-Roman art. On the one hand were

---

[1] MGH, Epist. 2.2, 270: 'It is one thing to adore a picture, another to learn from narrative pictures what should be adored. For what scripture is to those who can read, a picture offers to the illiterate who look at it, for in it the ignorant see what should be imitated and those who do not understand writing read from it. For this reason painting is above all a substitute for reading to the ordinary people.'

cycles of narrative scenes and on the other portraits. Unlike the narrative scenes, which merely recorded events, the portraits, like the imperial portraits from which some of them developed, were substitutes for the persons they represented. Instead of simply reminding the viewer of the existence of Christ or one of his saints they acted, like relics, as sources of divine power. It was these power-invested images against which the Byzantine church reacted in 727, and when the veneration of images was restored by the Council of Nicaea in 787 approval was restricted to two-dimensional images, which were presumably thought less likely to lead to idolatry.[2] One of the texts quoted in support of the reinstatement of images at this council came from a letter written by St Nilus in 451. Like the later letter from Pope Gregory to Serenus (quoted above), it suggests an emphasis on narrative painting:

It is fitting that the nave should on all sides be filled with stories from the Old and New Testaments, represented by the hand of a skilled painter, in order that the unlettered and those who cannot read the divine Scriptures may know in this manner the high deeds of the servants of God and may be prompted to imitate them.[3]

The instruction envisaged by St Nilus and Pope Gregory was of a moral kind: pictures of historical events were to offer an example which could be imitated, in accordance with the orthodox belief that faith should result in action. Carolingian writers, on the other hand, assigned a much more limited role to religious art. They responded to the reinstatement of images by the eastern church with the production of an official statement on the role of art in the church, the *Libri Carolini*. The authors of this work, who were reacting to what they saw as the excesses of the eastern church, accepted that painting could be useful for the instruction of the illiterate, but they omitted any reference to imitation in the passages they quoted from Gregory's letter.[4] For them, the function of painting was to call to mind historical events.[5] The rather grudging acceptance they gave to painting was constantly accompanied by references to the inadequacy of art in comparison with the written word. They pointed out that God gave man

---

[2] Kitzinger, 'Christian Imagery', pp. 147–58.

[3] Salaville, *Eastern Liturgies*, p. 116.

[4] *LC* II.xxiii (ed. Bastgen, p. 82). The question of date and authorship is discussed in Freeman, 'Theodulf of Orleans', 'Further Studies' and 'Carolingian Orthodoxy'.

[5] *Ibid.* II.xiii (p. 73), III.xvi (p. 138) and xxiii (p. 150).

the scriptures, not paintings, for his instruction,[6] that paintings could not be considered as a means of demonstrating the truth of what was written since much of scripture could not be pictured,[7] and that even the subject of a picture was often unclear without an explanatory inscription.[8] This last statement gives a new twist to the comparison between poetry and painting found in the *Rhetorica ad Herennium* of the first century BC: 'Poema loquens pictura, pictura tacitum poema.'[9] For the authors of the *Libri Carolini* the inscription was necessary so that the silent picture could speak.[10] One consequence of this view of the relative importance of art and writing was that the use of paintings for teaching purposes was seen as a temporary expedient, suitable only for beginners in the faith.[11] Pictures were intended to lead the mind from things seen to things unseen, not to recall the mind from the invisible to the visible.[12] If they were an aid to the memory this was the result of man's weakness,[13] for if Christ were present in man's heart, as he should be, there would be no need to recall him.[14]

It is clear from this reference to Christ's presence in man and from several other passages in the *Libri Carolini* that the authors were contrasting the Byzantine cult of images, which involved the recollection of God or of a saint through the medium of a painting, with the teaching of the church on God's creation of man in his own image.[15] It was generally held that the divine imprint on man resided in the three faculties of the soul: the memory, the understanding and the will. The importance of this idea lay in the belief that man possessed an image of God within himself which enabled him to remember, know and love his creator. This image, which had been damaged by Adam's rebellion, had been restored when Christ, the true image of God, became man.[16] Echoes of this teaching are found

---

[6] *Ibid.* II.xxx (pp. 92–100).   [7] *Ibid.* III.xxiii (p. 153).

[8] *Ibid.* IV.xvi and xxi (pp. 204 and 213).

[9] *Rhetorica ad Herennium* IV.xxviii.39 (ed. Caplan, p. 326): 'A poem is a speaking picture, a picture a silent poem.'

[10] *LC* IV.xvi (ed. Bastgen, p. 204).   [11] *Ibid.* II.xiii (p. 73).

[12] *Ibid.* II.xiii (p. 73).

[13] *Ibid.* II.xxii (p. 81).   [14] *Ibid.* IV.ii (p. 176).

[15] Set out in Augustine, *De Trinitate*; for an outline of Augustine's teaching, see Gilson, *Introduction*, pp. 138–40 and *Christian Philosophy*, pp. 219–24.

[16] Augustine, *De Trinitate* X.xii.19, XI.ii.6–iii, XII.iv.4, XIV.viii.11, XIV.xii.15, XIV.xvi.22–xviii.24 and XV.xx.39–xxi.40 (ed. Mountain I, 332, 339–41 and 358; and II, 435–8, 442–3, 451–6 and 516–18).

in the emphasis of the *Libri Carolini* on Christ as the true image of God,[17] on the presence of Christ in man's heart[18] and on the eucharist as the true memorial of Christ's Passion.[19] In contrast to the direct contact with God which took place in the eucharist, painting was thought to be concerned solely with the recording of historical events. It was an aid to memory but had no role in the other two activities of the soul: the understanding and the will.

The view of art set out in the *Libri Carolini* led to the production of extensive cycles of narrative paintings in Carolingian churches, a trend which continued into the Ottonian period. The royal church at Ingelheim, begun by Charlemagne in about 777 and completed by Louis the Pious in the early ninth century, was decorated with scenes from the Old and New Testaments[20] and the ninth-century church at St Gallen contained narrative paintings of scenes from the gospels.[21] These paintings have disappeared but examples of eighth-, ninth- and tenth-century illustrations of events from the New Testament survive at Saint-Germain of Auxerre, Santa Maria foris Portas at Castelseprio, Sankt Johann at Müstair and Sankt Georg at Oberzell on the island of Reichenau.[22] The decoration of these churches was not confined to narrative painting, however. The east wall of the church of San Benedetto at Malles was painted with standing figures of Christ, SS Stephen and Gregory and what are probably the two founders of the church.[23] The paintings on the walls of the nave at Oberzell include figures of apostles and portraits of the abbots of Reichenau as well as the main narrative scenes. The crypt at Oberzell contains fragments of a Crucifixion painting of a devotional rather than a historical type. Moreover, the narrative paintings often involved interpretation of the gospel story as well as simple record. The paintings at Ingelheim were arranged in parallel to show how Old Testament prophecy was fulfilled in the gospels. The scenes at Oberzell, which were drawn entirely from the miracles, offered proofs of Christ's

---

[17] *LC* II.xv and xvi (ed. Bastgen, p. 75).   [18] *Ibid.* IV.ii (p. 176).

[19] *Ibid.* II.xxvii (pp. 88–9).

[20] Ermoldus Nigellus, *In honorem Hludowici* IV, 179–284 (MGH, PLAC 2, 63–6; trans. Godman, *Poetry*, pp. 250–5).

[21] Schlosser, *Schriftquellen*, pp. 326–32.

[22] See Dodwell, *Painting*, pp. 15–23; Hubert *et al.*, *Carolingian Art*, pp. 5–11 and 15–28; Martin, *Reichenau-Oberzell*.

[23] Hubert *et al.*, *Carolingian Art*, pp. 21–3.

divine power rather than an account of his earthly life. In practice, therefore, Carolingian and Ottonian wall-painting went beyond the narrow limits laid down in the *Libri Carolini*.

Carolingian and Ottonian manuscript art, which was intended for a more educated public than was wall-painting, shows greater freedom in its choice of subjects. Many manuscripts contain pictures whose meaning is theological rather than historical, for instance the frontispieces to the gospels and the Apocalypse in the ninth-century bibles from Tours,[24] the Crucifixion picture in the Uta Gospels or the frontispieces to the Gospels of Bernward of Hildesheim. Yet the interest in narrative painting remains. The Pauline Epistles and many of the Old Testament books in the Tours bibles were prefaced by elaborate sequences of narrative pictures, often identified by inscriptions as wall-paintings were. Several Ottonian gospel-books were illustrated throughout with narrative pictures placed within the text.[25] In the Codex Egberti the figures were usually labelled with their names; in other manuscripts such as the Golden Gospels of Henry III or the Pericopes of Henry III the pictures themselves were identified by inscriptions. The same interest in narrative art can be seen in ivory carving and work in precious metals. Scenes from the life of Christ surround the central image of Christ on the front of the Golden Altar of Milan and representations of the donor, Angilbert II (824–59), and the artist, Wolvinius, are accompanied by scenes from the life of St Ambrose on the back. Ivory bookcovers such as that on Douce 176 in the Bodleian Library or gold covers such as that on the Codex Aureus of St Emmeram were decorated with narrative scenes as well as with images of Christ.

In England the balance between narrative and non-narrative art was quite different. Much of the public art of church buildings was designed to make men aware of their role as citizens of heaven rather than to teach them about Christ's earthly life. The decoration of churches had to make clear to those who entered them that they were in the house of God, a place which could rival the most wealthy of secular halls. If gold was fitting on a man's sword, as one of the gnomic poets claimed, it was equally so on the ornaments of the church.[26] Even Æthelwold, who reproved Edith of Wilton for her gold-embroidered garments – and received a tart reminder that she could be as holy as he in his ragged skins – filled his church at

---

[24] Gaehde, 'Turonian Sources', pp. 381–6 and 392–4; Kessler, *Illustrated Bibles*, pp. 36–58 and 69–83.

[25] See below, pp. 72–3.   [26] *Maxims I* 125 (ASPR III, 161).

Abingdon with spectacular works in precious metals: a golden wheel with lamps and bells, a retable of gold and silver, three large crosses, two bells, silver candlesticks and a massive chalice.[27] At Winchester he broke up the ornaments and silver vessels of the cathedral and gave the proceeds to the poor because, as he said, 'se equanimiter ferre non posse muta metalla integra perdurare, hominem vero ad imaginem Dei creatum et precioso Christi sanguine redemptum mendicitate et inedia perire'.[28] Yet it was during his time at Winchester that the scriptorium there produced some of the most sumptuous liturgical books of the late Anglo-Saxon period; at least one of these books was written and decorated on his orders and for his personal use.[29] Wilfrid's church at Ripon possessed altar hangings of purple and gold, a gold cross and a gospel-book written in gold letters on purple vellum and enclosed in a jewelled gold case.[30] Æthelwulf's poem, *De abbatibus*, written in the early ninth century, describes a church belonging to a cell of Lindisfarne which was filled with lamps and hanging bowls, decorated with metal panels depicting Christ's miracles, its books and altars covered in gold.[31] King Athelstan's gifts to the shrine of St Cuthbert (in *c*. 934) included gold and silver altar vessels, a gold and ivory cross and two gospel-books covered in gold and silver, as well as vestments and hangings.[32] Leofric, abbot of Peterborough from 1052 to 1066 and nephew of Earl Leofric of Mercia, gave his church of Peterborough so many treasures of gold and silver that its name was changed from Burh to Gildeneburh, the Golden City.[33]

The justification for this display lay in the parallel which was drawn

---

[27] William of Malmesbury, *Gesta pontificum* II.87 (ed. Hamilton, p. 189): 'quocirca puto quod tam incorrupta mens potest esse sub istis auratis vestibus quam sub tuis discissis pellibus'; L-B 13 (citing *De abbatibus Abbendoniae*) and 14 (citing *Chronicon monasterii de Abingdon*). For an account of Æthelwold's gifts to Peterborough see Way, 'Gifts of Æthelwold' and Robertson, *Anglo-Saxon Charters*, p. 72.

[28] Wulfstan, *Vita S. Æthelwoldi*, ch. 29 (ed. Winterbottom, p .50): 'He could not calmly endure that voiceless metal should remain intact while man, created in the image of God and redeemed with the precious blood of Christ, died of poverty and starvation.'

[29] London, BL, Add. 49598 (the Benedictional of St Æthelwold).

[30] Eddius, *Life of Bishop Wilfrid*, ch. xvii, (ed. Colgrave, pp. 34–7); Bede, *HE* v.19 (ed. Colgrave and Mynors, pp. 528–31).

[31] *De abbatibus* 625–45 (ed. Campbell, p. 51).   [32] Battiscombe, *Relics*, p. 33.

[33] ASC E, 1052; L-B 3454 (citing *The Chronicle of Hugh Candidus*); for a detailed account of the evidence of the documents see Dodwell, *Anglo-Saxon Art*.

between the earthly and heavenly churches. Anglo-Saxon sermon-writers emphasized the spiritual nature of the parallel: the people of God were the living stones from which the church would be built.[34] The liturgy, on the other hand, stressed the physical resemblance. The lesson for the mass of dedication of a church implies that the building being dedicated resembles in some way the jewelled city of St John's vision in the Apocalypse (XXI.2): 'I saw the holy city, and the new Jerusalem, coming down from God out of heaven, as beautiful as a bride all dressed for her husband.'[35] The psalms and antiphons for the dedication ceremony are chosen from those in praise of the earthly and heavenly cities of Jerusalem.[36] The earliest examples of these parallels between the earthly and heavenly churches date from the fourth century when Eusebius described the buildings erected by Constantine round Christ's tomb as the new Jerusalem.[37] Of course Constantine's buildings replaced the buildings of the Jewish city of Jerusalem and were therefore literally the new Jerusalem. For Eusebius, however, they had a further significance. They symbolized the heavenly Jerusalem of the Apocalypse (XXI.3 and 22), the true tabernacle and temple of God. At about the same time an artist in Rome chose to portray Christ in glory by showing him seated among his disciples in front of the Constantinian buildings of Jerusalem and Bethlehem.[38] Just as the Christian churches of Jerusalem were understood as symbols of the heavenly Jerusalem, so too were the Ark of the Covenant and Solomon's temple, which had been replaced by these churches. The parallels were well-known to English writers. Wilfrid building his church at Ripon was compared to Moses fashioning the Ark of the Covenant; Bede justified the use of paintings and carvings in churches through a comparison with Solomon's temple; Alcuin nicknamed Einhard, poet, artist and biographer of Charlemagne, Bezaleel

---

[34] Ælfric, *CH* II.xl (ed. Godden, pp. 337–8); *Homilies of Wulfstan*, no. xviii (ed. Bethurum, p. 248).

[35] See *Benedictional of Archbishop Robert*, ed. Wilson, pp. 97–8.

[36] *Fundamenta eius* (Ps. LXXXVI), *Lauda Hierusalem* (Ps. CXLVII), *Lapides pretiosi* (*Benedictional of Archbishop Robert*, ed. Wilson, pp. 76, 78, 81, 85, 86 and 87); see also the prayers at the entry to the church, in *The Missal of Robert of Jumièges*, ed. Wilson, pp. 279–80; on the parallel between churches and the heavenly Jerusalem see Heitz, 'Iconography'.

[37] Eusebius, *Vita Constantini* III.xxxiii (PL 8, 58).

[38] E. D. Hunt, *Holy Land Pilgrimage*, pp. 17–18; the mosaic is in the church of Santa Pudenziana and is reproduced in Grabar, *Byzantium*, pl. 145.

after the biblical craftsman who made the Ark of the Covenant.[39] Further support for the beautifying of churches was found in a verse from Psalm xxv: 'Domine, dilexi decorem domus tuae.'[40] The passage is quoted by the twelfth-century author of the treatise *De diversis artibus* who compares the role of the artists and craftsmen of the church to that of David who left gold, silver and other metals to his son for the building of the temple.[41] It is a phrase which recurs. Æthelwold is said to have enriched the church at Abingdon because he remembered this verse;[42] Byrhtnoth, abbot of Ely, 'dilexit autem gloriam ac decorem domus Dei, quam diversis ornamentis insignire appetebat';[43] Emma and Ælfwine vied with each other to ornament the church of St Swithun at Winchester, 'sed ille superatus est; quia vel illa plus potuit, vel plus dilexit decorem domus Dei'.[44]

Much of the decoration in Anglo-Saxon churches was related to this role of the church as a symbol of the heavenly city. The first requirement was magnificence, achieved through friezes and panels carved with geometric or foliage designs and through the use of costly hangings. Athelstan's gifts to St Cuthbert included seven palls, three curtains and three tapestries, while Bishop Leofric's bequest to Exeter in 1072 included two wall-hangings as well as seat-covers and other textiles.[45] Æthelric's gifts to Crowland (984–92) included a large number of palls for hanging on the walls next to the altars on feast days: many were of silk, some woven with golden birds, some patterned, others plain.[46] Sigeric, who in 990 became archbishop of Canterbury, sent Glastonbury, his former home, seven palls decorated with white lions which entirely covered the walls of the old church on its anniversary.[47] When details are given of these hangings they invariably turn out to be purely ornamental. If religious equivalents existed to the Bayeux Tapestry or to the tapestry given by Byrhtnoth's widow to Ely

[39] Eddius, *Life of Bishop Wilfrid*, ch. xvii (ed. Colgrave, pp. 34–5); Bede, *De templo* II (ed. Hurst, pp. 212–13); Meyvaert, 'Wearmouth-Jarrow', p. 69; Hubert *et al.*, *Carolingian Art*, p. 81.

[40] Ps. xxv.8.   [41] Theophilus, *De diversis artibus* (ed. Dodwell, pp. 61–2).

[42] L-B 14 (citing *Chronicon monasterii de Abingdon*).

[43] *Liber Eliensis* II.6 (ed. Blake, p. 79): 'He loved the glory and beauty of God's house which he sought to beautify with various ornaments.'

[44] L-B 4706 (citing *Annales monasterii de Wintonia*): 'But he was defeated, either because she was able to do more or because she loved the house of God more.'

[45] Battiscombe, *Relics*, p. 33; *Exeter Book*, pp. 22–3.

[46] L-B 1159 (citing *Historia Croylandensis auctore Ingulfo*).

[47] *De antiquitate Glastoniensis ecclesie*, ch. 67 (ed. Scott, p. 136).

and embroidered with scenes from her husband's life no Anglo-Saxon writer seems to have thought the fact worth recording.[48]

Figural decoration did, of course, exist in Anglo-Saxon churches but, like non-figural art, it was usually related to the conception of the church as a place where man shared in the worship of heaven rather than a place of instruction about the past. This link between art and worship applies equally to the many manuscript portraits of Christ, Mary, the saints and angels intended simply for contemplation and to the pictures or sequences of pictures which recall ideas or events. The one example of a work of art from the Anglo-Saxon period which offers a coherent programme of instruction in the historical and theological aspects of Christian belief – the eighth-century Ruthwell Cross – did not form part of the decoration of a church.[49] There are no parallels to the series of biblical scenes on the Ruthwell Cross in the architectural sculpture of the Anglo-Saxon period and very few parallels in painting and metal-work. Much late Anglo-Saxon art was iconic rather than narrative: the Virgin and Child or Christ in Majesty rather than the Adoration of the Magi or Christ entering Jerusalem. Even when artists chose to depict events rather than persons they often represented them in a theological rather than a historical way or selected and arranged them to illustrate non-narrative themes. When biblical scenes do occur in churches they are often single items like the Crucifixion groups placed over doorways and arches.

The best evidence for the existence of cycles of biblical paintings in Anglo-Saxon churches comes from Wearmouth and Jarrow. Benedict Biscop, the founder of the two monasteries, brought a large collection of panel-paintings from Rome to decorate the walls of his churches. The subjects are listed by Bede in his *Historia abbatum*.[50] The nave of St Peter's, Wearmouth, was decorated on one side with scenes from gospel history and on the other with scenes from the Apocalypse; further pictures of Christ's life decorated the walls of the church of St Mary. At St Paul's, Jarrow, there were pictures of scenes from the Old and New Testaments, arranged in pairs to show the fulfilment of the prophecies about Christ. Bede's discussion of painting in his work on Solomon's temple shows that he saw it as a way of offering a living reading of Christ's life to those who could not

[48] *Liber Eliensis* II.63 (ed. Blake, p. 136).

[49] The scenes on the Ruthwell Cross are described by Saxl, 'Ruthwell Cross' and discussed by Henderson, 'John the Baptist Panel' and Ó Carragáin, 'Ruthwell Crucifixion Poem'.

[50] *Historia abbatum*, chs. vi and ix (ed. Plummer, pp. 369–70 and 373).

read: 'et eis quoque qui litteras ignorant quasi vivam dominicae historiae pandere lectionem'.[51] He saw a further justification for painting, however. Whereas the authors of the *Libri Carolini* contrasted painting with verbal communication, Bede seems to have seen them in the same way, relating painting not only to the work of memory but also to that of the understanding and the will. He praised Cædmon's poems because they stirred the listener to prefer heavenly things to earthly ones, to abandon sin and love virtue; in the same way he claimed that the Wearmouth paintings moved those who saw them to compunction, gratitude and repentance.[52] Bede also saw an important role for the portrait image. Benedict Biscop's gifts to the church at Wearmouth included paintings of Mary and the apostles which were placed across the centre of the church, possibly in the manner of an iconostasis. Bede's comment that these paintings ensured that all who entered the church could see all round them the loving faces of Christ and his saints, even if only in an image,[53] shows a clear understanding of the way in which paintings displayed in a church could remind men that they worshipped in the presence of the saints, a conception of church decoration more akin to that of the Byzantine church than to that of the Carolingians and Ottonians.

It is sometimes assumed that most Anglo-Saxon churches were decorated with cycles of pictures similar to those in Biscop's churches, particularly in view of the widespread use of wall-painting on the Continent in the tenth and eleventh centuries. The evidence for such paintings is very slight. Remains of Saxon wall-painting have been discovered on the chancel-arch of the church at Nether Wallop; when complete the painting must have been similar to the upper part of the frontispiece to Edgar's charter for the New Minster and have shown Christ enthroned among angels.[54] The position of this painting shows that it is

---

51 *De templo* II (ed. Hurst, p. 213): 'And also to set before those who were ignorant of letters, as it were, a living reading of divine history'; see also Bede, *Homeliae evangelii* I.13 on Benedict Biscop (ed. Hurst, p. 93), also quoted by Gougaud, 'Muta praedicatio', p. 168.

52 *HE* IV.24 (ed. Colgrave and Mynors, pp. 418–19); *De templo* II (ed. Hurst, pp. 212–13); *Historia abbatum*, ch. vi (ed. Plummer, pp. 369–70).

53 *Historia abbatum*, ch. vi (ed. Plummer, pp. 369–70).

54 Gem and Tudor-Craig, 'Nether Wallop'. It is not known whether the other walls of the church were decorated. However, at the church of St Oswald, Gloucester, excavation has shown that whereas the dividing wall between nave and chancel was decorated, the side walls of the nave were plain (Carolyn Heighway, personal communication).

unlikely to have formed part of a series of pictures. The subject, too, is not one which belongs to a sequence setting out the story of Christ's life, and the function of the picture is not educational. The high altar of Anglo-Saxon churches was traditionally associated with Christ's resurrection and was frequently decorated with an image of Christ in Majesty.[55] In addition, the east end of the church was often linked with Christ's ascension into heaven.[56] The painting at Nether Wallop was a way of giving these associations visual form, of reminding people that they were in the presence of the risen and glorified Christ.

Stronger evidence for the existence of paintings of gospel scenes in the late Anglo-Saxon period comes from a fragment of painted stone recovered in 1966 from the foundations of the New Minster at Winchester and dating from the ninth century.[57] The painting is usually identified as part of a scene of the heavenly choirs, similar to those in the Athelstan Psalter, but the gesture of the figure to the right of the picture, who points with one finger to his head, suggests that it is more probably from a representation of the washing of the feet, similar to that in the mid-eleventh-century Tiberius Psalter. The painting could have formed part of a series of scenes from the life of Christ but there is no incontestable evidence on the point and it could equally well have come from a single scene. It is unlikely to have come from the pre-tenth-century church, which is described in the record of its acquisition by Edward as 'windciric' and was therefore probably of wattle not of stone.[58] The monastic buildings, on the other hand, were of stone.[59] The washing of the feet, or *mandatum*, would have been an appropriate decoration for a monastic refectory since Christ's act of humility took place as he and his disciples were sitting at table. The many references in the *Regularis concordia* to the need to imitate Christ's action suggest that the painting was designed to offer a constant reminder of the humility required of the monk rather than a simple recollection of an event in Christ's life.[60]

---

[55] See below, pp. 46 and 48.   [56] See below, p. 185.

[57] *Golden Age*, p. 44 (no. 25).

[58] *Liber vitae*, ed. Birch, pp. 155–6, n. 9.

[59] Quirk, 'Winchester New Minster', pp. 51–2; the buildings included both a dormitory, which was certainly of stone, and a refectory; the document is listed Finberg, *Early Charters of Wessex*, p. 34, no. 33 and ptd *Liber vitae*, ed. Birch, pp. 155–6, n. 9.

[60] *Regularis concordia*, ed. Symons, pp. 22, 39, 40, 48 and 61–3; cf. the prayer said at the *mandatum*, *The Missal of Robert of Jumièges*, ed. Wilson, p. 275. Schapiro has pointed out that the drawing of the washing of the feet in the Tiberius Psalter represents the event

A teaching role of the kind envisaged by the *Libri Carolini* is equally unlikely for the wall-paintings which existed at the Old Minster in the late Anglo-Saxon period. The numerous fragments of painted plaster recovered during excavation of the Old Minster show that the decoration included representations of human figures, but the fragments are too small to show whether the paintings consisted of portraits or scenes. Wulfstan of Winchester does not mention wall-paintings in his description of the rebuilt church and Ælfric says only that the nave was filled with the stools and crutches of cripples who had been healed.[61] It seems unlikely that Ælfric, who was educated at the Old Minster and who had a keen interest in education, would have failed to mention the paintings had they had any educational function. He was aware of some of the effects produced by painters for he comments in one place on the contrast produced by placing a dark figure next to a pale one[62] but his main reference to painting, drawn from St Augustine's commentary on St John's Gospel, contrasts it unfavourably with writing. He says: 'On oðre wisan we sceawiað metinge, and on oðre wisan stafas. Ne gæð na mare to metinge buton þæt þu hit geseo and herige: nis na genoh þæt þu stafas sceawige, buton ðu hi eac ræde, and þæt andgit understande.'[63] There is no recognition here of the fact that pictures, too, can be read and their meaning understood.

The only reliable evidence for the decoration of a late Anglo-Saxon church with paintings of scenes from the gospels comes from Wilton. Goscelin describes how Edith built a chapel in the shape of a cross and had it painted with scenes from the Passion.[64] The work was done shortly before 984 by a German painter, Benno of Trier. Benno must have been familiar with manuscripts such as the Codex Egberti, which was made for Egbert, archbishop of Trier, between 978 and 993, and it is possible, therefore, that the paintings he produced for Wilton resembled the narrative scenes which illustrate the gospel text in this book. However,

according to contemporary monastic practice, 'Disappearing Christ', p. 150; see also below, p. 60.

[61] Ælfric, *LS*, no. xxi (ed. Skeat I, 468–9).

[62] Ælfric, *CH* I.xxiii (ed. Thorpe, p. 334).

[63] Ælfric, *CH* I.xii (*ibid.*, p. 186): 'We look in one way at painting and in another at letters. No more is necessary in the case of painting than that you see it and praise it; it is not enough that you look at letters without also reading them and understanding the meaning'; cf. Augustine, *In Iohannis evangelium tractatus cxxiv*, xxiv.2 (ed. Mayer, p. 245).

[64] *De Sancta Editha* I.vii.20, in Wilmart, 'La légende de Ste Edith', pp. 86–7.

Goscelin's remark that the pictures showed the Passion story as Edith had pictured it in her heart suggests that they were devotional rather than historical in emphasis.[65] Meditation on Christ's Passion was not primarily a matter of recalling past events. Gregory the Great saw such meditation as a way of entering the next world: 'Vir itaque qui apparuit in porta stetit atque ita locutus est, quia Mediator Dei et hominum Christus Iesus in ipso quoque passionis suae tempore praecepta vitae discipulis dedit, ut hi qui in eum credunt ad portam semper aspiciant, et passionem eius sollicita consideratione pensantes, a suo quoque exitu cordis oculos non avertant.'[66] For Gregory, the significance of Christ's Passion was that it was a point of transition from the seen to the unseen.[67] By contemplating Christ's death man, too, could pass through the door to the unseen world where Christ had preceded him.

The passage from Gregory suggests that the Wilton paintings may have been intended, like the painting at Nether Wallop, to focus the mind on the present rather than on the past, to make people aware of Christ as a living reality rather than as an actor in past events. The same emphasis on the church as a place where man could enter into communion with the citizens of heaven is seen in the statues and portrait images of the Anglo-Saxon period. The antiphon sung during the translation of the relics at the dedication of a church speaks of the church as the home of the saints: 'Ingredere, benedicte Domine: preparata est habitatio sedis tue.'[68] This view of the nature of the church is reflected in many of the carvings of the Anglo-Saxon period. The rows of figures under the arcading on the Hedda Stone from Peterborough and on the friezes from Breedon and Fletton were not intended to teach; instead they made present the persons they represented. They reminded the viewer that he was constantly surrounded by the saints and angels: that he worshipped in the presence of the church in heaven as well as of the church on earth. Many of the statues mentioned

---

[65] See also below, p. 60.

[66] *In Hiezechihelem prophetam* II.i.16 (ed. Adriaen, p. 221): 'Therefore the man who appeared stood in the door and spoke thus because the mediator between God and man, Jesus Christ, gave the commands of life to his disciples at the time of his Passion so that those who believe in him should always look towards the door, and meditating about his passion with careful thought should not turn the eyes of their hearts away from his death'; see also Leclercq *et al.*, *Spirituality* II, 16.

[67] Cf. above, p. 6.

[68] *The Benedictional of Archbishop Robert*, ed. Wilson, p. 96: 'Enter, O blessed Lord: the dwelling-place of your home is prepared.'

in records were of this kind: the Virgin and Child seated on a huge throne above the altar in one of the side-chapels at Ely, and the apostles who decorated Æthelwold's retable at Abingdon and Harold's altar at Waltham.[69] Like the panel-paintings of Mary and the apostles which spanned the central area of Benedict Biscop's church at Wearmouth, these statues ensured that those who entered the church would see all around them the faces of Christ and his saints, even if only in an image.[70]

The idea behind these images goes back to the early church. In early Christian art the portrait played an important part in the decoration of burial chambers, where it evoked the presence of the dead person. When Christian art moved out of the catacombs the practice developed of decorating churches with portraits of the saints whose relics were enshrined there.[71] These portraits had a similar purpose to that of the earlier funerary portraits: they made visible the saints who, as it were, lived on in the relics. During the eighth century the popes transferred many relics from the catacombs to churches above ground, filling the churches with frescoes, mosaics and statues of the saints, apparently in protest against the iconoclasm of the Byzantine church. In the early ninth century Pope Paschal I built the church of Sta Prassede to house relics from the catacombs and decorated the apse with a mosaic showing Praxedes and her sister Pudentiana being presented to Christ by SS Peter and Paul; other saints whose remains were buried in the church were depicted on the sanctuary arch.[72] Similar developments can be traced in English churches at the time of the monastic revival. At Glastonbury paintings of some of the Anglo-Saxon abbots seem to have been placed above their tombs[73] and at Ely Byrhtnoth (*ob. c.* 996), the first abbot after the refoundation, placed four jewelled images of the virgins of Ely round the high altar near which they were buried.[74] Like the mosaics in the apses of certain Roman churches

---

[69] *Liber Eliensis* II.60 (ed. Blake, p. 132), L-B 13 (citing *De abbatibus Abbendoniae*) and 4473 (citing *De inventione sanctae crucis Walthamensis*).

[70] See above, p. 13.   [71] See Kitzinger, 'Christian Imagery', p. 150.

[72] Mâle, *Early Churches*, pp. 76–97, esp. 87–91.

[73] Dodwell, *Anglo-Saxon Art*, p. 93.

[74] *Liber Eliensis* II.6 (ed. Blake, p. 79). Quirk, 'Winchester Cathedral', p. 54, suggests that the Ely saints may have been buried in a west-work. This cannot be correct, since they were buried near the high altar and this is unlikely to have been placed within a western tower. St Æthelthryth's tomb was placed to the south of the high altar and remained there until the translation of the relics into the new church in 1106 (*Liber Eliensis* II.52 and 146, ed. Blake, pp. 120 and 231); Sexburg was buried to the north of

these statues made visible the saints who rested there. They did more than this, however. Some statues, like the relics they personified, brought with them miraculous powers as did the statue of St Swithun which Ælfwold, bishop of Sherborne from 1045 to 1058, acquired from Winchester.[75] Others, like the crucifix at Waltham, sometimes behaved as though they were alive.[76] The stories of crucifixes which were believed to have spoken, trembled, bled, lost their crowns or intervened in human affairs in various ways, show that statues were believed to have supernatural powers quite independent of any association with relics. They acted as channels of divine power, linking this world with the next. Devotion to the saints, like the bond between lord and retainer, worked in two ways. Just as the retainer promised loyalty and received protection in return, so churches and altars were dedicated to God and his saints with a firm expectation of benefits in return. These dedications were often given visual expression. At Ely a golden statue of the Virgin and Child reminded people of the dedication of one of the side-chapels to Mary;[77] a carved figure of the Virgin and Child in the church at Deerhurst showed that the church was under the protection of the mother of God. The most elaborate example of such a reminder was the series of six carvings placed by Æthelgar on the outside of the tower at the New Minster, Winchester, between 980 and 988. The carvings represented the dedication of the ground floor of the tower to Æthelgar's special patron, the Virgin Mary, and of the upper floors to the Holy Trinity, the cross, all saints, St Michael and the heavenly powers, and finally the four evangelists.[78]

The protective function of such carvings can be inferred from their use on tombs and shrines as well as on buildings. The outside of the apse at Deerhurst carries a carving of an angel. The apse was originally seven-sided and it is likely, therefore, that it was decorated with a series of seven

the same altar (I.35 and II.146 (pp. 51 and 231)); Eormenhild was buried near Sexburg (I.36 (p. 52)); her body seems to have remained there until 1106 (II.145 (p. 231)), though in the following chapter her remains are said to have been moved four years earlier (II.146 (p. 231)). The body of Wihtburg was moved from Dereham to Ely by Byrhtnoth (II.53 (p. 123)); the exact position of her tomb is not stated, though it may have been near that of Eormenhild (II.146 (p. 231)).

75 L-B 4215 (citing Goscelin, *Vita S. Swithuni*).

76 L-B 4478–80 (citing *Vita Haroldi regis* and *De inventione sanctae crucis Walthamensis*).

77 *Liber Eliensis* II.60 (ed. Blake, p. 132).

78 *Liber vitae*, ed. Birch, p. 10; Quirk, 'Winchester New Minster', pp. 21–2, 33–5 and 38–9.

angels, recalling the seven angels carved on the coffin of St Cuthbert. The decoration of this coffin with carvings of Christ in Majesty, Mary with the Christ Child, apostles and angels, is thought to illustrate the litany of intercession offered for the saint at his burial,[79] but it was probably also a way of protecting the body of the saint until the time of the general resurrection. The sarcophagus of Bernward of Hildesheim, which was carved with figures of nine angels together with a cross and the *Agnus Dei*, expresses a similar belief.[80] The church in which Bernward was buried was dedicated to Michael and his angels and the carving on the tomb clearly alludes to this dedication. Michael was traditionally thought to conduct the souls of the righteous to heaven and the prayer for the dying, *Subvenite sancti Dei*, calls on the saints and angels to meet the soul of the dead person and to present it to God.[81] The passage from the Book of Job (XIX.25–7) carved on the Bernward sarcophagus reminds the reader that eternal life includes the body as well as the soul and suggests that the protection invoked by the carved angels was intended to extend to the body in the tomb.

In contrast to the images which surrounded the bodies of Cuthbert and Bernward, some tombs and shrines were decorated with biblical and religious scenes. These, too, were linked to belief in a bodily resurrection, but whereas the carved angels on the Cuthbert and Bernward Coffins protected the body directly, these scenes asserted man's faith in the power of Christ to raise man from the dead. The eighth-century Wirksworth Slab, which has as its central motif representations of Christ's ascension into heaven and the Apocalyptic Lamb, includes a carving of the burial of the Virgin. This scene, with St John carrying the palm branch in front of the bier and a group of angels in a cloud above, reminded the viewer that man could share in Christ's victory over death. The shrine made by Edgar for St Swithun was decorated with representations of the Crucifixion, Resurrection and Ascension, the central events of salvation history; the shrine made by Cnut for Edith added reminders of the Holy Innocents and Jairus's daughter.[82] This last scene was considered appropriate to funerary art from early Christian times, partly because the words of Christ, 'Non est mortua puella sed dormit' (Matt. IX.24), were a reminder of the belief that death

---

[79] Battiscombe, *Relics*, p. 279. [80] Tschan, *Bernward* I, 205–9.

[81] *The Missal of Robert of Jumièges*, ed. Wilson, p. 297.

[82] Wulfstan of Winchester, *Narratio metrica de Sancto Swithuno* II.i (ed. Campbell, p. 141); *De Sancta Editha* II.xii.13, in Wilmart, 'La légende de Ste Edith', pp. 280–1.

was nothing but a sleep from which one would awake. Goscelin's *Vita S. Edithae* makes it clear that a parallel was drawn between Edith and Jairus's daughter when he describes the saint's mother as saying that her daughter was not dead but asleep.[83] The scene was of course particularly appropriate on the shrine of a female saint who had died at the age of twenty-three.

The biblical scenes on these shrines, like those in the catacombs and on early Christian sarcophagi, were subordinated to a theme: the individual Christian's hope of salvation. Other carvings, such as those on the New Minster tower, had a more general application. Richard Gem has suggested that the division of the tower into six storeys was related to Augustine's interpretation of the number six in relation to God's work of creation.[84] This is unlikely, however, for the diagram in Byrhtferth's *Enchiridion* which illustrates the Augustinian interpretation and which shows a tower-like structure divides the tower into four parts, not into six.[85] Moreover, although the author of the description of the tower in the *Liber vitae* was clearly aware of the importance of six as a perfect number there is no correspondence between the sixfold work of creation described by Augustine and the dedications of the six storeys of the tower. These dedications and the carvings which Quirk suggested illustrated them offered a statement about salvation, though of a more abstract kind than that of the carvings on the much earlier Ruthwell Cross, which set out a programme of instruction based on historical events. The difference in approach can be seen particularly clearly in the first carving on the tower, that of Mary and her virgins. The ground floor was appropriately dedicated to Mary because she was the source of Christ's human nature, the door by which he entered this world to redeem it; in the same way, the stucco of the Nativity at Saint-Riquier was placed in the entrance to the church.[86] On the Ruthwell Cross, Mary's role in the redemption was expressed through carvings of the Annunciation and the flight into Egypt, or possibly the return from Egypt;[87] on the tower, however, Mary was shown glorified in heaven, the supreme example of virginity rather than a human mother. This iconic approach was continued in the other carvings. The form taken by the carving of the cross is not known, but those of the Trinity, all saints,

---

[83] *De Sancta Editha* I.x.25, *ibid.*, p. 99.   [84] Gem, 'Iconography', pp. 16–18.

[85] Byrhtferth, *Manual*, ed. Crawford, p. 206.

[86] Cf. *Christ I* 301–25, Burlin, *Old English Advent*, pp. 147–9. The Saint-Riquier stuccoes are discussed by Taylor, 'Tenth-Century Church Building', p. 148 and fig. 12.

[87] See Henderson, 'Ruthwell Cross'.

St Michael and all angels and the four evangelists were certainly non-narrative representations; the symbolic nature of the last of these carvings is made clear in the description of the tower in the New Minster *Liber vitae* where the group of evangelists is linked to the account of the four rivers of paradise in the Book of Genesis (II.8–17) and to the allegory of the fountain of life.[88] Ælfric talks of the evangelists as the four streams which spring from one source[89] and in two Carolingian manuscripts – the Gospels of Saint-Médard of Soissons and the Codex Aureus of St Emmeram – one of the pictures over the canon tables shows a fountain surrounded by the symbols of the evangelists.[90] The order in which the New Minster carvings were placed was symbolic too. The carving of the Trinity, placed above that of Mary, showed Christ's divine origin; the carving of the cross recalled the redemption which came through his incarnation, made possible by the assent of a human mother. The carving of all saints portrayed those people redeemed by Christ who had already reached their home in heaven; that of St Michael and all angels reminded the viewer of the powerful forces who protected him. Finally, the figures of the four evangelists symbolized the spreading of the message of redemption throughout the world. The arrangement of the three lower carvings can be related to the arrangement of the altars in a number of continental churches which contained crypts below the high altar. In the church of St Michael at Hildesheim, where the crypt was an internal one, the high altar and the crypt altar were both visible from the nave of the church; the high altar was dedicated to the Saviour while that in the crypt was dedicated to Mary. At Halberstadt the crypt altar was again dedicated to Mary; the high altar had a double dedication to the Trinity and the cross. At Luxemburg the crypt altar was dedicated to Mary and her virgins; the high altar was dedicated to the Saviour, the cross and all saints.[91] Bandmann has argued persuasively that the arrangement of these altars was intended to show the link between the incarnation and the redemption.[92] Christ, who was God, humbled himself to be born of the Virgin Mary and was then restored to his divine glory by dying on the cross. It is possible, too, that there was an implied parallel between Christ's ascent from Mary's womb to the cross and

---

[88] Quirk, 'Winchester New Minster', pp. 38–9.

[89] 'Đas synd þa feower ean of anum wyllspringe, þe gað of Paradisum ofer Godes folc wide' (*Heptateuch*, ed. Crawford, pp. 53–4).

[90] See also below, pp. 70–1 and 126–7.

[91] Bandmann, 'Altaranordnung', pp. 400–2.   [92] *Ibid.*, p. 401.

his ascent from the tomb.[93] The main altar of early churches was often associated with Christ's tomb[94] and a passage in Ælfric's Palm Sunday homily shows that the parallel between Mary and the tomb was known in Anglo-Saxon England.[95] Bandmann's quotation from Migne's edition of Peter Damian's sermons[96] cannot be used as evidence because the sermon is by the twelfth-century writer, Nicholas of Clairvaux.[97] There may be some similar, earlier, text, however, for the content of the sermon has parallels with the New Minster carvings: in particular, both link Christ's ascent from Mary's womb to the cross with the image of the four rivers of paradise. Mary is both the altar and the garden from which the spring goes out to water the earth, while Christ is the spring which takes its origin from Mary and from God: 'Fluvius iste est Deus meus Iesus, qui a duobus locis voluptatis egreditur, ex utero patris, ex utero virginis.'[98] The image of Mary as the *hortus conclusus* was, of course, well-known and occurs in Paschasius Radbertus's commentary on St Matthew's Gospel.[99] Paschasius also links the outpouring of divine grace on Mary at the incarnation to the similar outpouring at Christ's death[100] and to the eucharist celebrated on the altar of the church.[101] Alcuin talks of Mary as the *fons vitae*[102] and in the Godescalc Gospels the picture of the Lateran Baptistry, the *fons vitae*, is placed opposite the gospel for the Vigil of the Nativity, so linking the fountain of life with Mary's life-giving womb.[103] A similar link is found in the pictures above the canon tables in the Gospels of Saint-Médard of Soissons where a picture of Emmanuel, God with us, appears opposite one of the fountain of life.[104]

---

93 *Ibid.*, p. 401, nn. 170 and 171.

94 See above, p. 14, and below, pp. 46–9 and 82.

95 Ælfric, *CH* II.xiv (ed. Godden, p. 149); see also *CH* I.xv (ed. Thorpe, p. 222).

96 Bandmann, 'Altaranordnung', p. 401, n. 170; PL 144, 557.

97 See Leclercq, 'Nicolas de Clairvaux', p. 276, no. 16.

98 *Sermo xi, De annunciatione* (PL 144, 558): 'This river is Jesus, my God, who went out from the two places of delight, from the womb of the Father and from the womb of the Virgin.'

99 Paschasius, *In Matheo* II.i.18 (ed. Paulus I, 120). 100 See below, p. 103.

101 See below, pp. 122 and 154.

102 Underwood, 'Fountain of Life', p. 49, MGH, PLAC 1, 314 (xc, no. ii). For a discussion of the motif of the fountain of life and the painting of the Virgin and Child in the Book of Kells see Henderson, *Durrow to Kells*, pp. 153–4.

103 Underwood, 'Fountain of Life', pp. 62–4.

104 *Ibid.*, pp. 68–70; Hrabanus, on the other hand, equates the fountain with God the

The decoration of Anglo-Saxon manuscripts follows the same principles as the more public arts of carving and wall-painting. Much of it was purely ornamental, designed like the costly hangings in Anglo-Saxon churches for splendid effect rather than for intellectual stimulation. Even in the late Anglo-Saxon period, when figural decoration had become common, some very sumptuous manuscripts like the Bosworth Psalter were decorated only with acanthus initials and borders. Contemporary comments show the value placed on ornament of this kind: the dedication poem in the Benedictional of Æthelwold (which contains one of the most extensive collections of figure paintings of the late Anglo-Saxon period) lays far greater stress on the ornamental frames than on the figure scenes. Many of the figure scenes in Anglo-Saxon manuscripts have a structural function rather than an illustrative one. Evangelist portraits act as markers for the divisions between the gospels and much of the decoration in psalters consists of pictures and initials used to mark the divisions of the psalms into three groups of fifty and their distribution between the days of the week in the divine Office. The eighth-century Vespasian Psalter distinguishes the psalms which begin the Office each day by large decorative initials, three of which contained scenes from the life of David.[105] The tenth-century Junius Psalter marks the threefold and eightfold divisions of the text with large initials, placing a picture of David killing the lion at Psalm CIX, while the eleventh-century Eadwig Psalter, which marks only the threefold division, has a painting of David and Goliath at Psalm CI. In other psalters pictures of Christ are used to mark the divisions of the text. In the Athelstan Psalter a painting of the Nativity was placed opposite Psalm I and a picture of the Ascension opposite Psalm CI; originally there may have been a picture of the Crucifixion at Psalm LI as there is in the Winchcombe Psalter (pl. X). Most of these pictures represent events, but many figure-scenes in manuscripts, like those in stone carving, were iconic. The paintings of the choirs of confessors, virgins and apostles which preface the Benedictional of Æthelwold or the saints and angels who gaze from the canon tables and decorative borders of some gospel-books, the

Father, *Commentarii in Genesim* I.xii (PL 107, 479): 'Fluvius de paradiso exiens, imaginem portat Christi de paterno fonte fluentis.'

[105] Pss. I, XXVI and LII; the initial to Ps. I is now missing but is thought to have contained a picture of Samuel anointing David: see Alexander, *Insular Manuscripts*, p. 55.

portraits of evangelists, of David playing the harp, of St Æthelthryth in the Benedictional of Æthelwold or of St Andrew in the Sacramentary of Robert of Jumièges were not intended as illustrations of the texts in which they occur. They convey no message. Instead they serve to unite the worshipper using these books with the worship of the saints in heaven.[106]

This awareness of the presence of the saints was sometimes given a more personal application. Edith made an alb for Wilton which was embroidered round the hem with golden figures of Christ and the apostles.[107] The theme is similar to that of the apostles on the Abingdon retable and the Waltham altar,[108] but there is one important difference. Edith included herself in the picture, in the guise of the penitent Mary Magdalen, embracing Christ's feet. Judith of Flanders, wife of Tostig of Northumbria, had herself painted in the same role embracing the foot of the crucifix (pl. xvi).[109] Dunstan drew himself kneeling at the feet of Christ, drawing inspiration from a painting of Hrabanus Maurus adoring the cross, and the deacon Ælfwine was shown standing at the feet of St Peter, the patron of his monastery.[110] These pictures allowed their owners to escape the constraints of time in two ways: first, they could share in events which had taken place centuries earlier and secondly they could remain praying at the feet of Christ or one of his saints through the medium of the picture even when they were unable to do so in fact. The pictures of Edith and Judith provide valuable evidence of the practice which became very common later in the Middle Ages of imagining oneself as actually present at and participating in events from the life of Christ. Further evidence of the desire to share in what is commemorated is found in the small portraits placed in the borders of some paintings. Usually the portraits are of saints and angels but occasionally they show unhaloed figures who seem to be present as witnesses to the main picture. Three paintings in the Sacramentary of Robert of Jumièges – those of the Crucifixion (pl. xv), the deposition and the adoration of the Lamb – include busts of two male figures in the

---

[106] BL, Add. 49598, 1r–4r and 90v; Cambridge, Trinity College B. 10. 4, 17v and 60r; BL, Royal 1. D. IX, 111r; BL, Harley 76, 8v and 10r; Cambridge, Pembroke College 301, 2v and 10v; Rouen, Bibl. Mun., Y. 6 [274], 164v.

[107] *De Sancta Editha* I.iv.16, in Wilmart, 'La légende de Ste Edith', p. 79.

[108] L-B 13 (citing *De abbatibus Abbendoniae*) and 4473 (citing *De inventione sanctae crucis Walthamensis*).

[109] See below, p. 160.

[110] Oxford, Bodleian Library, Auct. F. 4. 32, 1r (Dunstan); BL, Cotton Titus D. xxvi, 19v (Ælfwine).

borders, holding up their hands in admiration.[111] No such figures occur in the borders to the other pictures in the sacramentary and this suggests that the desire to share in the events of salvation may have centred on the Crucifixion and the communion of saints. Similar figures appear in the borders to a painting of Ecclesia in a historiated initial in the Bury Psalter,[112] a figure associated, like the adoration of the Lamb, with the doctrine of the communion of saints.

In contrast to the intimate, devotional quality of these pictures, the pictures of Edgar and Cnut with the saints of Winchester are public commemorative items, though they, too, have a devotional theme. The picture of Cnut forms the frontispiece to the *Liber vitae* of the New Minster; the names of the monastery's benefactors were read out at mass from this manuscript which was then placed on the altar.[113] The painting of Edgar forms the frontispiece to his charter for the New Minster;[114] it, too, was almost certainly displayed on the altar of the church. The inscription to the painting of Edgar echoes the role of humble adoration seen in the pictures of Edith, Dunstan and Judith:

> Sic celso residet solio qui condidit astra
> Rex venerans Eadgar pronus adorat eum.[115]

In the painting, however, Edgar, far from being prostrate before Christ, stands between the Virgin Mary and St Peter, apparently on equal terms. The text of the charter describes how Edgar, remembering the duty of kings as set out by Jeremiah (I.10: 'Look, today I am setting you over nations and over kingdoms, to tear up and to knock down, to destroy and to overthrow, to build and to plant'), and wishing to win salvation, had restored the monks to Winchester.[116] The charter continues by defining the terms of the refoundation. The king promised to support the monks; they in turn were to pray for him. The *Regularis concordia* emphasized the key role of the king as patron of the refounded monasteries and the painting at the beginning of the charter shows the king in this role, standing between SS Mary and Peter, the heavenly patrons of the monastery.[117]

[111] See below, p. 158.   [112] See below, pp. 89 and 152.

[113] *Liber vitae* (ed. Birch, p. 12).

[114] BL, Cotton Vespasian A. viii, 2v.

[115] *Liber vitae* (ed. Birch, p. 232): 'Thus he who formed the stars sits on his throne on high: King Edgar, prostrate, adores and venerates him.'

[116] *Liber vitae*, ed. Birch, pp. 233–46, esp. p. 237.

[117] On the king's role as mediator see John, *Orbis Britanniae*, p. 177.

In the drawing of Cnut and Ælfgifu presenting a cross to New Minster the position of the figures has been changed. At the top of the picture are Christ, Mary and Peter; at the bottom are the monks in their stalls. Filling the centre of the composition, and drawn on a larger scale than either saints or monks, are Cnut and Ælfgifu; above them two angels point with one hand to Christ and with the other grasp the crown and veil of the king and queen. The varying scale of the figures indicates the artist's view of the relative importance of the participants; the arrangement of the figures shows the king's role as mediator between the world of the monks and the heavenly court from which the royal power derives. The picture has a further meaning, however. As Edgar's charter said, those who gave to the monks and whose names were written in the book of life would have a place in heaven. The book of life was, of course, the book opened at the Judgement (Apoc. XX.12) and shown in the hands of an angel in the drawing of the Judgement on the two pages following the drawing of Cnut. Its earthly parallel was the monastic *Liber vitae*. Whereas in the painting of Edgar the king joins SS Mary and Peter as the patron of the monks, here Cnut is placed below Mary and Peter and relies on their intercession as he stands before Christ.[118]

Both these pictures record historical events, but they do not present them in a historical way. The abstract quality of the Edgar painting is particularly clear if it is compared with Carolingian paintings of royal occasions, for example the presentation picture at the beginning of the Vivian Bible. The painting of Edgar places the figures against a plain vellum background, producing a flat, diagrammatic composition; the painting of Charles the Bald on the other hand shows the king seated on his throne at the centre of a circle of guards, courtiers and ecclesiastics arranged to give an impression of depth and space. The drawing of Cnut shows the king placing his cross on the altar, but there is no depth to the picture and no coherent spatial relationship between the monks in their stalls and the altar. The change in style is even more apparent if the two English pictures are compared with a painting in the Codex Aureus of St Emmeram, which shows Charles seated on his throne and, on the opposite page, the saints in heaven worshipping the Lamb. Charles's participation in the heavenly scene is portrayed in a completely realistic way: he observes it, as if watching a vision, while he himself remains firmly on earth.

[118] See below, p. 63.

The pictures of Edgar and Cnut are related to the texts with which they occur but they are not textual illustrations, something which is true of much of the religious art which remains from tenth- and eleventh-century England. Straightforward textual illustrations of the kind found in Ottonian gospel-books are limited to a small number of manuscripts, mostly of a non-liturgical kind. The most extensive sets of textual illustrations occur in a small group of manuscripts of Prudentius's *Psychomachia*, a work which was illustrated at a very early date and of which many illustrated copies survive, and in two Old English versions of parts of the Old Testament.[119] The Prudentius manuscripts contain glosses to the text and in two of them the drawings are identified by inscriptions in Old English as well as in Latin, details which suggest that they were intended for readers who were not fluent in Latin.[120] The two Old Testament manuscripts contain vernacular texts and may have been intended for laymen. The pictures in these manuscripts, like those described by Pope Gregory the Great, could act as substitutes for the written text; their function was to convey information, particularly information of a narrative kind. Illustration of this kind is extremely rare in Anglo-Saxon liturgical books. Fragments remain of one fully illustrated gospel-lectionary[121] comparable to Ottonian gospel-books such as the Codex Egberti, but most tenth- and eleventh-century English gospels are illustrated with theological scenes, portrait images or small sequences of narrative scenes placed at the beginning of the text rather than being distributed throughout it.[122] This difference in artistic practice suggests that the gospel text was seen differently in England and in Germany. For the Ottonians the gospels provided a record of historical events; for the Anglo-Saxons they were a symbol of Christ, the *Logos* or Word of God.[123] The idea is similar to the Jewish belief that God was present in the Ark of the Covenant in the temple in Jerusalem and goes back at least to the Council of Ephesus (AD 431) when a copy of the gospels was solemnly enthroned to show that Christ was present, presiding over the council.[124] It seems likely that the practice of decorating the covers or opening pages of gospel-books with ornamental

---

[119] Oxford, Bodleian Library, Junius 11 and BL, Cotton Claudius B. iv.

[120] They may have been used as school texts: see Wieland, 'Glossed Manuscripts', p. 171.

[121] The Damme Fragments: see Catalogue below, p. 225.

[122] See below, pp. 83–5.

[123] See also below, p. 106.

[124] *DACL* 5, 673, s.v. 'Etimasie'; see also Beissel, *Entstehung der Perikopen*, pp. 3–4.

crosses, sometimes accompanied by symbols of the evangelists, or with representations of Christ in Majesty or Christ crucified, was intended to indicate this symbolic value of the text.[125]

In England the main sets of gospel illustrations are found in liturgical books and psalters rather than in gospel-books. The scenes chosen for illustration and the order in which they occur depend on allegorical criteria or on the order of the feasts in the liturgy, not on the historical order of the gospel text. The most extensive of these liturgical cycles is that in the Benedictional of Æthelwold, a manuscript containing the solemn blessings given by the bishop and intended for his personal use. Because the pictures in this manuscript are used to mark the major feasts they depict events such as the Nativity, the Presentation in the Temple or the entry to Jerusalem and omit Christ's miracles and ministry. The cycle even omits the Crucifixion, the central event in the history of salvation, because there was no mass on Good Friday and therefore no episcopal blessing. The constraints of liturgical order mean that representations of events from Christ's infancy such as the Nativity and the Circumcision are separated by pictures of much later events such as the martyrdom of Stephen, simply because the feast of St Stephen occurs on 26 December. In the same way, events such as the Adoration of the Magi and the Baptism which occurred many years apart are portrayed on adjacent pages because both events were celebrated on 6 January, the feast of the Epiphany.

The pictures in the Benedictional commemorate the great events of salvation, just as the blessings do, but their emphasis is different. For example, the painting of the Annunciation (5v) is placed before the blessings for the first Sunday in Advent. Its position is not inappropriate, for the mass of the day contains a *Memoria de Sancta Maria* which refers to the Annunciation. The blessings however are almost entirely concerned with Christ's second coming and make only the briefest reference to the incarnation in the words, 'Sanctifica plebem tuam domine, qui datus es nobis ex virgine, et benedic hereditatem tuam in pace.'[126] The picture is not only a commemoration of Christ's incarnation: it interprets the event in a way which is not even hinted at in the text of the manuscript. Mary is shown seated with an open book on a lectern in front of her, recalling the belief, set out by Ambrose and Bede, that she had read Isaiah's prophecy of

---

[125] Cf. Steenbock, 'Kreuzförmige Typen'.

[126] *Benedictional of Æthelwold*, ed. Warner and Wilson, p. 2 (7r): 'Sanctify your people Lord, given to us through a virgin, and bless your inheritance in peace.'

the virgin birth: 'Quia ergo legerat, Ecce virgo in utero habebit, et pariet filium, sed quomodo id fieri posset non legerat, merito credula iis quae legerat, sciscitatur ab angelo quod in propheta non invenit.'[127] Just as the painting of the Annunciation reaches back into the Old Testament the painting for the third Sunday in Advent (9v) looks forward to Christ's second coming. The parallel between the longing of the Jews for the coming of the Messiah, imitated by the Christian church in the period before Christmas, and the longing of the Christian for the consummation of the world was a traditional theme for the season of Advent, as was the contrast between Christ's first appearance as a helpless child and his return as judge. The first set of blessings alludes briefly to these themes: 'Ut qui de adventu redemptoris nostri secundum carnem devota mente laetamini, in secundo cum in maiestate sua advenerit, praemiis vitae aeternae ditemini.'[128] The painting, however, links Christ's second coming to his Passion and Resurrection, not to his birth. The words on his robe, 'Rex regum et Dominus dominantium' are taken from the description of the Word of God in the Apocalypse (XIX. 16), but the painting does not illustrate either this passage or the text of the blessings. Instead it shows Christ carrying the cross of the Resurrection and accompanied by angels carrying the symbols of his Passion, the source of his kingship.[129] This theme of kingship is also emphasized in the painting of Christ's Baptism (25r). Above the biblical figures of Christ and John the Baptist cluster angels holding crowns and sceptres, while the dove of the Holy Spirit, mentioned in the gospels,[130] carries a double flask of oil, an allusion to Christ's roles as king and priest.[131] Again, these details are not mentioned in the text.

These paintings in the Benedictional present the gospel events as part of

---

[127] Bede, *In Lucam* 1.i.34 (ed. Hurst, p. 33): 'For she had read, Behold a virgin shall conceive and bear a son, but how this would come about she had not read; believing those things she had read, she asked the angel about what she had not found in the prophet.' See *St Albans Psalter*, ed. Pächt *et al.*, pp. 63–6. The motif occurs in a more developed form in Odilo of Cluny's homily on the Assumption, see *St Albans Psalter*, p. 66; the parallel supports the argument set out below (pp. 141 and 157–8), for a link between Anglo-Saxon crowned crucifixes and Odilo's teaching on kingship and suffering, and between pictures of Mary grieving and Odilo's wish to share her sorrow.

[128] *Benedictional of Æthelwold*, p. 3 (10v): 'That you who rejoice with devout mind at the coming of our Redeemer according to the flesh, may receive the rewards of eternal life when he comes again in majesty.'

[129] See below, p. 146.   [130] Matt. III.16.

[131] Oppenheimer, *Ste Ampoule*, pp. 140–5; see also below, pp. 133 and 147–9.

a vast plan of redemption, conceived by God long before the time of Christ's birth and extending far into the future. The paintings in the Sacramentary of Robert of Jumièges, on the other hand, show scenes from Christ's life as events from the past, made present for the congregation through the liturgy.[132] The feast of the Nativity is marked by pictures of the Nativity itself, the annunciation to the shepherds and the flight into Egypt; four further infancy scenes – Herod consulting the priests and scribes, the Magi following the star, the Adoration of the Magi and the warning by an angel – are placed between the texts for the vigil and feast of Epiphany, and a sequence of four full-page paintings of the arrest of Christ, the Crucifixion (pl. xv), the deposition and the three Maries at the tomb stands before the text of the Easter vigil service.[133] These three groups of pictures differ from the paintings in the Benedictional because they illustrate the gospel story in step by step narrative fashion. They are not textual illustrations, however, for the Sacramentary contains only the prayers of the mass, not the readings, and the pictures relate to the readings. The four pictures of Herod and the Magi placed next to the prayers for the feast of Epiphany derive from the gospel for that feast, Matthew II.1–12. The pictures of the Nativity and of the angels with the shepherds, on the other hand, are placed before the prayers for the third mass of Christmas but are based on the readings for the first two masses, taken from St Luke's Gospel, II.1–20; the third picture for the Nativity, that of the flight into Egypt, relates to the gospel for the feast of the Holy Innocents, Matthew II.13–18. The Easter paintings similarly bring together events commemorated on different days. The pictures of the arrest, the Crucifixion and the deposition belong to the Passion story, read on Palm Sunday and the Tuesday, Wednesday and Friday of Holy Week. Only the final painting, that of the Maries at the tomb, belongs to the Easter vigil service. These paintings offer an imaginative reconstruction of the events commemorated in the mass, allowing the mind to dwell on them stage by stage. They elaborate on the human detail of the gospel story – the presence of the midwife, the ox and ass next to the manger, the angel's appearance to simple shepherds, the pathos of the descent from the cross – in order to aid the imagination in its attempt to relive the event and to respond to it as if actually present. This reliving of the gospel events played a central part in the liturgical cycle[134] and in the various

[132] See also below, pp. 67 and 183–5.   [133] See below, pp. 88 and 158.
[134] See below, pp. 54–6 and 82.

semi-dramatic ceremonies such as the Palm Sunday procession, the Good Friday Veneration of the Cross and the Easter Day visit to the tomb which were added to the mass and Office. [135] The paintings in the sacramentary can be seen as a small-scale and less public equivalent to these memorials.

The groups of narrative paintings in the Sacramentary, like the paintings of the Nativity or of the visit to the tomb in the Benedictional, are tied to the detail of the moment. Other pictures, such as the painting of the Annunciation in the Benedictional, are concerned with theological truths, with God's time rather than with man's. Both use the power of sight to prove but they do so in different ways. The pictures of the Nativity or of the visit to the tomb allowed the viewer to experience the biblical event for himself. They were a kind of substitute for the holy places in Palestine which provided a visible witness to pilgrims of the truth of the bible story, or for the relics which carried this witness to other lands. Jerome said of the holy places, 'quae prius ad me fama pertulerat, oculorum iudicio comprobavi'. [136] The author of the Blickling Homilies describes how Christ's footprints were preserved in the Church of the Ascension on the Mount of Olives as a sign to men that his human body had ascended into heaven and Ælfric tells his congregation that they should imitate the shepherds whose memory is preserved one mile east of Bethlehem and is manifested to those who visit the place. [137] In contrast to this physical proof the painting of the Annunciation offered intellectual proof: the gospel was known to be true because it fulfilled the Old Testament prophecies. The function of these pictures was not simply to recall the historical events commemorated in the liturgy. They served the faculties of understanding and of will as well as that of memory, first by causing those who saw them to reflect on the significance of what was remembered and secondly by inviting a response of faith or love. The decoration of Anglo-Saxon psalters functions in a similar way though it lays greater stress on the operation of the second faculty of the soul, the understanding, as might be expected in a prophetic text.

---

[135] See below, pp. 162–3.

[136] Jerome, *Epistula adversus Rufinum*, xxii (ed. Lardet, p. 94): 'I have proved with my own eyes what first rumour brought to me'; see also E. D. Hunt, *Holy Land Pilgrimage*, p. 100, n. 88 and below, p. 43. For a discussion of early Christian art and the holy places see Loerke, '"Real Presence"'.

[137] *Blickling Homilies*, no. xi (ed. Morris, pp. 125–9); discussed by Schapiro, 'Disappearing Christ', pp. 140–1; Ælfric, *CH* I.ii (ed. Thorpe, pp. 42–4).

Representations of Christ were placed in psalters because the psalms were habitually interpreted as prophecies about the Messiah. Some of these pictures relate to the interpretation of specific psalms[138] but others merely indicate the prophetic nature of the psalter as a whole, rather as the pictures of Christ in gospel-books were used to indicate the relationship between the *Logos* and the written word of the gospels.[139] The random nature of some of these pictures can be seen in the treatment of the scene of Christ trampling on the asp and the basilisk. This scene derives from a verse of Psalm XC, 'You will tread on lion and adder, trample on savage lions and dragons', but it is not used to illustrate this text. In the Douce Psalter it is placed opposite Psalm LI, in the Tiberius Psalter opposite Psalm CI and in the Winchcombe Psalter opposite Psalm CIX. The scenes from the life of David in the Vespasian, Junius and Eadwig Psalters[140] are similarly unrelated to the adjacent texts and although they offer a kind of narrative cycle, their distribution at intervals through the psalter means that the historical and biographical element is not readily apparent. They, too, relate to the psalter as a whole rather than to individual psalms. They act as reminders of the authorship of the psalms and also, through their use as images of Christ, as reminders of theological truths.[141]

In contrast to this structural and symbolic form of decoration, three eleventh-century English psalters are illustrated with extensive cycles of pictures. The scenes in the Harley Psalter, like those in the Utrecht Psalter from which they are partly derived, are composite scenes illustrating and commenting on the text of the psalms verse by verse. The Bury Psalter is decorated with marginal drawings which provide textual and interpretative illustrations to specific passages in the psalms. The Tiberius Psalter, which has full-page paintings marking the three main divisions of the text, contains sixteen drawings of scenes from the lives of David and Christ placed before the text itself as a sort of independent picture-book. The pictures in the Bury Psalter include representations of all the major events in Christ's life. A drawing of the Nativity illustrates Psalm LXXXVI, '"Here so and so was born" men say'; pictures of the Massacre of the Innocents and of the death of Stephen accompany Psalm LXXVIII, 'They have left the corpses of your servants to the birds of the air for food and the flesh of your devout to the beasts of the earth. They have shed blood like water

138 See below, pp. 32–3 and 85–7.   139 See above, p. 27.
140 See above, p. 23.   141 See below, p. 34.

throughout Jerusalem.' A picture of the Adoration of the Magi is placed next to Psalm LXXI, 'The kings of Tarshish and of the islands will pay him tribute. The kings of Sheba and Seba will offer gifts.' The Crucifixion is represented opposite Psalm XXI, 'My God, my God, why have you deserted me?' (pl. XIIa), and the Ascension at Psalm LXVII, 'God, you have ascended to the height, and captured prisoners, you have taken men as tribute.' These pictures are placed next to the texts to which they refer but they are not textual illustrations in the strict sense; instead, they offer a commentary on the text, reminding the reader of the New Testament events which the text in question prefigures. Reflection of this kind forms an integral part of the recitation of the Office, where attention is constantly drawn to the prophetic meaning of the psalms through the antiphons and responsories which accompany them. An illustrated psalter would be an appropriate adjunct to this recitation.

The pictures in the Tiberius Psalter differ from those in other psalters of the period because they have no practical function as text-markers, nor do they illustrate the text either literally or figuratively. The psalter played an important part in private prayer and it seems likely that the manuscript was designed for this purpose since it includes a number of devotional texts[142] together with the psalter collects which, by this date, were only recited privately.[143] One of the most striking features of the pictures in this manuscript is that in almost all cases they are identified by inscriptions. All the inscriptions except for that to the Crucifixion picture (pl. XIII) describe actions and in all but four cases the text begins with the word *hic* instead of the more common formula *ubi*.[144] The intention must have been to draw attention to the immediacy of what was represented: the historical event was made present to the viewer through the medium of the picture.[145] Some of the pictures in the psalter may come from a liturgical book, for two of the inscriptions have liturgical associations. That on 11r reads, 'Hic aequitavit Iesus Cristus in Palma Dominica' and that on 11v, 'Hic fecit Iesus mandatum cum discipulis suis.'[146] In their original context these pictures must have functioned like those in the Sacramentary of Robert of Jumièges, recalling the unity of historical event and liturgical commemor-

---

[142] BL, Cotton Tiberius C. vi, 21v–27v.   [143] *Psalter Collects*, ed. Brou, p. 10.

[144] On the significance of this for the Crucifixion picture see below, p. 150.

[145] For a discussion of the use of the corresponding Old English formula *her* in the *Anglo-Saxon Chronicle*, see Clemoes, 'Language in Context'.

[146] See also above, p. 14, n. 60 and below, p. 60.

ation. In the psalter, however, their context and therefore their meaning is different. The combination of pictures of David and pictures of Christ implies that the theme is that of the Epistle to the Romans (1.3–4): 'This news is about the Son of God who, according to the human nature he took, was a descendant of David: it is about Jesus Christ our Lord who, in the order of the spirit, the spirit of holiness that was in him, was proclaimed Son of God in all his power through his resurrection from the dead.'[147] The scenes from David's life included in the series are particularly apt for this purpose. David's rescue of the lamb from the lion and his defeat of Goliath were thought to symbolize Christ's defeat of the devil and his rescue of believers from him; the anointing, which initiated David's kingship, prefigured Christ's baptism and its recognition of his sacral kingship.[148] The New Testament pictures continue this royal theme. In the drawings of the Temptation, Betrayal and Crucifixion Christ is shown wearing a jewelled diadem; when he returns to heaven he leaves his disciples a crown and cross which symbolize his power. The true nature of his kingship is revealed by two pictures: in the Temptation scene he rejects the treasures of this world, represented by the gold torques and decorated swords of contemporary Anglo-Saxon society; in the *mandatum* scene he demonstrates his humility by washing his disciples' feet. The form of the inscriptions draws attention to the narrative element in the cycle; the selection and arrangement of the scenes indicates their theological and practical significance. The mind is not only invited to reflect on the parallels between David and Christ, on the scale of God's plan of salvation or on the truth of the Resurrection; the moral implications of the pictures of the Temptation of Christ, the washing of the feet, the betrayal by Judas and the doubts of Thomas require the will to act on what is seen.[149]

The cycles of scenes in the Benedictional of Æthelwold, the Sacramentary of Robert of Jumièges and the Tiberius Psalter have a devotional function, then, but it is of a different kind from that of the devotional images described earlier.[150] Whereas the images exist as ends in themselves and are therefore free to respond to the needs of the person confronting them, the commemoration of events for devotional purposes directs the viewer's attention to specific historical, theological and moral points. This

---

[147] I owe this reference to Herbert McCabe, OP.

[148] Ælfric, *Heptateuch*, ed. Crawford, pp. 35–6; *CH* II.iv (ed. Godden, p. 36); Bailey, *Durham Cassiodorus*, pp. 5 and 10–11.

[149] See below, pp. 60, 88 and 107.   [150] See above, p. 24.

difference in function between portrait-images and representations of historical events is marked by a difference in style. The drawings of St Peter welcoming the blessed into heaven or saving a soul from the devil in the *Liber vitae* of New Minster, or the paintings of Peter's miraculous release from prison in the Hereford Troper have narrative features completely missing from the drawing of a statuesque St Peter venerated by the monk Ælfwine. The material reality of events is indicated partly by the movement of the participants and partly by the use of furniture and landscape. In the painting in the Troper, for instance, the story is shown in three separate scenes which are arranged to simulate the movement of Peter from his prison cell, through the door and along the street to the point where the angel leaves him. In the drawing in the *Liber vitae* the saint is shown moving up the steps of the heavenly city with a welcoming gesture of the hand or fending off the devil with a well-aimed blow from his keys. A painting in the Sacramentary of Robert of Jumièges shows the Magi riding across country towards a walled city on the summit of a hill. The pictures of the entry to Jerusalem in the Benedictional of Æthelwold and the Tiberius Psalter pay attention to depth and perspective: the crowd surges out of the city gate and the spectators climb up on towers and into trees. Even when allegorical figures are added to historical ones, as is the case in the Baptism picture of the Benedictional, the event is still tied to a particular place and time. The arrangement of these pictures in a related sequence, whether it is chronological, historical or liturgical, implies that the scenes belong to a world in which there is change from one moment to another. The very sequence inevitably implies this, for in eternity where there is no time, there can be no succession of events.

There are, however, other pictures which do not imply such a chronological development. The main function of these pictures is to represent ideas rather than to record events. Sometimes they are diagrammatic; sometimes they include figures from more than one period who could not come together in normal time; sometimes they are grouped together, like the more historical scenes, not for narrative purposes but to express ideas which are related.

The simplest of these pictures are the diagrams in Byrhtferth's *Enchiridion* or the paschal hands associated with the computistical material in the Leofric Missal and the Tiberius Psalter. More complex are the circular Creation pictures in the Royal Bible and the Tiberius Psalter, where God is depicted with scales and compasses to illustrate his creation through number, weight and measure. Unlike the analytical Creation pictures of the Old English Hexateuch which follow the text of the opening chapters of Genesis stage by stage, the pictures in the bible and the psalter are synthetic, abstract compositions. Other pictures are less easily defined. The opening psalm in the Tiberius and Winchcombe Psalters is accompanied by a picture of David with his four musicians based on the text of the *Origo psalmorum*, one of the prefaces to the psalms. Pictures of David with his musicians are commonly found as frontispieces to psalters: the eighth-century Vespasian Psalter includes such a picture. The arrangement of the figures in the eleventh-century miniatures, however, is quite different from that in the earlier manuscript. Instead of the naturalistic grouping of the Vespasian figures the later compositions divide the picture into separate compartments to create a formal pattern reminiscent of Carolingian pictures of Christ among the evangelists, though with standing figures rather than seated ones. David and his musicians were in fact considered to be types of Christ and the evangelists and the inscription to the David picture in a ninth-century Carolingian manuscript, the San Callisto Bible, draws attention to the parallel.[151] It is possible therefore that the pictures in the two English psalters are to be interpreted symbolically. Certainly this would be appropriate, for both manuscripts include complex Christological scenes in their decoration.

Many of the pictures in late Anglo-Saxon manuscripts convey their meaning through formal devices of the kind seen in these two psalters. One of the most striking examples is the Last Judgement picture at the beginning of St John's Gospel in the eleventh-century Grimbald Gospels. The portrait of the evangelist and the opening words of his gospel are enclosed in panelled frames filled with figure scenes instead of the more usual acanthus patterns. The border on the left-hand page depicts the Trinity, accompanied by angels, apostles and other saints, receiving a group of souls from two angels; the right-hand page shows the Virgin and Child with seraphs, saints and angels. Illustrations are also placed in the margins of the text in the Bury Psalter, but the effect is quite different. In the Psalter, pictures are distributed round the text in such a way as to form a single composition. In the Gospels, by contrast, the figures are arranged singly or in groups in the medallions and panels of the frame in such a way that the scene cannot be viewed as a whole. Instead, the observer is invited

[151] Kessler, *Illustrated Bibles*, p. 107.

to study each detail of the picture individually and to relate it to the rest of the composition for himself. The intellectual approach implied by the borders in the gospel-book recurs in a painting of St Benedict with the monks of Canterbury in the Eadwig Psalter from Christ Church, Canterbury. At first sight the picture seems to be a presentation scene, for the volume offered to St Benedict by the group of monks contains the opening words of his rule, 'Ausculta o fili precepta.' Further inscriptions on scrolls and vestments indicate that the picture requires a more complex interpretation. The saint's mitre carries the words, 'Timor dei', a reference to the fear of the Lord which is the beginning of wisdom; the words recall the prologue to the *Regula S. Benedicti*, 'Venite, filii, audite me: timorem domini docebo vos.' The clasp on his cape is inscribed 'iustus' and three of the flowers on his tunic are labelled 'castus, obediens, humilis'. The figure therefore symbolizes the wisdom attained through the monastic vows of poverty, chastity and obedience. At the top of the picture a scroll in the outstretched hand of God reminds the monk of his duty of obedience: 'Obedientes estote propositi vestro. Qui vos audit me audit.' Finally the humility which characterized the true monk is vividly portrayed by the monk crouching beneath St Benedict's feet and holding the book of psalms whose recitation occupied so much of the monastic day; his belt is inscribed 'zona humilitatis'. The theme of the picture is the monastic vocation and the part played in it by the psalter, not the interpretation of the psalter itself. [152]

These pictures, like the carvings and paintings in Anglo-Saxon churches, go far beyond the remembrance of biblical events envisaged by Gregory or by the authors of the *Libri Carolini*. Far from being intended for beginners in the faith, many of them embody complex and difficult theological ideas and require prolonged and attentive consideration. Almost all these works of art – the elaborate liturgical manuscripts, the gold and silver statues, the decorated bookcovers, shrines and portable altars – were associated with monastic houses. Some monastic art was accessible to lay people of course. Pilgrims flocked to the shrine of St

[152] One of my students, Mr E. Griffin, has suggested to me that the picture is designed to involve the viewer in the scene: the monks to the right of the picture and the figure at St Benedict's feet direct their attention to the main figure and remain within the context of the picture; the figure of Benedict, on the other hand, looks out of the picture in the manner of a portrait-image, inviting a response from the viewer like that of the monks within the picture.

Swithun at Winchester and must have gazed on the biblical scenes with which it was covered.[153] The four statues of the virgins of Ely are said to have offered an imposing spectacle to the people.[154] But smaller items like illuminated manuscripts, embroidered vestments, ivories and portable altars – even if they were on public view – could have been studied only by those who saw them at close quarters. Many ivories are only three or four inches high. The portable altar from the Musée de Cluny measures just over ten inches from end to end (pl. VII). Even large manuscripts such as the Benedictional of Æthelwold or the Arundel Psalter measure only about ten inches by eight; others, like the Ælfwine Prayer-book, are only a quarter this size. These items were not intended for the instruction of the illiterate, who would have had no opportunity to see them. Some, like the Gospels of Judith of Flanders or Margaret of Scotland, belonged to wealthy and educated lay people. The majority, however, were seen and used by monks; they are related to a contemplative vocation, not a teaching one.

The monastic life did not involve the kind of instruction in Christian belief which was necessary for lay people. It was essentially a life of prayer, a quest for God rather than a quest for knowledge.[155] The experience of God's presence which the monk sought involved two things: first, an objective understanding of God's relationship with man throughout history; second, an interior awareness of God's presence to man and man's presence before God. In the liturgy the monk relived the great events of salvation history; in private prayer he became aware of God's presence in his own soul; in both, he remembered the goal to which human and individual history was moving. Although meditation could be based on the memory of past events, its real focus was the future. The art which served it, therefore, could not be limited to the recollection of the past. Moreover, narrative art, with its preoccupation with the physical and temporal, could play only a very limited part in a life which was concerned with what was spiritual and eternal. This concern with the ultimate significance of historical events can be seen particularly clearly in the first two paintings in the Athelstan Psalter and in the decorated frames to St John's gospel in the Grimbald Gospels. The paintings in the Psalter, which are associated with the calendar and other preliminary material, are inscribed with texts from the litany. They are pictorial expressions of the constant intercession of the saints in heaven. Unlike the rather similar choirs of saints and angels in the

[153] See above, p. 19.   [154] See above, p. 17.

[155] On the monastic vocation see Leclercq, *Love of Learning*, pp. 1–9.

Benedictional of Æthelwold these figures are grouped around pictures of Christ showing his wounds, a scene associated in sermons and in Old English poetry with the Last Judgement. The theme of these passages is Christ's great love for man, and his desire that this love should be returned. As Wulfstan said in a sermon on parts of Matthew XXIV:[156]

And on þam dome, þe ealle men to sculan, ure Drihten sylf eowað us sona his blodigan sidan and his þyrlan handa and ða sylfan rode þe he for ure neode on ahangen wæs, and wile þonne anrædlice witan hu we him þæt geleanedan, and hu we urne cristendom gehealden habban. Leofan men, utan beon þe wærran and don swa us þearf is, lufian God over ealle oðre þing and his willan wyrcan swa we geornost magan. þonne geleanað he hit us swa us leofast bið.[157]

The paintings in the Psalter, like the passage from the sermon, link Christ's death to his return as judge. More than this, they demand an emotional response. The scene in the Grimbald Gospels is more intellectual. The figures in the roundels at the top of the two frames – the Trinity on the left and the Virgin and Child on the right – contrast the eternal existence of the *Logos* with Christ's birth in time, a contrast which forms the main theme of the opening chapter of St John's Gospel. The figures of angels and saints and, in particular, the angels with the group of souls at the bottom of the first frame, link the scene with the end of the world, with the theme of Christ as *alpha* and *omega*, the end of man as well as his beginning. It is pictures like these, far more than the narrative scenes of Carolingian wall-painting, which lead the mind from the visible to the invisible.[158]

The Crucifixion pictures which form the main subject of this book have to be seen as a part of this monastic world where art was intended not, as the *Libri Carolini* claim, for beginners, but for those who had already gained a foretaste of heaven through their prayers.

[156] Matt. XXIV. 1–14, 36 and 42.
[157] *Homilies*, no. ii (ed. Bethurum, pp. 121–2): 'And at that judgment to which all men must come, our Lord himself will show us at once his bloody side and his pierced hands and the same cross on which he was hung for our need, and then will quickly demand how we have repaid him for that and how we have kept our Christian faith. Beloved men, let us be more careful and do what is necessary for us, love God above all other things and do his will as eagerly as we can. Then he will repay us for it in the most pleasing way for us.' See also below, pp. 65–6.
[158] *LC* II.xiii (ed. Bastgen, p. 73); see above, p. 6.

2

The place of the crucifix in Anglo-Saxon religious life

The sole purpose of the monastic life was to seek God. To achieve this end the monks pictured heaven in their minds; they cultivated the desire to come there; they remembered the saints who had already reached their goal; above all, they revered the cross, the symbol of man's reconciliation to God. The cross, which recalled what Christ had suffered for them and which reminded them of his future return in glory, was visible everywhere they went: in the refectory and chapter-house; on shrines, bookcovers and portable altars; in the shape of pectoral and processional crosses. Christ's sufferings were remembered in the ceremonies of Holy Week; his triumph in the two feasts of the Invention and Exaltation of the Cross. Each Friday his death was recalled through a votive mass and Office in honour of the cross.[1] Each day was punctuated by memorials of the cross: the antiphons after Lauds and Vespers[2] and the collects for the hours of Terce, Sext and None.[3] Devotion to the cross formed the mainstay of private prayer. The importance of the cross in the life of the Anglo-Saxon church can be inferred from the large numbers of crosses and crucifixes owned by churches. Hereward and his outlaws were able to steal fifteen, all of gold or silver, when they broke into the abbey church at Peterborough in 1070.[4] An inventory of the treasures of Ely made in 1075 or 1076 notes that the abbey possessed nineteen large crosses and eight smaller ones, including two processional crosses given by Archbishop Wulfstan and Bishop

---

[1] *Regularis concordia*, i.24 (ed. Symons, p. 20); Ælfric, *Epistula*, v.11 (ed. Hallinger, p. 158); *Dicta Einsidlensia*, xviii.62 (ed. Hallinger, p. 239); *Portiforium*, ed. Hughes II, 59–60.

[2] *Regularis concordia*, i.19 (ed. Symons, pp. 14–15); Ælfric, *Epistula*, v.12 (ed. Hallinger, p. 158).

[3] Discussed below, pp. 163–6.   [4] ASC E, 1070.

Athelstan.[5] Worcester possessed fifteen crosses at the time of the Norman Conquest.[6] Earlier in the century Brihtwold, bishop of Ramsbury (*ob.* 1045), gave his former monastery of Glastonbury twenty-six crosses together with other ornaments.[7] Crosses were a favourite gift to monasteries. Edgar gave crosses to Ely and Glastonbury, Eadred presented a gold cross to the Old Minster at Winchester and Cnut gave a jewelled one to the New Minster.[8]

The most spectacular of these crosses were the life-size crucifixes and Crucifixion groups, often in precious metals, which dominated the interior of late Anglo-Saxon churches. At Peterborough a huge crucifix of silver and gold, the gift of Abbot Leofric (1052–66), towered over the altar. When Hereward and his followers broke into the church in 1070 they tried at first to remove the crucifix bodily, but having climbed up to it they found it too heavy to move and had to content themselves with stealing the gold crown and footrest.[9] Bury possessed a large robed crucifix said to have been copied by Abbot Leofstan (1044–65) from the Volto Santo at Lucca.[10] At Harold's church of Holy Cross, Waltham, a figure of the crucified Christ carved out of flint, or possibly black marble, stood near the altar. It was visible from the doors of the church and must have presented a strange sight, for Tovi, Cnut's standard-bearer, had attached his own sword to it and then fixed the body to a wooden cross with silver bands; Tovi's wife added a golden crown and footrest and placed her own headband round its thigh.[11] By the end of the Anglo-Saxon period at least five churches possessed large Crucifixion groups. The earliest was given by Leofric of Mercia (*ob.* 1057) and his wife Godgifu to the church at Evesham.[12] At Durham Tostig of Northumbria (*ob.* 1066) and his wife Judith placed a large crucifix in the church accompanied by figures of Mary and John, all

---

[5] *Liber Eliensis* II.65, II.114 and III.50 (ed. Blake, pp. 138, 196 and 290).

[6] Robertson, *Anglo-Saxon Charters*, p. 242.

[7] *De antiquitate Glastoniensis ecclesie*, ch. 68 (ed. Scott, p. 138)

[8] *Liber Eliensis* III.50 (ed. Blake, p. 290); *De antiquitate Glastoniensis ecclesie*, ch. 62 (ed. Scott, p. 130); Wulfstan, *Vita S. Æthelwoldi*, ch. 10 (ed. Winterbottom, p. 40); L-B 4758 (citing Florence of Worcester, *Chronicon ex chronicis*).

[9] ASC E, 1070; L-B 3454 and 3458 (citing *The Chronicle of Hugh Candidus*).

[10] See below, p. 92 and James, 'S. Edmund at Bury', pp. 139 and 161.

[11] L-B 4469–71 (citing *De inventione sanctae crucis Walthamensis*) and 4479–80 (citing *Vita Haroldi regis*); see also Dodwell, *Anglo-Saxon Art*, p. 35.

[12] L-B 1613 (citing *Chronicon abbatiae de Evesham*).

covered in gold and silver.[13] Stigand (*ob.* 1072) had at least three large Crucifixion groups made, all in precious metals, for the churches of Bury, Ely and Winchester.[14]

These crucifixes and Crucifixion groups were placed in churches for three main reasons: first, they reminded people of the central truths of Christian belief; secondly, they played an important part in the liturgy and, finally, they had a devotional function. It might have been expected that representations of Christ's death would have played a major part in the decoration of churches from the beginning but this was not so. The earliest Christian paintings, on the walls of the catacombs, belong to an age when the church was persecuted and when martyrdom was common; their aim was to strengthen belief in an after-life and trust in God's power to save. The commonest scenes are the examples of God's protection invoked in the prayer for the dead – the stories of Noah, Jonah and the children in the fiery furnace – together with peaceful pastoral scenes showing the dead standing in the fields of paradise.[15] Even after the conversion of Constantine and the end of the persecutions church art remained focused on the joys of the next world. The lambs and doves which symbolized the peace of heaven in early Christian art were retained in the art of fifth- and sixth-century Ravenna: a representation of Christ as the Good Shepherd decorates the lunette over the entrance to the mausoleum of Galla Placidia and at Sant'Apollinare in Classe the apse mosaic shows the saint standing in an idyllic landscape filled with trees, flowers, lambs and birds.[16] Side by side with these pastoral scenes are others which depict heaven in more imperial terms. At Sant'Apollinare Nuovo two long processions of saints and martyrs, holding crowns in their hands, approach the twin thrones of Christ and his mother.[17] At San Vitale, Christ, accompanied by angels, crowns the youthful saint, Vitalis, and, to the sides, the emperor, Justinian, and his empress, Theodora, join in the worship of heaven with their attendants.[18] These mosaics reminded men of the rewards promised by Christ to those who followed him and of their own ability, even in this world, to share in the

---

[13] L-B 1355 (citing Simeon, *Historia Dunelmensis ecclesiae*).

[14] Jocelin of Brakelond, *Cronica* (ed. Butler, pp. 5 and 108); *Liber Eliensis* III.50 (ed. Blake, p. 290); L-B 4709 (citing *Annales monasterii de Wintonia*).

[15] Mâle, *Early Churches*, p. 24; Grabar, *Beginnings of Christian Art*, pp. 67–121.

[16] Bovini, *Ravenna Mosaics*, pls. 2 and 44–5; Grabar, *Byzantium*, pl. 148.

[17] Bovini, *Ravenna Mosaics*, p. 31, pls. 20–2 and 26.

[18] *Ibid.*, pls. 28 and 33; Grabar, *Byzantium*, pls. 147 and 171–2.

glory of the next; they made visible the splendour by which the believing Christian was already surrounded. The whole emphasis in these scenes is on life: on Christ reigning in heaven; on the eternal happiness promised to his followers. Christ's death is not mentioned. When the cross is portrayed it is the triumphal jewelled cross which symbolizes the transfigured Christ or which announces his second coming.

These scenes reflect the theology of the early church. Easter was not originally a feast which celebrated historical events. It was the feast of an idea: the new passover in which God saved his people as he had once led the Jews out of Egypt. [19] The story of the exodus was in fact one of the earliest readings for the Easter vigil and Christ himself was described as the new passover sacrifice in the epistle, *Alleluia* and communion of the Easter mass. [20] With the excavation of the holy places under Constantine in the early fourth century and the building of the churches of the Anastasis over the tomb of Christ and of the Martyrium over the site where the cross had been discovered, interest shifted to the historical basis of the Christian faith. Pilgrims came to Jerusalem seeking proof of the reality of what they believed. Even Jerome, who argued in one of his sermons that the sight of the relics and of the holy places was irrelevant to a religion with universal claims, reacted quite differently when he first saw Jerusalem. [21] By the late fourth century the central feast of the Resurrection had been surrounded by commemorations of all the details of the last stages of Christ's life on earth at the sites where they had taken place. At the centre of these ceremonies was the Good Friday veneration of the relics of the cross in the chapel behind the rock of Golgotha. The Holy Week services were arranged so that the pilgrim relived the events surrounding Christ's death and Resurrection; moreover the buildings of Christian Jerusalem were arranged in such a way that in moving through them one passed, as it were, through the Crucifixion to the Resurrection. The entrance to the precinct was through an arcaded court, the western side of which formed the porch of the basilica of the Martyrium; in the porch were three crosses recalling the death of Christ between the two thieves; the actual wood of the crosses

---

[19] Ælfric, *CH* II.xv (ed. Godden, pp. 159–60); see also E. D. Hunt, *Holy Land Pilgrimage*, p. 118, n. 54; Dix, *Shape of the Liturgy*, pp. 337–41.

[20] I Cor. v.8.

[21] E. D. Hunt, *Holy Land Pilgrimage*, pp. 91–2; Jerome, *Tractatus* (ed. Morin, pp. 154–5, on Ps. xcv), *Epistula adversus Rufinum*, 22 (ed. Lardet, p. 94); see also above, p. 31, n. 136.

discovered on the site was preserved in the crypt beneath the Martyrium. Beyond the apse of the Martyrium was an open court leading to the circular church of the Anastasis, built over the tomb itself. The Anastasis therefore lay to the west of the whole complex. The site of the Crucifixion, which is not mentioned in the earliest accounts of the buildings, was in the court between Anastasis and Martyrium and by the middle of the fourth century was marked by a jewelled cross. Adomnán, who wrote his account of the holy places in the seventh century, says that there was a second cross over the building which covered the tomb.[22]

The Jerusalem liturgy and its setting influenced the Christian church in two main ways: first, the feasts of the church's year became more historical in character and secondly the church buildings themselves were influenced by the Jerusalem arrangements. This influence is apparent in a number of circular churches, built in imitation of the church of the Anastasis, in the placing of an altar dedicated to the cross in the centre of the nave of churches and in the use of western sanctuaries, reflecting the position of the Anastasis in relation to the site of Golgotha and the Crucifixion. One of the clearest examples of this influence is the church of Saint-Riquier, built in 799, with its altar of the Saviour in the western transept surmounted by a circular staged tower and the altar of the cross in the centre of the nave.[23] The Easter liturgy was celebrated in this western church while the Good Friday Veneration of the Cross, imitated from the veneration of the relics in Jerusalem on Good Friday, took place at the altar of the cross. The St Gallen plan of an ideal monastery, dating from the early ninth century, also has an altar dedicated to the cross in this position, though here the dedication to the Saviour is combined with that to the cross: 'altare Sancti Salvatoris ad crucem'.[24] The much later church of Saint-Bénigne at Dijon, built in the eleventh century and partly modelled on the abbey church at Cluny, is even closer to the plan of the Jerusalem churches. The main basilica, with its central altar of the cross placed to the west of the choir, was joined by a rotunda to the eastern chapel of St Mary in clear imitation of the alignment of Martyrium and Anastasis.[25] The rotunda built by Wulfric at St Augustine's, Canterbury, to link the church of SS Peter and

[22] Conant, 'Holy Sepulchre', pp. 1–48 and Coüasnon, *Holy Sepulchre*.

[23] Heitz, 'Architecture et liturgie', pp. 30–47 and 'Iconography', pp. 93–4.

[24] Horn and Born, *St Gall* I, 135–6 and 142.

[25] Conant, 'Cluny II', pp. 179–94; see also Martindale, 'Church of S. Bénigne', pp. 44 and 53.

Paul to that of St Mary was almost certainly influenced by the church at Dijon.[26] Whether Wulfric's church also had an altar dedicated to the cross is unknown. Centrally placed altars with this dedication were very common on the continent – the churches of Fulda, Corvey, Saint-Vaast and Le Mans all had such altars – and an altar dedicated to the cross normally stood just to the west of the choir-screen in early Norman churches.[27] Two pre-Conquest churches which probably had an altar of the cross in the nave are Ramsey and the Old Minster at Winchester. The church at Ramsey was built in 970 in the form of a cross and it is clear from the account of its construction that its plan was intended to recall Christ's death on the cross.[28] The church was of the open-plan type with a central tower and tall arches supported on columns between the crossing and the rest of the building.[29] Evidence for the existence of a cross in the nave comes from the history of Ramsey Abbey under the year 1043, which mentions the monks celebrating Vespers and 'iuxta consuetudinem antiquitus usitatam, ad stationem ante crucem in navem ecclesiae procedentibus'.[30] In some Norman churches the crucifix over the choir-screen is referred to as in the nave, but the Ramsey reference is rather early for a rood-screen of this kind and the open structure of the church would preclude a crucifix over the chancel-arch. The evidence for Winchester is more complex. Excavation of the Old Minster has revealed three sets of foundations on the axis of the nave between the high altar, which stood at the east end of the nave, and the western entrance. These foundations must have been for altars or standing crosses.[31] Thomas Rudborne, writing in the fifteenth century, refers to a crowned crucifix which at that time stood in front of the high altar of the medieval cathedral. He believed that the crucifix was the one said to have been crowned by Cnut after his failure to command the waves. The story was first recorded in the twelfth century by Henry of Huntingdon, and a similar story was told at Canterbury.[32] The story is late but there is probably some truth in it for the earliest crowned crucifixes in English manuscript art are those in the Ælfwine Prayer-book, written and

---

[26] For a different view see Gem, 'Iconography', pp. 9–11.
[27] Horn and Born, *St Gall* I, 136.
[28] Gem, 'Iconography', p. 13; *Vita Sancti Oswaldi* (ed. Raine, p. 434).
[29] *Historia Rameseiensis*, 22 [xx] (ed. Macray, p. 41).
[30] *Historia Rameseiensis*, 92 [ciii] (*ibid.*, p. 156).
[31] Biddle, 'Winchester, 1965', p. 321.
[32] Discussed below, pp. 143–5.

decorated at the New Minster, Winchester, between 1023 and 1035 (pl.
VIII), and the Bury Psalter, written and decorated at Christ Church,
Canterbury, at about the same time (pl. XIIa). The most likely position for
the Winchester crucifix is in the nave, near an altar dedicated to the cross.
By the time of Cnut the Old Minster had been remodelled. The high altar
had been moved further east and was approached by a flight of steps leading
up from the nave, while the earlier structures to the west had been covered
by a fresh floor. If there was an altar of the cross – and such altars seem to
have been almost the rule in monastic churches of the eleventh century – it
must have stood in the western part of the nave, below the steps to the new
choir and sanctuary.

The imitation of the Jerusalem plan in later churches implied two
parallels. The first was between the site of the Crucifixion and the centrally
placed altar of the cross; the second was between the site of the tomb and
the high altar.[33] Just as the tomb was covered by a small house-like
building placed within the circular church of the Anastasis so the high altar
of many early churches was covered by a ciborium. At Saint-Riquier the
altar of the Saviour with its ciborium was placed under a circular tower
recalling the circular form of the church of the Anastasis. Excavations have
revealed the supports for a ciborium over the high altar of the Old Minster
at Winchester and the picture of Æthelwold celebrating mass at the end of
his Benedictional shows a ciborium and also a staged circular bell-tower
over the centre of the church. This drawing should probably not be taken as
an accurate picture of Æthelwold's Old Minster but it is suggestive that the
drawing of the three Maries at the sepulchre in another Winchester
manuscript – the mid-eleventh-century Tiberius Psalter – shows the tomb
as a circular staged tower with a square base and a crypt beneath, which is
closely similar to the western church of the Saviour at Saint-Riquier and
which may perhaps have been modelled on the tower built by Bishop
Ælfheah at the Old Minster and dedicated in 993–4.[34] This tower,
described by Wulfstan of Winchester as square below but circular above
and surmounted by a golden weathercock, was probably built over the

[33] Cf. a fifth-century Syriac homily quoted by Hardison, *Christian Rite*, p. 37, n. 5: 'The
altar is a symbol of our Lord's tomb, and the bread and wine are the Body of the Lord
which was embalmed and buried.'

[34] See Heitz, 'Iconography', p. 96.

crossing of the church.[35] The instructions for the Good Friday ceremonies in the *Regularis concordia* state that the model of the tomb in which the cross used for the Good Friday veneration was ceremonially buried until Easter Day stood close to the altar.[36] If this arrangement continued into the eleventh century the ritual tomb must have stood under Ælfheah's tower and it would have been appropriate to represent the historical tomb by a picture of this tower in the Psalter. Another picture which suggests that English artists were familiar with architectural parallels to the Jerusalem buildings is the painting of the visit to the tomb in the Sacramentary of Robert of Jumièges, written and decorated in about 1020. Here the tomb is represented as a church with a nave and rotunda, the angel being seated under the rotunda.

The association of the high altar with the Resurrection of Christ rather than with his death may explain the late introduction of altar crosses, which were not actually prescribed until the time of Innocent III. The frontispiece to the New Minster *Liber vitae* shows Cnut placing a cross on the altar of the monastery, but it is very unlikely that crosses were kept permanently on the altar at this date. Many of the crosses and crucifixes of the late Anglo-Saxon period were far too large to have stood on the small square altars of the time and the liturgical pictures of the tenth and eleventh centuries do not suggest that altar crosses were used. The picture at the end of the Benedictional of Æthelwold shows only a chalice and paten on the altar and the mass scene on the early eleventh-century St Lawrence Box shows only a candlestick. The same is true of continental pictures. The painting of Bernward of Hildesheim at the beginning of the gospel-book which he presented to his cathedral between 1012 and 1022 shows a chalice and paten, together with what may be a small portable altar, on the richly draped altar-table; the painting of Erhard saying mass in the Uta Gospels, dating from the early eleventh century, shows a portable altar (the Arnulf Ciborium), a book (the Codex Aureus of St Emmeram), a chalice and paten on the main altar-table; there is a hanging crown above the altar but again no altar cross. The usual arrangement

[35] Wulfstan, *Narratio metrica de Sancto Swithuno*, Ep. spec. 175–84 (ed. Campbell, pp. 70–1); Quirk, 'Winchester Cathedral', pp. 28–68, esp. 61–3; Gem, 'Iconography', p. 7 says the tower was probably at the west end; for a detailed discussion of the vocabulary of this passage see the notes to the edition of Wulfstan of Winchester by Lapidge, *The Cult of St Swithun*, forthcoming.

[36] *Regularis concordia*, iv.46 (ed. Symons, p. 44).

seems to have been for the cross to stand behind or to one side of the altar or to be raised above it, often on a decorated beam.

From the Norman period onwards it was the practice to place a large crucifix or Crucifixion group above the screen which separated the choir from the nave of the church. This was the case in Lanfranc's cathedral at Canterbury, built between 1070 and 1077: 'Pulpitum vero turrem praedictam a navi quodammodo separabat, et ex parte navis in medio sui altare S. Crucis habebat. Supra pulpitum trabes erat, per transversum ecclesiae posita, quae crucem grandem et duo cherubin et imagines S. Mariae et S. Iohannis apostoli sustentabat.'[37] At Winchester the Crucifixion group made by Stigand for the Anglo-Saxon cathedral was later placed above the *pulpitum* built by Walkelin between 1070 and 1097 to separate the nave of the new Norman cathedral from the choir and at St Augustine's, Canterbury, the great silver crucifix made by Stigand stood on the westernmost of the two screens built by Abbot Hugh Flori, 'in navi ecclesiae super pulpitum erectam'.[38] The position of the altar of the cross under the screen at Canterbury – and in other medieval monastic churches – suggests that these arrangements developed from the earlier practice of placing an altar dedicated to the cross in the centre of the nave. The St Gallen plan shows that a large cross some ten feet high was placed next to the altar of the cross in the nave and it is likely that the arrangements in other churches were similar.[39] In contrast, the high altar was sometimes associated with a representation of Christ in Majesty indicating its symbolic relationship to the resurrection and the life of the next world. The late tenth-century church at Barton-on-Humber probably had a carving of Christ in Majesty above the chancel-arch.[40] Emma made an altar frontal for Ely which was decorated with a picture of Christ in Majesty[41] and later in the Middle Ages both the Canterbury churches had figures of Christ in Majesty over the high altar. Gervase of Canterbury describes the choir at Christ Church, built during the time of Anselm (1093–1109) and

---

[37] Gervase of Canterbury, *Chronica* (ed. Stubbs, pp. 9–10): 'A screen separated the previously mentioned tower to some extent from the nave and had the altar of the Holy Cross in the centre of the side facing the nave. Above the screen was a beam, placed across the church, which supported a large cross, two cherubs and figures of St Mary and St John the apostle.'

[38] L-B 653 and 720 (citing William Thorne, *Chronica*).

[39] Horn and Born, *St Gall* I, 142.

[40] Rodwell and Rodwell, 'St Peter's Church', p. 295.

[41] *Liber Eliensis* III.50 (ed. Blake, p. 292).

destroyed by fire in 1174. Behind the high altar were two wooden pillars decorated with gold and silver which supported a beam covered in gold; on top of the beam were images of Christ in Majesty and of SS Dunstan and Ælfheah together with seven shrines; between the columns stood a gilded cross.[42] A fifteenth-century drawing of the high altar of St Augustine's shows a similar arrangement. Immediately behind the high altar is a reredos with a beam supporting a shrine. Behind this are two columns which support a second beam decorated with foliage scrolls on which are two shrines and images of Christ in Majesty and two angels.[43] Some tenth- and eleventh-century churches, however, had a cross or crucifix over the high altar. King Edgar gave a large cross to the high altar at Glastonbury; it is not clear whether this is the same as the large silver crucifix which was damaged when Thurstan's archers broke into the choir and attacked the monks in 1083 and which was still displayed to visitors in the late twelfth century.[44] More important are the three Crucifixion groups made by Stigand. According to the chronicle of Jocelin of Brakelond, Stigand's Crucifixion group at Bury was displayed on a beam above the high altar in the late twelfth century.[45] An inventory of the treasures of Ely made after the installation of Bishop Nigel in 1133 shows that here too Stigand's statues stood on a decorated beam above the high altar.[46] In both cases the statues had been moved from their original position: the church at Bury was built by Abbot Baldwin and the sanctuary was completed in 1095 when the body of St Edmund was placed in its shrine behind the high altar; the church at Ely was started by Abbot Simeon between 1081 and 1093 and the sanctuary, with its shrines of the four virgins of Ely, was completed by Simeon's successor in 1106. However, the description of the Crucifixion group given by Stigand to Winchester includes a beam and it seems likely therefore that all three groups were mounted originally on beams above the high altars of their respective churches and that they were placed in the same position at Bury and Ely when they were moved into the new buildings. At Winchester, where the *pulpitum* was built very early, they were placed on that instead.

---

[42] L-B 804 (citing Gervase of Canterbury, *Chronica*).

[43] Dugdale, *Monasticon* I, before p. 121.

[44] *De antiquitate Glastoniensis ecclesie*, ch. 62 (ed. Scott, p. 130); ASC E, 1083; *De antiquitate Glastoniensis ecclesie*, chs. 28 and 78 (ed. Scott, pp. 80 and 156–8).

[45] Jocelin of Brakelond, *Cronica* (ed. Butler, p. 108).

[46] *Liber Eliensis* III.50 (ed. Blake, p. 290).

The presence of crucifixes and Crucifixion groups in association with the high altar indicates a change in religious beliefs. Of course there was a cross over the ciborium which covered the tomb in the church of the Anastasis, but this was a decorative cross intended, like the jewelled crosses in the mosaics at Santa Pudenziana in Rome and Sant'Apollinare in Classe at Ravenna, to symbolize the glorified Christ. Stigand's Crucifixion groups had a quite different meaning and must have been intended to link the high altar with the death of Christ rather than with his Resurrection.[47] The large Crucifixion groups of the kind presented by Stigand no longer exist, but the decoration of altar-tables and portable altars indicates a similar change in attitude. Many are decorated with crosses but representations of the Crucifixion are rare.[48] The golden altar of St Ambrose in Milan which dates from the ninth century includes a Crucifixion scene among the series of scenes from Christ's life, but it is not prominent, particularly when compared with the centrally placed Maiestas, and the associations of the altar are better expressed by the panels at its ends which show jewelled crosses adored by angels in heaven.[49] The design on the tenth- or eleventh-century Anglo-Saxon portable altar in the Musée de Cluny on the other hand links this theme of adoration to the historical event of Christ's death and to the Old Testament prophecies (pl. VII).[50] At the top is Christ on a tree-cross; to the sides are Mary and John with two angels, one of whom holds a mass-bread; at the bottom is the *Agnus Dei* and in the corners are the symbols of the four evangelists. This complex scene links Christ's death to the celebration of the mass taking place over the altar, to the passover Lamb and to the triumphal Lamb of the Apocalypse, emphasizing the sacrificial nature of Christ's death and of the mass.[51] The Heinrichsportatile in the Schatzkammer at Munich, made at Fulda or Reichenau in the early eleventh century, has a similar meaning. In the upper compartment are two angels supporting a circle with the *Agnus Dei* from whose wounds blood pours into a chalice held by Ecclesia: to Ecclesia's right is a figure holding a chalice and host and below is a picture of the sacrifice of Isaac, one of the Old Testament types of Christ's sacrificial death. For the early church it was Christ's Resurrection which offered the hope of eternal life; by the

---

[47] Cf. Amalarius, *Liber officialis* III.xxv.8 (ed. Hanssens II, 342).

[48] See Elbern, *Das erste Jahrtausend* I, 436–70.

[49] Hubert *et al.*, *Carolingian Art*, pl. 221.

[50] Okasha and O'Reilly, 'Anglo-Saxon Portable Altar', pp. 32–51.

[51] For a discussion of the angels see below, pp. 123–6; see also p. 182.

eleventh century man's hope of salvation was based instead on Christ's death. As the first reading for the Friday Office of the cross says:

Crux igitur dominica angelis et hominibus veneranda, merito nobis est adoranda, quia iustissimum est salutis nostrae signum totis veneremur laudibus gloriae. Nam dum sanctae crucis insignia recolimus ad memoriam reducimus quod pro nobis in ipsa passus est dominus. Per crucem quippe diabolus est captivatus, et mundus liberatus, sed et infernus despoliatus et paradysus iocundatus, omnisque per orbem christianus populus ad regna caelestia invitatus.[52]

In addition to the crosses and crucifixes associated with the altar of the cross in the nave of the church and the high altar in the sanctuary some churches had a crucifix or Crucifixion group at the entrance to the choir. The tenth-century churches of St Mary in Tanner Street, Winchester, and St Peter, Barton-on-Humber, both had rood-beams across the arch leading into the sanctuary.[53] In Norman churches, as was mentioned earlier, the monastic choir was separated from the nave by a solid screen or screens surmounted by a large crucifix. The earliest reference to such a screen comes from Beverley where Ealdred built a *pulpitum* with a cross above it at the entrance to the choir of the minster between 1060 and 1069.[54] It is possible too that a solid screen existed at Christ Church, Canterbury, before the Norman Conquest. Eadmer describes the monks' choir of the Saxon cathedral, which was burned down in 1067, as 'decenti fabrica a frequentia turbae seclusus' and Gervase's description of the misery of the monks during the five years after the fire of 1174 when they had to pray at the altar of the cross to the west of Lanfranc's screen, 'in aula ecclesiae muro parvulo a populo segregati', suggests that he, at least, felt that decency required a solid wall between monks and public.[55] Of course the choir and sanctuary of Christian churches were screened from the nave from

---

[52] *Portiforium* (ed. Hughes II, 59–60): 'Accordingly, the Lord's cross is to be venerated by angels and men, and is rightly to be adored by us, because it is most just that we should venerate the sign of our salvation with all the praise of glory. For while we honour again the symbol of the holy cross we are led to remember what our Lord suffered for us on it. Through the cross the devil is truly taken captive, the world is freed, hell is plundered and paradise made glad, and the whole Christian community throughout the world is invited to the heavenly kingdom.'

[53] Biddle, 'Winchester, 1971', pp. 312–13; Warwick Rodwell, private communication; Rodwell and Rodwell, 'St Peter's Church', p. 293 gives a plan.

[54] L-B 326 (citing *Chronica pontificum ecclesiae Eboracensis*).

[55] L-B 658 (citing Eadmer, *Vita S. Audoeni*) and 801 (citing Gervase of Canterbury, *Chronica*); Taylor, 'Cathedral Church at Canterbury', pp. 101–30.

earliest times, though not by a *pulpitum*. Sometimes curtains were used as in the liturgical scenes on the ivory cover of the ninth-century Drogo Sacramentary or the eleventh-century St Lawrence Box; sometimes the division was made through low screens or pillared arcades.[56] At Angilbert's church of Saint-Riquier six columns supporting a beam with thirteen shrines on it stood across the entrance to the apse with the altar of St Riquier.[57] The early churches of St Pancras at Canterbury, St Peter, Bradwell-on-Sea and St Mary, Reculver, had a triple arcade between the nave and apse which could have supported curtains or infilling screens.[58] However, the foundation in front of the arcade at Reculver suggests that the altar lay to the west of the arcade not to the east and additional screens may have been necessary further west. The same arrangement can be seen in the ninth- or tenth-century church at Raunds.[59] The St Gallen plan shows the complex system of screening possible in a large church where access had to be provided for pilgrims while at the same time offering privacy for the monks and seclusion for the altars.[60]

Whereas the early Kentish churches had only one structural division some larger churches had two, suggesting an arrangement closer to that of Norman churches. At Brixworth there was at one time either a triple arcade or, more probably, a wall pierced by a tall arch flanked by two windows and two smaller arches between the nave and choir; a single arch separated the choir from the apse.[61] It is possible that the outer arches were intended to provide access to the crypt while the central arch gave access to the choir; nevertheless, the arrangement of the doors is similar to that in the choir-screens of the Norman period and later, where the western screen had two doorways with an altar between them while the eastern screen had a single central doorway. At Gloucester a wall pierced by an arch was placed between the crossing and the nave of the church of St Oswald in the early tenth century.[62] Other Saxon churches which had a division to the west of the crossing in addition to the arch between crossing and chancel are Breamore, Deerhurst, Repton and St Mary in Castro, Dover.[63] Like the

[56] Bond and Camm, *Roodscreens* I, 5–6.
[57] Hariulf, *Chronicon* II.v–vi (PL 174, 1247–8); Clapham, *Romanesque Architecture*, pp. 79 and 81.
[58] Taylor, *Architecture* III, 785–6; Taylor, 'Reculver', pp. 291–6.
[59] Parsons, 'Sacrarium', p. 106, fig. 78.
[60] Horn and Born, *St Gall* I, 205.   [61] Taylor, *Architecture* III, 793.
[62] Heighway and Bryant, 'St Oswald, Gloucester', p. 190, fig. 129.
[63] Taylor, *Architecture* III, 794; Taylor and Taylor, *Architecture* I, 216.

later rood- and choir-screens these walls were sometimes decorated with crucifixes or Crucifixion groups. At Bibury in Gloucestershire traces of two standing figures remain above the string-course over the Anglo-Saxon chancel-arch and at Bitton, also in Gloucestershire, the string-course on the east wall of the nave supports a stone carved with a serpent and the feet of a crucifix; to the right a stone marks the position of one of the accompanying figures.[64] At Bradford-on-Avon the two carved angels high above the chancel-arch must have belonged to a Crucifixion scene similar to those in the Sherborne Pontifical and the Arenberg Gospels (pls. I and II).[65] The carvings have been moved but it seems likely that they have been replaced in their original position, for the large area of blank wall above the chancel-arch demands some form of decoration and there is ample room for a crucifix below the angels. The Crucifixion group over the south door of the church at Breamore may originally have stood over a chancel- or choir-arch. The church at Breamore is cruciform in plan with a central tower separated by a small arch from the southern porticus. The original arch between tower and chancel is known to have been 6′8″ wide and there must have been a similar arch between the nave and the central tower; both have been replaced by wide fifteenth-century arches. A comparison with Wootton Wawen where all four tower-arches remain is useful in reconstructing the arrangements at Breamore. The arch to the north of the tower at Wootton measures 4′1″ by 8′10″ compared to the 4′5″ by 10′ of the southern arch at Breamore. The arches on the axis of the church are larger. The largest, between nave and tower, measures 6′10″ by 13′1″, and is therefore comparable in width to the original chancel-arch at Breamore. If the axial arches at Breamore were similar in size to those at Wootton there would have been ample room for the Crucifixion panel now over the entrance door to have stood above the arch between nave and tower.[66] Alternatively, it could have been placed on the outside of the present west wall of the church, within a western annexe like the Crucifixion group at Headbourne Worthy.[67] These crucifixes parallel the 'stations' of Saint-Riquier: carved stucco panels with scenes of the Nativity, Passion, Resurrection and Ascension which were placed in the entrance to the church and over the arches which divided the nave and its aisles from the eastern

---

[64] Taylor and Taylor, *Architecture* I, 65 and 75.

[65] *Ibid.* I, 87.

[66] *Ibid.* I, 96 and II, 687; Taylor, *Architecture* III, 784.

[67] Rodwell and Rouse, 'Anglo-Saxon Rood', pp. 298–325.

transept, and which played an important part in the daily processions after Vespers.

From at least the sixth century it had been customary to say the end of the Offices of Lauds and Vespers in a different oratory from the main part of the services.[68] By the late tenth century Lauds and Vespers of all saints and of the dead had been added to the Office of the day and it was these additional Offices which were said in the second oratory.[69] At Cluny the oratory used for this purpose was that of St Mary.[70] Between the main Office and the additional ones came the *memoriae* of the cross, St Mary and the saint to whom the church was dedicated. The procession to the cross after Vespers described in the *History of Ramsey* must have taken place in connection with the *memoriae* of the cross.[71] Angilbert's *Ordo* for his church at Saint-Riquier shows that the processions there involved prayers at each altar and at the three stations of the Passion, Resurrection and Ascension. When the main part of the service was said at the eastern altar of St Riquier the monks moved first to the representation of the Passion in the centre of the church and, after praying in front of it, divided into two groups to visit various altars before meeting again at the altar of the cross; there they prayed again before moving to the altar of St Maurice for Vespers of the dead. When the main service was said at the western altar of the Saviour, the procession separated to visit the carvings of the Resurrection and Ascension and the altars of St John and St Martin before meeting at the carving of the Passion; after the prayers in front of this station they moved east to the altar of St Riquier and then separated once more to visit the altars of St Stephen and St Lawrence before moving to the altar of the cross; the service ended with a procession to the altars of St Maurice and St Benedict where the final part of the Office was recited.[72]

Another ceremony which involved the cross in the nave of the church or at the entrance to the choir was the *Asperges*: the procession before the Sunday high mass at which the main buildings of the monastery were sprinkled with holy water.[73] The Cluny Customary describes the route of the procession and the five stations made during it: in the chapel of St

---

[68] E. Bishop, *Liturgica Historica*, p. 222, n.1.

[69] *Regularis concordia*, i.19 (ed. Symons, pp. 14–15).

[70] Ulrich, *Consuetudines* I.iii and xli (PL 149, 646–7 and 686–9).

[71] See above, p. 45.

[72] E. Bishop, *Liturgica Historica*, pp. 328–9.

[73] *Regularis concordia*, i.23 and iv.36 (ed. Symons, pp. 19 and 34).

Mary, in front of the dormitory and refectory, in the vestibule of the church and finally, from Easter to Pentecost, 'ad sanctam crucem'.[74] These processions involved a cross or crucifix kept permanently in the church. Their function, as can be seen from the collects and antiphons listed in the Durham Ritual for the *memoriae* of the cross, was one of praise and thanksgiving: Christ was imagined reigning from the cross; the cross was the symbol of his triumph.[75] The church itself was seen as the heavenly Jerusalem, the place where men joined in the worship of heaven.[76] This triumphal element explains why the crosses were covered during Lent and a veil was hung between the sanctuary and the congregation. As Ælfric said, 'absurdum putamus crucem adorare dum *Alleluia* relinquimus. Si quis crucem adorare vult in Quadragesima, non habet opus in die Passionis Domini eam adorare nobiscum.'[77] In the Good Friday services, by contrast, the church became the historical city of Jerusalem, the scene of Christ's earthly sufferings, and the cross, which formed the focus of the ceremony, became a substitute for the actual cross on which Christ died and also for Christ himself.[78] The veneration of the cross took place in the area below the altar which, as was said above, was traditionally connected with the place of Christ's death. Like the early pilgrims to the Holy Land, the congregation imagined themselves to be actually present at the events they recalled. Amalarius compares the Good Friday Veneration of the Cross to the reaction of the wealthy Roman widow Paula when she saw the relics of the cross: ' "Prostrataque ante crucem, quasi pendentem Dominum cerneret"; et ego iacens ante crucem, passus Christus pro me proscriptus est in corde meo; virtutem sanctae crucis quam accepit ex Dei Filio, adoro.'[79]

---

[74] Ulrich, *Consuetudines* I.x (PL 149, 653–4).

[75] 45r and 68[72]v, *Durham Ritual*, pp. 47–8; ptd Thompson and Lindelöf, *Durham Collectar*, pp. 93–4 and 149–51.

[76] See above, p. 10.

[77] *Epistula*, viii.30 (ed. Hallinger, p. 165): 'We consider it ridiculous to venerate the cross during the time when *Alleluia* is not sung. If anyone wishes to venerate the cross during Quadragesima he does not need to venerate it with us on the day of the Lord's Passion.' The implication is that the proper occasion on which to venerate the cross is Good Friday, not during Lent; cf. *Epistula*, viii.31 (p. 166): 'Conformat se sancta aecclesia capiti suo et de glorificatione eius reticetur, usquedum exaltetur per triumphum victoriae.'

[78] Cf. above, p. 46.

[79] Amalarius, *Liber officialis* I.xiv.7 (ed. Hanssens II, 101): ' "Prostrate before the cross as though she saw the Lord hanging there"; and I, lying before the cross, have Christ suffering for me written on my heart; I adore the power of the holy cross which it received

During the reading of the Passion, Christ was imagined visibly present on the cross, and the sense of reliving Christ's Passion was enhanced by the reading of the Passion in three tones of voice to simulate the different participants in the action. The reproaches, 'Quia eduxi vos per desertum' and 'Quid ultra debui facere vobis', which were sung during the Veneration of the Cross implied that Christ was speaking directly to the congregation from the cross. The sense of participation in the historical event was further enhanced by the introduction of semi-dramatic incidents such as the ritual burial of the cross in a tomb next to the high altar.[80]

The remembrance of Christ's sufferings was not confined to the Good Friday ceremonies, however. The four versions of the Passion story from the gospels were used as a basis for private prayer and appear as independent texts associated with the collections of private prayers in the Book of Cerne and the Book of Nunnaminster.[81] A copy of the Passion according to St John precedes the prayers to be said before a crucifix in the Ælfwine Prayer-book.[82] Many of the prayers from the mass and Office were used privately as well as in the public prayer of the church. The collects from the day hours of the Office appear as independent items in at least three Anglo-Saxon manuscripts.[83] In addition, the prayers of the Good Friday ceremonies were copied for separate use and became the basis for further devotions in honour of the cross. The collection of private prayers at the end of the *Portiforium Wulstani* includes a ceremony with texts which are similar to those in the Good Friday rite of the *Regularis concordia*;[84] the devotion occurs twice and includes English translations of some of the texts. A similar set of private devotions but with one extra psalm occurs in two separate places in a manuscript of the *Regularis concordia*;[85] the first copy of these devotions is headed, 'Sing these psalms as often as you can in praise

from the Son of God.' Cf. Jerome, *Epistula* cviii *(Epitaphium Sanctae Paulae)*, 9 (ed. Hilberg, p. 315).

[80] *Regularis concordia*, iv.46 (ed. Symons, pp. 44–5).

[81] CUL, Ll. 1. 10, 3r–20v and 22r–40r (Kuypers, *Book of Cerne*, pp. 5–40 and 43–79); Book of Nunnaminster, 1r–16r (ed. Birch, pp. 39–57).

[82] BL, Cotton Titus D. xxvii, 57r–64r.

[83] BL, Cotton Titus D. xxvi, 45v–46r; BL, Cotton Galba A. xiv, 105v–107v; *Durham Ritual*, 60r–v and 76[69]r (Thompson and Lindelöf, *Durham Collectar*, pp. 123–4 and 144); the collects are discussed below, pp. 164–6.

[84] *Portiforium* (ed. Hughes II, 18–23).

[85] BL, Cotton Tiberius A. iii, 58r–59r and 114v–115v, part of the second set ptd Dewick, *Facsimiles of Horae BMV*.

and honour of the cross.' These manuscripts, together with the Ælfwine Prayer-book, also contain elaborate arrangements of psalms, antiphons and prayers in honour of the cross which are not based on the Good Friday ceremonies. The *Portiforium Wulstani* and the *Concordia* manuscript both include a set of prayers to the cross for protection against one's enemies;[86] the Ælfwine Prayer-book contains an extensive set of devotions to be said in front of a crucifix which seem to be unique to this manuscript.[87] The Book of Nunnaminster, thought to have belonged at one time to Alfred's wife, contains a series of forty-seven prayers on the theme of salvation history from the creation of the angels to the Last Judgement, twenty of which are concerned with Christ's Passion in all its detail. In these prayers the narrative commemoration made through reading the gospel texts was supplemented by a meditative commemoration in which each stage of Christ's Passion and glorification was made the basis of a specific petition related to the needs of the person reciting the prayer.

The simplest of these prayers is the first of the three recited during the Good Friday Veneration of the Cross in tenth-century England:

Domine Iesu Christe, adoro te in cruce ascendentem; deprecor te ut ipsa crux liberet me de diabolo percutiente.
Domine Iesu Christe, adoro te in cruce vulneratum; deprecor te ut ipsa vulnera remedium sint animae meae.
Domine Iesu Christe, adoro te in sepulchro positum; deprecor te ut ipsa mors sit vita mea.
Domine Iesu Christe, adoro te descendentem ad inferos liberantem captivos; deprecor te ut non ibi me dimittas introire.
Domine Iesu Christe, adoro te resurgentem ab inferis ascendentem ad caelos; deprecor te, miserere mei.
Domine Iesu Christe, adoro te venturum iudicaturum; deprecor te ut in tuo adventu non intres in iudicio cum me peccante, sed deprecor te ut ante dimittas quam iudices.[88]

An earlier and more elaborate version of the prayer, found in the eighth- or ninth-century Book of Cerne, includes references to the crown of thorns, the gall and vinegar in addition to the general reference to Christ's wounds in the *Concordia* prayer.[89] The most detailed recollection of Christ's

86 *Portiforium* (ed. Hughes II, 24), BL, Cotton Tiberius A. iii, 59r–v.
87 BL, Cotton Titus D. xxvii, 66r–70r.
88 Trans. in *Regularis concordia*, iv.45 (ed. Symons, p. 43).
89 Kuypers, *Book of Cerne*, pp. 114–17.

sufferings, however, is contained in the series of prayers in the Book of Nunnaminster where each detail is separately invoked: the kiss of Judas, the crowning with thorns, the taunting, the removal of Christ's clothes, the darkness which descended on the earth, the promise to the repentant thief, the closing of Christ's eyes in death, the wound in his side.

Many of these prayers indicate that they were recited in front of a crucifix: some are headed, 'Ante crucem domini deprecatio sancta legenda' or, 'Ante crucem domini oratio sancta'; others include phrases such as 'prostratum coram adoranda tua cruce sancta', 'tibi flecto genua mea' or, 'deprecor coram sancta cruce tua'.[90] Some may have been said in front of the large crucifixes associated with the high altar, the entrance to the choir or the altar of the cross, for the *Regularis concordia* provides for private prayer between Matins and Lauds, before Vespers and after Compline and this prayer must have taken place in the choir of the church. At other times those wishing to pray could do so 'secretis oratorii locis', in the side-chapels where private masses were said.[91] Some of the small stone panels such as those at Romsey and Stepney may have been placed in these chapels to serve as a focus for prayer and it is probable that some bookcovers functioned in the same way. The decoration of bookcovers, which often doubled as reliquaries, frequently included crosses or crucifixes. The Ely inventory of 1134 lists fifteen decorated bookcovers, ten of which were ornamented with crucifixes or Crucifixion groups; five of the ten were made in the Anglo-Saxon period.[92] One of the four gospel-books owned by Judith of Flanders still has its jewelled gold cover, decorated with raised figures of Christ in Majesty and Christ crucified, and a gospel-book given by Ælfgar of Mercia to Rheims in the 1060s in memory of his son Burchard once had a similar binding.[93] The Ely bookcovers were of metal, like that on the Judith Gospels, but Carolingian bookbindings show that ivory was a favoured medium for bindings and it is likely that some at least of the small ivory panels preserved from the late Anglo-Saxon period come from bookcovers. Elaborately decorated bindings of this kind normally belonged to books displayed in the church, often on the altar, and it was therefore

90 BL, Cotton Titus D. xxvii, 71r; BL, Arundel 155, 173r; CUL, Ff. 1. 23, 277v and 278r; BL, Cotton Vespasian A. i, 158r.
91 *Regularis concordia*, i. 19, 25 and 27, Proemium 6 and xii.67 (ed. Symons, pp. 14, 21–2, 23–4, 4 and 66).
92 *Liber Eliensis* III.50 (ed. Blake, pp. 290–1).
93 Needham, *Bookbindings*, pl. xxi; M. C. Ross, 'Bookcover', pp. 83–5, fig. 1.

possible to create scenes in high relief, giving the impression of small sculptured panels. The two ivory figures of Mary and John at Saint-Omer probably came from a binding of this kind (pl. VI); they are very close to the ninth-century ivory figures placed either side of a cross – the figure of Christ being missing – on the cover of an eleventh-century missal from Saint-Denis.[94] Some manuscript pictures of the Crucifixion such as the frontispieces to the Ramsey and Arundel Psalters (pls. XIV and IX respectively) and the Weingarten Gospels (pl. XVI) were probably used in the same way, as was the drawing in the Ælfwine Prayer-book (pl. VIII).

The structural similarity between some of the prayers and cycles of prayers and the cycles of pictures in the Tiberius Psalter and the Sacramentary of Robert of Jumièges, suggests that these too were used as aids to meditative prayer.[95] The cycle of pictures in the Psalter, like the prayer in the Book of Cerne and the collection of prayers in the Book of Nunnaminster, encloses the events of Christ's life within references to the creation and Last Judgement.[96] In the Nunnaminster cycle Christ's life is presented as the means by which God reformed human nature, the overall theme being set out in the prayer, 'Deus formator reformatorque humanae naturae qui incondita condidisti, qui caelum extendisti, et terram fundasti, Paradisum plantasti, et hominem de limo terrae formasti, et errantem eum ad viam vitae revocasti.'[97] In the prayer of the Book of Cerne Christ's life is similarly portrayed as part of the movement of creation from the first appearance of light, through the judgement of Adam, the rescue of Noah and the destruction of Pharaoh's army in the Red Sea to the final judgement of the world.[98] In the psalter cycle this movement from creation to judgement is filled out by a parallel between David and Christ.[99] In all three sequences Christ's death is seen as part of the total plan God is working out for his world. Both cycles of pictures resemble the prayers in their concern with the human details of Christ's life as well as with its theological significance.[100] The paintings in the sacramentary include

---

[94] Beckwith, *Ivory Carvings*, pls. 57–8; H. Swarzenski, *Monuments*, pl. 12 (26–7); Goldschmidt, *Elfenbeinskulpturen* II, 60, fig. 40, pl. lxx. 194.

[95] See above, pp. 30 and 33–4.   [96] See also below, pp. 175–8.

[97] Book of Nunnaminster, 19v–20r (ed. Birch, p. 62): 'God, the creator and re-creator of human nature, who formed the unformed, who spread out the sky and founded the earth, who planted Paradise and formed man from the dust of the earth, and when he erred called him back to the way of life.'

[98] Kuypers, *Book of Cerne*, pp. 114–17.   [99] See above, p. 34.

[100] See above, p. 30.

scenes of devotional rather than doctrinal importance: the betrayal by Judas and the deposition from the cross. The psalter cycle includes incidents which have an immediate and practical application to the lives of the readers – Christ washing his disciples' feet, the betrayal by Judas, doubting Thomas – as well as the great doctrinal pictures of the Crucifixion (pl. XIII), the empty tomb, the Ascension and the descent of the Holy Spirit. [101] The picture of Christ washing his disciples' feet is labelled, 'Hic fecit Iesus mandatum cum discipulis suis.' The word *mandatum* and the use of the verb *fecit* relate the scene to the liturgical washing of feet which took place on Maundy Thursday fulfilling Christ's commandment, 'Mandatum novum do vobis, ut diligatis invicem sicut dilexi vos.' [102] The two scenes in which Judas is shown kissing Christ as he betrays him can be related to the omission of the kiss of peace during the Maundy Thursday mass in memory of the betrayal by Judas. [103] The scene with doubting Thomas provides reassurance to those whose faith is weak. [104]

Some pictures may have derived from meditative prayer as well as being a stimulus to it. Goscelin describes Benno painting the walls of Edith's church at Wilton with scenes of Christ's Passion, 'as she had pictured them in her heart'. [105] Elsewhere, he compares Edith, her mother and Benno to Paula, Eustochium and Jerome, [106] a comment which suggests that, like Paula, they may have imagined themselves as actually present at the gospel events. [107]

Whereas the manuscript representations of Christ's death and the crucifixes and Crucifixion groups displayed permanently in the church offered a focus for extended meditation, other items must have provided quite brief reminders of the redemption. Leofric's gifts to Exeter included

[101] See above, p. 34.

[102] John XIII.34; see also John XIII.14–15; Schapiro, 'Disappearing Christ', p. 150 and above, p. 14, n. 60.

[103] Amalarius, *Liber officialis* I.xiii.18 (ed. Hanssens II, 98); compare also the laments which accompanied the readings about the betrayal by Judas in the Jerusalem ceremonies, *Itinerarium Egeriae*, xxxiv and xxxvi.3 (ed. Franceschini and Weber, pp. 78 and 80).

[104] Cf. *CH* I.xvi (ed. Thorpe, p. 234).

[105] *De sancta Editha* I. vii.20, in Wilmart, 'La légende de Ste Edith', pp. 86–7; see also above, p. 16.

[106] *De sancta Editha* I.iv.14 (*ibid.*, p. 73).

[107] See above, p. 55 and *Epistula* cviii (*Epitaphium Sanctae Paulae*), 9–10 (ed. Hilberg, pp. 314–18).

processional and pectoral crosses among the necessary equipment of a church and there are many examples and illustrations of such items. [108] The drawing of Æthelgar, archbishop of Canterbury (988–90) and earlier abbot of New Minster, in the *Liber vitae* of New Minster, shows him carrying an episcopal cross; a similarly shaped cross is held by Christ in the pictures of doubting Thomas in the Benedictional of Æthelwold and in the Tiberius Psalter. The eighth- or ninth-century Rupert cross, usually described as an altar cross, may have been the upper part of a processional cross. [109] Other Winchester pictures show smaller crosses being carried in the hand. Mary holds such a cross in the frontispiece to the New Minster Charter and similar crosses are held by Peter in one of the paintings at the beginning of the Benedictional of Æthelwold, by Christ in a painting in the Tiberius Psalter and by one of the apostles in the drawing of the Ascension in the same manuscript. In addition to four seventh-century pectoral crosses – the Cuthbert cross, the Wilton and Ixworth pendants and the Thurnham cross – two particularly magnificent reliquary crosses have been preserved from the later Anglo-Saxon period. [110] The first, which dates from the end of the tenth century, consists of an ivory figure mounted on a cedarwood cross covered in gold filigree. The second, which probably dates from the second quarter of the eleventh century, consists of an ivory box with foliage scrolls and figures of the Lamb among the evangelist symbols. [111] Both crosses have suspension loops and shows signs of wear on the back. Many liturgical objects were decorated with crucifixes. The Alcester tau, which dates from the early eleventh century, has a carving of the Crucifixion on one side of the head and of the Resurrection on the other. [112] An ivory and silver tau of about the same date, now at Cologne Cathedral, has a Crucifixion scene on one side and a carving of Christ in Majesty on the other; the silver mounts below the head are decorated with representations of the Harrowing of Hell and of the Maries at the sepulchre. [113]

At its most basic, devotion to the cross was concerned with protection against both physical and spiritual enemies. This is reflected in the practice of crossing oneself seven times each day, [114] in the use of the sign of the

[108] *Exeter Book*, ed. Chambers *et al.*, p. 21.
[109] Campbell, *Anglo-Saxons*, p. 108, pl. 101.
[110] Beckwith, *Ivory Carvings*, nos. 20 and 45. [111] Raw, 'Archer', pp. 391–4.
[112] British Museum, MLA 1903, 3–23, 1.
[113] Cologne, Cathedral Treasury, Tau cross.
[114] *Blickling Homilies*, no. iv (ed. Morris, p. 47).

cross in the leechdoms[115] and in the raising of crosses in hermitages and on battle-sites. Guthlac protected himself against devils by raising a cross[116] and Oswald raised a cross before his battle against Ceadwalla. [117] Harold prayed in front of the crucifix at Waltham before the Battle of Hastings in order to ask for help in battle. [118] One of the antiphons commonly sung in front of the cross read, 'Per signum crucis de inimicis nostris libera nos, Domine, Deus noster'[119] and a collection of prayers, psalms and antiphons in the *Portiforium Wulstani* is headed, 'Gyf ðe ðynce þæt ðine fynd þwyrlice ymbe þe ðrydian ðonne gang þu on gelimplicere stowe and þe ða halgan rode to gescyldnesse geciig and asete þe aðenedum earmum and cweð þus ærest.'[120]

The desire for protection at the moment of death was another potent reason for venerating the cross. People recalled Christ's forgiveness of the repentant thief and asked for the same mercy for themselves. [121] Many of the prayers to the cross reiterate this point. The most striking is probably the prayer 'O Iesu clementissime' in the Ælfwine Prayer-book, with its refrain, 'Dum supervenerit mihi mortis hora horribilis', [122] but the same theme is there, even if less dramatically expressed, in the public prayer of the Good Friday veneration with its appeal, 'deprecor te ut in tuo adventu non intres in iudicio cum me peccante'. [123] The belief that devotion to the cross would ensure one's entry to heaven is set out at length in the explanatory lines which follow the vision of the cross in the Old English poem, *The Dream of the Rood*. The poet places his hope of protection in the cross which has told him:

> ðurh ða rode sceal   rice gesecan
> of eorðwege   æghwylc sawl,
> seo þe mid Wealdende   wunian þenceð. [124]

---

[115] *Leechdoms*, ed. Leonhardi, pp. 34, 41, 106, 135, 147 and 150.   [116] *Guthlac* 180.

[117] *LS*, no. xxvi (ed. Skeat II, 126).

[118] L-B 4478 and 4480 (citing *Vita Haroldi regis* and *De inventione sanctae crucis Walthamensis*); see below, p. 143.

[119] *Durham Ritual*,. 68[72]v (Thompson and Lindelöf, *Durham Collectar*, p. 150).

[120] *Portiforium* (ed. Hughes II, 24): 'If it seems to you that your enemies deliberate evilly around you go to a suitable place and call on the holy cross for protection and set yourself down with outstretched arms and first say as follows'; also in BL, Cotton Tiberius A. iii, 59r.

[121] BL, Cotton Titus D. xxvii, 72r.   [122] BL, Cotton Titus D. xxvii, 69r.

[123] *Regularis concordia*, iv.45 (ed. Symons, p. 43).

[124] *Dream of the Rood* 119–21: 'Every soul which thinks to live with God must seek the way from earth to the kingdom of heaven through the cross.'

If the cross would protect one at the hour of death or — as the poet of *The Dream of the Rood* saw it — would fetch one to the next world, what better gift could one make to a church than a cross or crucifix? Æthelwold gave three crosses to Peterborough 'for the redemption of his soul'.[125] Byrhtnoth gave two gold crosses to Ely for burial rights just before the battle at Maldon in which he lost his life and King Eadred bequeathed two gold crucifixes to Winchester for the same purpose.[126] Cnut, who was buried in the Old Minster, gave a large cross to the New Minster; the picture recording this gift forms the frontispiece to the monastery's *Liber vitae*, suggesting that it was intended to secure the monks' prayers for the king's welfare in the next world. This drawing of Cnut is usually compared to the painting of King Edgar offering his charter to Christ,[127] but there is another, and perhaps better, parallel. The upper part of the drawing, which shows Christ flanked by SS Mary and Peter, is very close to the Byzantine scene of the *deesis* in which the Virgin Mary and St John the Baptist intercede with Christ at the Last Judgement. A very similar composition, in which St Peter replaces St John as he does in the Winchester drawing, fills the upper part of a late Anglo-Saxon ivory panel in the Museum of Archaeology and Ethnology at Cambridge; on the ivory, however, the Last Judgement reference is certain for Christ is displaying his wounds and the lower half of the carving shows a cross held by two angels. The drawing of Cnut presenting his cross is followed in the manuscript by a double-page representation of the Last Judgement and of St Peter welcoming the blessed into heaven, confirming the suggestion that the figures of Mary and Peter in the first drawing are interceding for the king. Their intercession is gained by Cnut's gift of the cross which forms the central point of the drawing. The drawing therefore is more than a simple record of a splendid gift or a fitting frontispiece to the minster's list of benefactors. It links this particular gift quite specifically to the future judgement to assert the belief that devotion to the cross would bring one safely to heaven. This belief may explain the pictures of Judith of Flanders (pl. XVI) and of a number of continental kings and monks like Charles the Bald or Hrabanus Maurus kneeling before a cross or crucifix.[128] These pictures reminded their owners

[125] Robertson, *Anglo-Saxon Charters*, p. 72.
[126] *Liber Eliensis* II.62 (ed. Blake, p. 135); L-B 5952 (citing *Liber monasterii de Hyda*).
[127] See above, pp. 25–6.
[128] New York, Pierpont Morgan, 709, 1v; Munich, Schatzkammer, 38v–39r; Cambridge, Trinity College B. 16. 3, 30v.

of the attitude they wished to cultivate: the painting of Hrabanus Maurus illustrates the poem, 'De adoratione crucis ab opifice' in his *De laudibus sanctae crucis*, and the picture of Charles the Bald is inscribed,

> In cruce qui mundi solvasti crimina Christe;
> Orando mihimet tu vulnera cuncta resolve.[129]

By having themselves painted in front of a crucifix pious people were, as it were, able to remain permanently in front of the crucifix in will if not in deed.

This desire for protection is reflected in the first two reasons given for venerating the cross in a text copied into two late Anglo-Saxon manuscripts:

Prima causa est, qui in una die septem cruces adit, aut septies unam crucem adorat, septem porte inferni clauduntur illi, et septem porte paradisi aperiuntur ei. Secunda causa est, si primum opus tuum tibi sit ad crucem, omnes demones si fuissent circa te, non potuissent nocere tibi. Tertia causa est, qui non declinat ad crucem non recipit pro se passionem Christi; qui autem declinat recepit eam et liberabitur. Quarta causa est, quantum terrae pergis ad crucem, quasi tantum de hereditate propria offeras domino.[130]

The third reason is more subtle. Prayer before a crucifix was not simply a matter of calling on the power inherent in the cross; it was a way of praying to Christ and of laying claim to the benefits of his Passion. As Amalarius said: 'Prosternor corpore ante crucem, mente ante Deum; veneror crucem per quam redemptus sum, sed illum deprecor qui redemit.'[131] Ælfric pointed out that the cross was honoured in order to honour Christ who

---

[129] 'Christ who cancelled the sins of the world on the cross, as I pray cancel again all that wounds me'.

[130] BL, Cotton Titus D. xxvii, 70r–v and BL, Cotton Tiberius A. iii, 59v–60r: 'The first reason is that if a man recites seven prayers to the cross in one day, or venerates a cross seven times, the seven doors of hell will be closed to him and the seven doors of paradise will be opened to him. The second reason is, if your first duty is to the cross, if all the demons should be around you, they will not be able to harm you. The third reason is, who does not bow to the cross does not receive for himself the Passion of Christ; the man who bows receives it and is freed. The fourth reason is that whatever land you give to the cross, it is as if you offer to the Lord that much from your own inheritance.'

[131] *Liber officialis* I.xiv.8 (ed. Hanssens II, 102): 'I prostrate my body before the cross, my mind before God; I venerate the cross through which I am redeemed, but I pray to him who redeemed me.'

redeemed us through it.[132] It was not enough simply to treat the cross as a source of help; man had to make some response to Christ whose power was invoked through the cross. In a sermon for mid-Lent Sunday Ælfric compared the crucifix to the brazen serpent raised up by Moses. Just as the Israelites were healed physically through looking at the serpent, so the Christian was healed spiritually through contemplating the crucifix, provided that he did so with faith in Christ's death and Resurrection.[133] In a homily for the feast of the Invention of the Cross Ælfric pointed out that the crucifix was a reminder of Christ's sufferings and of his love in redeeming mankind, a love which demanded gratitude in return.[134] This gratitude could be expressed in different ways. For Ælfric it was shown through a life devoted to good works.[135] For other writers it was a more emotional affair. Wulfstan visualized Christ the judge reminding man of his sufferings and demanding some return.[136] There is a similar passage in the Blickling homily for Easter Day,[137] but the most dramatic expressions of this theme come in the poem *Christ III* and in one of the Vercelli homilies where Christ reproaches man for his lack of love:

Loca nu and sceawa þa dolg on minum handum and on minum fotum, and gesioh ðas mine sidan, þe wæs spere þurh-stungen. þynum sare þe ic on minum lichoman onfeng, to þan þæt ic wolde, þæt ðu wære rixiende in heofona-rices wuldre. Forhwan, la man, forlur ðu þis eal, þe ic for þe þrowode? Forhwan wær ðu swa unþancul þinre onlysnesse?[138]

In *Christ III* the poet links the sins of his contemporaries even more closely to Christ's sufferings by making Christ ask:

Forhwon ahenge þu mec hefgor on þinra honda rode
þonne iu hongade?[139]

---

[132] *CH* II.xviii (ed. Godden, pp. 175–6).

[133] *CH* II.xiii (*ibid.*, p. 136); see below, p. 172.

[134] *CH* II.xviii (*ibid.*, pp. 175–6). [135] *CH* II.vii (*ibid.*, pp. 65–6).

[136] See above, p. 39.

[137] *Blickling Homilies*, no. vii (ed. Morris, p. 91).

[138] *Vercelli Homilies*, no. viii (ed. Förster, pp. 154–5): 'Look now and see the wounds in my hands and in my feet and see my side which was wounded by the spear. I received your punishment in my body because I wished you to reign in the glory of heaven. Why, O man, did you lose all this that I suffered for you? Why were you so unmindful of your redemption?'

[139] *Christ* 1487–8: 'Why do you hang me more heavily on the cross of your hands than I once hung?' (Caesarius, *Serm.* lvii.4 (ed. Morin I, 253)).

In these passages the two themes kept separate in the early church – the hope of heaven and compassion for Christ's sufferings – come together. The same point is made in two of the paintings added to the Athelstan Psalter at Winchester in the second quarter of the tenth century. These pictures show the saints in heaven, but they are grouped round figures of Christ showing his wounds or throned in front of the symbols of his Passion.[140]

It is clear from these and other passages that the theme of compassion for Christ's sufferings was well-known in the writings of the late Anglo-Saxon period, but it was almost invariably linked with the subject of the Last Judgement. Many of the prayers to be said in front of a crucifix were similarly concerned with the Judgement. The emphasis in the art of the period was different. In the Last Judgement passages man is placed in the position of the sinner who has caused Christ's sufferings and who has failed to return his love. In the prayers he is linked to the thief, a sinner in need of God's mercy. Most representations of the Crucifixion from the late Anglo-Saxon period, on the other hand, show Christ accompanied by Mary and John. If man is to respond to these scenes it must be by associating himself with Mary and John, the two people who stayed with Christ when most of his friends had deserted him. The relationship is no longer one of guilt but of love. The implications of this choice of iconography are discussed in ch. 4 with particular reference to the manuscript art. Detailed discussion of this kind is not possible in relation to the Crucifixion scenes placed in churches because most of the stone carvings which remain have been mutilated or are too worn for the details to be visible and the large-scale pieces of goldsmith's work have long since disappeared. Some suggestions will be made in ch. 8 about the way in which the large Crucifixion groups with figures of Mary and John may have functioned in the liturgy. As regards private prayer, it is clear that it must have included elements other than those found in the written prayers of the period. As will be shown later,[141] it seems likely that the meditative prayer of the late Anglo-Saxon period was much closer to that of the time of Anselm and Ailred than the texts would suggest.

---

[140] See above, pp. 38–9.   [141] See below, pp. 99, 157 and 160.

3

Crucifixion pictures in context

The pictures of the Crucifixion in late Anglo-Saxon manuscripts resemble the stone crucifixes and Crucifixion groups which formed part of the decoration of Anglo-Saxon churches and the gold or ivory Crucifixion groups which decorated bookcovers from an iconographic point of view. They differed from them in one respect, however, for they had a textual context even though most of them were not textual illustrations in the strict sense. Carvings have to be seen in relation to the church buildings and the actions which took place in them. Manuscript pictures must be seen additionally in relation to the words of the gospels, the psalter and the different liturgical texts and to the way in which these words were understood.

When Christians recall Christ's death on the cross they are concerned with an abstract idea (man's redemption) as well as with a historical event (Christ's death in time). In Christ's life and death God, who is infinite and outside time, entered the finite world of human history. This interpenetration of the infinite and the finite finds clear expression in the liturgy, the central act of the Christian church. In the action of the mass the church makes Christ's death present, not by recalling or repeating an event which happened at a particular moment in history, but by sharing in the perpetual offering of Christ to his Father in the eternal present of heaven. This timeless action, repeated in every mass, is enclosed within the historical cycle of the liturgical year, with its two sequences of commemorations, the first recalling the main events of Christ's life, the second placing those events within the whole of salvation history from the fall of man to the consummation of the world. The mass, then, combines an escape from human time (in the unchanging prayers of the canon and the actions they accompany) with a commemoration of historical events (in the prayers and readings proper to the various feasts). The Office, on the other hand, while recalling the events of salvation in readings from the Old and New Testaments, demonstrates the coherence and unity of God's plan as it unfolds in history by linking Old Testament prophecy with gospel event.

The decoration of the gospel-books, psalters and sacramentaries used in the mass and Office, like the texts of these services, relates Christ's death on the cross to the gospel sequence of events, to salvation history as a whole and to the timeless state of the next world.

The gospels are primarily narrative works, recording the events of Christ's life: they are therefore appropriately illustrated by cycles of narrative pictures. Even in the gospels, however, the events are interpreted: in particular, Christ's life is presented as the fulfilment of the Old Testament prophecies. Both approaches are reflected in the decoration of three sixth-century gospel-books: the Gospels of St Augustine, the Greek Rossano Gospels and the Syriac Rabbula Gospels. The St Augustine's Gospels contain two sets of narrative pictures, the first at the end of St Mark's Gospel, the second at the beginning of that of St Luke. The first consists of a full-page arrangement of twelve pictures of the Passion, from the entry to Jerusalem up to the carrying of the cross. The second consists of a series of scenes from Christ's ministry, placed in the frame of the portrait of St Luke. Other pictures have been lost but offsets show that there were probably similar scenes in the borders to the portraits of the other three evangelists[1] together with a second full-page painting divided into compartments at the end of St John's Gospel.[2] The two sets of paintings which remain differ from each other in that the scenes from the ministry which accompany the evangelist portrait are based on events from that gospel whereas the Passion scenes include episodes from all four gospels. The episode of Pilate washing his hands is found only in St Matthew's Gospel; the raising of Lazarus and the washing of the disciples' feet, on the other hand, appear only in St John's Gospel while the scene in which Simon of Cyrene carries the cross comes from the synoptic gospels not from that of St John. These scenes were not intended to help the reader to visualize one particular gospel text; instead they provide an independent narrative which could be studied independently of any text.

In the Rossano Gospels and those of Rabbula this separation between

---

[1] St Augustine's Gospels, before 3r, 78r and 206r.   [2] *Ibid.*, after 265v.

text and pictures is even clearer, for the pictures are placed at the beginning of the manuscript as a whole. Those in the Rossano Gospels, which cover the narrative from the raising of Lazarus to Pilate's condemnation of Christ, include scenes mentioned only by Matthew, Luke or John as well as episodes which occur in three or more of the gospels. The scenes in the margins of the canon tables of the Rabbula Gospels again combine material from all four gospels. The Massacre of the Innocents[3] is described only by St Matthew, the Annunciation to Zechariah[4] only by Luke and the marriage at Cana[5] only by John. But whereas the pictures in the St Augustine's Gospels are purely historical and narrative in content, those in the Rossano and Rabbula Gospels involve an interpretative, prophetic element. In the Rossano Gospels all but two of the gospel pictures are accompanied by figures of prophets displaying Old Testament texts which relate to the gospel scenes. In the Rabbula Gospels Old Testament figures accompany the gospel scenes in the borders to the canon tables.

The practice of placing groups of pictures at the beginning of the text continues in ninth-, tenth- and eleventh-century gospel-books but with a major difference in emphasis. The pictures in the St Augustine and Rossano Gospels provide an independent gospel harmony, a narrative in visual form. Carolingian gospel frontispieces, by contrast, are theological or symbolic rather than narrative in form. The Grandval and Vivian Bibles include narrative frontispieces to Genesis, Exodus and the Pauline Epistles and there are further narrative frontispieces to Old Testament books in the San Callisto Bible.[6] The gospel frontispieces, on the other hand, offer complex theological statements rather than stories in pictures. In the Bamberg Bible, the earliest of the illustrated bibles from Tours, the gospel frontispiece (which serves as frontispiece to the whole of the New Testament) shows a lamb with spear, sponge and chalice, accompanied by symbols of the four evangelists and busts of the four major prophets; a nearly identical picture forms the frontispiece to the St Gauzelin Gospels at Nancy. The inscription to this picture shows that the scene symbolizes the unity of the gospels in the person of Christ:

---

[3] Rabbula Gospels, 4v.   [4] *Ibid.*, 3v.   [5] *Ibid.*, 5r.

[6] Kessler, *Illustrated Bibles* and Gaehde, 'Turonian Sources', 'Carolingian Interpretations' and 'Pictorial Sources'.

Quattuor hic rutilant uno de fonte fluentes
Matthei, Marci, Lucae libri atque Iohannes.[7]

The composition is probably derived from Apocalypse pictures of the Adoration of the Lamb but there are extra elements. The spear and sponge relate the scene to Christ's death on the cross; the chalice relates it to the mass; the figures of the prophets stress the fulfilment in Christ of Old Testament prophecy. In the Grandval, Vivian and San Callisto Bibles the Lamb is replaced by a figure of Christ enthroned. The artist of the Grandval Bible shows Christ surrounded by the four beasts, representing the evangelists, and by the four major prophets: Isaiah, Jeremiah, Ezekiel and Daniel. In the Vivian and San Callisto Bibles the scene is further extended by the addition of writing figures of the evangelists. The scene is based on Jerome's gospel preface, *Plures fuisse*, in which the biblical descriptions of God enthroned among the four beasts[8] are used as evidence for the unity of the four gospel accounts of Christ's life. These pictures are making the same point as the gospel cycles in the Rossano and Rabbula Gospels but in a different way. Whereas the sixth-century manuscripts asserted the unity of the gospels by creating a single composite narrative from them and accompanied this by figures of the prophets to indicate the unity of Old and New Testaments, the Carolingian manuscripts offer an abstract, diagrammatic statement of the theme. Another scene with a similar meaning is that of the fountain of life. The inscription to the frontispiece of the St Gauzelin Gospels alludes to the interpretation of the four rivers of paradise springing from one source as a reference to the evangelists with their source, Christ.[9] This allegory is made explicit in the group of six pictures which precedes the text of the late eighth-century Godescalc Gospels. Portraits of the four evangelists are followed by a painting of Christ enthroned. The sixth picture, a painting of a fountain based on the baptistry of the Lateran, indicates the link between the first five. The fountain represents the spring in the Garden of Eden (Christ) from which the four rivers (the evangelists) spread out to water the garden (the church). But the fountain is also the font and this links the scene to Christ's death. As one of the fifth-century inscriptions on the font at the Lateran stated:

---

[7] 'Four books shine out here flowing from one source, those of Matthew, Mark, Luke and John.' *Rutilant*, strictly speaking, implies a red colour; the couplet may, therefore, embody an allusion to the blood from Christ's side. See below, p. 71.

[8] Ezekiel I.5–12, Apoc. IV.7.   [9] Gen. II.10

Fons hic est vitae, qui totum diluit orbem
sumens de Christi vulnere principium. [10]

The scene of the fountain, like that of the Lamb with the chalice, spear and sponge, relates the theme of the common origin of the gospels to that of the source of the two chief sacraments, the baptism and the eucharist, in the blood and water which flowed from Christ's side on the cross. [11]

Carolingian gospel-books did contain straightforward gospel scenes but they differed from the pictures in sixth-century gospel-books in being linked to the gospel text or the gospel prefaces. The Gospels of Saint-Médard of Soissons, which contain paintings of the symbolic scenes of the Adoration of the Lamb and the fountain of life, also include small paintings of gospel scenes such as the Baptism of Christ, the Annunciation to Zechariah or the turning of water into wine at the marriage of Cana; these are found in the margins of the evangelist portraits and initial pages. [12] These scenes are not in chronological order nor do they provide a coherent gospel cycle. Their selection and arrangement are probably related to the contents of the Priscillian Prologues to the gospels which attempt to define the distinctive features of each gospel. [13] In other manuscripts the pictures are more closely integrated with the gospel text. The initial to St Luke's Gospel in the Harley Gospels contains a painting of the Annunciation to Zechariah, described in Luke I.11, and a gospel-book from Metz, contemporary with the Drogo Sacramentary, includes historiated initials with scenes of the Annunciation, Nativity, birth of John the Baptist and the journey of Mary and Joseph to Bethlehem, introducing the texts in which these events are described.

Carolingian artists also produced fully illustrated gospel-books though only one fragment now remains: a painting of the Annunciation to Zechariah pasted into BL, Cotton Claudius B. v. [14] The main examples of

[10] 'This is the fountain of life which waters the whole earth, taking its source from the wound of Christ'; quoted in Underwood, 'Fountain of Life', p. 55.
[11] See below, pp. 119–20 for a discussion of this theme in the Arenberg Gospels; note too the baptismal ceremonies of the Easter vigil in which men were symbolically buried with Christ to rise with him: 'You have been taught that when we were baptised in Christ Jesus we were baptised in his death; in other words, when we were baptised we went into the tomb with him and joined him in death' (Rom. VI.3–4); cf. *Missal of Robert of Jumièges*, ed. Wilson, pp. 97–9.
[12] Paris, BN, lat. 8850, 82r, 123v, 124r, 180v and 181r.
[13] Walker, 'Priscillian Prologues', pp. 1–10.
[14] BL, Cotton Claudius B.v, 132v.

illustrated gospel-books however come from the Ottonian period. But although the pictures in late tenth-century manuscripts such as the Codex Egberti or the Gospels of Otto III are intended to help the reader visualize the events described in the text they are still to some extent independent of the text. The selection and arrangement of the scenes depend on the order of events in Christ's life, not on the order of the text. In the Gospels of Otto III all the infancy pictures are placed opposite St Matthew's Gospel and all the Passion scenes opposite that of St John. The problem of creating a single sequence of pictures is not as acute in the Codex Egberti, which is a gospel-lectionary with readings already arranged in a single chronological sequence. The readings for Holy Week however include all four Passion narratives. The problem of maintaining a single sequence of pictures in this part of the manuscript was solved by leaving the accounts of Christ's Passion by Matthew, Mark and Luke unillustrated and by placing all ten pictures of Christ's Passion opposite St John's account, read on Good Friday. In addition to maintaining the correct chronological order of the scenes by confining the illustrations to one of the Passion narratives the artist of the Codex Egberti fused the four gospel accounts together, including incidents or details from gospels other than that to which the pictures ostensibly belong.[15] The first of the three Crucifixion scenes is based on the synoptic gospels and shows Simon of Cyrene carrying the cross; St John states that Christ carried his own cross.[16] The next scene includes elements from all four gospels. The gambling soldiers at the foot of the cross are mentioned by all the evangelists; the different attitudes of the two thieves, one of whom turns towards Christ while the other turns away, are based on St Luke's Gospel, the only one to mention the penitent thief; the soldier with the sponge full of vinegar, on the other hand, is not mentioned by Luke, while the presence of St John, who stands to the right of the picture, is mentioned only in the fourth gospel. The role of these pictures as a semi-independent gospel harmony is enhanced by their narrative style, each stage in the narrative being represented in a separate picture. For example, the drink of vinegar offered to Christ before he died and the spear-wound made in his side after death are placed in separate pictures, emphasizing that these are events which took place in historical time. In the Gospels of Otto III, by contrast, the incidents of the vinegar and the spear-wound are placed in the same picture as though they

[15] See below, p. 93.   [16] John XIX.17.

happened simultaneously. The picture is still not a symbolic one however. All its details derive from the text of the gospels; even the figures of the sun and moon are simply a metaphorical way of expressing a historical event for they are hiding their faces, an allusion to the darkness at the death of Christ.

Crucifixion pictures of the type found in the Gospels of Otto III or the Codex Egberti are to be understood within the world of history. They form part of a narrative sequence; they include only material of a historical kind; they illustrate the text with which they are associated but do not interpret it. Some Carolingian and Ottonian gospel-books however use Crucifixion pictures as frontispieces or as items in groups of pictures prefixing the gospel texts. Some, like the painting in the Gospels of Gundold, are clearly devotional items for they contain donor figures: their function is to express an attitude of mind not to interpret a text. This particular picture, which shows Christ dead on the cross, blood dripping from his wounds, is placed opposite a picture of Christ in Majesty;[17] the two scenes represent the two aspects of the act of redemption: the human suffering and the divine glory. Like the pictures of the Lamb among the evangelists or the fountain of life in Carolingian gospel-books, they involve an abstraction. The same is true of the Crucifixion picture in the Uta Gospels. This painting combines allegorical figures like Vita and Mors, Ecclesia and Synagogue with pictures of gospel events surrounding Christ's death: the tearing of the temple veil and the dead emerging from their graves. All the details, whether historical or allegorical, have inscriptions drawing attention to their symbolic meaning. The context of the picture, too, indicates that it is to be understood in a symbolic, non-narrative way. The Crucifixion painting is the third of four scenes. The first shows the hand of God; the second is a dedication scene showing the abbess Uta with the Virgin and Child; the fourth is a mass scene. In these pictures Christ's death on the cross is related on the one hand to the mystery of his incarnation and on the other to the mystery of his presence in the mass.[18]

The pictures in two slightly later manuscripts, the Odbert Gospels, produced at Saint-Bertin round about the year 1000, and the early eleventh-century Gospels of Bernward of Hildesheim, are harder to classify. The opening words of the gospels of Luke and John in the Odbert Gospels have historiated initials like those in some Carolingian gospel-books. The

[17] Stuttgart, Württembergische Landesbibl., Cod. Bibl. 402, 9v and 10r.
[18] See below, pp. 100–1, for a discussion of this relationship in early Christian art.

scene at the beginning of St Luke's Gospel is the traditional one of the Annunciation to Zechariah, described in chapter 1 of the gospel;[19] the initial also includes a picture of the Nativity with the ox and ass. The initial and frame at the beginning of St John's Gospel include four scenes: the Crucifixion, the Harrowing of Hell, the three Maries at the tomb and the Ascension.[20] These pictures do not relate specifically to St John's Gospel. Unlike the other evangelists John does not mention the conversation of the women with the angel at the tomb. The Ascension is not mentioned explicitly by any of the evangelists, though there may be an allusion to it in Luke XXIV.51. The Harrowing of Hell belongs to church tradition, not to the gospel story. The pictures are not only independent of the text; they interpret the events of Christ's life as well as recording them. The Crucifixion scene includes figures of Ecclesia and Synagogue as well as those of Mary and John and presents Christ's death as an event which replaced the rule of law by that of grace. Four figures with water jars represent the four rivers of the Garden of Eden and, in turn, symbolize the four evangelists. Their source, Christ, is indicated by the picture of Christ on the cross. The figures of Gaia and Oceanus in the lower margin draw attention to the cosmic significance of Christ's death. Despite its apparent narrative context, therefore, this scene is closer to symbolic scenes such as that in the Uta Gospels than it is to the historical, narrative scenes of the Codex Egberti.

The paintings in the Bernward Gospels are similar in emphasis to those in the Odbert Gospels. Each of the gospels is preceded by a group of paintings including evangelist portraits, gospel scenes and theological pictures. The Crucifixion is represented twice: once at the beginning of St Luke's Gospel, where it is combined with the symbol of St Luke,[21] and once among the pictures preceding St John's Gospel.[22] The gospel scenes are not a narrative cycle for they are not arranged in chronological order. The scenes relating to Christ's early life are divided among the four groups and relate to the early part of each gospel. The Adoration of the Magi appears before St Matthew's Gospel, the Annunciation to Zechariah and the Visitation accompany that of St Luke and the Baptism of Christ that of St

---

[19] New York, Pierpont Morgan, 333, 51r; for the Nativity see Luke II.6–20; the ox and the ass are not mentioned in the gospels: they derive from the *Liber de infantia* (or *Pseudo-Matthew*), ch. xiv, in James, *Apocryphal New Testament*, p. 74.

[20] New York, Pierpont Morgan, 333, 85r.   [21] Hildesheim Cathedral, 18, 118v.

[22] *Ibid.*, 175r.

John. Other pictures, however, are unrelated to the text. Christ's appearance to Mary Magdalen, described in John XX.11–17, is placed at the beginning of St Mark's Gospel in which it is not mentioned. The first of the two Crucifixion pictures is preceded by scenes of the Last Supper and of Judas receiving his reward, suggesting that it should be understood in a literal, narrative way. However, the combination of this scene with the symbol of St Luke and the composition of the scene, with a tree at each side of the cross and personifications of Oceanus and Gaia, suggests that its primary meaning is not a historical one. It seems likely that the picture alludes to the common interpretation of St Luke's symbol of the bull as a reference to the sacrificial nature of Christ's death: 'Hostia Christus erat, quam Lucas in bove monstrat.'[23] In the same way, the eagle, the symbol of St John, is placed below a representation of the Ascension which it was thought to symbolize: 'Alta Dei scandens aquilae gerit ora Iohannes.'[24] This picture comes after a series of five paintings of events described in St John's Gospel: the Baptism, the raising of Lazarus, the entry to Jerusalem, the Crucifixion and the empty tomb. They are not simple illustrations of the gospel story however. Instead, they illustrate a doctrinal point. The events chosen for illustration all reveal Christ's dual nature as God incarnate and develop the theme of the opening picture to St John's Gospel, which shows Christ in human form as a child in the crib and, under the form of a lamb, as the *Logos*, the Word with God.

The illustrations in ninth-, tenth- and eleventh-century gospel-books, then, can be divided into two groups. On the one hand are straightforward illustrations of the gospel story which are distributed throughout the text or used in historiated initials. They normally relate to the adjacent text though they may incorporate details from other gospel texts in the manner of a gospel harmony. On the other hand are pictures placed at the beginning of the gospels as a whole or at the beginning of the separate gospels. These pictures are normally not related to the gospel texts though they may illustrate the prefatory material such as Jerome's *Plures fuisse* or the Priscillian Prologues to the individual gospels. Their emphasis tends to be theological rather than historical though they also include author portraits and scenes from the lives of the evangelists.

A similar distinction between pictures distributed throughout the text

---

[23] 'Christ was the sacrifice which Luke revealed through the bull'; Tschan, *Bernward* II, 42.

[24] 'John displays the face of an eagle, ascending to the heights of God'; *ibid.* II, 43.

and pictures placed at its major divisions is found in psalters, though with one significant difference. The psalter is not a narrative work and is not normally illustrated with narrative pictures. Fully illustrated psalters such as the Stuttgart and Utrecht Psalters, both dating from the ninth century, contain two kinds of picture: first, literal representations of the words of the psalms and secondly typological scenes in which the text is interpreted with reference to New Testament events. Psalters in which illustrations are confined to the main structural divisions tend to contain pictures of David with his musicians or playing the harp, corresponding to the evangelist portraits of gospel-books, scenes from the life of David, corresponding to the scenes from the lives of the evangelists, and pictures of the Crucifixion, Christ in Majesty or Christ above the beasts, corresponding to the theological scenes in gospel-books. Because the psalter is not read in the same way as the gospels these scenes do not necessarily have the same meaning when placed in a psalter as they do in a gospel-book.

The Stuttgart Psalter contains five paintings of the Crucifixion, the first opposite Psalm I, two opposite Psalm XXI, which was believed to have been recited by Christ while hanging on the cross, one opposite Psalm LXVIII and one opposite Psalm LXXXVII, both of which were interpreted by St Augustine with reference to Christ's Passion. The literal, verbal nature of these pictures is seen in that on 27r, illustrating Psalm XXI.18–22, where a lion and unicorn accompany the gambling soldiers of the gospel story to illustrate the words:

> Save me from the lion's mouth,
> my poor soul from the wild bulls' horns.[25]

The illustration to Psalm LXVIII,[26] on the other hand, is purely prophetic. The picture shows one of the soldiers offering Christ vinegar on a sponge, an incident linked by St John[27] with the psalm verse:

> They gave me poison to eat instead,
> When I was thirsty they gave me vinegar to drink.[28]

The Utrecht Psalter includes four drawings of the Crucifixion as well as a drawing of the instruments of the Passion placed before Psalm XXI. Two of these drawings[29] illustrate the Canticle of Habbakuk and the Apostles'

---

[25] Ps. XXI.22, Vulgate, *a cornibus unicornium.*

[26] Stuttgart, Württembergische Landesbibl., Cod. Bibl. fol. 23, 80v.

[27] John XIX.28–9.   [28] Ps. LXVIII.22.

[29] Utrecht, Universiteitsbibl. 32, 85v and 90r.

Creed and show Christ with the two thieves and the spear- and sponge-bearers and Christ with Mary and John and the two soldiers. The other drawings illustrate Psalms LXXXVIII and CXV. The first[30] shows Christ with the spear- and sponge-bearers. The second[31] shows Christ dressed in a long robe and hanging from a cross surmounted by a wreath; to the left of the cross are Mary and John and to the right a man holding a paten of bread in his right hand and catching the blood from Christ's side in a chalice held in his left; below the cross is a soldier with a spear. This drawing illustrates the verse, 'I will take the chalice of salvation and I will call upon the name of the Lord.'[32] It relates Christ's death to the sacrifice of the mass and asserts the identity of Christ's historical body and blood with the bread and wine of the eucharist. The figures of Mary and John and of the soldier with the spear are based on the gospel text.[33] The man with the paten and chalice, however, has no such historical basis. He does not represent either the psalmist who originally spoke the verse or some person actually present at Christ's death. Instead he illustrates an idea: the link between Old Testament prophecy, New Testament fulfilment and contemporary sacrament. In these drawings the Crucifixion is placed within a series of abstract relationships. The links with Old Testament prophecy demonstrate the truth of Christ's claim to be the Messiah; the links with the ritual of the contemporary church assert the identity of the sacrifice of the mass and of Christ's sacrifice on Calvary. The drawing placed next to Psalm XXI shows a simple cross supporting the spear, sponge, scourge and crown of thorns. Psalm XXI was always interpreted as a prophecy of the Crucifixion and the lot-casting machine below the cross in the Utrecht Psalter relates to verse 19:

> They divide my garments among them
> and cast lots for my clothes.

The rest of the drawing, however, has no direct relationship to the text of the psalm. Instead, it links the allusion to Christ's death to an assertion of his triumph; the instruments of Christ's Passion become triumphal objects, the *arma Christi* with which he conquered death.

The illustrations to the Stuttgart and Utrecht Psalters invite reflection on specific passages from the psalms. The Odbert Psalter, which dates from about the year 1000, carries prophetic interpretation much further. This

---

[30] *Ibid.*, 51v.   [31] *Ibid.*, 67r.   [32] Ps. CXV.4, see below, pp. 119–20.
[33] John XIX.26–7 and 34.

manuscript contains an extensive gospel cycle in its historiated initials. The scenes are in chronological order and, in general, have little to do with the psalms they accompany. A picture of the Crucifixion, together with scenes of the Maries at the tomb and the Harrowing of Hell, fills the initial to Psalm CI.[34] Augustine's commentary on Psalm CI, verse 24, points out the necessity of Christ's death if he was to rise from the dead,[35] but it seems unlikely that this is the basis of the Odbert picture. The initial to Psalm C[36] is decorated with a picture of Judas and Psalm CVI[37] has a picture of the descent from the cross. The Crucifixion picture here is related to a sequence of pictures illustrating Christ's life, not to the text of an individual psalm, and the logical relationship of prophecy and fulfilment is abandoned for the much vaguer idea that everything in the psalter speaks of Christ. As Augustine said: 'Modo ergo tota intentio nostra est, quando psalmum audimus, quando prophetam, quando legem, quae omnia antequam veniret in carne Dominus noster Iesus Christus, conscripta sunt, Christum ibi videre, Christum ibi intellegere.'[38] In using this manuscript the reader was invited to meditate on the life of Christ while reciting the psalms but the actual text of the psalms did not form part of the meditation. It was simply a background, much as the prayers of the rosary were in later times.

Sacramentaries, like gospel-books and psalters, can have their decoration placed at the major structural divisions or distributed throughout the text. In this case, however, the two kinds of illustration correspond to different kinds of text: the central, unchanging prayer of the mass and the prayers and prefaces proper to each of the feasts of the liturgical year. The central prayer (the canon) made the events of salvation present, and was, in a sense, a commentary on them; the proper prayers, like the readings from the gospels and epistles, commemorated the individual events of salvation history and applied them to the needs of the present. The distinction made between these two kinds of text is clearly seen in the historiated initials of the Drogo Sacramentary, written and decorated at Metz between 844 and 855. The texts of the Preface and Sanctus at the beginning of the

---

[34] Boulogne, Bibl. Mun., 20, 109r.

[35] *Enarrationes in Psalmos* (ed. Dekkers and Fraipont III, 1442, on Ps. CI).

[36] Boulogne, Bibl. Mun., 20, 108r.   [37] *Ibid.*, 119v.

[38] *Enarr. in Ps.* (ed. Dekkers and Fraipont II, 1378, on Ps. XCVIII): 'Therefore our whole intention, when we hear the psalm, the prophet, the law, all that was written before our Lord Jesus Christ came in the flesh, is to see Christ there, to understand Christ there.'

manuscript[39] are illustrated by mass scenes, with a painting of a seraph opposite the Sanctus; the initial to the *Te igitur* at the beginning of the canon includes figures of Abel, Abraham and Melchisedech, all of whom are mentioned in the prayer of the canon as having offered sacrifices which prefigured Christ's sacrifice, commemorated in the mass.[40] Some of the proper prefaces later in the manuscript are illustrated by historiated initials; they too contain liturgical scenes, not historical, biblical ones. These scenes, which direct attention to the meaning of the action which they accompany, are quite different from the narrative and symbolic pictures elsewhere in the sacramentary, which direct attention away from the action and invite the reader to meditate on the meaning of the events commemorated. The first text entered for each feast is the collect; the initial to each of these prayers is decorated with a scene which relates to the feast being celebrated. Some, like the Nativity scenes with the shepherds and the Magi[41] in the initials for Christmas and Epiphany, are narrative pictures, comparable to those in the Ottonian gospel-books. In these scenes the gospel event is relived in all its historical detail and attention moves outwards from the central event to other events surrounding it. Other pictures, like that of the Crucifixion in the initial to the Palm Sunday collect,[42] are more symbolic. Instead of dividing attention between a number of related events they focus attention on the inner meaning of the event being commemorated. Both approaches belong to the techniques of meditative prayer: the first is designed to produce an emotional response, the second a more intellectual one. The Crucifixion painting in the Drogo Sacramentary expresses at least six different ideas. Above the cross are two angels with a wreath representing the martyr's crown. To the sides are two small crowned heads representing the sun and moon; they are cosmic symbols, drawing attention to Christ's role as lord of creation. At the foot of the cross a coiled serpent recalls man's fall. The prophet Hosea is shown seated under the cross because of his prophecy that Christ would destroy death:

> And am I to save them from the power of Sheol?
> Am I to rescue them from Death?
> Where is your plague, Death?
> Where are your scourges, Sheol?[43]

---

[39] Paris, BN, lat. 9428, 14v, 15r and 15v.
[40] The *Te igitur* initial is discussed by Suntrup, '*Te igitur*-Initialen', pp. 303–13.
[41] Paris, BN, lat. 9428, 23v, 24v and 34v.   [42] *Ibid.*, 43v.
[43] Hos. XIII.14, cf. I Cor. XV.55.

The fulfilment of the prophecy is represented by two tiny figures of the dead rising from their graves. On the other side of the cross stands Ecclesia, catching the blood from Christ's side in a chalice. She asserts the identity of the blood from Christ's side and the sacramental wine and, in addition, emphasizes the church's role as guardian of the sacraments. The grieving figures of Mary and John appear at the edges of the painting, where they act as witnesses to the historical event. The picture contains historical elements – the figures of Mary and John and the dead rising from their graves – but its main significance lies in the central figures who relate the historical event to salvation history, to the messianic prophecies and to the church of the ninth century.

In contrast to the Drogo Sacramentary, which uses gospel scenes only in relation to the liturgical cycle, some sacramentaries contain Crucifixion pictures at the *Te igitur*, the prayer which begins the canon of the mass. An early example is that in the eighth-century Sacramentary of Gellone, which shows Christ hanging from the cross with blood streaming from his wounds, including the wound in his side; above the cross are two flying angels.[44] A painting in a ninth-century sacramentary from Metz[45] is similar; Christ is shown alive, with open eyes, yet the wound in his side is present, for the blood from Christ's side was believed to symbolize the eucharist. Bede, for instance, says: 'passione illius in cruce completa *unus militum lancea latus eius aperuit, et continuo exivit sanguis et aqua*. Haec sunt etenim sacramenta quibus ecclesia in Christo nascitur et nutritur aqua videlicet baptismatis qua abluitur a peccatis et sanguis calicis dominici quo confirmatur in donis.'[46] These pictures do not focus on the Crucifixion as a historical event; instead, they remind the priest that the mass he is celebrating makes present Christ's death on the cross. The painting in the Sacramentary of Gellone is particularly appropriate for this purpose. It draws attention to Christ's blood, the source of the sacrament, and to the presence of angels, believed to assist at the mass as they assisted at Christ's death.[47] Yet some manuscripts illustrate the *Te igitur* by pictures of the

---

[44] See below, p. 116.   [45] Paris, BN, lat. 1141, 6v.

[46] *Hom.* II.xv, *In ascensione Domini* (Luc. XXIV.44–53) (ed. Hurst, p. 284): 'When his Passion on the cross was finished *one of the soldiers opened his side with a spear and immediately there went forth blood and water*. For these are the sacraments by which the church is born and nourished in Christ: the water, that is, of baptism by which she is cleansed of sins and the blood of God's chalice by which she is strengthened in gifts.'

[47] See below, pp. 120–2.

crucified Christ with SS Mary and John.[48] This iconography usually recalls the incident when Christ committed his mother to the protection of his favourite disciple. In Byzantine pictures of the Crucifixion, Christ's words are often placed next to the figures of Mary and John and they are included in the Crucifixion picture at the *Te igitur* in a sacramentary of the second half of the tenth century from Verdun Cathedral.[49] Mary and John are mentioned in the *Communicantes* of the canon, together with other saints, but although Mary is singled out and placed at the beginning of the list, St John is not distinguished from the other disciples. Moreover, the incident in which Christ entrusted Mary and John to each other has little relevance to the central prayer of the mass or to the action it accompanies. St Augustine suggests another emphasis. In his commentary on Psalm XXI he argues that Christ's Passion, re-enacted each year, stirs the emotions of those who are present as though they were assisting at Christ's death: 'Tamen ne obliviscamur quod factum est semel, in memoria nostra omni anno fit. Quoties pascha celebratur, numquid toties Christus moritur? Sed tamen anniversaria recordatio quasi repraesentat quod olim factum est, et sic nos facit moveri tamquam videamus in cruce pendentem Dominum, non tamen irridentes, sed credentes.'[50] The final phrase of this passage contrasts the mockery of the Jews with the faith of Mary and John and invites the Christian to associate himself with the latter. Mary and John, then, are put forward as models for imitation and the priest celebrating mass is invited to stand with them at the foot of the cross. Mary and John also had an intercessory role.[51] A fragment of a tenth-century sacramentary stitched into a gospel-book from Reichenau contains a painting of a crucifix with Mary and John.[52] Inscriptions on the frame and background of this painting read as follows:

> Fulgida stella maris pro cunctis posce misellis.
> Et tu iunge preces cum virgine virgo Iohannes.

[48] E.g. Hildesheim Cathedral, 19 (Bernward Sacramentary), 4v.

[49] Munich, Bayerische Staatsbibl., Clm. 10077, 12r; for Byzantine examples see Goldschmidt and Weitzmann, *Elfenbeinskulpturen* II, pls. xv.38, xvi.39, xvii.40 and xviii.42.

[50] *Enarr. in Ps.* (ed. Dekkers and Fraipont I, 121, on Ps. XXI): 'Nevertheless, in case we forget what happened once only, it is repeated each year in memory. As often as Easter is celebrated, does not Christ die as often? In the same way, the yearly remembrance as it were makes present once more what was done once and thus makes us respond as though we saw the Lord hanging on the cross, not however scorning but believing.'

[51] See below, pp. 101–2.   [52] Leipzig, Stadtbibl., cxc, IV.

Annuat hoc agnus mundi pro peste peremptus.
In cruce, Christe, tua confige nocentia cuncta.

Stella maris.
Virgo Iohannis.[53]

The priest calls on the help of the saints as he does in the *Communicantes* of the mass, but singles out Mary and John from the long list of apostles and early popes, martyrs and other saints mentioned in the prayer. In this way the prayer of the church is brought closer to the historical event commemorated. One manuscript goes even further in linking the timeless action of the mass to historical events. An early eleventh-century sacramentary from Bamberg includes scenes of the three Maries at the tomb and the Resurrection as well as one of the Crucifixion before the *Te igitur*.[54] The prayer *Unde et memores* which follows the consecration prayers of the canon recalls Christ's Resurrection and Ascension as well as his Passion and this may account for the inclusion of the extra scenes. Bede relates St Luke's description of the women and the angels at Christ's tomb to the contemporary celebration of the mass, linking the altar to the tomb[55] and a similar point is made by Amalarius in his *Liber officialis*.[56] It is possible, therefore, that the pictures express contemporary understanding of the action of the mass.[57]

Tenth- and eleventh-century English manuscript art differs noticeably from French and German art of the period in that most pictures of scenes from the gospel story occur in missals, sacramentaries, pontificals and psalters rather than in gospel-books. The scenes chosen for illustration and the order in which they occur depend on criteria other than the historical order of the gospel text. Narrative sequences illustrating New Testament scenes are therefore rare in late Anglo-Saxon art and most Crucifixion pictures form part of schemes of decoration where the pictures are related to the structural divisions of the text or to its overall meaning rather than illustrating the text itself.

Crucifixion pictures appear in thirteen late Anglo-Saxon manuscripts:

53 'Shining star of the sea, intercede for all wretched people, and do you join your prayers with the virgin, O virgin John. May the Lamb killed for the sickness of the world assent to this. Transfix all harmful things on your cross, O Christ. Star of the sea, virgin John'.
54 Munich, Bayerische Staatsbibl., Clm. 4456, 15v, 15r and 16r.
55 *In Luc.* VI (Luke XXIV.1) (ed. Hurst, pp. 410–11).
56 *Liber officialis* III.xxx.1–5 (ed. Hanssens II, 359–61).
57 See also below, pp. 183–4.

two gospel-books, five psalters, three pontificals, sacramentaries or missals, one book of private prayers, a collection of homilies and, finally, a copy of Bede's *Historia ecclesiastica*. In addition, an unfinished sketch of the Crucifixion was added in the tenth century to a ninth-century French manuscript.[58] Six of the sixteen Crucifixion pictures in these manuscripts are frontispieces or form part of a group of pictures used as a kind of multiple frontispiece. Two are placed opposite the beginning of Psalm LI to mark one of the three major divisions of the psalter. One forms part of a cycle of biblical scenes without any accompanying text. Two are sketches unrelated to a text, though the first has been overwritten with a homily on the Passion, and the second with a series of devotional texts in various hands of the eleventh and twelfth centuries. Another decorates the initial to the chapter of Bede's *Historia ecclesiastica* which describes the vision of Drihthelm;[59] it has no connection with the text it accompanies. The remaining four pictures are contained within the text. One illustrates Psalm XXI and another the *Te igitur* of the mass. Of the other two, the first relates to a series of private prayers in honour of the cross. Only one forms part of a narrative sequence: the painting placed before the vigil mass of Holy Saturday in the Sacramentary of Robert of Jumièges (pl. XV). Even this is not a textual illustration, for the sacramentary does not include the gospel readings to which the pictures refer.

The two Crucifixion pictures in Anglo-Saxon gospel-books are both frontispieces. Fragments remain of one extensively illustrated late Anglo-Saxon gospel-lectionary (the Damme Fragments) with pictures of the Gadarene swine, Peter and the tribute money and Christ teaching his disciples, but it seems unlikely that large numbers of such gospel-books were produced. More than twenty illuminated gospel-books and gospel-lectionaries remain from the late Anglo-Saxon period but in most cases their decoration is confined to evangelist portraits, decorated *incipits* and ornamental canon tables. When other pictures are included they are

---

[58] The manuscripts are: NY, Pierpont Morgan, 709 and 869; CCCC 41, 421 and 422; CUL, Ff. I. 23; BL, Arundel 60, Cotton Tiberius C. vi, Cotton Titus D. xxvii and Harley 2904; Paris, Bibliothèque Nationale, lat. 943; Rouen, Bibliothèque Municipale, A. 292 [26] and Y. 6 [274]; Vatican, Biblioteca Apostolica, Reg. lat. 12. The illustrations in BL, Royal I. E. VI, which may have included a Crucifixion, are not discussed here, since the manuscript is earlier than the period under discussion; the probable subjects of the pictures in Royal I. E. VI are discussed in Budny, 'Royal I E. vi' and Ohlgren, *Catalogue*, pp. 28–30 and 137 (nos. 32 and 160).

[59] CCCC 41, p. 410.

grouped at the beginning of the manuscript or at the beginning of each gospel. The Trinity Gospels, for example, include a painting of Christ enthroned as well as portraits of the four evangelists. The Boulogne Gospels contain groups of pictures at the beginning of each gospel. Some scenes, like the portraits of Christ's ancestors at the beginning of St Matthew's gospel, the picture of the Annunciation to Zechariah at the beginning of that of St Luke or the drawing of Christ with Isaiah and John the Baptist at the beginning of that of St Mark, relate to the opening chapters of these particular gospels. The pictures of the Annunciation, Visitation, Nativity and annunciation to the shepherds at the beginning of St Matthew's gospel, on the other hand, illustrate passages from St Luke's gospel.[60] These scenes provide a short narrative sequence but they are not textual illustrations and the manuscript contains no complete gospel cycle. The Crucifixion pictures at the beginning of the Arenberg Gospels (pl. 11) and the Weingarten Gospels have even less connection with the text. The picture in the Weingarten Gospels (pl. XVI) shows Christ accompanied by Mary and John with a second female figure at the foot of the cross. The manuscript belonged to Judith of Flanders and it is likely that this figure represents Judith herself.[61] The picture, then, is a devotional one similar to that in the Gundold Gospels discussed above. It exists as an item in its own right, independent of the text. The Crucifixion picture in the Arenberg Gospels (pl. 11) is placed immediately before the elaborately decorated canon tables. The pictures above these tables, which show angels, the Virgin and Child, Mary with the Trinity, Christ with Peter and Paul, Christ with saints and angels and Christ triumphing over the beasts, do not represent gospel scenes nor do they provide a narrative context for the picture of the Crucifixion. The drawing of Christ above the beasts derives originally from an illustration to Psalm XC[62] though the scene was frequently used in other contexts. The picture of Christ with Peter and Paul relates to the foundation of the church. The pictures of the Virgin and Child and of the Trinity embody a reference to Christ's dual nature as God and man. The drawing of Christ holding a lamb and accompanied by saints suggests a reference to the eucharist. The Crucifixion picture has to be seen within this context. As the first picture in the sequence it states the main theme: the redemption. The iconography chosen for this picture is that with angels above the cross and a chalice below it: as will be explained

[60] Luke I.26–56 and II.6–20.   [61] See below, p. 160.   [62] Ps. XC.13.

later, this iconography emphasizes the continuation of Christ's offering in the eucharist and also the role of the eucharist as a sharing in the worship of heaven.[63] These themes are taken up in the picture of Christ holding a lamb. Other pictures elaborate the theology of the redemption: the picture of the Virgin and Child celebrates Christ's incarnation while the following picture, of Mary with the Trinity, emphasizes his divinity. Whereas the Crucifixion picture shows the cross as an instrument of punishment, the picture of the cross accompanied by angels shows its triumph. Where the Crucifixion picture shows Christ apparently overcome by evil, the final picture, of Christ above the beasts, shows him triumphing over evil. The redemption theology which is implicit in the Crucifixion picture is made explicit in the series of scenes which follow.[64] These scenes are far more intellectual than the painting in the Weingarten Gospels (pl. XVI), which is concerned with the emotional response of the individual to Christ's death. In both cases, however, the function of the scenes is similar: to aid meditation.

The Crucifixion pictures in tenth- and eleventh-century English psalters include both textual illustrations and structural pictures. The Harley copy of the Utrecht Psalter, written at Canterbury in the 1020s, suggests that the English were less inclined to see allusions to the Crucifixion than Carolingian artists were. The Crucifixion pictures at Psalms LXXXVIII and CXV are omitted and only the drawing of the instruments of the Passion is preserved.[65] The Bury Psalter, which is lavishly illustrated with marginal drawings, including representations of the Nativity, the Massacre of the Innocents, the Adoration of the Magi and the Ascension[66] includes only one Crucifixion picture, opposite Psalm XXI (pl. XIIa). This psalm is usually taken as a prophecy of Christ's sufferings on the cross, but the artist chose to focus on verse 29: 'For Yahweh reigns, the ruler of nations.' He showed Christ reigning from the cross, a crown on his head and, above, the hand of God holding a sceptre. Beneath his feet are a serpent and a chalice to symbolize the defeat of evil and the redemption of man through Christ's blood which becomes the wine of the eucharist.[67] The picture may owe something to a comment on this psalm by Cassiodorus, who quotes Augustine: 'Ille irrisus, ille crucifixus, ille derelictus hoc regnum acquirit

---

[63] See below, ch. 5.
[64] See Rosenthal, 'Arenberg Gospels', pp. 169–278, though I differ in some details.
[65] BL, Harley 603, 12r, see below, p. 94.   [66] See above, pp. 32–3.
[67] See below, p. 147.

et tradet in fine Deo et Patri, non ut ipse amittat, sed quod in fide seminavit cum venit minor Patre, hoc perducat in speciem in qua aequalis non recessit a Patre.'[68]

The other English psalters with Crucifixion pictures place them at the beginning of the manuscript or at Psalm LI, to mark the start of the second major division of the psalter.[69] The simplest of these psalters is that known as the Ramsey Psalter, written at Winchester towards the end of the tenth century. It contains only one picture: the drawing of the Crucifixion placed opposite the beginning of Psalm I (pl. XIV). The picture does not relate to this particular psalm and should probably be interpreted as a devotional item in its own right, like other Crucifixion pictures used as frontispieces. The Crucifixion picture at the beginning of the Arundel Psalter (pl. IX) had a similar function, but a second picture of the Crucifixion which was added later, opposite Psalm LI, does relate to the text. Augustine interpreted this psalm with reference to Christ's Passion, drawing a parallel between David, persecuted by Saul, and Christ dying on the cross. He stressed that Christ's glory was the result of his suffering and that we too must follow this path. The Crucifixion picture opposite Psalm LI in the Winchcombe Psalter (pl. X), like that in the Arundel Psalter, illustrates the hidden meaning of Psalm LI but it also has to be seen in relation to the total illustrative scheme of the manuscript. The picture of David with his musicians opposite Psalm I is the traditional author portrait, placed opposite the beginning of the text. The picture of Christ with angels at Psalm CI forms a pair with the Crucifixion picture at Psalm LI; it shows Christ, as Augustine says in his commentary, 'non infirmus in cruce, sed fortis in caelo'.[70] The fourth picture, which shows Christ above the beasts (Ps. CIX) has a similar function to the corresponding picture in the Arenberg Gospels.[71] It shows Christ's final triumph over evil. In this group of scenes the sufferings of Christ, the descendant of David, are contrasted with his glory in heaven and the evil which seemed to triumph at Christ's death is shown to be ultimately powerless. A rather different

---

[68] Cassiodorus, *Expos. Ps.*, xxi.29 (ed. Adriaen, I, 206): ' Mocked, crucified, abandoned, he gains this kingdom and surrenders it at last to God the Father, not so that he should abandon it, but that what he sowed in faith when he came, inferior to the Father, he should bring in the form in which, as his equal, he never left the Father.'

[69] See above, p. 23.

[70] *Enarr. in Ps.* (ed. Dekkers and Fraipont III, 1442, on Ps. CI).

[71] See above, pp. 84–5.

emphasis is given to the Crucifixion in the illustrations to the Athelstan Psalter. Originally the manuscript seems to have included a painting of the Crucifixion opposite Psalm LI, in addition to the surviving pictures of Christ with saints and angels (placed before the calendar and the computus), of the Nativity opposite Psalm I and of the Ascension at Psalm CI.[72] If this was the case, Christ's death was portrayed in relation to his coming to earth, his ascent to heaven and his return as judge to show his wounds to man and remind him of his debt.[73]

Whereas in these manuscripts the pictures are distributed throughout the text, the Crucifixion scene in the Tiberius Psalter (pl. XIII) forms part of a cycle of pictures placed at the beginning of the manuscript. It was suggested in ch. 2[74] that these pictures were used as an aid to meditative prayer. Some of the pictures are based on scenes in a liturgical book, the Benedictional of Æthelwold, and the choice of New Testament scenes resembles that of a liturgical cycle in some respects, but it seems unlikely that the pictures were intended as a basis for meditation on part of the liturgical cycle. Their meaning must be sought in the combination of scenes from the life of David with scenes from the life of Christ, an arrangement clearly devised for use with a psalter. The interpretation of David as a type of Christ was, of course, a commonplace of medieval thought.[75] As Ælfric said in his *Preface to the Old and New Testaments*, 'He [David] hæfde getacnunge þæs Hælendes Cristes, þe ys stranghynde, þe þone hetolan deofol eaðelice gewilde, and him of gewann ealle þa geleafullan on his gelaðunge, swa swa David gelæhte þæt scep of þam deorum.'[76] The pictures are not simply typological, however. The series as a whole treats the theme of redemption in a chronological way in contrast to the more abstract approach of other psalters. In addition there is an emphasis on the theme of Christ's kingship, something which would be particularly appropriate in Winchester which was not only the royal seat but which possessed a crucifix said to have been crowned by Cnut in acknowledge-

---

[72] BL, Cotton Galba A. xviii, 2v and 21r; Oxford, Bodleian Library, Rawlinson B. 484, 85r and BL, Cotton Galba A.xviii, 120v. The Crucifixion picture has been lost but traces of paint show that there was once a painting opposite Ps. LI; see Wood, 'Æthelstan's Empire', p. 268, n.84.

[73] See above, pp. 38–9.   [74] See above. p. 59.   [75] See above, p. 34.

[76] *Heptateuch* (ed. Crawford, p. 36): 'He symbolized the Saviour Christ, who is strong of hand, who easily overpowered the wicked devil and gained from him for his kingdom all the faithful as David freed the sheep from the wild beasts.'

ment of Christ's sovereignty.[77] The Crucifixion scene in the Psalter shows Christ wearing a crown and the royal element is emphasized by the inclusion of a picture of Christ before Pilate, recalling the question, 'Are you the king of the Jews?' and Christ's reply, 'Mine is not a kingdom of this world.'[78] The theme of Christ reigning from the cross is found elsewhere in late Anglo-Saxon art but it is given a particular slant in the Tiberius Psalter by the surrounding pictures of the third temptation (the goods of this world), the washing of the disciples' feet and Christ before Pilate, in which the implications of this kingship are explored. Another theme in the Crucifixion picture which is emphasized through the choice of supporting pictures is that of the physical reality of Christ's death and consequently of his Resurrection.[79] The picture which follows those of the Crucifixion and the Maries at the tomb shows doubting Thomas placing his hand in Christ's side. The selection and arrangement of the scenes is designed, like that of the pictures at the beginning of the Arenberg Gospels, to illustrate a series of theological points: they do not simply record events from Christ's life even though they are chronologically arranged.

The nature of the Tiberius cycle can be clearly seen if it is compared with the series of Passion pictures in the Sacramentary of Robert of Jumièges. This manuscript includes three small narrative sequences of pictures illustrating the feasts of the Nativity, Epiphany and Easter.[80] The third group consists of four full-page pictures showing the arrest of Christ, the Crucifixion (pl. xv), the deposition and the Maries at the tomb, placed before the text of the Easter vigil service. Three of these scenes were included in the Tiberius cycle, but whereas the psalter added a picture of Christ before Pilate, the sacramentary added one of the descent from the cross, so changing the whole emphasis of the series. The picture of Christ before Pilate embodied a theological point: the nature of Christ's power. The picture of the descent from the cross, like the Good Friday liturgy from which it derives, was intended to evoke an emotional response. This difference in approach is seen also in the different Crucifixion iconographies chosen by the two artists. That in the Tiberius Psalter (pl. xiii) shows Christ with the two soldiers. The main emphasis is on the dual nature of Christ, though there is also an allusion to the healing effect of Christ's death, for the picture shows the cure of Longinus's blindness.[81] The

---

[77] See below, pp. 144–5.   [78] John XVIII.33 and 36.

[79] See below, pp. 107–8.

[80] See above, p. 30, and below, p. 158.   [81] See below, p. 151.

Crucifixion picture in the sacramentary shows Christ between the grieving figures of Mary and John; the scene, like that of the deposition, shows the compassion man should feel at the memory of Christ's death. The different emphasis is significant, for the liturgy of Holy Week with which the pictures in the sacramentary are associated involved a reliving of the events surrounding Christ's death. The more intellectual approach of the Tiberius cycle would have been quite out of place in such a context.

The pictures in the Sacramentary of Robert of Jumièges and in a second liturgical manuscript, the Sherborne Missal, illustrate the two methods of decorating sacramentaries seen in continental manuscripts such as the Drogo Sacramentary and the sacramentaries of Gellone and Metz. Whereas the decoration of the Sacramentary of Robert of Jumièges is related to the commemoration of historical events in the cycle of the year, and specifically to Christ's passover from death to life between the Saturday and Sunday of Easter, that of the Sherborne Missal is associated with the unchanging prayers of the canon of the mass. The emphasis is accordingly different. This manuscript contains two pictures: one of Christ enthroned between angels at the *Vere dignum* and one of the Crucifixion at the *Te igitur* (pl. XIIb).[82] The two pictures together illustrate the traditional theme of the suffering humanity and triumphant divinity of Christ. In addition, the Crucifixion picture draws attention to the meaning of the action of the mass.[83] The cross is presented as the tree of life, with new leaves springing from the dead wood where it is touched by Christ's blood. Christ is shown alive and erect before the cross. To the right is the *Dextera Dei*, symbolizing God's approval and, to the left, a dove, possibly representing the Holy Spirit, flies down with a crown. Beneath the cross is a female figure, possibly Ecclesia but more probably Mary, who points to the blood flowing from the wound in Christ's side.[84] The picture does not illustrate the text of the canon; instead it proclaims the life-bringing power of Christ's death, renewed by the church in the action of the mass.

These pictures illustrate the way in which a relatively limited range of iconographic types can vary their meaning through being placed in different textual and artistic contexts. Some, like the frontispieces to the Weingarten Gospels (pl. XVI), the Ramsey Psalter (pl. XIV), the Cambridge Homilies (pl. XI)[85] and the drawing in the Ælfwine Prayer-book

---

[82] CCCC 422, pp. 52 and 53.   [83] See below, pp. 151–5.
[84] See below, pp. 151–2.
[85] CCCC 421.

(pl. VIII), were probably devotional items: substitutes for actual crucifixes. Others, like the cycles of pictures in the Arenberg Gospels, the Tiberius Psalter or the Sacramentary of Robert of Jumièges, suggested themes for meditation of a theological or affective kind. Still others, like the drawings in the Harley 603 and Bury Psalters (pl. XIIa) and that in the Sherborne Missal (pl. XIIb), comment on and expand the text with which they are associated. None is concerned simply to convey information about a gospel event.

4

Anglo-Saxon Crucifixion iconography and the theology of the early medieval period

English artists of the late Anglo-Saxon period used a very limited number of iconographic formulae for the Crucifixion. With few exceptions the main figures are limited to three, and within these limits there is a strong preference for compositions in which the crucifix is accompanied by Mary and John. Nine of the fourteen manuscript pictures and five of the thirteen ivory carvings are of this type as are most of the stone carvings from the south of the country. [1] There are a few unaccompanied crucifixes and one or two examples of the iconography with the two soldiers which had been the preferred type in the early Anglo-Saxon period. There are, however, no examples of the complex narrative scenes with the crosses of the two thieves, the soldiers sharing out Christ's clothes and the dead rising from their graves or of the elaborate symbolic pictures with personifications of Oceanus and Gaia, Ecclesia and Synagogue, all of which were common elsewhere in early medieval art. In addition there is no evidence that Anglo-Saxon artists followed Carolingian and Ottonian artists in distinguishing between large-scale public works such as stone carvings and smaller, more intimate objects such as ivory carvings and manuscript illustrations. The same iconographic types were used for both.

These works of art were produced over a period of about seventy years during which the main features of the iconography remained virtually unchanged. Christ is invariably depicted in the manuscripts and on the ivories as a bearded long-haired figure dressed in a loincloth reaching to the knees. There are no examples of the loose full-length robe which had been common in early Christian and Hiberno-Saxon art and which reappeared in Ottonian art. One stone carving – the crucifix outside the church at

---

[1] The later of the two pictures in Arundel 60 and the initial in CCCC 41 are excluded from this count.

Langford in Oxfordshire – shows Christ dressed in a long robe with a cord at the waist but this probably derives from a model similar to the Volto Santo of Lucca, a copy of which is said to have been brought to England by Leofstan, abbot of Bury from 1044 to 1065.[2] Christ's head is normally framed by a cruciferous nimbus and in some cases he also wears a crown. The hand of God commonly appears above his head. In contrast, the *titulus* – the inscribed board over Christ's head – is rare and appears in only five manuscripts: the Ramsey Psalter (pl. XIV), the Ælfwine Prayer-book (pl. VIII), the Tiberius Psalter (pl. XIII), the Bury Psalter (pl. XIIa) and the Weingarten Gospels (pl. XVI). All except the Bury Psalter are probably Winchester manuscripts. Some stylistic variations are found within the basic figure type: the loincloth may be draped or knotted in different ways; the angle of the arms or the curve of the body may vary; sometimes the hair falls in separate strands across the shoulders. There is, however, no coherent chronological development from pictures of Christ triumphing over death to ones of Christ suffering. The drawings in the Ramsey Psalter (pl. XIV) and the Arenberg Gospels (pl. II), both of which date from the end of the tenth century, show Christ dead on the cross, his body sagging and his head sunk below his shoulders; a drawing in the Sherborne Missal made sixty years later shows him standing erect with open eyes (pl. XIIb). Crowned crucifixes, which might have been expected to be early and to carry a triumphal meaning, do not develop until the 1020s; only two of the six manuscript examples could be described as triumphal images; the other four show Christ dead on the cross. Variations in the subsidiary figures are similarly unrelated to date. A drawing in the Sherborne Pontifical, dating from the 990s, shows Mary and John standing without any visible emotion under the arms of the cross (pl. I); the nearly contemporary Ramsey Psalter shows Mary overcome by grief (pl. XIV). The only detail which may be related to date is the practice of representing the cross as a roughly cut tree. All four examples date from the closing years of the Anglo-Saxon period.[3]

The Crucifixion pictures which show Mary and John standing under the cross and those in which one of the soldiers pierces Christ's side with a spear derive from two passages found only in St John's Gospel. The other evangelists describe Christ's death between two thieves, the division of his clothes, the mockery of the bystanders, the inscription above his head, the darkness from the sixth to the ninth hour, the vinegar offered to Christ to

---

[2] See above, p. 41.

[3] For discussion of the tree-cross see O'Reilly, 'Rough-Hewn Cross'.

quench his thirst, the tearing of the temple veil and the centurion's affirmation that Christ was the Son of God. Matthew describes the dead emerging from their tombs and Luke the scene with the repentant thief. Only John records the conversation in which Christ entrusted his mother to his favourite disciple and the wounding of Christ's side after his death.[4]

St John's account of the Passion was read on Good Friday and it might have been expected that artists would have based their pictures on it in preference to the accounts by the other evangelists which were read in the earlier part of Holy Week. This was not the case however. German artists used details from all four gospels even when they were ostensibly illustrating that of St John.[5] The Crucifixion scene in the Codex Egberti,[6] which is placed next to the Good Friday readings, omits any reference to Christ entrusting his mother to his disciple and shows the women standing well to the side of the scene as described in the synoptic gospels; in addition it includes a reference to the darkness from the sixth to the ninth hour, a detail not mentioned by St John. The painting of the Crucifixion in the Gospels of Otto III, again associated with St John's Gospel,[7] includes details such as the sun and moon veiling their faces or the different attitudes of the two thieves which do not derive from St John's account. Of course, Carolingian and Ottonian artists did use the iconography showing only Mary and John under the cross, but it was only one of a variety of types. Anglo-Saxon artists, on the other hand, ignored entirely the material from the synoptic gospels concentrating instead on the two incidents noted only by St John.

The very restricted range of iconographies used in tenth- and eleventh-century English art must have been the result of deliberate choice, for alternatives were certainly available. The ninth-century Utrecht Psalter was at Canterbury in the late tenth and early eleventh centuries and some of its illustrations had an enormous influence on Anglo-Saxon art. The drawing of Christ at the right hand of God which illustrates Psalm CIX and the drawings of the Trinity and of Mary at the *Gloria* and the Apostles' Creed were copied and adapted at Winchester as well as at Canterbury and continued in use into the twelfth century. The drawings in the Utrecht Psalter include four different representations of the Crucifixion in addition to the drawing of the instruments of the Passion opposite Psalm XXI, but

[4] John XIX.26–7 and 33–4.   [5] See above, p. 72.
[6] Trier, Stadtbibl., 24, 83v.
[7] Munich, Bayerische Staatsbibl., Clm. 4453, 248v; see above, p. 72.

this rich iconographic series seems to have had virtually no influence on tenth- and eleventh-century English art. When the Psalter was copied at Canterbury in the early eleventh century the English artists omitted all four Crucifixion pictures, retaining only the drawing of the instruments of the Passion.[8] The figure of Mary in the Crucifixion picture of the Arenberg Gospels (pl. II) may owe something to one of the Utrecht Psalter drawings,[9] but there is no indication that the ideas about the Crucifixion expressed in these drawings captured the imagination of Anglo-Saxon artists as the drawings of the Trinity did. The artists of the Benedictional of Æthelwold are known to have had access to a series of New Testament pictures of a type associated with Metz and it is likely that this included a representation of the Crucifixion.[10] The paintings in the Benedictional itself do not include such a picture, Good Friday not being a feast day, but the Crucifixion panel on the Brunswick Casket and the painting of the Crucifixion in the Drogo Sacramentary, both of which come from Metz, show that the repertoire of gospel scenes at Metz included at least two iconographies for this subject.[11] Evidence that similar pictures were known in England, even though they were not copied *in toto*, comes from both Canterbury and Winchester. The drawings of the Crucifixion in the Arenberg Gospels and the Sherborne Pontifical (pls. II and I) include flying angels which are very close to those on the Brunswick Casket and the Crucifixion drawing in the Ælfwine Prayer-book (pl. VIII) includes classical figures of the sun and moon which could have been inspired by similar figures on the Casket.[12] In addition, the Crucifixion painting in the Sacramentary of Robert of Jumièges (pl. XV), written and illuminated about forty years later than the Benedictional of Æthelwold, was copied from something similar to the Brunswick Casket, for it uses the same formulae for the figures of Mary and Christ, including the sideways draping of Christ's loin-cloth. Other paintings in this manuscript have affinities to scenes on carvings from Metz and to paintings in the Benedictional of Æthelwold and in a second benedictional, also from Winchester.[13] The likelihood is that all three manuscripts were based on the same continental model.[14]

[8] Cf. above, pp. 76–7 and 85.   [9] See below, p. 115.

[10] Homburger, *Malschule von Winchester*, pp. 8–10 and 'L'art carolingien', p. 36.

[11] See above, pp. 79–80 and below, pp. 116–17.   [12] See also below, p. 132.

[13] Rouen, Bibl. Mun., Y. 7 [369].

[14] Homburger, 'L'art carolingien', pp. 41–2; *St Albans Psalter*, pp. 55–6; see also below, p. 117.

All the evidence suggests that English artists made a deliberate choice among the models available to them and that they preferred the iconography with Mary and John to those with the soldiers or the crucified thieves. The omission of the thieves and of the soldiers implies a wish to move away from a record of the historical event, while the presence of Mary and John means that more was intended than a simple reminder of Christ's sufferings, for which an unaccompanied crucifix would have been sufficient. The choice of the iconography with Mary and John is particularly striking since the Good Friday liturgy and the private prayers of the period lay more stress on Christ's forgiveness to the repentant thief than on his words to his mother and his disciple. The collect for Good Friday contrasts the punishment of Judas with the reward given to the thief. The Office prayer for None recalls how Christ sent the repentant thief to paradise.[15] The Book of Nunnaminster includes a prayer *De latrone*.[16] The Ælfwine Prayer-book contains a prayer which mentions the crowning with thorns, the thieves, the nails, the wound in Christ's side, the gall and vinegar.[17] The prayers added to the Vespasian Psalter in the early eleventh century include a reference to Christ's mercy to the thief.[18] The only references to Christ's words to his mother and his disciple are in the Good Friday reading of the Passion and in one prayer in the Ælfwine Prayer-book and the Arundel Psalter.[19] The reason for this difference in emphasis between the prayers and the art must lie in the significance which was attached in the tenth and eleventh centuries to the moment when Christ entrusted his mother to his disciple.

One of the earliest writers to explore the implications of this incident was St Ambrose.[20] In his commentary on St Luke's Gospel he claimed that St John's account of Christ's death was to be preferred to the others because John was the only evangelist to record Christ's words to his mother.[21] Ambrose interpreted the situation in a human way and argued that John's testimony showed that this act of piety on the part of the victor over suffering and the devil was more important than his gift of the kingdom of

---

[15] *Benedictine Office*, ed. Ure, p. 98.

[16] Book of Nunnaminster, 28v (ed. Birch, pp. 74–5).

[17] *Deus qui voluisti*, BL, Cotton Titus D. xxvii, 71v–72r.

[18] In the prayer, *O bone pastor*, BL, Cotton Vespasian A. i, 158r–v.

[19] *O virgo virginum*; see below pp. 102–3 and n. 61.

[20] T. Koehler, 'Jean xix.25–27', pp. 119–55.

[21] *In Luc.* x.130 (ed. Adriaen, p. 383).

heaven for, as he says, if it was a religious act to show mercy to the repentant thief how much greater was it for the mother to be honoured by the son.[22] This passage helps explain why Anglo-Saxon artists chose to represent Christ with Mary and John even though the antiphons and responses of the Good Friday liturgy and most of the private prayers of the late Anglo-Saxon period concentrated on Christ's forgiveness of the thief. They were restoring a proper balance. Yet the fact that in most late Anglo-Saxon Crucifixion pictures Christ is represented with his eyes closed shows that the artists were not concerned with the literal portrayal of the gospel event but with its theological and devotional significance. The painting in the Sacramentary of Robert of Jumièges which shows Mary and John standing sadly under the cross is the only picture which could be described as a straightforward representation of the gospel scene (pl. xv). The pictures in the Ramsey Psalter and the Weingarten Gospels (pls. xiv and xvi), which emphasize the human and emotional aspects of Mary's role, show St John writing, apparently indifferent to anything except his role as a reporter of events. In the drawings in the Winchcombe Psalter (pl. x) and the Sherborne Missal (pl. xiib) Mary, too, is shown addressing an audience outside the picture, drawing attention to the wound in Christ's side. The iconic nature of these scenes is emphasized by the symbolic details such as the hand of God above the cross, the chalice or serpent below it, the crown on Christ's head, the angels round the cross or the leaves sprouting from it, all of which involve interpretation of the historical event. These motifs appear in various combinations in practically all late Anglo-Saxon Crucifixion pictures. Sometimes they are brought together to create distinct iconographic types, discussed in chs. 5 to 7; sometimes they move from one type to another to represent ideas which were central to the understanding of the Crucifixion in the late Anglo-Saxon period.

One of the major themes in the Crucifixion pictures of this period is the witness of St John. The description of the piercing of Christ's side in St John's Gospel is presented as a reliable account because it is that of an eye-witness: 'One of the soldiers pierced his side with a lance; and immediately there came out blood and water. This is the evidence of one who saw it – trustworthy evidence, and he knows he speaks the truth – and he gives it so that you may believe as well.'[23] These verses are probably the basis of the Crucifixion scenes which show John holding a book to indicate

[22] *In Luc.* x.130 (*ibid.*, p. 383) and *De inst. virg.*, vii (PL 16, 317–19).
[23] John xix.34–5.

his status as an evangelist and raising one hand in a gesture of witness. However, four Anglo-Saxon artists chose to represent John writing on a scroll or in a book.[24] These pictures belong to three separate iconographic types. The drawings in the Ælfwine Prayer-book and the Winchcombe Psalter (pls. VIII and X), which show Christ crowned and accompanied by symbols of the sun and moon, are concerned with the theme of Christ's kingship;[25] the drawings in the Ramsey Psalter (pl. XIV) and the Weingarten Gospels (pl. XVI) depict Mary's sorrow at Christ's death and her compassion for her dying son.[26] The artist of the Winchcombe Psalter included a text on St John's book: 'Et ego vidi et testimonium' (pl. X). The use of the verb *vidi* suggests that the text is based on John XIX.35 and that John's witness relates to the blood and water from Christ's side; this is confirmed by the figure of Mary who points to the wound in Christ's side. The text on the scroll in the Ramsey Psalter drawing, on the other hand, is based on John XXI.24: 'Hic est discipulus qui testimonium perhibet' (pl. XIV). Unlike the passage from ch. XIX, this verse continues with a reference to St John's written testimony, though the testimony relates more generally to Christ's life. It is possible that the artist of the Ramsey Psalter applied these words to John's presence at Christ's death of his own accord and that this explains his use of a writing figure, but it is also possible that he took the idea from some written source. In a sermon for the Assumption Ælfric described John making a written record of his presence with Mary under the cross.[27] This sermon is based on the so-called *Epistola ad Paulam et Eustochium*, attributed in the Middle Ages to St Jerome but probably by Paschasius Radbertus.[28] The reference to the writing St John does not occur in the Latin text and Ælfric has modified his source in other ways. He recalls Gabriel's words to Mary at the Annunciation but then moves straight to a description of Christ's words to Mary and John from the cross, omitting the reference to the events of Christ's infancy which occurs in the Latin text. He emphasizes the human element in Christ's relationship with his mother and his disciple, introducing a reference to the sorrow of Mary and John at the

[24] The manuscripts are the Ramsey Psalter, the Ælfwine Prayer-book, the Winchcombe Psalter and the Weingarten Gospels.

[25] See below, ch. 6.   [26] See below, pp. 155–8 and 159.

[27] *CH* I.xxx (ed. Thorpe, p. 438).

[28] Lambot, 'L'homélie du Pseudo-Jérôme', pp. 265–82; Barré, 'La lettre du Pseudo-Jérôme', pp. 203–25; text in PL 30, 122–42.

cross.[29] He retains the original reference to Mary's great love for her son, which increased her own sufferings, and the comment that she made Christ's death her own,[30] but adds: 'Hire sawul wæs swiðe geangsumod mid micelre þrowunge, þa ða heo stod dreorig foran ongean Cristes rode, and hire leofe cild geseah mid isenum næglum on heardum treowe gefæstnod.'[31] He describes Mary teaching the disciples about Christ's humanity after the Ascension.[32] His main theme, however, is revealed at the end of the sermon: that his hearers should ask Mary to pray for them because Christ, who was true God and true man and who allowed himself to become man through Mary, will grant her requests.[33] These passages indicate an emphasis in Ælfric's writing on Christ's human nature which came to him from Mary, on the connection between the incarnation and the redemption and on Mary's role as an intercessor for man. Ælfric was educated at Winchester and it is of interest that the first evidence for the use of these ideas in the art comes from Winchester. The earliest representation of St John writing is that in the Ramsey Psalter, written at Winchester in the last quarter of the tenth century (pl. XIV).[34] The same drawing also provides the earliest English representation of Mary's sufferings at Christ's death.[35] The next manuscript to show the writing St John is the Ælfwine Prayer-book, written at Winchester between 1023 and 1035 (pl. VIII). This drawing does not show the sufferings of Mary and Christ but is the earliest of a group of pictures in which Mary is represented as an orant figure, an image which traditionally recalls her faith in God's promises, manifested at the Annunciation, and her role as intercessor for man.[36]

Ælfric does not explain why he describes John as writing, but the answer may lie in a passage in Ambrose's commentary on St Luke's Gospel. Ambrose presented Christ's provision for his mother as a will which was signed by John: 'Testabatur de cruce Christus et testamentum eius signabat Iohannes, dignus tanto testatore testis. Bonum testamentum non pecuniae, sed vitae, quod non atramento scribitur, sed spiritu dei vivi. *Lingua*

---

[29] *CH* I.xxx (ed. Thorpe, p. 438).   [30] *CH* I.xxx (*ibid.*, p. 444); PL 30, 138.

[31] *CH* I.xxx (*ibid.*, p. 444): 'Her soul was greatly troubled with great suffering when she stood sadly opposite Christ's cross and saw her dear child fastened to the hard tree with iron nails.'

[32] *CH* I.xxx (*ibid.*, pp. 438–40).   [33] *CH* I.xxx (*ibid.*, pp. 452–4).

[34] See below, p. 156.

[35] See below, pp. 156–8.   [36] See below, pp. 100–3.

mea calamus scribae velociter scribentis.'[37] Christ's action was not simply a matter of piety: for Ambrose it provided proof of Mary's perpetual virginity[38] and it was this to which John was a witness. The belief that Christ entrusted his mother to St John because both were virgins was certainly known to Ælfric[39] though it cannot be shown that he was borrowing from Ambrose, and he does not mention him in the list of sources at the beginning of the Catholic Homilies. Mary and John were praised as examples of the monastic ideal of virginity from the patristic period. Jerome argued that John's privileged position among the disciples, his seat next to Christ at the Last Supper and his being asked to care for Mary were the reward for his virginity.[40] Aldhelm placed Mary and John at the head of the list of exemplary figures in his *De virginitate*, written for the nuns of Barking:

> Christus passus patibula
> Atque leti latibula
> Virginem virgo virgini
> Commendabat tutamini.[41]

The idea that the link between Christ, his mother and his disciple was based on the fact that all three were virgins formed a constant theme in monastic writing. Goscelin's *Liber confortatorius*, written for Eva of Wilton between 1082 and 1083, described how Christ commended his weeping mother to his beloved disciple, even though angels were watching over her, because all three were virgins.[42] By the twelfth century Ailred of Rievaulx could claim that the reason for placing a crucifix with figures of Mary and John in the recluse's cell was that it reminded one of the value of virginity.[43] There can be little doubt that the pictures of Mary and John beneath the cross in late Anglo-Saxon manuscripts, most of which belonged to monastic houses, were intended as a reminder to those who had chosen a celibate life of the value Christ placed on virginity.

[37] *In Luc.* x.131 (ed. Adriaen, p. 383): 'Christ made his testimony from the cross and John signed his testament, a worthy witness for such a testator. It was a good will, not concerned with money but with life, written not with ink but with the spirit of the living God. *My tongue is the pen of a scribe writing swiftly.*'

[38] *In Luc.* II.4 (*ibid.*, p. 32).   [39] *CH* I.xxx and I.iv (ed. Thorpe, pp. 438 and 58).

[40] *Adv. Jov.* 1.26 (PL 23, 245–8).

[41] MGH, Auct. antiq. 15, 235; trans. Lapidge and Herren, *Aldhelm*, p. 64.

[42] *Liber confortatorius* (ed. Talbot, p. 31).

[43] *De inst. incl.*, ch. 26 (ed. Talbot, pp. 658–9).

Another moral lesson to be drawn from Christ's words concerned faith in Christ's victory on the cross. Christ had promised that some of his disciples would not die before seeing the kingdom of God[44] and Ambrose explains how his readers can imitate these disciples by praying before a crucifix: 'Eris filius tonitrui [i.e. like James and John], si fueris filius ecclesiae. Dicat et tibi de patibulo crucis Christus: *ecce mater tua*, dicat et ecclesiae: *ecce filius tuus*; tunc enim incipies esse filius ecclesiae, cum in cruce victorem videris Christum.'[45] Here Mary becomes a symbol of the church and John a symbol of the individual Christian. Just as John became the adopted son of Mary and so was able to follow her divine son into the next life, so man must become a son of the church through contemplating the triumph of Christ on the cross if he, too, is to escape death. He does not simply associate himself with Mary and John by standing under the cross; he brings about an actual change in his status.

For Ambrose, imitation of John involved belief in Christ's victory on the cross. The same attitude to Christ's death can be seen in his description of Mary standing under the cross, when most of Christ's followers had run away, and looking forward to the salvation of the world.[46] Mary is not simply an example of courage but a symbol of faith. Bede argued that she maintained her firm belief in Christ's divinity even though she could not help grieving at his death[47] and Ælfric makes the same point in his homily for the feast of the Purification.[48] In early Christian art the symbol of faith was the *orans*. Mary is portrayed as an orant in the Ascension scenes of the Rabbula Gospels and the Monza Ampullae,[49] partly to represent the continuous prayer of Mary and the apostles between the Ascension and Pentecost,[50] but partly because these scenes combine the Ascension with the second coming. The praying figure of Mary is a sign of faith in Christ's future return to earth. An important variant on these scenes shows Christ's incarnation. In the wall-paintings at the Coptic monastery of Bawit the

---

[44] Luke IX.27.
[45] *In Luc.* VII.5 (ed. Adriaen, p. 216): 'You will be a son of thunder if you have been a son of the church. May Christ say to you from the gibbet of the cross: *Behold your mother* and may he say to the church, *Behold your son*; then, truly, you will begin to be a son of the church when you see Christ victorious on the cross.'
[46] *In Luc.* X.132 (*ibid.*, p. 383), *De inst. virg.*, vii (PL 16, 317–19).
[47] *Hom.* I.18, *In purificatione S. Mariae* (Luc. II.22–35) (ed. Hurst, p. 132).
[48] *CH* I.ix (ed. Thorpe, p. 146).
[49] Nos. 1, 2, 10 and 11: Grabar, *Ampoules*, pls. 3, 5, 17 and 19.
[50] Acts I.9–14.

orant figure of Mary in Ascension pictures is sometimes replaced by a representation of Mary holding the Christ Child.[51] This image contrasts the enthroned and glorified Christ above and the incarnate Christ below. The same idea was sometimes expressed through an orant figure of Mary instead of by a picture of the Virgin and Child. One of the sixth-century ampullae at Bobbio shows Christ enthroned among angels; in the lower half of the scene are Mary, John the Baptist and Zechariah.[52] The meaning of the scene is defined by the star and the symbols of the sun and moon above Mary's head and by the text on the scroll held by John the Baptist which refers to Christ as the *Agnus Dei*.[53] Representations of the enthroned Christ with figures of the apostles and either an orant figure of Mary or a representation of her holding the Christ Child were often placed in the apses of churches and Grabar has argued that the intention of these pictures was to remind the congregation that their communion with Christ in the eucharist was dependent on his incarnation. There is a seventh-century mosaic of such a scene in the chapel of San Venanzio next to the baptistry of St John at the Lateran in Rome but the clearest evidence for the eucharistic meaning comes from a painting in the apse of chapel fifty-one at Bawit where the apostles are shown holding the bread and wine.[54] Anglo-Saxon artists were familiar with the Palestinian Ascension iconography used at Bawit and on the Monza Ampullae and it is likely that the praying figures of Mary in their Crucifixion pictures, which seem to have no parallels in non-Anglo-Saxon Crucifixion scenes, were derived from pictures of the Ascension.[55] The meaning of these figures was threefold. First, they offered an example of faith in the redemption which those who looked at the picture could imitate.[56] Secondly, they recalled Mary's prayer for the church. Thirdly, they reminded people of the incarnation and Mary's part in the redemption.

Mary's role as an intercessor was well-established long before the late tenth century, but it was linked with her position as Christ's mother, not with her presence beneath the cross and her relationship to St John. The earliest example of the belief that Mary had become the mother of mankind

[51] Grabar, *Christian Iconography*, pl. 324.
[52] *Ibid.*, pp. 74–6 and 132–3, pl. 319.
[53] John 1.29; cf. also the words of Zechariah, Luke 1.78.
[54] Grabar, *Christian Iconography*, pp. 133–5 and pls. 322 and 327; cf. the Uta Gospels, discussed above, p. 73.
[55] See below, p. 132.   [56] See ref. to Ælfric above, p. 100, n.48 and also p. 81.

when she accepted John as her adopted son and that she could therefore be relied on to pray for all Christians seems to be a passage in a prayer written by Anselm of Lucca for Matilda of Tuscany between 1076 and 1086.[57] There is some evidence, however, that Mary's prayer for the church was linked to her presence beneath the cross before this date. A picture of the Crucifixion in a sacramentary fragment linked with Reichenau has inscriptions asking Mary and John for their prayers.[58] Pictures of Mary in the orant position were certainly associated with prayers asking for her help in the late tenth century: a picture of this type is placed before two prayers to Mary in a manuscript which belonged to Archbishop Arnulf of Milan.[59] Ælfric's Assumption homily, discussed above, links Mary's intercessory role to her position as the source of Christ's human nature and this in turn is linked to her role at the Annunciation and at Christ's death.[60] Two of the four manuscripts which contain drawings of Mary as an orant figure beneath the cross include a prayer to Mary which links her intercession specifically to her presence with John beneath the cross:

O virgo virginum ... per pretiosum sanguinem filii tui unigeniti domini nostri Iesu Christi, quem in pretium nostrae salutis effudit; et per sanctam et venerabilem et salubrem crucem eius in qua adfixus stare dignatus est pro salute generis humani qui est fabricator mundi, et inter mortis supplicium, quod ipse Dei filius sponte pro nobis in cruce pati voluit, te suo discipulo sancto Iohanni commendavit dicens: *Ecce mater tua*, Adiuva nos.[61]

The only other known example of this prayer is in the eleventh-century Psalter of Nonantola,[62] but there is an important difference. The Nonantola prayer invokes the help of all the saints whereas the English prayer

---

[57] Barré, 'Maternité spirituelle', p. 89; T. Koehler, 'Jean xix.25–27', p. 145; prayer ptd in Wilmart, 'Cinq textes de prière', pp. 49–57.

[58] See above, pp. 81–2.

[59] AD 998–1018. See BL, Egerton 3763, 102v, reprod. Barré, *Prières*, frontispiece; described in Turner, 'Prayer-book', pp. 360–92.

[60] See above, pp. 97–8, *CH* I.xxx (ed. Thorpe, pp. 436–54).

[61] BL, Cotton Titus D. xxvii, 84r–85r, Arundel 60, 142r–v (ptd Barré, *Prières*, pp. 137–8): 'O virgin of virgins ... through the precious blood of your only son our lord Jesus Christ, which he poured out as the price of our salvation; and through his holy, venerated and life-giving cross, fixed to which the creator of the world deigned to stand for the salvation of the human race and during the torment of death, which the same Son of God willingly wished to suffer for us on the cross, commended you to his disciple St John, saying, *Behold your mother*: Help us.'

[62] Vatican, Biblioteca Apostolica, Vat. lat. 84, 280r–v (Barré, *Prières*, p. 211).

concentrates on the invocation to Mary and John. Moreover, the passage quoted above does not occur in the Nonantola prayer and may therefore be an English feature, possibly even a Winchester feature.

Evidence that Mary's role beneath the cross was linked to her acceptance of God's will at the incarnation is provided by the *Epistola ad Paulam et Eustochium* which was used by Ælfric for his homily on the Assumption.[63] In this treatise the link between Mary and John is based partly on their virginity but partly also on John's testimony to the Word being made flesh through Mary.[64] Paschasius describes the descent of the Spirit on Mary, using the traditional image of the dew on Gideon's fleece and linking it to the grace which flowed from the cross: 'Coelestis plane imber in virgineum vellus, placido se infudit illapsu: tota divinitatis unda se contulit in carnem, quando Verbum caro factum est: ac deinde per crucis patibulum expressum, terris omnibus salutis pluviam effudit, et stillicidia gratiae humanis praestitit mentibus.'[65] A passage in an unidentified homily for the feast of the Assumption included in Migne's edition of Paul the Deacon's Homiliary interprets the stones of the heavenly Jerusalem as symbols of Mary's virtues and links her faith at the incarnation with her faith at Christ's death.[66] But the most important contribution to the belief that Mary's presence below the cross witnessed to the truth of the incarnation came from Augustine, who interpreted Christ's words to Mary and John from the cross in relation to his words to Mary at the marriage at Cana. He saw the statement, 'My hour has not come yet'[67] on this earlier occasion as a reference to Christ's death and drew a contrast between the miracle at Cana, which was the work of his divinity, and his death on the cross which belonged to his humanity.[68] For Augustine, the important

---

[63] See above, p. 98 and n. 28.

[64] John 1.14; *Epistola ad Paulam et Eustochium*, iii (PL 30, 124–5).

[65] PL 30, 127: 'The heavenly dew poured itself completely on to the virgin fleece with gentle rain; the whole river of the divinity passed into the flesh when the Word became flesh; and then, squeezed out through the wood of the cross, it poured the rain of salvation on all lands and offered an assurance of the falling drops of grace to human minds.'

[66] PL 95, 1493. It is likely that the homily dates from after the time of Odo of Cluny (*ob.* 942) since it refers to Mary as *mater misericordiae* (PL 95, 1496), a title associated with Odo; cf. PL 133, 47 and 72 and Barré, *Prières*, pp. 111–12.

[67] John 11.4.

[68] *In Iohannis Ev.* VIII.9 and CXIX.1 (ed. Mayer, pp. 87–8 and 658); cf. Haymo: PL 118, 441.

point about Mary at the cross was that she was the source of the human nature through which Christ was able to redeem man: 'Non enim de Maria sumpserat quod habebat in divinitate, sicut de Maria sumpserat quod pendebat in cruce.'[69] The point was elaborated by Bede in a homily for the second Sunday after Epiphany:

Nondum venit hora mea ut fragilitatem sumptae ex te humanitatis moriendo demonstrem; prius est ut potentiam aeternae deitatis virtutes operando patefaciam. Venit autem hora ut quid sibi et matri commune esset ostenderet cum eam moriturus in cruce discipulo virgini virginem commendare curavit. Carnis namque infirma perpetiens matrem de qua haec suscepit pie cognitam ei quem maxime diligebat discipulo commendavit quam divina facturus quasi incognitam se nosse dissimulat quia hanc divinae nativitatis auctorem non esse cognoscit.[70]

Ælfric was certainly familiar with these passages for he makes the same contrast in one of the second set of Catholic Homilies intended for the second Sunday after Epiphany: 'Drihten cwæð to his meder: Fæmne, hwæt is me and ðe to ðan? swilce he cwæde, ne wyrcð seo menniscnyss ðe ic of ðe genam þæt tacn þe ðu bitst, ac seo godcundnys þe ic ðe mid geworhte. þonne min ðrowungtima cymð, þonne geswutelað seo menniscnys hire untrumnysse.'[71] Ælfric returns to this point in his second Palm Sunday homily where he interprets the words, 'Woman, this is your son'[72] as a reference to Christ himself instead of using the more usual interpretation of them as a reference to John:

---

[69] *Sermo* ccxviii, x.10 (PL 38, 1086): 'Truly, he did not take from Mary what he possessed in his divinity as he took from Mary what hung on the cross.' I owe this reference to Malcolm Godden.

[70] *Hom.* I.14, *Post Epiphaniam* (Ioh. II.1–11) (ed. Hurst, p. 97): 'My hour has not yet come when I shall show clearly by my death the weakness of the humanity taken from you; first I must make clear the power of the eternal godhead by works of power. But the hour came for him to show what was common to him and his mother when he took care to entrust the Virgin to his virgin disciple as he was about to die on the cross. For, enduring the weakness of the flesh, he dutifully recognized the mother from whom he received it and commended her to the disciple whom he loved most – the mother whom he pretended not to know when about to exercise his divinity because he knew that she was not the author of his divine nativity.'

[71] *CH* II.iv (ed. Godden, p. 30): 'The Lord said to his mother: Woman, what is that to you and me? as if he said, The human nature which I received from you does not work the miracle that you ask but the divine nature with which I created you. When the time for my Passion comes, then the human nature will show its weakness.'

[72] John XIX.26.

Seo halige Maria þæs hælendes moder, stod wið ða rode, ðearle dreorig, and
Iohannes samod, hire swuster bearn. Ða clypode drihten, to his dreorian meder:
Efne her hangað nu ðin sunu, fæmne. Swilce he cwæde, þis is ðin gecynd, ðus
ðrowigendlic, ðe ic of ðe genam. He cwæð to Iohanne, Her stænt ðin modor. þa
hæfde Iohannes, hire siððan gymene, mid geswæsum ðenungum, a on ðisum
life.[73]

These passages suggest that one reason for the preference for the
Crucifixion iconography with Mary and John was that it reminded people
of the reality of the incarnation. This view is borne out to some extent by
the fact that seven of the ten manuscript pictures which include the figure
of Mary portray Christ dead on the cross. But although it was important to
assert that Christ was truly man and that he had truly died there was a
danger of losing sight of his divinity: in emphasizing Mary's role as the
source of Christ's human nature it was possible to imply that Christ had not
existed before his birth on earth. There are indications in tenth- and
eleventh-century manuscript pictures that artists were alert to this possibility of doctrinal error. The orant figures of Mary discussed earlier were
one way of emphasizing Christ's divine nature. Another was to depict Mary
as the source of wisdom. In two Crucifixion pictures and on two ivories
Mary is shown holding a book, a detail which seems to be quite new in
Crucifixion iconography.[74] The book had been used as an attribute of Mary
in Annunciation scenes from Carolingian times[75] and Mary was shown
reading in the Annunciation picture in the Benedictional of Æthelwold.[76]
In these representations the book has a narrative function and a better
parallel to the use of the book in Crucifixion scenes is the non-narrative
image of Mary with the Trinity above the fourth and fifth canon tables in
the Arenberg Gospels. This scene shows Mary with the dove of the Holy
Spirit perching on her head. It is related to the drawing of Mary and the
Trinity opposite the *Gloria* in the Utrecht Psalter,[77] but with one
important difference: Mary holds an open book instead of the Christ Child.

---

[73] *CH* II.xiv (ed. Godden, p. 146): 'The holy Mary, the Saviour's mother, stood by the
cross, grieving greatly, and John with her, her sister's son. Then the Lord said to his
grieving mother: Here now hangs your son, mother. As though he said, This is your
nature suffering thus which I received from you. He said to John, Here stands your
mother. Then after that John took care of her with gentle service for the rest of this life.'

[74] The Arundel Psalter, the Weingarten Gospels and the Cambridge and Copenhagen
ivories.

[75] E.g. the Annunciation scene on the Brunswick Casket; see *St Albans Psalter*, p. 66.

[76] See above, pp. 28–9.   [77] Utrecht, Universiteitsbibl., 32, 89v.

Jane Rosenthal has suggested that the book represents the gospels and that it is a symbol of Christ's body, which was equated with the book of the gospels.[78] The book is more likely to represent Christ's divine nature, however: the *Logos* or Word of God.[79] The figure of Mary with the dove in the drawing next to the Apostles' Creed in the Utrecht Psalter[80] illustrates the words, 'qui conceptus est de Spiritu Sancto, natus ex Maria Virgine'. It is a symbol of the incarnation. St John's account of the incarnation[81] draws on a number of Old Testament descriptions of the Word of God and his wisdom, present before the world was created.[82] Christ was celebrated as the wisdom of God in the first of the antiphons sung at the *Magnificat* during the eight days before Christmas and therefore linked specifically to the theme of the incarnation.[83] One of the two main churches at York in the eighth century was dedicated to the Holy Wisdom.[84] Moreover, a passage from the Book of Proverbs[85] which describes wisdom as co-operating in God's creation was applied to Mary and used as the epistle for the feast of her nativity from the tenth century onwards.[86] The figure of Mary with the book in the Trinity picture of the Arenberg Gospels asserts that she was not simply the mother of Christ's human nature but the mother of God. Further evidence of this concern to emphasize Mary's position as *Theotokos*[87] can be seen in the illustrations of the Ælfwine Prayer-book and the related *Liber vitae* of New Minster. Mary holds a book in the frontispiece to the *Liber vitae*[88] and the Christ Child holds a book in the drawing of Mary with the Trinity in the Prayer-book.[89] The dove on Mary's head in this second picture represents the overshadowing of the Holy Spirit, as it does in the drawings in the Utrecht Psalter, and the chained figure of Arius beneath Mary's feet indicates that the picture is

---

[78] Rosenthal, 'Arenberg Gospels', p. 238; Pseudo-Jerome, *Breviarium in Ps.*, cxlvii (PL 26, 1258–9).

[79] See also above, p. 27.   [80] Utrecht, Universiteitsbibl., 32, 90r.

[81] John I.1–14.

[82] E.g. Prov. VIII.22–35 and Wisdom VII.22–30.

[83] Hesbert, *Corpus antiphonalium* I, 16(a), pp. 28–9: 'O Wisdom who camest out of the mouth of the Most High, reaching from end to end and ordering all things mightily and sweetly: come and teach us the way of prudence.'

[84] Morris, 'Alcuin, York and the *alma sophia*'.   [85] Prov. VIII.22–35.

[86] Capelle, 'Epîtres sapientiales', p. 320.

[87] The term is used by Bede, *In Luc.* I.i.35 (ed. Hurst, p. 34).

[88] BL, Stowe 944, 6r.

[89] BL, Cotton Titus D. xxvii, 75v.

intended as a refutation of his claim that Christ did not exist before his conception by Mary.[90]

The wish to emphasize the union of the human and the divine in the person of Christ can also be found in the one eleventh-century drawing of Christ between the spear- and sponge-bearers, that in the Tiberius Psalter (pl. XIII). St John presents the two episodes of the drink of vinegar offered to Christ just before his death and the wounding of his side with a spear after his death as fulfilling the Old Testament prophecies and so confirming the truth of Christ's claim to be the Messiah:

After this, Jesus knew that everything had now been completed, and to fulfil the scripture perfectly he said: *'I am thirsty'* . . . When they came to Jesus, they found he was already dead, and so instead of breaking his legs one of the soldiers pierced his side with a lance . . . all this happened to fulfil the words of scripture: *Not one bone of his will be broken*, and again, in another place scripture says: *they will look on the one whom they have pierced*.[91]

Whereas the fulfilment of the prophecies was evidence of Christ's divine nature, his physical sufferings proved his humanity. He suffered thirst on the cross. His death was not a trick. The practical purpose of the wound made in Christ's side was to ensure that he was dead. The point was theologically important because the basis of the Christian faith was belief in Christ's Resurrection from the dead and this in turn depended on assurance that he had truly died. As Augustine said: 'Quare autem credimus eum mortuum? Quia credere eum resurrexisse non possumus, nisi prius mortuum fuisse credamus.'[92] St John stresses the importance of the point by adding: 'This is the evidence of one who saw it – trustworthy evidence, and he knows he speaks the truth – and he gives it so that you may believe as well.'[93] St John returns to this point in the following chapter when, alone among the evangelists, he describes Thomas's attempt to prove the physical reality of Christ's Resurrection by thrusting his hand into his side. Christ's comment, as recorded by St John, echoes the words of the previous chapter: 'You believe because you can see me. Happy are those who have not seen and yet believe.'[94]

[90] Cf. *CH* I.xx (ed. Thorpe, p. 290).
[91] John XIX.28, 33–4 and 36–7, refs. to Ps. LXVIII.22, Ps. XXXIII.21 and Zech. XII.10.
[92] *Enarr. in Ps.* (ed. Dekkers and Fraipont III, 1442, on Ps. CI): 'Why do we believe him to have been dead? Because we cannot believe him to have risen from the dead unless we first believe him to have been dead'; cf. above, p. 88.
[93] John XIX.35.   [94] John XX.29.

The drawings in the Tiberius Psalter present this Johannine view of Christ's death.[95] On 13r Christ is shown hanging from the cross, his eyes closed in death, a jewelled crown on his head (pl. XIII). Blood streams from the wound in his side. Beneath the cross are the soldiers with spear and sponge. The picture is inscribed, 'Iesus Nazarenus rex Iudeorum' and the crown, which replaces the crown of thorns of the gospel narrative, asserts that despite all appearances Christ was truly a king. The sagging body and the closed eyes are equally insistent that he died a human death. Three pages later a drawing of Thomas placing his hand in Christ's side proclaims the reality of the Resurrection.[96]

The paintings of Christ between the two soldiers in the much earlier Durham and St Gallen Gospels differ from the drawing in the Tiberius Psalter in that they relate Christ's death to his second coming rather than to his resurrection. The prophecy of Zechariah, quoted in St John's Gospel to show that Christ fulfilled the Old Testament prophecies about the Messiah, lies behind a passage in the Apocalypse:

Jesus Christ, *the faithful witness, the First-born* from the dead, *the Ruler of the kings of the earth.* He loves us and has washed away our sins with his blood, and made us a *line of kings, priests to serve* his God and Father . . . It is he who *is coming on the clouds*; everyone will see him, even *those who pierced him*, and *all the races of the earth will mourn over him.*[97]

It was a commonplace of early medieval writing that Christ's wounds would be visible at doomsday. Ælfric wrote in a sermon for Ascension Day: 'þa twegen englas sædon þæt Crist cymð swa swa he uppferde, forðan ðe he bið gesewen on ðam micclum dome on menniscum hiwe, þæt his slagan hine magon oncnawan, þe hine ær to deaðe gedydon, and eac ða ðe his lare forsawon, þæt hi ðonne rihtlice onfon þæt ece wite mid deofle.'[98] According to Bede, the wicked would see Christ as he was when he died, whereas the just would see him in his glory: 'Se enim cunctis hominibus, seipsum vero solis manifestabit electis. Nam et reprobi in iudicio Christum videbunt, sed, sicut scriptum est, *videbunt in quem transfixerunt*, soli autem

---

[95] See above, p. 88 and below, p. 151.   [96] BL, Cotton Tiberius C. vi, 14v.

[97] Apoc. 1.5–7.

[98] *CH* I.xxi (ed. Thorpe, p. 300): 'The two angels said that Christ will come as he ascended, because he will be seen at the great judgement in the form of a man so that his killers can recognize him, whom they previously put to death, and also so that those who despised his teaching may justly receive eternal punishment with the devil.'

regem in decore suo videbunt oculi iustorum.'[99] The artist of the eighth-century Durham Gospels expressed this idea through a picture of the Crucifixion which looks forward to the Last Judgement. Christ is shown nailed to the cross. His side is wounded yet his eyes are open and he stands erect in front of the cross, apparently alive. The two soldiers under the arms of the cross allude to the scene on Golgotha. The A and ⍵ and the words *initium* and *finis* placed next to Christ's head refer to the words of the Son of Man in the Apocalypse: 'It is I, *the First* and *the Last*; I am the Living One, I was dead and now I am to live for ever and ever, and I hold the keys of death and of the underworld.'[100] The implications of the Durham painting are clear because the inscription round the frame links Christ's sufferings to his glory and promises the same glory to those who have suffered with him.[101] In the St Gallen Gospels, also of the eighth century, a painting of Christ, apostles and angels, which symbolizes both the Ascension and the second coming, is placed opposite the painting of the Crucifixion to convey the same idea.[102] Both pictures come at the end of the manuscript instead of opposite one of the descriptions of Christ's Passion, presumably to indicate that both were connected with the end of the world.

Whereas the eighth-century paintings of Christ between the two soldiers linked Christ's death with his second coming, the artist of the Tiberius Psalter linked it with his Resurrection, first, by representing Christ with closed eyes to show the reality of his death and secondly by associating the scene with pictures of the Maries at the tomb and of doubting Thomas. He was making the same point as the artists of the pictures which showed Mary and John below the cross: Christ was truly God and truly man; he died and rose from the dead. The presence of his human mother, her faith in his divinity, the testimony of John, the experience of Thomas all witness to the truth of the Christian message and to the link between Christ's incarnation and his redemption of man on the cross. This central truth underlies all tenth- and eleventh-century English representations of the Crucifixion. Meditation and the art which served it expanded this doctrinal statement with points of devotional importance:

---

[99] Bede, *Homilia* xi. *In Vigilia Pentecostes* (PL 94, 193): 'Truly, he will show himself to all men, but as he is, only to the elect. For the wicked will see Christ at the Judgement but, as it is written, *they will look on the one they pierced*; only the eyes of the just will see the king in his glory.'

[100] Apoc. I.17–18.   [101] Mynors, *Durham Cathedral Manuscripts*, pp. 16–17.

[102] St Gallen, Stiftsbibliothek, 51, pp. 266–7.

the relationship between Christ's death and the mass; the role of angels in the church; the relationship between Christ's rule and that of earthly kings; the forgiveness offered by Christ to the individual sinner; the compassion required of man by Christ. These themes formed the basis of the main variants on the crucifix with Mary and John discussed in chs. 5 to 7: the crucifix with angels; the crowned crucifix; the crucifix with the weeping Virgin or with Mary Magdalen.

5

The crucifix with angels

The first and best-defined of the Crucifixion iconographies with Mary and John in use in late Anglo-Saxon England is characterized by two flying angels above the arms of the cross, the *dextera Dei* above Christ's head and a chalice at the foot of the cross. The only complete examples of this iconography are the drawings in two late tenth-century manuscripts, both probably from Christ Church, Canterbury: the Sherborne Pontifical and the Arenberg Gospels. In addition three ivory Crucifixion panels dating from the late tenth or early eleventh century and now in Brussels, Cambridge and Copenhagen, show the main features of the type, omitting only the chalice. A gold and ivory crucifix in the Victoria and Albert Museum, two unfinished sketches of Christ crucified in manuscripts at Cambridge and Rouen[1] and the ivory figures of Mary and John at Saint-Omer are linked to the Arenberg and Sherborne drawings by details of the drapery and it is possible that the flying angels above the chancel-arch of the church of St Laurence, Bradford-on-Avon, should also be associated with this group.[2] The portable altar in the Musée de Cluny includes many of the elements of the Arenberg/Sherborne iconography though they have been rearranged to suit the format of an altar (see pls. I–VII).[3]

It is clear from the detailed parallels between these items that they derive from a common source. The Arenberg and Sherborne drawings, the sketches in Cambridge and Rouen and the crucifix in the Victoria and Albert Museum all show Christ's loincloth fastened in a distinctive way. Whereas in most tenth- and eleventh-century English Crucifixion pictures the material is swathed round the waist or knotted on the left hip, here the central triangular fold is secured by a loop which passes behind the

---

[1] CCCC 41 and Rouen, Bibl. Mun., A. 292.   [2] See above, p. 53.

[3] See above, p. 50.

waistband in the manner of a highwayman's knot. In the Arenberg drawing, the Saint-Omer ivory and the ivory panels at Brussels, Cambridge and Copenhagen, Mary raises the folds of her mantle in her hands; in the Arenberg drawing she holds the material in her right hand, on the ivory panels in the left and on the Saint-Omer ivory in both, but the pose is sufficiently distinctive to suggest that the figures are related despite these differences. The Arenberg and Sherborne drawings and the Saint-Omer ivory of Mary all show the same padded fold round the ankles, the diagonal fold across the body and the loose panel of drapery below the left arm. The Arenberg and Sherborne drawings of St John both lack the falling curve of the over-garment where it is tucked into the waistband, a detail found in virtually every other Anglo-Saxon drawing of St John below the cross.

There are also differences between the items in the group. The Sherborne and Arenberg drawings and the crucifix show Christ with eyes closed, dead on the cross. The sketches in the Cambridge and Rouen manuscripts and the three ivory panels show him with open eyes. The Brussels ivory lacks the distinctive knot in the loincloth and shows it falling in a triangular curve similar to that in a Crucifixion picture in the Arundel Psalter. In the Sherborne drawing Mary stands with hands folded on her breast and in this drawing and the Saint-Omer ivory St John is shown without the traditional book. The angels on the Brussels ivory carry crowns in their hands; Christ himself is crowned on the ivory crucifix, and on the Copenhagen ivory both Christ and Mary are crowned. On the Cambridge and Copenhagen ivories Mary holds a book in her right hand. These are the kind of minor variations which tend to occur in any iconography as it is adapted for different ends. Two differences between the Arenberg and Sherborne drawings may be more significant. First, the chalice at the foot of the cross is represented quite differently. In the Arenberg drawing it is of the normal type, without handles and with a prominent knob; in the Sherborne drawing it is shown as a narrow-necked jar with two handles, similar to the wine-jar in the drawing of a feast in the Cambridge Prudentius.[4] Secondly, the Arenberg drawing shows Christ with his head sunk below the level of his shoulders and his left foot turned sideways as though he were standing on the *suppedaneum*.

There are many Byzantine, Carolingian and Ottonian representations of

[4] CCCC 23, 17v.

the Crucifixion which are broadly similar to these English works but none shows the detailed correspondences which would allow one to claim it as a model. It seems likely therefore that the Arenberg/Sherborne iconography was an English creation which combined elements from several different sources. The inspiration for the central figure probably came from a crucifix rather than from a drawing or painting. The cross in the Arenberg drawing is of an unusual form with a stepped base and arms. There is a rather similar cross in the painting of the death of Peter in the Benedictional of Æthelwold (95v); the stepped ends of this cross may have been adapted from the stepped bases of the pillars in other paintings in the Benedictional. The closest parallels to the cross in the Arenberg Gospels, however, are three German gold crucifixes: the Lothar and Otto Crosses, both of the late tenth century, and the Matilda Cross which dates from the eleventh.[5] Crosses of this kind are very rare in manuscript art. A small historiated initial in the Bede manuscript which contains the sketch related to the Arenberg drawing contains a crucifix which could be related to the Arenberg one[6] and the drawing of Cnut in the New Minster *Liber vitae* shows a cross of similar form, though without the figure of Christ. The cross in the Arenberg picture was clearly intended to look like a processional or altar cross and it could well have been copied from one. The cross in the Sherborne drawing also has extended terminals to the arms, though they are simpler than the Arenberg ones. Parallels to these, too, can be found in the work of eleventh-century German goldsmiths: the Theophanu and Erpho Crosses.[7] Further evidence of links between the Arenberg group of crucifixions and Ottonian art comes from the crucifix in the Victoria and Albert Museum. The ivory figure on this crucifix is English but there have always been doubts as to whether the mount is English or German.[8] The front of the cross, which is decorated with gold ribbon filigree, was clearly made to fit the ivory figure and may well be English[9] though parallels to the filigree can be found on three Ottonian works: the Lothar Cross,[10] the Otto Cross[11] and the head of the Petrus Staff in Limburg.[12] The repoussé panels of the Lamb and evangelist symbols on the back of the crucifix, on the other hand, are probably German; they are

---

[5] Elbern, *Das erste Jahrtausend* III, pls. 303, 376 and 378.   [6] CCCC 41, p. 410.
[7] Elbern, *Das erste Jahrtausend* III, pls. 379 and 395.
[8] Mitchell, 'English or German?'
[9] *Golden Age*, p. 118.   [10] Elbern, *Das erste Jahrtausend* III, pl. 303.
[11] *Ibid.* III, pl. 376.   [12] *Ibid.* III, pls. 334 and 335.

similar to the decoration on the shaft of the Petrus Staff and have been taken over from a larger cross and re-used on the present one.[13] A number of arguments suggest that the enamel roundels of the evangelist symbols on the front of the cross are German too. In the first place, such symbols are rare in Anglo-Saxon representations of the Crucifixion. Apart from the portable altar in the Musée de Cluny (pl. VII), the only crucifixes with accompanying evangelist symbols are a panel on the ninth-century Sandbach Cross,[14] a small ivory reliquary cross in the Victoria and Albert Museum, an ivory panel in Dublin[15] and a painting added to the mid-eleventh-century Arundel Psalter after the Norman Conquest.[16] Secondly, the iconography of the roundels on the crucifix in the Victoria and Albert Museum is unknown in late Anglo-Saxon art. The four symbols, which are identical to those on the reverse of the cross, are shown as heads peering over unrolled scrolls instead of the usual books. Similar heads can be found in two eleventh-century gospel-books from Echternach: the Codex Aureus in the Escorial, written for Henry III between 1043 and 1046, and the Goslar Gospels at Upsala, also written for Henry between 1050 and 1056.[17] Thirdly, the symbols are framed by small gold tendrils ending in dots of red enamel. Rather similar tendrils, though with gold dots, appear on the front of the Alfred Jewel, but the best parallels are on the enamels of the evangelist symbols at the corners of the cover of the Gospels of Henry II.[18] Enamels are very common in Ottonian gold work: the Petrus Staff and the enamelled cross of Essen both have enamels of the evangelist symbols[19] and enamels also appear on the Otto and Matilda crosses. Since the back of the English crucifix is thought to be German work of the late tenth century it is likely that the enamels too came from a German crucifix and it is at least possible that this crucifix provided the model for the ivory figure on the English cross and for the central figure in the Arenberg and Sherborne drawings. The unusual position of the feet of the Arenberg figure of Christ and the distinctive knot in the loincloth are further pointers to Ottonian influence. The only Anglo-Saxon examples of

[13] *Golden Age*, p. 118.   [14] Kendrick, *Anglo-Saxon Art*, pl. xciv.

[15] Beckwith, *Ivory Carvings*, nos. 32 and 37.

[16] Dodwell, *Canterbury School*, pp. 118–19.

[17] Goldschmidt, *German Illumination* II, pls. 57 and 63.

[18] Mitchell, 'English or German?', p. 329; Munich, Bayerische Staatsbibl., Clm. 4452, reproduced in Lasko, *Ars Sacra*, frontispiece.

[19] Elbern, *Das erste Jahrtausend* III, pls. 334, 335 and 377.

Christ standing on the cross are the Arenberg drawing, the sketch in Corpus Christi College 41, the ivory reliquary cross in the Victoria and Albert Museum mentioned above in connection with the evangelist symbols and the painting in the Arundel Psalter. Standing figures of Christ are found in Byzantine Crucifixion pictures; the figure of Christ in the *Te igitur* painting of the Sacramentary of Gellone may derive from a Byzantine model of this kind.[20] The best parallels to the English scenes, however, are the crucifix incised on the back of the late tenth-century Lothar Cross,[21] the early eleventh-century silver crucifix of Bernward of Hildesheim[22] and an incised crucifix on an eleventh-century bookcover from Mainz.[23] Crucifixes and Crucifixion pictures in which Christ is draped in a centrally knotted loincloth are common in Byzantine, Carolingian and Ottonian art. The best parallel to the distinctive knot of the Arenberg and Sherborne drawings and the ivory crucifix, however, comes from the Gero Cross, made at Cologne between 969 and 976.[24]

Whereas the figure of Christ in the Arenberg drawing is related to Ottonian crucifixes, the figure of Mary seems to derive from a Carolingian model.[25] The drawing of the Crucifixion opposite the Apostles' Creed in the Utrecht Psalter[26] shows Mary raising both hands with a fold of her mantle clutched in the left hand; the position is a mirror copy of the figure in the Arenberg drawing. A very similar figure is found on a Carolingian ivory of about 820 in the Liverpool Museum.[27] The artists of the Arenberg Gospels were certainly familiar with the Utrecht Psalter, for two of the drawings above the canon tables are copied from it. The drawing of the Trinity with Mary on 11v is taken from the illustration to the *Gloria* on 89v of the Psalter and the drawing of Christ above the asp and the basilisk on 13v derives from the illustration to Psalm LXIV or from that to Psalm XC. It seems likely therefore that the artist of the Arenberg Crucifixion picture, or of his model, took the figure of Mary directly from the Utrecht Psalter. The artist of the Sherborne Pontifical, on the other hand, was probably borrowing from Byzantine art where Mary is frequently shown

---

[20] See below, p. 116 and n. 32.
[21] Schiller, *Iconography* II, pl. 395; the back of the Lothar Cross, though not the front, may be English work, see Rosenthal, 'Arenberg Gospels', p. 105, n. 47.
[22] Tschan, *Bernward* III, pl. 91.   [23] H. Swarzenski, *Monuments*, pl. 30 (72).
[24] Elbern, *Das erste Jahrtausend* III, pl. 365.
[25] See above, p. 94.   [26] Utrecht, Universiteitsbibl., 32, 90r.
[27] Goldschmidt, *Elfenbeinskulpturen* I, pl. lix.139; Lasko, *Ars Sacra*, p. 37, pl. 31.

with hands crossed on her breast.[28] The figure of St John in the Arenberg drawing is less distinctive; the pose, with a book in the left hand and the right hand raised towards the cross, is so common as to give little indication of any specific source. The Sherborne St John, who raises both hands towards the cross, can be paralleled in the Crucifixion picture in the Gospels of Otfrid of Weissenburg which date from the third quarter of the ninth century[29] and on an Alemannic ivory dating from about 900.[30]

Further evidence of borrowing from Carolingian art comes from the flying angels above the cross. The earliest example of a crucifix with flying angels is the painting at the *Te igitur* of the mass in the Sacramentary of Gellone, a manuscript which dates from the eighth century.[31] This painting shows Christ hanging from a jewelled cross above which are two angels with peacock wings. No source has been found for this painting, though Reil believed that the distorted position of the feet and legs indicated that it was derived from a Byzantine model which showed Christ standing in front of the cross instead of hanging from it.[32] The central knot in the loincloth and the blood which flows from the wounds, in particular the blood from the wound in the side, would also be in accordance with Byzantine tradition. By the middle of the ninth century two further iconographies were available which included flying angels. The simpler is found on the later of the two covers of the Lindau Gospels, Rheims work of about 870. This gold relief shows Christ accompanied by four flying angels while, beneath the cross, Mary and John are accompanied by two female figures, possibly the other Maries.[33] A more complex iconography in which the angels, Mary and John are accompanied by representations of the soldiers, Ecclesia and Synagogue, symbols of earth and ocean and of the sun and moon, appears on several ivories associated with Rheims and Metz and in the Palm Sunday initial of the Drogo Sacramentary.[34] These scenes usually show the dead rising from their graves and the serpent crushed under foot in accordance with the

---

[28] Thoby, *Le crucifix*, pls. xlix.113, lii.122 and liii.124; Schiller, *Iconography* II, pls. 341 and 342.

[29] Boinet, *Miniature*, pl. 160; Goldschmidt, *German Illumination* I, pl. 62.

[30] Goldschmidt, *Elfenbeinskulpturen* IV, pl. lxxix.308.

[31] See above, p. 80.   [32] Reil, *Christus am Kreuz*, p. 38.

[33] H. Swarzenski, *Monuments*, pl. 11 (22); for discussion see Reil, *Christus am Kreuz*, pp. 56–69 and Friend, 'Carolingian Art', p. 68.

[34] Goldschmidt, *Elfenbeinskulpturen* I, pls. xxxvi.85 and 86, xxxvii.88, xxxviii.89 and xliv.96; see also above, pp. 79–80.

1   Paris, Bibliothèque Nationale, lat. 943 (Sherborne Pontifical), 4v, Crucifixion

11　New York, Pierpont Morgan Library, 869 (Arenberg Gospels), 9v,
Crucifixion

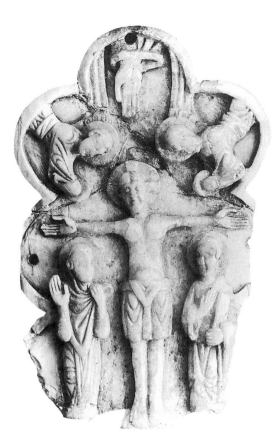

IIIa   Brussels, private collection, ivory panel of the Crucifixion

IIIb   Cambridge, Fitzwilliam Museum, no. M 24–1938, ivory panel of the
Crucifixion

iva   Copenhagen, Nationalmuseet, inv. no. D 13324, ivory
panel of the Crucifixion

ivb   London, Victoria and Albert Museum, M 7943–1862,
gold and ivory crucifix

va   Cambridge, Corpus Christi College, 41, p. 484, sketch of the Crucifixion

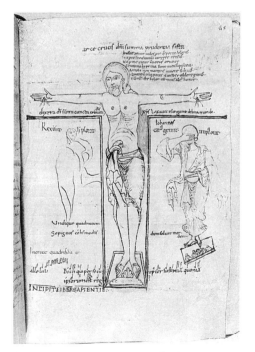

vb   Rouen, Bibliothèque Municipale, A. 292 [26], 48r, sketch of the Crucifixion

VI   Saint-Omer, Musée Sandelin, no. 2822, ivory figures of Mary and John

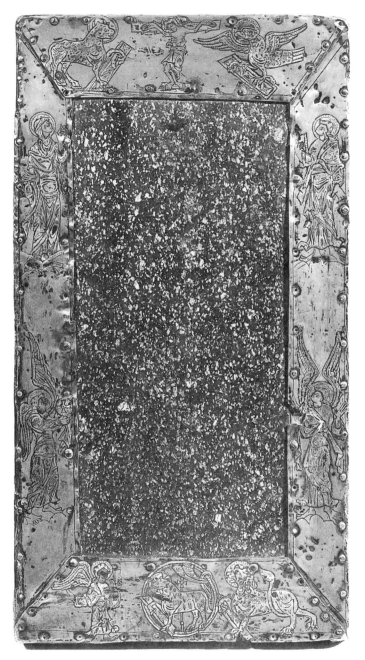

VII   Paris, Musée de Cluny, portable altar with Crucifixion

VIII   London, British Library, Cotton Titus D. xxvii (Ælfwine
Prayer-book), 65v, Crucifixion

ix   London, British Library, Arundel 60 (Arundel Psalter), 12v, Crucifixion

x   Cambridge, University Library, Ff. 1. 23 (Winchcombe
Psalter), 88r, Crucifixion

XI   Cambridge, Corpus Christi College, 421 (Cambridge Homilies), p. 1, Crucifixion

esemen eorum afilnf hominum·
qm declinauerunt inte mala· cogitauerunt
confilia quae non potuerunt stabilire·
Qm ponef eof dorfum· mreliquinf
tuif preparant uultum eorum·
Gxaltare dne inuirtute tua·
cantabim̄ & psallem̄ uirtutes tuas·
XXI· IN EIH PASSUMPTIOHE MATUTINA·
ps· DAUID UEL ̄I XP̄I CU PATER ETUR·
Ds̄ dms̄ respice inme· quare me
dereliquisti· longe asalute mea
uerba delictorum meorum·
Ds̄ms̄ clamabo pdiem & non exaudief·
& nocte· & non adinsipientiam mihi·
Tu aut̄ insc̄o habitas lausIfrl̄· intespauere
patref nostri spauerunt & libasti eos·
Adte clamauerunt & salui facti sunt·
intespauerunt & non sunt confusi·
Ego aut̄ sum uermis & non homo·
obpbrium hominu & abiectio pleb·
Oms̄ uidentes me deriserunt me·
locutisunt labiis & mouerunt caput·
S perauit indn̄o eripiat eum·

XIIa   Vatican City, Biblioteca Apostolica Vaticana, Regin. lat. 12
(Bury Psalter), 35r, Crucifixion

XIIb   Cambridge, Corpus Christi College, 422 (Sherborne
Missal), p. 53, Crucifixion

XIII London, British Library, Cotton Tiberius C. vi (Tiberius Psalter),
13r, Crucifixion

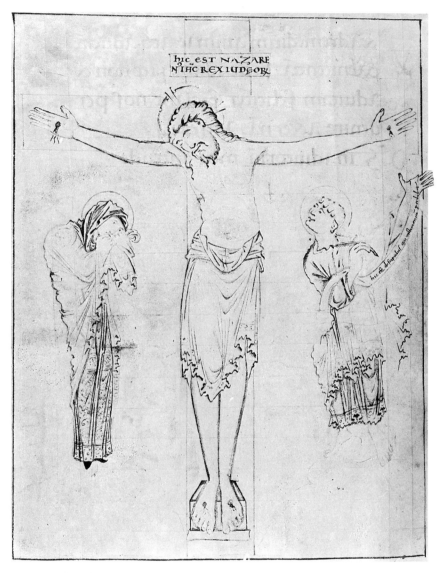

XIV   London, British Library, Harley 2904 (Ramsey Psalter), 3v, Crucifixion

xv   Rouen, Bibliothèque Municipale, Y. 6 [274] (Sacramentary of Robert of Jumièges), 71v, Crucifixion

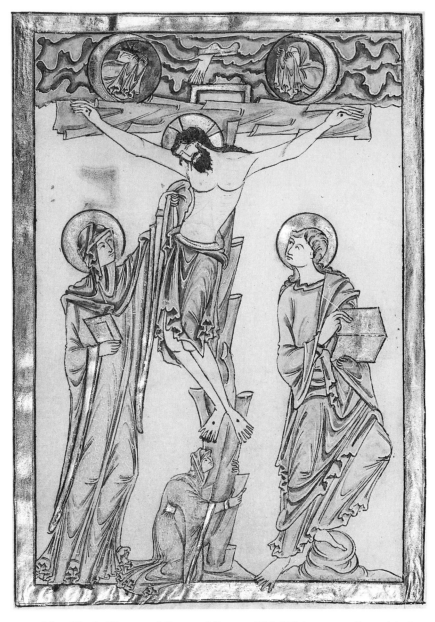

XVI   New York, Pierpont Morgan Library, 709 (Weingarten Gospels), 1 v,
Crucifixion

prophecy of Genesis.[35] Some later ivories show a more restricted version of the iconography. An eleventh-century ivory bookcover with multiple scenes on it includes a Crucifixion scene with a single flying angel overhead and figures of Mary and John below.[36] Another ivory, dating from about 1100, shows two flying angels above the cross and Mary and John below.[37] A portable altar dating from the second half of the eleventh century includes two standing angels behind the figures of Mary and John.[38] Anglo-Saxon artists almost certainly had access to a gospel cycle from Metz which included a Crucifixion scene with flying angels.[39] Some of the paintings in the Benedictional of Æthelwold are very close to the carvings on a ninth-century ivory casket from Metz in the Brunswick Museum and the Nativity and Passion paintings in the Sacramentary of Robert of Jumièges are also related to work from Metz.[40] The casket is decorated with scenes of the Baptism and the Crucifixion on the long sides and with scenes of the Annunciation and the Nativity on the ends; the lid is carved with flying angels. The angels who hover above the cross are similar to the angels in the English drawings though they do not have the same draped hands; the angels above the Baptism scene, on the other hand, have their hands covered and correspond very closely to the angels in the two English drawings. The Crucifixion panel itself is very different from the Sherborne and Arenberg pictures. Like most Crucifixion ivories from Metz, it shows Christ's loincloth knotted on the left hip instead of centrally;[41] the figures of Mary and John, too, are quite different and the ivory includes the figures of Ecclesia, the soldiers and the holy women as well as those of Mary and John. The figures of the angels in the Sherborne and Arenberg drawings could have been taken from a scene of this type but the scene on the Brunswick Casket does not explain the overall conception of the English pictures. An alternative possibility is a Byzantine Crucifixion panel similar to that on a tenth-century diptych in the Hanover Museum.[42] This panel shows Christ draped in a centrally knotted loincloth and accompanied by Mary and John; above the cross are the busts of two angels. It is likely that a

[35] Gen. III.15.   [36] Goldschmidt, *Elfenbeinskulpturen* II, pl. xxi.62.
[37] *Ibid.* II, pl. xlvi.161.
[38] *Ibid.* II, pl. xl.139.   [39] See above, p. 94.
[40] Goldschmidt, *Elfenbeinskulpturen* I, pls. xliv.96 and xlv.96; see above, p. 94; for discussion see Homburger, *Malschule von Winchester* and 'L'art carolingien', pp. 42–3.
[41] Cf. above, p. 94.
[42] Elbern, *Das erste Jahrtausend* III, pl. 318; cf. an ivory from Constantinople, s. x[ex], Schiller, *Iconography* II, pl. 338.

composition of this type was known in late Anglo-Saxon England for the small Crucifixion panel in the church at Romsey includes the busts of two angels above the arms of the cross.

Parallels to the chalice at the foot of the cross are harder to find. Byzantine artists often showed the blood flowing from Christ's wounds into a chalice placed at the side of the cross or held by Ecclesia, but they never placed the chalice at the foot of the cross.[43] A chalice sometimes appears at the foot of the cross in Carolingian and Ottonian art. A ninth-century painting on the altar wall of the crypt of the church of St Maximin at Trier[44] and a painting in the Gospels of Otfrid of Weissenburg dating from about 868[45] show a narrow-necked jar at the foot of the cross. The reference in the wall-painting may be to the container for the vinegar, for the painting includes the figures of the spear- and sponge-bearers as well as those of Mary and John. In the Otfrid picture, however, the blood flows from Christ's feet into the jar showing that it must be interpreted as a chalice. An ivory dated by Goldschmidt to about 900 includes a chalice at the foot of the cross and standing angels above[46] and some latish ivories also include a chalice below the cross.[47] A better parallel is the Erpho Cross,[48] mentioned earlier as a parallel to the shape of the cross in the Sherborne drawing,[49] which includes two angels at the end of the arms of the cross as well as a chalice at the foot.

Jane Rosenthal has argued that the Arenberg and Sherborne drawings were copied from two separate Carolingian models, one from Rheims and the other from Metz or from the school of Charles the Bald, but that both these models were based on a common source.[50] The lack of any really close parallels in Carolingian art and the links with Ottonian goldsmith's work suggest a different explanation. The central figure was probably based on an Ottonian crucifix which showed Christ standing against the cross draped in a loincloth with a central knot, possibly of the highwayman's type; this crucifix may have included the chalice and angels as the Erpho Cross does.

[43] Thoby, *Le crucifix*, pls. xliv.100 and xliv.bis.101. For a discussion of the chalice in the Arenberg Gospels drawing see Rosenthal, 'Arenberg Gospels', pp. 92–100.

[44] Schiller, *Iconography* II, pl. 347.

[45] Boinet, *Miniature*, pl. 160; Goldschmidt, *German Illumination* I, pl. 62.

[46] Goldschmidt, *Elfenbeinskulpturen* IV, pl. lxxix.308.

[47] *Ibid.* II, pls. xv.48, xviii.59, xxix.89, xlvi.163 and xlvii.167.

[48] Elbern, *Das erste Jahrtausend* III, pl. 395.   [49] See above, p. 113.

[50] Rosenthal, 'Arenberg Gospels', pp. 109 and 127–31.

Because English artists preferred an iconography which included the figures of Mary and John[51] they added these figures, basing that of Mary on a drawing in the Utrecht Psalter,[52] and transferred the angels to the spaces above the arms of the cross, perhaps in imitation of something similar to the Crucifixion panel on the Brunswick Casket. This new iconography provided the basis for the Arenberg drawing, the sketches in the Cambridge and Rouen manuscripts and the ivories. The artist of the Sherborne Pontifical drew on the same English prototype but made changes to the figures of Mary and John and to the chalice, possibly using a Byzantine Crucifixion picture as a model for the figure of Mary.

The artist who first devised the Crucifixion iconography of the Arenberg and Sherborne drawings must have done so in order to express some specific theological or devotional point about Christ's death. If it is accepted that the iconography with Mary and John was preferred in the late Anglo-Saxon period because it embodied an allusion to the incarnation and to the reality of Christ's human nature, then the angels and chalice which mark out the Arenberg/Sherborne iconography must be linked in some way to the incarnation.

The motif of the chalice relates Christ's death on the cross to the sacrifice of the mass. The blood and water which flowed from Christ's side on the cross were traditionally interpreted as symbols of the two major sacraments: the eucharist and baptism. Augustine says in his commentary on St John's Gospel: 'Dormit Adam ut fiat Eva; moritur Christus ut fiat Ecclesia. Dormienti Adae fit Eva de latere; mortuo Christo lancea percutitur latus ut profluant sacramenta, quibus formetur ecclesia.'[53] The baptismal associations of the water from Christ's side are brought out very clearly in the prayer for the blessing of the font on Holy Saturday: 'Unde benedico te creatura aquae per deum vivum, per deum sanctum . . . qui te una cum sanguine de latere suo produxit.'[54] The eucharistic associations, based on Christ's words at the Last Supper,[55] can be seen in the drawing of the

---

[51] See above, ch. 4.   [52] Utrecht, Universiteitsbibl., 32, 90r.

[53] *In Iohannis ev.* IX.10 (ed. Mayer, p. 96): 'Adam sleeps so that Eve may come into being; Christ dies so that the church may come into being. Eve springs from the side of the sleeping Adam; the side of the dead Christ is wounded with a spear so that the sacraments may flow forth, by which the church is formed.'

[54] Underwood, 'Fountain of Life', p. 60; *Missal of Robert of Jumièges* (ed. Wilson, p. 98): 'I bless you, creature of water, through the living and holy God . . . who brought you forth from his side, mingled with blood.'

[55] Matt. XXVI.26–8; Mark XIV.22–4; Luke XXII.19–20.

Crucifixion at Psalm CXV in the Utrecht Psalter, where a man holding a paten and chalice catches the blood from Christ's side.[56] The verse from this psalm, 'I will take the chalice of salvation and I will call upon the name of the Lord',[57] was used during the celebrant's communion from the early eleventh century[58] and was already linked with the communion by Paschasius Radbertus in the ninth century.[59] On many Carolingian ivories, as in Byzantine art, Ecclesia holds a chalice to Christ's side to symbolize the role of the church as the guardian of the sacraments and Elbern has suggested that the scenes in which the chalice is placed at the foot of the cross are a reduced form of this iconography.[60] The omission of Ecclesia must mean that the emphasis is not so much on the church's sacramental system as on the relationship between the eucharistic chalice and Christ's blood: the fact that the chalice now catches the blood from Christ's feet implies a more literal identification of the blood and the sacramental wine. If the wavy lines under the chalice in the Arenberg drawing are identified with the hill of Golgotha, as has been suggested in one discussion of the drawing,[61] it would, of course, draw attention to this identity of sacramental commemoration and historical event.

The angels, like the chalice, connect the historical event of Christ's death to its commemoration in the mass. There was a widespread belief in both the Greek and Roman churches that angels were present at the Crucifixion. Angels are shown above the arms of the cross in many Byzantine ivories and several Greek theologians mention their presence at Christ's death. One writer describes how the sun and moon acknowledged Christ by their darkness at the time of his death and the angels shuddered to see the creator and ruler of the world hanging on the cross: 'Nam stupor invasit omnem animatam creaturam, Christum videntem ligno affixum, conditorem et rectorem universi lancea in sacro latere confossum . . . Exhorruerunt ordines incorporeorum angelorum; triste moestumque caelum fuit, stellarum lux et splendor extinctus est; magnus ille gigas sol lampadas subduxit, tenebrae aethera occuparunt, dies versa est in densam

---

[56] See above, p. 77.   [57] Ps. CXV.4.   [58] Jungmann, *Mass*, p. 495.

[59] *De corpore et sanguine Domini*, xix and xxi (ed. Paulus, pp. 103 and 110); cf. above, pp. 77 and 80.

[60] Elbern, 'Der eucharistische Kelch', p. 144.

[61] Rosenthal, 'Arenberg Gospels', pp. 92 and 148.

vesperam.'[62] One of the most striking examples of this idea comes in a speech attributed to the thief on the cross: 'Angelos circumstantes video, solem fugientem, velum scissum, terram trementem, mortuos fugam iam meditantes.'[63] A passage in the Syrian liturgy names the angels grieving at Christ's death as Michael and Gabriel: 'Commotus fuit Gabriel et Michael caput suum inclinavit, quia viderunt Filium Dei inter latrones suspensum et elatum supra lignum.'[64] This identification must have been known to Greek artists for the angels who appear above the arms of the cross are sometimes labelled Gabriel and Michael.[65] There is no evidence that the texts cited above were known in the west, though the belief that angels were present at Christ's death was clearly familiar to Carolingian writers. Hrabanus Maurus, for instance, refers to their presence in his *De laudibus sanctae crucis*:

Merito quippe sanctorum angelorum ordines et coelestis militiae exercitus, nomine et numero sanctae cruci concordant, ut aeterni Regis victoriam collaudent, et magnitudinem laetitiae suae honesto officio praedicent; cum non solum in hora nativitatis Christi laudasse, et post in deserto illi ministrasse sacer Evangelii textus commemoret, verum etiam in tempore passionis et resurrectionis eius, debito ei officio ipsos affuisse manifeste narret.[66]

[62] Pseudo-Chrysostom, *In adorationem venerandae crucis* (PG 62, 747): 'For numbness fell upon every living creature, seeing Christ fixed to the wood of the cross, the creator and ruler of the universe wounded by a spear in his sacred side . . . The ranks of bodiless angels shuddered; the sky became sad and full of grief, the light and splendour of the stars was extinguished; that great giant, the sun, withdrew his torches, darkness filled the sky, day was turned into deep evening.' Cf. Alexander of Alexandria, *Sermo de anima et corpore deque passione Domini*, 6 and additions (PG 18, 599 and 606).

[63] Pseudo-Chrysostom, *In sancta et magna parasceve* (PG 50, 816): 'I see angels standing around, the sun fleeing, the veil torn apart, the earth trembling, the dead already meditating flight.' Cf. John Damascene, *Homilia in sanctam parasceven et in crucem*, 8 (PG 96, 599).

[64] 'There was an earthquake, Gabriel and Michael bowed their heads, because they saw the Son of God hanging between thieves and raised up on the wood of the cross'; quoted in Reil, *Kreuzigung Christi*, p. 74 n. 5.

[65] Schiller, *Iconography* II, pl. 338; Thoby, *Le crucifix*, pls. xlviii.110 and xlix.112.

[66] *De laudibus sanctae crucis* I.iii (PL 107, 161): 'Rightly, indeed, the orders of holy angels and the army of celestial soldiers agree in name and number with the holy cross, in order that they may praise the victory of the eternal king and make known the greatess of their joy by their attentive service; since the sacred text of the gospel not only commemorates their praise at the hour of Christ's birth and their later ministry to him in the desert, but also clearly records that they were present at the time of his Passion and Resurrection with the service they owed to him.'

It was also believed that angels were present in the church during the mass. The Preface of the mass asks that the worship of the earthly congregation should be joined to that of heaven and the presence of angels in the church was noted in the Anglo-Saxon law-codes.[67] Paschasius Radbertus, quoting Gregory the Great, said: 'Quis enim fidelium habere dubium possit, in ipsa immolationis hora ad sacerdotis vocem caelos aperiri, in illo Iesu Christi mysterio angelorum choros adesse, summis ima sociari, terram coelestibus iungi, unum quid ex visibilibus atque invisibilibus fieri?'[68] The idea of a heavenly liturgy in which, as Augustine puts it, 'Adiungitur ista Ecclesia, quae nunc peregrina est, illi coelesti Ecclesiae, ubi Angelos cives habemus'[69] is represented on one of the most elaborate pieces of ninth-century goldsmith's work, the golden altar in the church of Sant'Ambrogio, Milan. The ends of this altar are decorated with scenes in which men and angels honour a jewelled cross placed among the trees of paradise.

These ideas were commonplaces of early medieval religious thought. In the ninth century, however, they were placed in a new and intimate relationship to the theme of Christ's humanity through Paschasius Radbertus's work on the eucharist, the *De corpore et sanguine Domini*. Paschasius argued that the bread and wine offered in the mass became the same human body that was crucified and buried.[70] In the *Epistola ad Fredugardum* he quoted Augustine on the subject: 'Immolatur pro nobis cottidie in mysterio, ut percipiamus *in pane quod pependit in cruce*, et bibamus *in calice quod manavit* de *latere*.'[71] Paschasius saw the change in the bread and wine brought about by the words of consecration as analogous to Mary's conception through the Holy Spirit: in both cases, the earthly was transmuted into the divine.[72] Moreover, he drew a distinction between the

---

[67] *Ecclesiastical Institutes*, x (Thorpe, *Ancient Laws* II, 408) and I Cnut, 4, 2 (Liebermann, *Gesetze* I, 284).

[68] *Epistola ad Fredugardum* (ed. Paulus, pp. 151–2): 'Furthermore, which of the faithful can have any doubt that at the hour of sacrifice itself the heavens open at the priest's voice, earth is joined to heaven and the visible is made one with the invisible?' Cf. Gregory, *Dial.* IV.lx (ed. Moricca, p. 323).

[69] *Sermo* cccxli. 9 (PL 39, 1500): 'This church, which is now a pilgrim, is joined to that heavenly church where we have angels as citizens.'

[70] *De corpore et sanguine*, iv (ed. Paulus, p. 30).

[71] *Epistola ad Fredugardum* (ed. Paulus, p. 151): 'He is sacrificed for us daily in a mystery, so that we may perceive in the bread what hung on the cross and may drink in the chalice what flowed from his side', and cf. a passage earlier in the work (p. 149).

[72] *De corpore et sanguine*, iv (ed. Paulus, p. 30).

bread and the wine, drawing on the Old Testament images of communion. As was common, he linked the bread to the manna given to the Israelites in the desert and to a passage in Psalm LXXVII: 'He rained down manna to feed them, he gave them the wheat of heaven; men ate the bread of Immortals.'[73] The wine was linked to the water from the rock struck by Moses and mentioned in the same psalm.[74] But whereas the bread, the food of angels, came from heaven and made men like the angels, the wine, Christ's blood, was poured out for man alone: the angels had no need to drink it for they had never sinned.[75]

The Arenberg and Sherborne drawings are a clear expression of this view of the mass. Mary is present as a testimony to the incarnation, the precursor of the change in the eucharistic bread and wine. Christ is shown dead on the cross because the breaking of his body and the pouring out of his blood are the reality which lies behind the breaking of the bread and the pouring out of the wine. The angels, placed above the cross, adore Christ's body, the bread of angels which has become the food of man. Below the cross stand Mary, the source of Christ's humanity, and John, the witness to the reality of his death; between them is the chalice, the drink of mankind.

The eucharistic associations of this Crucifixion iconography are exploited in the decoration of the Anglo-Saxon portable altar in the Musée de Cluny (pl. VII).[76] The design on this altar differs in several respects from that in the Arenberg and Sherborne drawings and on the ivory panels, though it must be related to it. Some details seem to be related to date. Christ is shown slumped against a tree-cross, a motif which first appears in English drawings of the mid-eleventh century.[77] Whereas the other items in this group show Christ's hands straight, the thumbs separated from the fingers, the altar shows the hands drooping from the wrists, the thumbs crossed over the palms; the detail of the crossed thumbs appears in the Crucifixion picture of the Bury Psalter which dates from about 1020 (pl. XIIa) and in two mid-eleventh-century works, the Tiberius Psalter and the Weingarten Gospels (pls. XIII and XVI), both of which show the pronounced bend of Christ's body at the knees which also appears on the altar. Other differences, such as the mass-bread held by the left-hand angel, emphasize the eucharistic meaning of the scene. The major difference, however, is the presence of the four evangelist symbols and the

---

[73] Ps. LXXVII.24–5.   [74] Ps. LXXVII.20; Exod. XVII.6.

[75] *De corpore et sanguine*, v and x (ed. Paulus, pp. 32 and 65).

[76] See above, p. 50.   [77] See above, p. 92, n. 3.

Agnus Dei. Decorative crosses of the tenth and eleventh centuries are typically decorated with a crucifix on the front, representing Christ's suffering, and with the apocalyptic scene of the lamb and evangelist symbols on the reverse, symbolizing his triumph. On the portable altar the two themes have been combined to express the paradox of Christ's death.[78] A further shift in the meaning of the scene is suggested by the inscription round the edge of the altar which reads:

> Discipulus plorat Raphael quem semper adorat.
> Genetrix meret Gabriel cui sanctus adheret.[79]

This couplet, which would be more appropriate to a composition which showed Mary and John weeping, directs attention away from the eucharist and back to the historical event of Christ's death. It seems unlikely that it was composed for the altar though it must have been thought appropriate to it. A rather similar couplet occurs among the inscriptions round the sketch of Christ crucified in the Rouen manuscript, which was copied from something similar to either the Arenberg or Sherborne drawings. The inscription reads:

> Rex obit, haec plorat,
> Carus gemit, impius orat.[80]

The hand may be twelfth century and the couplet occurs in several twelfth-century manuscripts.[81] The inscription cannot have been intended originally for the sketch it accompanies since this shows Christ alive not dead. The last half-line, which must refer to someone praying in front of a crucifix, suggests that it was intended for devotional use and the couplet on the altar probably had a similar function.

The identification of the angels on the altar as Gabriel and Raphael is highly unusual: normally the angels in Crucifixion pictures are identified as Michael and Gabriel.[82] Gabriel is associated with God's power: 'Gabriel

---

[78] See also below, pp. 182–3; for a more complicated explanation see Okasha and O'Reilly, 'Anglo-Saxon Portable Altar', pp. 41–4.

[79] 'The disciple weeps for the one whom Raphael always adores; the mother mourns the one to whom the holy Gabriel clings.'

[80] Rouen, Bibl. Mun., A.292 [26], 48r: 'The king dies, the woman weeps, the beloved sighs, the wicked one prays.'

[81] Walther, *Initia carminum*, no. 16748; I am indebted to Andrew Watson for help in dating this hand.

[82] See above, p. 121.

Hebraice in linguam nostram vertitur fortitudo Dei. Ubi enim potentia divina vel fortitudo manifestatur, Gabriel mittitur. Unde et eo tempore, quo erat Dominus nasciturus et triumphaturus de mundo, Gabriel venit ad Mariam, ut illum annuntiaret qui ad debellandas aerias potestates humilis venire dignatus est.'[83] The link made in this passage between Christ's birth and his triumph over the powers of evil would account for Gabriel's association with Mary beside the cross. Raphael is associated with God's healing power: 'Raphael interpretatur curatio vel medicina Dei. Ubicumque enim curandi et medendi opus necessarium est, hic archangelus a Deo mittitur; et inde medicina Dei vocatur.'[84] He seems to have no particular connection with St John though he is appropriately present at Christ's death which healed man's sickness. One of the prayers in the Book of Nunnaminster expresses the same idea:

O medicinae divinae mirabilis dispensator qui tibi lancea latus aperire permisisti, aperi mihi quaeso pulsanti ianuam vitae, ingressusque per eam confitebor tibi; per tui vulnus lateris omnium vitiorum meorum vulnera per misericordiae tuae medicamen sana, ne umquam indignus presumptor tui corporis et sanguinis reus efficiar, pro meritis propriis meorum peccatorum, sed ut anima mea miserationum tuarum abundantia repleta, ut qui mihi es pretium ipse sis et praemium, Domine Iesu Christe.[85]

Michael, whose name means *quis ut Deus?*, is associated with God's power.[86] Hrabanus Maurus linked Michael, Gabriel and Raphael with

---

[83] Isidore, *Etym.* VII.v.10–11 (ed. Lindsay): 'The Hebrew word Gabriel is translated in our language as *God's strength*. For wherever the divine power or strength is made manifest, Gabriel is sent. So, at that time when the Lord was to be born and to triumph over the world, Gabriel came to Mary so that he might announce the one who deigned to come in humility in order to conquer the powers of the air.'

[84] Isidore, *Etym.* VII.v.13 (*ibid.*): 'Raphael is interpreted as *healing* or *the medicine of God*. Wherever there is need of curing and healing, this archangel is sent from God; and therefore he is called *the medicine of God*.'

[85] Book of Nunnaminster, 30r–v (ed. Birch, p. 77): 'O wonderful dispenser of the divine medicine, who allowed your side to be opened with the spear, open to me knocking, I beg, the door of life and, having entered through it, I will acknowledge you; through the wound in your side, cure the wounds of all my sins through the medicine of your mercy, lest I should ever be made guilty of your body and blood by receiving it unworthily, as a punishment for what my sins deserve; but grant that my soul may be filled with the abundance of your mercies and that you who are my ransom may also be my reward, Lord Jesus Christ.'

[86] Isidore, *Etym.* VII.v.12 (ed. Lindsay).

Christ's death on the cross in his *De laudibus sanctae crucis*, associating Michael with Christ's immolation on the altar of the cross and with his defeat of the devil, Gabriel with the promise of Christ's kingdom at the Annunciation and Raphael with the bitterness of Christ's death.[87] Goscelin of Saint-Bertin, who came to England in 1058, draws a parallel between Michael killing the dragon and Christ defeating the devil.[88] We are the members of Christ, he says, our Michael having defeated the dragon. If this identification was known to the poet who composed the couplet it might account for the substitution of Raphael for the more usual Michael. The two angels, together with Christ, would complete the group of Michael, Gabriel and Raphael.

The drawings in the Sherborne and Arenberg manuscripts are not attached to eucharistic texts and although they retain their eucharistic meaning they have a further significance. As was said above,[89] the Crucifixion picture in the Arenberg Gospels forms part of the prefatory material and is placed immediately before the eight pages of canon tables to which it refers. The group of scenes as a whole sets out the theme of Christ's redemption of the world. The Crucifixion picture itself functions like the gospel frontispieces in some Carolingian manuscripts, in particular the scenes of the Lamb with the spear and chalice in the Bamberg Bible and the St Gauzelin Gospels[90] and the pictures of the fountain of life in the Godescalc Gospels[91] and the Gospels of Saint-Médard of Soissons. It shows Christ as the source of the four gospels as well as of the sacraments.[92] The wound in his side is equated with the font which, in turn, is related to the spring in the garden of Eden, the source of the rivers which symbolized the four evangelists.[93] The link was made quite explicitly in the Good Friday liturgy used in Jerusalem in the tenth century which included a chant sung in the church of the Holy Sepulchre, the atrium of which was known as the garden or the new Eden:

> And thy life-giving side, like a fountain bubbling forth from Eden,
> Waters thy church, O Christ, like a reasonable Paradise,

---

[87] *De laudibus sanctae crucis* II.iii (PL 107, 268); see also I.iii (PL 107, 160), which mentions only Gabriel and Raphael.

[88] *Liber confortatorius* (ed. Talbot, pp. 54–5).   [89] See above, p. 84.

[90] See above, p. 69.   [91] See above, pp. 21 and 70–1.

[92] Cf. the *incipit* to St John's Gospel in the Odbert Gospels, 85r, discussed above, p. 74.

[93] See above, p. 70.

Thence dividing into sources, into Four Gospels,
Watering the universe, purifying creation,
And teaching the nations faithfully to worship Thy Kingdom.[94]

The chalice too was associated with this theme of the fountain. A poem by
the ninth-century monk of Tours, Audradus Modicus, the *Liber de fonte
vitae*, has the refrain:

Incipe nunc mecum, caelestis gratia, carmen
Aeterni fontis, scyphi, paschalis et horae.[95]

In the Sherborne Pontifical the emphasis is more on the sacraments. Once
again the Crucifixion picture forms part of the prefatory material. It is the
first of a group of four pictures – the others are drawings of the three
persons of the Trinity – which form a kind of multiple frontispiece to the
text of the Pontifical.[96] The Pontifical contains those services which were
peculiar to the bishop, namely the dedication of churches, ordinations and
episcopal benedictions. The slightly later Lanalet Pontifical is prefixed by
two drawings which relate to the first of these texts and show first a bishop
with an acolyte and secondly the consecration of a church by a bishop.[97]
The Benedictional of Æthelwold illustrates the blessing for the dedication
of a church with a picture of a bishop giving the blessing.[98] The Sherborne
Pontifical illustrates the dedication itself. Christ Church, Canterbury,
where the manuscript was written, was dedicated by Augustine in the
name of the Holy Saviour and was normally known as *Ecclesia Christi* or
Ecclesia Salvatoris.[99] In the Middle Ages, however, it was also known as the
priory of the Holy Trinity and it is thought that the high altar may have
had this dedication whereas the matutinal altar was dedicated to Christ.[100]
The drawing of the Crucifixion shows the main dedication, to Christ as
Saviour, and the three standing figures the subsidiary dedication, to the
Trinity. If Jane Rosenthal's identification of the three standing figures as

[94] Underwood, 'Fountain of Life', pp. 105–6 and n. 247 for Greek text.
[95] MGH, PLAC 3.1, 77: 'Begin now with me, O heavenly Grace, the song of the eternal
font, of the cup and the Paschal season'; Kessler, *Illustrated Bibles*, p. 47; Underwood,
'Fountain of Life', p. 48, n. 27.
[96] 4v and 5v–6v; the text of the dedication ceremony starts on 10r, 7r–8v being occupied
by a copy of a privilege of John XII.
[97] Rouen, Bibl. Mun., A.27 [368], 1v and 2v.   [98] BL, Add. 49598, 118v.
[99] Bede, *HE* I.xxxiii (ed. Colgrave and Mynors, p. 115).
[100] Dugdale, *Monasticon* I, 98; Harmer, *Writs*, p. 166; Gem, 'Cathedral Church at
Canterbury', p. 199, n. 29; Morris, 'Alcuin', p. 82.

three manifestations of Christ were accepted all four pictures would refer to the main dedication, to Christ the Saviour.[101]

The meaning of the scenes on the three ivory Crucifixion panels (pls. IIIa-IIIb and IVa) is different from that of the two drawings because, although they have a general similarity to the Arenberg drawing, they introduce important changes of detail. The most striking difference is that none of them shows the chalice at the foot of the cross. Moreover all depict Christ with open eyes and without the nails in hands and feet or the wound in the side. The chalice, which embodies an allusion to the blood which flowed from the wound in Christ's side, a wound made only after his death, belongs to pictures in which Christ's death is emphasized. The three ivory panels revert to an earlier tradition in which Christ was shown living and triumphant. If the sacrificial, eucharistic element is removed then the meaning of the angels must change and this is confirmed in the case of the Brussels ivory where they carry crowns as do the angels in the Baptism painting in the Benedictional of Æthelwold. Whether the crowns are royal emblems or crowns of martyrdom the implication is the same: they signify Christ's triumph over death. The triumphal element is enhanced on the Copenhagen ivory by showing Christ wearing a crown as he does on the crucifix in the Victoria and Albert Museum, though in the latter case his eyes are closed. This detail links these ivories with a second group of Crucifixion pictures, most of them associated with Winchester, in which Christ is shown wearing a crown and accompanied by emblems of the sun and moon.

---

[101] Rosenthal, 'Three Drawings', pp. 547–62; the suggestion that the three figures are related to the texts from the dedication ceremony when Christ, the *rex gloriae*, enters the church, and that the Crucifixion picture shows the moment when Christ became the victorious king (pp. 560–1), is relevant to the question of the crowned crucifixes discussed below, ch. 6.

6

The crucifix with the crowned Christ

The second group of Crucifixion pictures comprises four drawings in which Christ is shown wearing a crown and accompanied by Mary and John. The hand of God appears above the cross in all four pictures and in three of them symbols of the sun and moon are placed above the arms of the cross. The individual motifs in these scenes are fairly common in late Anglo-Saxon art. The sun and moon appear on the ivory tau cross at Cologne,[1] on the stone Crucifixion panels at Stepney and Breamore and in the Crucifixion painting in the Weingarten Gospels (pl. XVI). Two of the ivories discussed in ch. 5 represent Christ with a crown (pls. IVa–IVb) as do the Crucifixion pictures in the Tiberius and Bury Psalters (pls. XIII and XIIa). The large stone crucifix at Romsey and the Breamore Crucifixion group are known to have had crowns at one time and there are records of crowned crucifixes at Canterbury, Glastonbury, Peterborough, Waltham and Winchester.[2] The four drawings discussed in this chapter are distinguished from these other representations partly by the combination of the crowned figure of Christ with the sun and moon and the figures of Mary and John, partly by details in the position and drapery of the figures and partly by the use of inscriptions to identify the figures, something found only in this particular iconographic group.

The earliest of the four manuscript pictures is a drawing in the Ælfwine Prayer-book, written and decorated at Winchester between 1023 and 1035 for Ælfwine, deacon and later abbot of New Minster (pl. VIII). This

[1] Beckwith, *Ivory Carvings*, no. 30, pl. 80.
[2] Robertson, *Anglo-Saxon Charters*, pp. 158 and 406–7; *De antiquitate Glastoniensis ecclesie*, ch. 27 (ed. Scott, p. 78); L-B 3458 (citing *The Chronicle of Hugh Candidus*), 4471 (citing *De inventione sanctae crucis Walthamensis*), 4700 (citing Thomas Rudborne, *Historia maior*) and Rodwell and Rouse, 'Anglo-Saxon Rood', p. 309.

picture shows Christ standing on the *suppedaneum*, his head turned to the right; his eyes are open even though the wound, made after his death, is visible in his side; he is fastened to the cross with four nails and wears a jewelled fillet on his head. At the top of the cross is a board inscribed, 'Hic est Iesus Nazarenus rex Iudeorum' and, above this, the hand of God is shown, extended in blessing. Above the arms of the cross are three-quarter length figures representing the sun and the moon; they hold torches in their left hands and wear symbolic head-dresses, a crescent for the moon and a spiked crown for the sun, who also carries a disk inscribed 'sol' in his right hand. Mary and John stand among flowering plants beneath the cross, the latter writing in a book. All the figures are identified by name: 'Sancta Maria' by Mary; 'Sanctus Iohannes' by John; 'sol' and 'luna' above. In addition there is a metrical inscription across the top of the picture: 'Hec crux consignet Ælfwinum corpore mente / in qua suspendens traxit Deus omnia secum.'[3]

The other pictures in the group are less complex, but their basic similarity shows that they belong to one coherent type. The picture which resembles that in the Ælfwine Prayer-book most closely is the frontispiece to the Arundel Psalter, written and decorated at the New Minster, Winchester, in about 1060 (pl. IX). The artist has simplified the composition considerably: there is no *titulus*, the sun and moon are represented by two simple crowned heads, the flowers have all disappeared and St John no longer writes in the book that he holds. The fillet is still there, however, as are some of the inscriptions, and the details of the drapery show that this drawing derives from that in the Prayer-book or from something very close to it. Whereas in the group of pictures with flying angels[4] Christ's loincloth was knotted above a central triangular fold, in these two pictures there are two such folds, one at each side, and the cloth is swathed round the waist with, in the Arundel Psalter illustration, a deep central loop. Mary is shown wearing a cloak which falls in a deep curve between the arms like a chasuble. In the Prayer-book she stands in a very distinctive attitude, her arms held close to the body, the hands fanning out from the waist. The gesture of the left hand is preserved in the Arundel Psalter, though this later manuscript shows her holding a book in the right hand. The best

---

[3] 'This cross, hanging on which God drew all things to himself, is a seal placed on Ælfwine's body and mind'; cf. John XII.32 and III.14–15; Ælfric, *CH* II.xiii (ed. Godden, p. 135).

[4] Discussed above in ch. 5.

parallels to these figures occur in the Ascension scenes in the Athelstan Psalter[5] and on a late tenth-century ivory in the Victoria and Albert Museum.[6]

The other two drawings in this group are found in the Winchcombe Psalter and in a collection of homilies associated with Exeter (pls. X and XI).[7] In both pictures the symmetrical arrangement of Christ's loincloth has been replaced by a diagonal draping which leaves the left thigh uncovered. Mary is depicted differently too. She still wears the chasuble-like cloak but her arms are placed in such a way that the whole of the forearm is visible, with the hands raised towards the shoulders instead of fanning out at waist level. The position is similar to that of Mary in the Ascension paintings in the Benedictional of Æthelwold and the Sacrament-ary of Robert of Jumièges. The drawing in the Winchcombe Psalter preserves the rare motif of St John writing in his book, and both pictures retain the details of the jewelled fillet and some of the inscriptions. These drawings show some interesting additional features. The artist of the Arundel Psalter had shown Christ hanging on a rough-hewn tree-cross; in the slightly earlier Winchcombe Psalter the idea of the cross as a tree is conveyed by inscribing it with the words 'lignum vitae'. In the Winchester Prayer-book and the Arundel Psalter the sun and moon are present, like Mithraic symbols, to assert the divinity of Christ; in the Winchcombe Psalter, by contrast, they have been replaced by two female figures who veil their faces to symbolize the sorrow and darkness of the natural world at Christ's death. In the manuscript of homilies the sun and moon have disappeared completely and a new and unusual element in English Crucifixion pictures has been introduced in the form of a winged dragon at the foot of the cross.

There are no real parallels to the overall composition of these pictures and this suggests that the iconography in which Christ is shown wearing a fillet and accompanied by symbols of the sun and moon may have been an English invention. The artist of the Ælfwine Prayer-book, which contains the earliest example of this iconography, was certainly capable of combin-ing elements from different sources to create new compositions. For his drawing of the Trinity he used parts of the illustrations to Psalm CIX and

---

[5] See below, p. 132.
[6] Victoria and Albert Museum, no. 254–1867, in Beckwith, *Ivory Carvings*, no. 22, pl. 52 and Goldschmidt, *Elfenbeinskulpturen* I, pl. xxviii.70.
[7] CCCC 421, p. 1.

the *Gloria* in the Utrecht Psalter, adding the details of the jaws of hell and the figures of Arius and Judas.[8] For his Crucifixion picture he seems to have drawn first on the illustrations to the Athelstan Psalter. The figure of Mary in the Crucifixion picture is strikingly like the Mary of the Ascension picture in the Athelstan Psalter. Both stand in the identical position, hands fanning out from the waist; in addition, the arrangement of the drapery, in particular the symmetrical folds of the cloak and the padded fold at the ankles, is very close. Both pictures contain the same spindly flowering plants which reappear in the David scenes in a later Winchester manuscript, the Tiberius Psalter. Finally, the pictures in the Athelstan Psalter contain identifying inscriptions which could have provided a model for the inscriptions in the four Crucifixion pictures.

The Ælfwine figure of Mary could have been taken directly from the Ascension picture in the Athelstan Psalter or from a derivative of it, but there is one other possibility. Originally the Athelstan manuscript probably contained a Crucifixion picture.[9] If this was based on an early Christian model, as the Ascension picture seems to have been, it might account for the late antique figures of the sun and moon in the Ælfwine Crucifixion picture.[10] Similar figures are fairly common in Carolingian art[11] but they are also found in the Crucifixion scenes on four of the Monza Ampullae[12] which provide one of the best parallels to the Athelstan Ascension scene.[13]

The second source which seems to have influenced the artist of the Ælfwine Prayer-book is the Crucifixion picture in the Ramsey Psalter (pl. xiv).[14] Both drawings show St John writing: in the Ramsey Psalter drawing he writes on an unrolled scroll, in the Ælfwine drawing on a book. It is likely that the two pictures are related, however, in spite of this difference, for the motif is too unusual for both artists to have arrived at it independently.[15] A further detail which may link the Ælfwine drawing to the work of the Ramsey Psalter artist is that St John is shown with a beard. The St John of the Ramsey Psalter Crucifixion picture is of the normal

---

[8] Cf. Ælfric, *CH* I.xx (ed Thorpe, p. 290).   [9] See above, p. 87, n. 72.

[10] Wood, 'Athelstan's Empire', p. 268, n. 84.

[11] E.g. Schiller, *Iconography* II, pls. 360 and 361; Goldschmidt, *Elfenbeinskulpturen* I, pl. lxxxiv.181; cf. above, p. 94.

[12] Nos. 5, 9, 10 and 11, Grabar, *Ampoules*, pls. 11, 14, 16 and 18.

[13] Deshman, 'Anglo-Saxon Art', pp. 186–90.

[14] Discussed below, pp. 155–8.   [15] See above, pp. 96–9.

youthful, beardless type, but the artist of this manuscript represents St John with a beard in the evangelist portraits of the Boulogne Gospels and the Anhalt-Morgan Gospels. A similarly bearded St John appears in the portraits of the Eadwig Gospels.

The meaning of the Crucifixion picture in the Ælfwine manuscript is defined by the fillet on Christ's head, though this has to be interpreted in relation to the other elements in the scene, in particular the symbols of the sun and moon. Pictures of Athelstan, Edgar and Cnut show that the royal crowns of the period consisted of a broad band surmounted by three or four knobs or fleur-de-lis. The enthroned Christ of the Trinity Gospels wears a crown of this type as does the first of the three standing figures in the Sherborne Pontifical (5v). Elsewhere Christ is shown crowned with a narrow circlet, sometimes plain, sometimes with a central jewel, sometimes studded all round with jewels.[16] Similar circlets were commonly used to distinguish angels, saints and evangelists in tenth- and eleventh-century English art but this does not necessarily mean that they have no royal significance, for the saints have royal status. Fleur-de-lis crowns of the normal royal type are worn by the choirs of confessors and virgins in the paintings at the beginning of the Benedictional of Æthelwold and are presented to Mary in the dormition pictures of this manuscript and the related benedictional in Rouen.[17] The crowns presented to Christ by the choirs of angels and saints in a painting in a sacramentary from Metz, probably produced for the coronation of Charles the Bald as king of Lorraine in 869, are similar;[18] they represent the crown of life given by Christ to those who follow him and mark his followers as the line of kings, the royal priesthood.[19] That the circlets have a similar meaning can be seen from the Baptism picture in the Benedictional of Æthelwold, where they are associated with royal sceptres, and from a drawing of Christ the judge wearing a circlet and inscribed with the words 'Rex regum'.[20] Some English kings seem to have worn circlets as well as the normal crowns. King John wore a narrow band with a rose ornament at the centre and

[16] E.g. Beckwith, *Ivory Carvings*, nos. 27 and 39; Boulogne Gospels, 10r; Florence, Bibl. Laurenziana, Plut. xvii. 20, 1r; BL, Cotton Tiberius C. vi, 10v, 12r and 114v. For a discussion of the question of crowned figures of Christ in late Anglo-Saxon art see Deshman, '*Christus rex*'.

[17] Rouen, Bibl. Mun., Y. 7 [369], 54v.   [18] BN, lat. 1141, 5v.

[19] Apoc. 1.5–6 and IV.10; I Peter II.9.

[20] Cambridge, Trinity College, B. 15. 34, 1r.

Henry III was crowned with a similar circlet at Gloucester though the ceremony was repeated later with a crown.[21] Reginald of Durham's description of the opening of St Cuthbert's tomb in 1104 suggests that similar circlets may have been worn in the tenth century: he describes the saint as wearing a gold fillet studded with jewels and it seems likely that this was the royal cap presented by King Athelstan in 934.[22]

By the twelfth century it was quite common to represent Christ on the cross wearing a fleur-de-lis crown.[23] An eleventh-century psalter from Saint-Germain-des-Prés[24] includes a figure of this type and a crucifix at Vercelli is decorated with a fleur-de-lis crown attributed to Otto III,[25] but most crowned crucifixes of the ninth to the eleventh centuries are more discreet. Crucifixion pictures in the Sacramentary of Drogo of Metz and the Utrecht Psalter[26] indicate Christ's victory in death by a wreath above his head as well as by the *titulus*, which the gospels describe as carrying the words, 'rex Iudeorum'.[27] A variant on this motif is a jewelled gold circlet which replaces the *titulus* and which is held either by the hand of God or by angels.[28] In these scenes Christ's kingship, which he possessed in virtue of his divine nature, is separated from his humanity, visible on the cross.[29] The church always emphasized, however, that Christ's divine nature was still present on the cross even though it could not suffer as his human nature did. Cassiodorus makes the point very clearly, quoting Augustine, in a comment on the verse, 'Quoniam Domini est regnum.'[30] Bede interpreted the inscription over Christ's head as a sign that his royalty shone from the cross even while he suffered in his humanity.[31] The words 'a ligno' were added to the psalm verse, 'Dicite in nationibus: Dominus regnavit', at an early date to show that Christ's rule was dependent upon his

[21] Schramm, *Herrschaftszeichen* III, 765.

[22] Battiscombe, *Relics*, pp. 33, 42, 63 and 109.

[23] Thoby, *Le crucifix*, pls. lxv.147–9, lxvii.153–4 and lxxii.164.

[24] BN, lat. 11550, 6r; Leroquais, *Psautiers* II, 105–10, pl. xxx.

[25] Heer, *Holy Roman Empire*, pl. 23.   [26] Utrecht, Universiteitsbibl., 32, 67r.

[27] Matt. XXVII.37, Mark XV.26, Luke XXIII.38 and John XIX.19.

[28] Goldschmidt, *Elfenbeinskulpturen* I, pl. l.114 and II, pls. xviii.57 and 58.

[29] Cf. below, p. 148.   [30] See above, pp. 85–6.

[31] *In Luc.* VI.xxiii.38 (ed. Hurst, p. 404); the identical passage appears in Hrabanus Maurus, *Comment. in Matt.* VIII.xxvii [iv] (PL 107, 1138); see also Paschasius Radbertus, *Exp. in Matt.* XII.xxvii.37 (ed. Paulus, p. 1369), where the *titulus* is interpreted as a symbol of the priestly crown.

death[32] and from there they passed into the *Vexilla regis* of Venantius Fortunatus, sung at Vespers on Palm Sunday:

> Impleta sunt quae concinit
> David fideli carmine,
> Dicendo nationibus:
> Regnavit a ligno Deus.[33]

From an early date artists had recalled Christ's kingship even on the cross by showing him clothed in a purple *colobium* as is the case in the Crucifixion painting in the Rabbula Gospels. It was only in the ninth century, however, that they began to portray him wearing a crown, possibly as a reaction to the introduction at this time of representations of the dead Christ. The crowned figure first appears, rather tentatively, in the illustrations to Hrabanus Maurus's *De laudibus sanctae crucis*. The halo which surrounds the head of the crucified Christ, and which is called *corona* in the accompanying poem, is inscribed with the words, 'Rex regum et Dominus dominorum'.[34] The artist of the Metz Coronation Sacramentary went further and placed a pearl-studded band round Christ's head in the Crucifixion painting at the *Te igitur* of the mass.[35] In both cases Christ is shown with open eyes, alive on the cross, and in the Sacramentary his kingship is emphasized by including the motifs of the sun, moon and serpent.

The motifs of the sun and moon were taken over by the early Christians from pagan art where they symbolized divine power.[36] Like the figures of Oceanus and Gaia who appear in scenes such as that of the enthroned Christ in the Metz Sacramentary[37] or the Crucifixion picture before St Luke's Gospel in the Bernward Gospels they convey Christ's dominion over the

---

[32] Ps. XCV.10, Capelle, 'Regnavit a ligno', pp. 211–14; cf. Augustine, *Enarr. in Ps.*, xcv.11 (ed. Dekkers and Fraipont II, 1350).

[33] *Portiforium* (ed. Hughes I, 44):
> Fulfilled is all that David told
> In true prophetic song of old;
> Amidst the nations, God, saith he,
> Hath reigned and triumphed from the tree.

[34] *De laudibus sanctae crucis* I.i and II.iv (PL 107, 151 and 268–70).

[35] BN, lat. 1141, 6v; Rosenthal, 'Three Drawings', p. 552.

[36] Hautecoeur, 'Le soleil et la lune', p. 14; Deonna, 'Sol et Luna', esp. article 1, p. 39 and article 2, pp. 61–77.

[37] BN, lat. 1141, 6r.

natural world. On a more literal level they were linked with the eclipse which took place at Christ's death and this is their meaning in the Crucifixion picture of the Uta Gospels, two of whose inscriptions read:

> Igneus sol obscuratur in aethere, quia sol iustitiae patitur in cruce.
> Eclypsin patitur et luna, quia de morte Christi dolet ecclesia.[38]

The meaning is not purely historical, however, for the darkness is seen as a sign of the grief of the natural world at the death of its lord and is therefore linked to the theme of Christ's kingship. The idea goes back at least to Gregory the Great, who listed the signs of Christ's dominion: the star at his birth, the sea over which he walked, the earth which hid its light and the rocks which were torn apart at his death.[39] It was recalled in the antiphon sung during the Good Friday Adoration of the Cross: 'Dum fabricator mundi mortis supplicium pateretur in cruce, clamans voce magna tradidit spiritum; et ecce velum templi scissum est, monumenta aperta sunt, terre motus enim factus fuerat magnus, quia mortem filii Dei clamabat mundus se sustinere non posse.'[40] The prayer *De tenebris* in the Book of Nunnaminster includes the passage: 'Expavit dies non solita nocte et suas tenebras mundus invenit, etiam lux ipsa visa est mori tecum ne a sacrilegis cernere videris, clauserat enim suos oculos caelum ne te in cruce aspiceret.'[41] Ælfric used the idea three times[42] and its connection with Christ's kingship is clearly stated in the poem *The Dream of the Rood*:

---

[38] 'The fiery sun is darkened in the sky because the sun of justice suffers on the cross; the moon suffers an eclipse because the church mourns the death of Christ.'

[39] Gregory, *Homilia in Ev.* I.x.2 (PL 76, 1111); compare also Friend's discussion of the figures of the sun and moon on the cover of the Lindau Gospels in relation to the account of the eclipse in the letter of Dionysius to Polycarp of Smyrna, 'Carolingian Art', pp. 67–8.

[40] *Concordia*, iv.44 (ed. Symons, p. 42): 'While the creator of the world was suffering the punishment of death on the cross, crying with a loud voice, he gave up his spirit; and behold, the veil of the temple was torn apart, the graves were opened, there was a great earthquake, because the world cried out that it could not bear the burden of the death of the Son of God.'

[41] Book of Nunnaminster, 28r–v (ed. Birch, p. 74): 'The day became afraid at the unaccustomed night and the world discovered its shadows, even light itself seemed to die with you lest you should be recognized by the sacrilegious, and the heaven closed her eyes lest she should see you on the cross.'

[42] *CH* I.vii and I.xv (ed. Thorpe, pp. 108 and 228); *CH* II.xiv (ed. Godden, p. 147); cf. Haymo, *Hom.* xv (PL 118, 110) and Paul the Deacon, *Hom.* xlviii (PL 95, 1188); see also below, p. 175.

Weop eall gesceaft,
cwiðdon cyninges fyll. Crist wæs on rode.[43]

The second triumphal symbol in the Metz Sacramentary Crucifixion picture, the serpent under Christ's feet, recalls the prophecy that the serpent of Genesis would be crushed under foot by the Messiah, the descendant of Eve.[44] This motif is very common in work from Metz but only three examples are known from Anglo-Saxon England: the Crucifixion picture opposite Psalm XXI in the Bury Psalter (pl. XIIa), the frontispiece to the Cambridge manuscript of homilies (pl. XI) and the fragments of a stone Crucifixion group at Bitton. In both manuscript pictures it is combined with the motif of the crowned Christ. The idea of victory over the devil, which is implicit in the motif of the serpent under Christ's feet, is often linked with the theme of Christ's kingship in Old English literature. In the Blickling Annunciation and Palm Sunday homilies Christ's death is described as the victorious expedition of a king against the traitor devil. The cross is described as Christ's throne from which he distributes gifts like an Anglo-Saxon ruler: 'þa swa se hyhtenda gigant, swa Drihten on middangearde bliðe wunode oþþæt he becom to þæm heahsetle þære rode on þæm upstige eall ure lif he getremede. He sealde his þone readan gim, þæt wæs his þæt halige blod, mid þon he us gedyde dæl-nimende þæs heofonlican rices.'[45] Christ's entry to Jerusalem is seen as the triumphant reception of a king returning from battle: 'þa bæron hie him togeanes blowende palmtwigu; forþon þe hit wæs Iudeisc þeaw, þonne heora ciningas hæfdon sige geworht on heora feondum, and hie wæron eft ham hweorfende, þonne eodan hie him togeanes mid blowendum palm-twigum, heora siges to wyorþmyndum. Wel þæt gedafenode þæt Drihten swa dyde on þa gelicnesse; forþon þe he wæs wuldres cyning.'[46] This passage

---

[43] *Dream of the Rood* 55–6: 'All creation wept, lamented the death of the king; Christ was on the cross.'

[44] Gen. III.15.

[45] *Blickling Homilies*, no. i (ed. Morris, pp. 9–11): 'Then, like the exulting giant, the Lord lived happily on earth until he came to the throne of the cross, in ascending which he raised up all our lives. He gave his red jewel, which was his holy blood, with which he made us sharers in the heavenly kingdom.'

[46] *Blickling Homilies*, no. vi (*ibid.*, p. 67): 'Then they carried waving palm-branches before him, because it was the Jewish custom, when their kings had won a victory over their enemies and they were returning home again, to go towards them with waving palm-branches in honour of their victory. It was very fitting that the Lord should act in the same way, because he was the king of glory.'

reflects the church's practice of commemorating Christ's entry to Jerusalem with chants which made his kingship explicit in a way which the gospel account of his entry to Jerusalem did not. The Palm Sunday procession involved an imaginative re-creation of Christ's journey from the Mount of Olives rather than a reminder of it. The *Regularis concordia* describes how the children went ahead as the procession returned to the church so that they could greet Christ with the chant, 'Gloria, laus et honor tibi sit rex Christe redemptor.'[47] A tenth-century treatise attributed to Alcuin, the *De divinis officiis liber*, describes how the congregation inclined towards the gospel-book, 'quod intelligitur Christus', at the singing of the 'Gloria, laus'.[48] In the Sarum rite the procession paused before the crucifix at the entrance to the choir and saluted it with the antiphon, 'Ave rex noster, fili David, redemptor mundi'.[49] This antiphon is not mentioned in the description of the ceremony in the *Regularis concordia* but it does occur in a tenth-century German customary before the singing of the hymn 'Gloria, laus'[50] and something similar was certainly known at Winchester in the early eleventh century for a prayer based partly on it occurs opposite the drawing of the Crucifixion in the Ælfwine Prayer-book, among the prayers to be recited in front of a crucifix.[51] The link between Christ's kingship and his death on the cross is made particularly clear in the German customary where the antiphon 'Salve rex' is sung during the Good Friday veneration of the cross.[52] Celebrations of Christ's kingship played a major part in the Cluny liturgy during the early eleventh century. The emperor Henry II had given the monastery his coronation robe together with his crown and sceptre, a cross and a gold globe which had been given him by the pope at his coronation in 1014.[53] The crown was hung above the high altar on the feasts of Easter and Pentecost.[54] The imperial *insignia* were placed on the

---

[47] *Concordia*, iv.36 (ed. Symons, p. 35): 'Glory, praise and honour to you, oh Christ, king and redeemer'; see also, *Portiforium*, ed. Hughes I, 43.

[48] *De divinis officiis*, xiv (PL 101, 1201); for the date see Hallinger, *Initia consuetudinis Benedictinae*, pp. xxxviii–xxxix.

[49] *Sarum Missal* (ed. Legg, p. 96): 'Hail, our king, son of David, redeemer of the world.'

[50] *Dicta Einsidlensia*, xviii.45 (ed. Hallinger, p. 220).

[51] BL, Cotton Titus D. xxvii, 66r–v.

[52] *Dicta Einsidlensia*, xviii.57 (ed. Hallinger, p. 232).

[53] Ademar, *Historiae* III.37 (PL 141, 54).

[54] *Liber Tramitis* I.ix.57.1 and I.xiii.74.1 (ed. Dinter, pp. 83 and 111).

altar on the feasts of Easter, Pentecost, St Peter and the Assumption[55] and were carried in the processions for Christmas, Candlemass, Palm Sunday, Easter, Ascension and Pentecost.[56] That these items were considered to be attributes of Christ, not of earthly kings, can be seen from the fact that they were not carried in the processions with which kings were welcomed to the monastery.[57]

In an age when it was held that the king's power derived from the royal power of Christ it was natural that Christ should be represented as a king. Several writers have seen this as a device for enhancing royal power. Robert Deshman has argued that the crowned figures of Christ and the Magi which appeared in England during the reign of Edgar were connected with his pretensions to imperial power, seen also in the episode after his coronation when a group of six kings did homage to him at Chester.[58] Deshman draws a parallel with Ottonian Germany where Otto III was shown enthroned among the evangelist symbols like Christ[59] and the emperor Henry II was depicted seated before a medallion-cross and wearing a crown and stole like those worn by Christ in the Crucifixion picture of the Uta Gospels.[60] There are no comparable portraits of Anglo-Saxon kings, however, and it seems more likely that the crowned figures of Christ in English art were intended to express a rather different royal ideal.

The idea that the king received his power from Christ existed long before the Ottonian period, and the parallels which were undoubtedly drawn between king and Christ involved elements other than power. The two Carolingian miniatures discussed earlier both have royal connections.[61] The Christ figure with the inscription 'Rex regum et dominus dominorum' round the halo in Hrabanus Maurus's *De laudibus sanctae crucis* follows a picture of the emperor Louis the Pious inscribed, 'Tu Hludovicum Christe corona.'[62] The crowned figure of Christ in the Metz Coronation Sacramentary is associated with a painting of a young prince, probably

---

[55] *Ibid.* I.x.58.1, I.xiii.75, I.xiv, 85.4 and I.xiv.100.3 (ed. Dinter, pp. 88, 115, 131 and 150).

[56] *Ibid.* I.ii.13.4, I.iv.31.3, I.vi.54.2, I.x.58.2, I.xii.72 and I.xiii.75 (ed. Dinter, pp. xlviii–l, 23, 42, 68, 89, 108 and 115).

[57] *Ibid.* II.xxvii.169 (ed. Dinter, p. 242).

[58] Deshman, '*Christus rex*', pp. 400–3; ASC E, 972; Ælfric, *LS*, no. xxi (ed. Skeat, I, 468); see also below, p. 149.

[59] Deshman, '*Christus rex*', p. 387.   [60] *Ibid.*, p. 384; Vat. Ottob. lat. 74, 193v.

[61] See above, p. 135.   [62] *De laudibus sanctae crucis* (PL 107, 141–50).

Charles the Bald, being crowned by the hand of God.[63] The eleventh-century artists who showed the emperor Henry II being crowned by Christ were not expressing some new idea.[64] The belief that the king shared in Christ's priesthood as well as his kingship similarly goes back to the Carolingian period. Charlemagne was addressed as 'Rex et sacerdos' at the 794 Synod of Frankfurt which debated the question of the veneration of images.[65] Charles the Bald emphasized his own priestly character by wearing a silk veil beneath his diadem on Sundays and feast days.[66] A similar veil can be seen under the crown in the painting of Christ in the early eleventh-century Trinity Gospels. However, the way in which the parallel between Christ and king was understood in the tenth and eleventh centuries differed from the Carolingian interpretation of the parallel. In the ninth century the emphasis was on the Old Testament. The Franks saw themselves as the new Israel and kings were compared to David, the ancestor of Christ. Charlemagne himself was known as David in court circles and Amalarius drew a parallel between David and Charlemagne's son, Louis the Pious.[67] The parallel implied the sacred character of the Carolingian kings, who were anointed as David was, but it also involved a comparison with Christ. David was interpreted as a prophetic symbol of Christ; the Carolingian king, the new David, was equally an image of Christ but this time a commemorative one. It was in this context that the *Laudes regiae* developed: the chants which were sung between collect and epistle or after the *Gloria* on great feast days when kings and bishops were present and which acclaimed Christ's kingship in the refrain, 'Christus vincit, Christus regnat, Christus imperat.' The Palm Sunday hymn, 'Gloria, laus', which consists of a series of acclamations addressed to Christ as he makes his royal entry to the city of Jerusalem, belongs to the same period.[68] By the late tenth century the king was seen more directly as an image of Christ. A German coronation *ordo* of this period makes the point explicitly in the words spoken when the king was invested with the sword, 'cum mundi Salvatore, cuius typum geris in nomine sine fine merearis

[63] BN, lat. 1141, 2v.

[64] Gospels of Henry II, Munich, Bayerische Staatsbibl., Clm. 4452, 2r; Sacramentary of Henry II, Munich, Bayerische Staatsbibl., Clm. 4456, 11r.

[65] Kantorowicz, *Laudes regiae*, pp. 47 and 57, n. 148; MGH, Concilia 2.1, 142.

[66] Kantorowicz, *Laudes regiae*, p. 93; *Annales Fuldenses*, AD 876 (ed. Pertz, p. 86).

[67] *Liber officialis*, Praefatio, 7 (ed. Hanssens II, 21).

[68] Kantorowicz, *Laudes regiae*, p. 72, n. 25.

regnare'.[69] But whereas the Carolingian parallel between king and Christ was concerned with power, the tenth-century parallel focused more sharply on the idea, applicable to all Christians and not simply to the king, that to reign with Christ one had first to suffer with him.[70] The king was reminded of his duty to imitate the suffering of Christ when he first entered the church for his coronation. Before his anointing, coronation and enthronement he prostrated himself in the form of a cross before the altar while the congregation sang the *Te Deum*.[71] Odilo of Cluny's life of the empress Adelaide sets out in detail the royal ideal of sharing the sufferings of Christ[72] and when the emperor Henry II presented the imperial globe to Cluny in 1014 he said that it could not be held more appropriately than by those who had abandoned the pomp of the world to follow the cross of the Saviour.[73]

The church was always very conscious of the difference between Christ's kingship and that of earthly kings. Christ himself had told Pilate, 'Mine is not a kingdom of this world',[74] and the prophecy of Zechariah, which lies behind the description of Christ's entry to Jerusalem, emphasized the humility of the Messiah: 'See now, your king comes to you; he is victorious, he is triumphant, humble and riding on a donkey, on a colt, the foal of a donkey.'[75] Odo of Cluny distinguished between the heavenly Jerusalem with its humble king, Christ, and Babylon with its proud king, the devil.[76] He described how Christ submitted to torture and death in order that the humble God should teach man not to be proud.[77] Even Odilo, who was responsible for the elaborate processions in which the imperial *insignia* were carried, made the connection between suffering and glory the central point in his teaching.[78] For Ælfric one of the most important points about Christ was that he was not like earthly kings. He came to be nailed to the cross with insults, not to be raised on a royal throne.[79] He wore a crown of thorns, not a royal crown. He rejected the transitory rule of this world

---

[69] Schramm, *Kaiser* I, 83 and III, 84: 'With the Saviour of the world, whose image you carry in your name, may you be worthy to reign without end.'

[70] II Tim. II.11–12.

[71] Schramm, *Kaiser* II, 235, n. 25 and III, 95; Bornscheuer, *Miseriae regum*, p. 200.

[72] Bornscheuer, *Miseriae regum*, pp. 41–59; *Epitaphium Adalheidae imperatricis* (ed. Pertz, pp. 633–45).

[73] Ralph Glaber, *Historiae sui temporis* I.v (PL 142, 626).   [74] John XVIII.36.

[75] Zech. IX.9, Matt. XXI.5.   [76] *Collationes* I.xiv (PL 133, 529).

[77] *Ibid.* I.xxxiv (PL 133, 543).

[78] Odilo, *Serm.* xv (PL 142, 1033).   [79] *CH* I.v (ed. Thorpe, p. 82).

for the eternal kingship of the next.[80] The same point is made in the crowned crucifixes of the period: the only example of a crowned crucifix from Anglo-Saxon England where the reason for the crowning is given, links the jewelled gold crown on the crucifix with the historical crown of thorns.[81]

The ideal of kingship set out by tenth-century Anglo-Saxon writers resembled their picture of Christ in being one of humility, as well as of power.[82] The *ordo* used for the coronation of Edgar in 973 included the prostration before the altar during the singing of the *Te Deum*.[83] That the parallel between Edgar and Christ was related to Christ's Passion is made clear by Byrhtferth of Ramsey in his life of St Oswald:

Non enim ita ad eum confluxerat suae gentis admirabilis et gloriosus exercitus ut eum expellerent, vel consilium facerent ut eum morti traderent, vel ligno suspenderent, sicut olim infelices Iudaei benignum gesserunt Iesum; sed tam rationabili scientia undique adventitabant, et cum gaudio accelerabant, ut eum episcopi reverentissimi benedicerent, unguerent, consecrarent, Christo largiente, ex Quo, vel a Quo summae benedictionis et sanctae religionis unctio beata processit.[84]

Ælfric described the king's role in a sermon for the Sunday after the Ascension. The king was Christ's deputy.[85] He was to defend his people against attackers and to pray to God for victory, but he also had the duty of giving up his life for his people as Christ sacrificed himself for man.[86] Ælfric was in no doubt about the reality of royal power but he believed equally in royal humility. In a sermon for the feast of the Exaltation of the Cross he described how an angel appeared above the Golden Gate of Jerusalem as the emperor Heraclius rode in triumph from the Mount of Olives to the city, carrying the relics of the cross which he had recovered from

---

[80] *CH* I.x (*ibid.*, p. 162).

[81] L-B 4471 (citing *De inventione sanctae crucis Walthamensis*); see above, p. 41.

[82] Cf. John, 'Abbot Ælfric', pp. 309–13.   [83] Schramm, *Kaiser* II, 235.

[84] *Vita Sancti Oswaldi*, iv (ed. Raine, *Historians of the Church of York* I, 436): 'For the admirable and glorious army of that race did not come together in order to drive him out, or to plot to betray him to death or to hang him on the cross, as the ill-fated Jews once acted to the kindly Jesus; but they approached from all sides with rational understanding and hastened with joy so that most reverent bishops should bless him, anoint and consecrate him, with Christ's blessing, from whom or by whom the blessed unction of perfect blessing and holy religion proceeds.'

[85] *Cristes sylfes speligend.*

[86] Ælfric, *Homilies* (ed. Pope I, 380–1); see also pp. 374–7 and Silverman, 'The King as "Cristes sylfes speligend" '.

the Persians. The angel reminded him that when Christ, the king of heaven, took this same road to his Passion he was not crowned or dressed in purple but rode humbly on an ass. The emperor then dismounted and, stripping off his royal robes, entered the city barefoot, carrying the relics of the cross in his hands.[87] Ælfric's *Life of St Edmund*, translated from the life by Abbo of Fleury, showed the king modelling himself on Christ by refusing to fight against the Viking invaders.[88] In a homily for Palm Sunday Ælfric reminded his listeners that the king may be chosen by the people but once he is consecrated they cannot shake his yoke from their necks.[89] The phrase invites comparison with the yoke of Christ which man must shoulder in order to learn gentleness and humility.[90] This yoke is, of course, the cross which man must take up if he is to follow Christ.[91] Harold Godwinsson is said to have made a habit of praying lying on the ground in the form of a cross, a practice which symbolized the relationship between his kingship and that of Christ. When he was on his way from Stamford Bridge to Hastings in 1066 he called at Waltham to pray in front of the crucifix there, the king of wretched mortals saluting the immortal and invisible king of the ages.[92] The crucifix at Waltham had been crowned by the wife of Cnut's standard-bearer[93] and it is of interest that Cnut himself is credited with the gift of crowns to crucifixes at Winchester and Canterbury.[94] The Canterbury gift is recorded in a charter conferring the port of Sandwich on Christ Church. The charter – thought by some to be spurious, but accepted as genuine by Robertson – is written in an eleventh-century hand and dated 1023, though the Parker manuscript of the Anglo-Saxon Chronicle claims that the gift of Sandwich was made on Cnut's return from Rome in 1031.[95] This may refer to a second visit to Rome or to that made by Cnut in 1027 for the coronation of Conrad II. A parallel to Cnut's action can be seen in the gift of a crown and other imperial items to Cluny a few years earlier by the emperor Henry II as he was returning with Odilo from his coronation

---

[87] *LS*, no. xxvii (ed. Skeat II, 148–50); based on Hrabanus, *Hom.* lxx (PL 110, 131–4); there is an illustration of the scene in the Mont Saint-Michel Sacramentary, New York, Pierpont Morgan Library, 641, 155v.

[88] *LS*, no. xxxii (ed. Skeat II, 320–2).

[89] *CH*, I.xiv (ed. Thorpe, p. 212); the word is *geoc*.

[90] Matt. XI.29–30.   [91] Matt. XVI.24.

[92] L-B 4478 (citing *Vita Haroldi regis*) and 4480 (citing *De inventione sanctae crucis Walthamensis*); see above, p. 62.

[93] L-B 4471 (citing *De inventione sanctae crucis Walthamensis*); see above, pp. 41 and 142.

[94] See above, p. 45.   [95] Robertson, *Anglo-Saxon Charters*, pp. 158 and 406–7.

in Rome.[96] According to the charter Cnut took the crown from his head and placed it on the altar with his own hands; a late list of benefactors from Canterbury states that the crown was still to be seen 'in capite crucis maioris in navi eiusdem ecclesie'.[97] A similar story is associated with Winchester, though here Cnut is said to have placed the crown on the head of the crucifix himself. The story was first recorded in the twelfth century by Henry of Huntingdon who associated the gift with Cnut's failure to command the waves.[98] Henry did not link the event with a specific church but later writers claimed that the crucifix was at Winchester[99] and Thomas Rudborne, writing in the fifteenth century, stated that the crucifix stood in front of the high altar of the medieval cathedral.[100] The story is plausible, for the earliest pictures of crowned crucifixes from Anglo-Saxon England come from Winchester and Canterbury and date from the time of Cnut.[101] There are several continental examples of gifts of royal crowns to statues[102] and the gift of more than one crown by Cnut need not invalidate the story: Charles the Bald owned at least four crowns.[103]

The story of Cnut's attempt to command the waves is late and sounds apocryphal, yet the moral of the story is similar to that of Ælfric's account of Heraclius and fits well with what is known of attitudes to kingship in the late Anglo-Saxon period. What seems never to have been noticed is the closeness of the story, and of the idea of a king commanding the waves, to one of the psalms. The moral of the story is that the power of earthly kings is vain: only Christ, who commands heaven, earth, sea and winds, is worthy to be called a king.[104] The speech attributed to Cnut by Matthew Paris stresses the king's humility before Christ, the one true king: 'Te solum decet, rex Domine Iesu Christe omnipotens, regem appellari et esse, qui coelos moderaris et infima, qui mari et ventis imperas. Te Deum veneror homo, te Dominum servus adoro. Unde nobis mortalibus, nobis

---

96 See above, p. 138.

97 Robertson, *Anglo-Saxon Charters*, p. 407: 'on the head of the great cross in the nave of the same church'.

98 *Historia Anglorum* VI.17 (ed. Arnold, p. 189).

99 Higden, *Polychronicon* VI.xx (ed. Lumby VII, 134); Richard of Cirencester, *Speculum historiale* III.xxxiv (ed. Mayor II, 185); Henry Knighton, *Chronicon* I.v (ed. Lumby, I, 28).

100 L-B 4700 (citing Thomas Rudborne, *Historia maior*).   101 See above, pp. 45–6.

102 Schramm, *Herrschaftszeichen* II, 400, 409 and 415.   103 Schramm, *ibid.* II, 389.

104 Henry of Huntingdon, *Hist. Angl.* VI.17 (ed. Arnold, p. 189); Matthew Paris, *Historia minor* (ed. Madden I, 308–9).

miseris peccatoribus tanta praesumptio, ut reges vel etiam reguli audeamus appellari vel esse? nedum corona et sceptro insigniri, et regalibus redimiri?'[105] In these passages Christ is presented as the ruler of the created world just as he is in the three drawings which show the sun and moon next to a crowned figure of Christ. Psalm LXXXVIII contrasts this cosmic figure with King David, the model of Anglo-Saxon kingship. In the opening verses of the psalm God promises David an everlasting dynasty, a throne which will outlast time, and the psalmist replies that no one is like God who controls the pride of the ocean and calms its waves.[106] The psalm goes on to describe how David was chosen by God, anointed and crowned, how he was promised victory over his enemies, control over the seas and a dynasty which would last for ever and yet he was defeated, stripped of crown and sceptre, covered in shame.[107] Augustine interpreted the psalm as a prophecy of Christ's death[108] and the Utrecht Psalter includes a drawing of the Crucifixion at this point,[109] but for a king who saw himself as another David it would have provided a powerful reminder of the limitations of royal power. Ælfric interpreted David as a symbol of power,[110] but it is noticeable that when the Anglo-Saxon coronation service compares the king to David it is to ask that he should be exalted, like David, because of his humility.[111]

This theme of glory through humility plays a major part in the decoration of the two Winchester manuscripts which celebrate the royalty of Christ most fully: the Benedictional of Æthelwold and the Tiberius Psalter. The Benedictional includes a painting of Christ enthroned and wearing a jewelled diadem and is the earliest English manuscript to portray him in this way.[112] It is noticeable, however, that Christ is not shown

---

[105] Matthew Paris, *Historia minor* (*ibid.* I, 308–9): 'Lord Jesus Christ, almighty king, you alone deserve to be called and to be a king, who restrain the skies and the depths, who rule sea and winds. You, O God, I venerate as man, you, Lord, I adore as slave. Where does such presumption come from in us mortals, wretched sinners, that we dare to be called or to be kings, or even sub-kings, or to be distinguished with crown and sceptre, and surrounded by royal symbols?'

[106] Ps. LXXXVIII.4–10.   [107] Ps. LXXXVIII.20–46.

[108] *Enarr. in Ps.* (ed. Dekkers and Fraipont II, 1231, on Ps. LXXXVIII).

[109] Utrecht, Universiteitsbibl., 32, 51v.   [110] *Heptateuch* (ed. Crawford, pp. 35–6).

[111] 'David humilitate exaltatus', Schramm, *Kaiser* II, 236; 'Humilem quoque David, plurum tuum regno fastigio sublimasti', *Benedictional of Archbishop Robert* (ed. Wilson, p. 142).

[112] BL, Add. 49598, 70r.

crowned in the two triumphal scenes of the entry to Jerusalem and the second coming. The second example is particularly striking for the Apocalypse description of the Word of God (from which the words 'Rex regum et Dominus dominantium' written on Christ's thigh are taken) states that he is crowned with many coronets.[113] In the manuscript painting, by contrast, his kingship is expressed through the cross, spear and sponge, the instruments of his Passion, which are carried as *insignia* by the angels.[114] Moreover, the Baptism of Christ, where the artist of the Benedictional shows angels presenting crowns and sceptres to Christ, is normally taken as an example of Christ's humility.[115] The pictures in the Tiberius Psalter are particularly relevant for a study of the relationship between the Anglo-Saxon king and Christ the king of kings because they present Christ's kingship as the fulfilment of what was shown symbolically by David, the type of the Anglo-Saxon king. The difference between the two figures is expressed by the royal fleur-de-lis crown worn by David and the simpler jewelled fillet worn by Christ. Moreover, Christ is shown crowned when he is at his most humble, in the scenes of the Temptation,[116] the Betrayal[117] and the Crucifixion (pl. XIII);[118] he does not wear a crown in the picture of the entry to Jerusalem.[119] The Tiberius Psalter offers one final comment on the relationship between Christ and his deputies on earth. In the picture of the Ascension Christ leaves a short cross-staff and an imperial crown to his disciples;[120] the crown is held by one of the apostles in the Pentecost illustration.[121] The crown, which is similar in form to that held over the head of Cnut in the frontispiece to the New Minster *Liber vitae*, and quite different from the jewelled fillet, must symbolize earthly dominion; the fact that it is left to the disciples, the forerunners of the bishops, implies the predominance of church over state.

---

[113] Apoc. XIX. 12–16.   [114] See above, p. 29.
[115] Ælfric, *CH* II.iii (ed. Godden, pp. 21–2).
[116] BL, Cotton Tiberius C. vi, 10v.   [117] *Ibid.*, 12r.   [118] *Ibid.*, 13r.
[119] *Ibid.*, 11r.
[120] *Ibid.*, 15r.   [121] *Ibid.*, 15v.

7

Minor iconographic types

The theme of Christ's kingship is not limited to the group of Crucifixion pictures with sun and moon discussed in ch. 6. The drawings in the Bury Psalter (pl. xIIa) and the Tiberius Psalter (pl. xIII) both include crowned figures of Christ though the implications of the crown are quite different in the two pictures. The Bury Psalter drawing shows Christ with open eyes. Above his head is a sceptre, held in the hand of God, and below his feet are a serpent and a chalice, details which link the picture with two separate iconographic types. The sceptre emphasizes the idea of Christ's kingship. The serpent symbolizes Christ's triumph over evil and was associated with the figure of the crowned Christ in the frontispiece to the Cambridge Homilies (pl. xI).[1] The chalice is a eucharistic symbol which has no necessary connection with the themes of kingship or of the defeat of evil. As was said above,[2] the Bury Psalter drawing is placed next to Psalm xxI, which was believed to have been recited by Christ while hanging on the cross.[3] The picture relates to verse 29 of the psalm, which refers to God's kingdom, but it is not, strictly speaking, a textual illustration, for the psalm includes nothing which would justify the presence of the serpent and the chalice.

The distinctive feature of the drawing is the sceptre in the hand of God. Some Carolingian ivories had shown Christ being crowned by the hand of God[4] and the angels carry sceptres as well as crowns in the Baptism painting of the Benedictional of Æthelwold.[5] The hand of God, which is almost universal in late Anglo-Saxon Crucifixion pictures, indicates God's approval of Christ's action in offering himself on the cross, his acceptance of

---

[1] See above, pp. 131 and 137.   [2] See above, p. 85.   [3] Matt. xxvII.46.
[4] See above, p. 134.   [5] See above, p. 133.

the sacrifice which atoned for man's sins. A sceptre is used as the attribute of God the Father on the Godwine Seal[6] and the addition of the sceptre in the Bury Psalter drawing, together with the crown on Christ's head, probably indicates that Christ's kingship is a sharing in that of his Father, rather as Christ shares his Father's throne in the pictures of the Trinity in the Ælfwine Prayer-book and on the Godwine Seal. Psalm CIX, which forms the textual basis for pictures of Christ seated on his Father's right, includes two of the themes of the Bury Psalter drawing. Christ is given a sceptre by his Father[7] and he is made a priest like Melchisedech, the priest-king of the Old Testament.[8] Augustine pointed out in his commentary on Psalm CIX that the sceptre belongs to Christ's human nature and symbolizes his rule over the church; it is to be distinguished from his rule over creation which belongs to his divine nature.[9] According to Cassiodorus, Psalm CIX refers to the two natures of Christ and, in particular, to the way in which, as a result of his triumph on the cross, his human nature received the royal status which he had always possessed in his divine nature.[10] The theme is similar to that of the first two chapters of the Epistle to the Hebrews. In ch. I Christ is portrayed as a king, anointed by God and given a throne and a sceptre: 'To his Son he says: *God, your throne shall last for ever and ever*; and: *his royal sceptre is the sceptre of virtue; virtue you love as much as you hate wickedness. This is why God, your God, has anointed you with the oil of gladness, above all your rivals.*'[11] In ch. II the theme of Christ's rule over all things is related to his death: 'We . . . see in Jesus one who was *for a short while made lower than the angels* and is now *crowned with glory and splendour* because he submitted to death.'[12] Later in the chapter Christ's incarnation, which made his death possible, is related to his defeat of the devil and to his role as the high priest who atones once and for all for men's sins:

Since all the children share the same blood and flesh, he too shared equally in it, so that by his death he could take away all the power of the devil, who had power over death, and set free all those who had been held in slavery all their lives by the fear of death . . . It was essential that he should in this way become completely like his brothers so that he could be a compassionate and trustworthy high priest of God's religion, able to atone for human sins.[13]

6 Beckwith, *Ivory Carvings*, no. 41; Harris, 'Bury St Edmunds Psalter', pp. 418–20.
7 Ps. CIX.2.   8 Ps. CIX.4 and Gen. XIV.18.
9 *Enarr. in Ps.*, CIX.10 (ed. Dekkers and Fraipont III, 1609–10); cf. above, p. 134.
10 *Exp. Ps.*, Ps. CIX.1 (ed. Adriaen II, 1006–8).   11 Heb. 1.8–9.
12 Heb. II.9.   13 Heb. II.14–15 and 17.

Christ's priesthood is symbolized by the chalice at the foot of the cross in the Bury Psalter drawing, and his defeat of the devil by the coiled dragon under his feet.

The psalm text 'Virga recta est, virga regni tui' which the author of the Epistle to the Hebrews applies to Christ[14] was used in the prayer over the staff in the Anglo-Saxon coronation service.[15] The same text is written on the rod held by Christ in the frontispiece to the Dunstan Classbook and John Higgitt has argued on the basis of this parallel that the Dunstan picture should be seen as an assertion of the alliance between king and monks during the reign of Edgar.[16] Robert Deshman has used a similar argument about the crowned figure of Christ and the crowned Magi in the Benedictional of Æthelwold[17] and R. M. Harris has suggested that the Crucifixion drawing in the Bury Psalter is an example of the imperialization of biblical imagery.[18] But the text in the Dunstan drawing does not necessarily have this kind of meaning. Paschasius Radbertus associates it with the theme of Christ's triumph through weakness, linking it with the reed placed in Christ's hand when he was mocked by Pilate's soldiers.[19] According to Paschasius, Christ received a fragile sceptre from our hands so that he could triumph by breaking it on the cross.[20] In view of this passage a political motive for the introduction of the sceptre into the Crucifixion picture seems unlikely. Moreover, the psalms, together with the early commentaries on them and certain New Testament texts, provide ample justification for the doctrine of Christ's kingship and for the inclusion of a sceptre among his attributes.

The theme of the drawing in the Tiberius Psalter (pl. XIII) is more devotional in emphasis than that in the Bury Psalter though it still embodies a theological point. As was said earlier,[21] several of the pictures in the Tiberius Psalter touch on different aspects of Christ's kingship and the importance of this theme to the Crucifixion picture is emphasized by the inscription above it: 'Iesus Nazarenus rex Iudeorum'. The words are taken from the inscription placed by Pilate on the board above Christ's head but by removing them from the body of the picture the artist has

---

[14] Ps. XLIV.6, Roman version; Heb. 1.8.

[15] Schramm, *Kaiser* II, 238; *Benedictional of Archbishop Robert*, ed. Wilson, p. 146.

[16] Higgitt, 'Glastonbury', p. 280.   [17] See above, p. 139.

[18] Harris, 'Bury St Edmunds Psalter', pp. 418–20.

[19] Matt. XXVII.29.   [20] *Exp. in Matt.* XII.xxvii.31 (ed. Paulus III, 1362–3).

[21] See above, pp. 87–8.

turned them into a statement about the scene as a whole. The inscription is particularly striking because it differs from those elsewhere in the manuscript. All the other inscriptions are concerned with actions and are of the form, 'Hic ascendit Cristus ad caelos' or 'Angelus tribus mulieribus loquitur.'[22] The inscription to the Crucifixion picture, on the other hand, defines the identity of the central figure. The picture is a representation of a person rather than a record of an event; it functions like Pilate's address to the Jews, 'Here is your king.'[23] The link between Christ's kingship and his death has already been discussed in relation to the group of Crucifixion pictures which include the symbols of the sun and moon[24] where it was connected with Christ's authority over the created world. The symbols of the sun and moon are not included in the drawing in the Tiberius Psalter where a different point is being made. Unlike the rule of earthly kings which ends with death, Christ's kingship is eternal and remains even in death. This temporal element is hinted at, though in a different way, by representing the cross as a roughly lopped tree. The same motif was used in the drawing in the Arundel Psalter (pl. IX) and its meaning was made clear by the inscription on the plain wooden cross in the drawing in the Winchcombe Psalter, 'lignum vitae' (pl. X).[25] The tree-cross emphasizes the antithesis between Adam's tree of death by which man fell and Christ's tree of life by which he was redeemed. It looks back to the story of the creation and forward to the description of the new Jerusalem with its river of life and the tree of life whose leaves were to heal the nations.[26] The most striking feature of the Tiberius drawing, however, is that it shows Christ accompanied by the two soldiers instead of by Mary and John. This iconography, which was usual in early Anglo-Saxon art, was very rare in tenth- and eleventh-century England. The Tiberius drawing is the only manuscript example; there are two ivories in the Victoria and Albert Museum[27] and carvings at Romsey, Daglingworth, Alnmouth, Aycliffe, Penrith and Gosforth, the last four being in the north of the country where there was less influence from Carolingian art and early iconographies were often retained. The use of this iconography in the Tiberius Psalter may be the result of copying from a Franco-Saxon model of the type found in the Gospels of Francis II[28] though simple imitation is not an adequate

[22] See above, p. 33.   [23] John XIX.15.   [24] See above, pp. 134–5 and 138.
[25] See above, p. 131.   [26] Apoc. XXII.2; see below, pp. 176–7.
[27] Beckwith, *Ivory Carvings*, nos. 33 and 34.
[28] BN, lat. 257, 12v; Hubert *et al.*, *Carolingian Art*, pl. 152.

explanation. Anglo-Saxon artists were perfectly capable of selecting and altering to suit their own ends and it must be assumed that the choice of this particular iconographic type was deliberate. As was explained in chapter 4[29] the inclusion of the two soldiers emphasizes the reality of Christ's death and therefore of his Resurrection, a point explored elsewhere in the Tiberius cycle of pictures. But the picture also includes a devotional point. The soldier with the spear raises his left hand to his eye in an allusion to the legend of Longinus's blindness which was cured by the blood from Christ's wounded side. The incident is depicted in the eighth-century St Gallen Gospels and in the Gospels of Francis II and a reference to the story occurs in one of the Anglo-Saxon charms.[30]

The Longinus story relates Christ's death to the needs of the individual and is appropriate in a series of pictures which, it has been suggested, were intended as a basis for private meditation.[31] References to the healing power of Christ's blood can also be used in a wider context. The Sherborne Missal contains a drawing of the Crucifixion at the *Te igitur* of the mass (pl. XIIb). Christ is shown standing against a tree-cross; his eyes are open but blood flows from a wound in his side. Above the cross are the *dextera Dei* and a dove holding a crown in its beak. A female figure pointing to the wound in Christ's side stands underneath the cross. One distinctive feature of this drawing is that new leaves are sprouting from the right-hand side of the cross; the dead wood has been brought back to life by the blood from Christ's side. A small Crucifixion panel at Romsey, which includes the two soldiers under the cross as well as Mary and John, also shows fresh shoots breaking from the wood of the cross. In these scenes the trees of Adam and of Christ are brought together to show that the death brought into the world by the first tree had been turned into life by the second. Other details in the *Te igitur* picture are harder to parallel. The female figure, who holds a fold of her cloak to her face, is similar in some respects to the ivory carving of Mary at Saint-Omer (pl. VI)[32] or to the weeping Virgin of the Ramsey Psalter (pl. XIV) and the Sacramentary of Robert of Jumièges (pl. XV), but the gesture of her right hand, which points to the wound in Christ's side, suggests that she is drawing attention to the source of the sacrament of the eucharist to which the accompanying text relates. It is just possible that the

[29] See above, pp. 107–8. [30] Storms, *Anglo-Saxon Magic*, p. 286 (no. 49).

[31] Cf. the prayer on Christ's side in the Book of Nunnaminster (ed. Birch, p. 77); discussed above, p. 125.

[32] See above, p. 112.

figure represents the church, the guardian of the sacraments, rather than Mary,[33] though the latter seems more likely. Mary is mentioned in the *Communicantes* of the mass and her presence in the drawing in the Sherborne Missal would be appropriate in a picture associated with the beginning of the canon of the mass.[34] Representations of Ecclesia, on the other hand, are very rare in Anglo-Saxon art, the only certain example being the crowned figure holding a sceptre and seated on a throne in the initial to Psalm LI of the Bury Psalter; this figure is labelled 'oliva fructifera'[35] and two commentaries on the psalms identify the olive tree of Psalm LI with the church.[36]

The other distinctive feature of the drawing in the Sherborne Missal is the dove with the crown in its beak. As was said in chapter 6,[37] there are several representations of the Crucifixion in which Christ is crowned by angels or by the hand of God, but this is the only English example of a crown brought by a dove and there is only one contemporary parallel from the continent: the crucifix engraved on the back of the Lothar Cross, where a dove enclosed in a wreath held by the hand of God is placed above Christ's head.[38] In early Christian funerary art, portraits of the deceased were often accompanied by a dove symbolizing divine peace and carrying a crown.[39] Later the dove came to be used as a symbol of the Holy Spirit, most commonly in pictures of Christ's Baptism where all four of the gospels refer to the descent of the Spirit in the form of a dove.[40] The association between the dove and the Holy Spirit was so strong that this symbol came to be used to indicate the presence of the Spirit in pictures of the incarnation or Pentecost where there was no textual justification for it. In the illustrations to the Utrecht Psalter, and in drawings in the Ælfwine Prayer-book and the Arenberg Gospels derived from them, a dove is shown perching on Mary's head to represent the overshadowing of the Spirit at the incarnation, and the Pentecost scenes in the Benedictional of Æthelwold, the Benedictional of Archbishop Robert, the Sacramentary of Robert of Jumièges and

---

[33] See above, p. 89.   [34] Ps. LI.8.
[35] Pseudo-Jerome, *Breviarium in Psalmos*, li (PL 26, 977); Pseudo-Bede, *In psalmorum librum exegesis*, li (PL 93, 758); Temple, *Anglo-Saxon Manuscripts*, p. 100, identifies the Bury Psalter figure as Mary.
[36] See also above, p. 81.   [37] See above, p. 134.
[38] See above, p. 115, n. 21, for the suggestion that the back of the Lothar Cross may be English.
[39] *DACL* 3.2, 2198–2231, s.v. 'Colombe', especially 2208–2216.
[40] Matt. III.16, Mark I.10, Luke III.22 and John I.32.

the Tiberius Psalter all show the descent of the Spirit on the apostles in the form of a dove. In the second of the two Benedictionals and in the Psalter, the dove is accompanied by the hand of God. The same two motifs appear in the Ascension scene on number 10 of the Monza Ampullae and are thought to indicate that the scene represents both the Ascension and Pentecost.[41] The addition of the dove to the more usual hand of God in the drawing in the Sherborne Missal and the engraving on the Lothar Cross must be intended to show that all three persons of the Trinity were present at Christ's death. The late Anglo-Saxon period saw the development of several different iconographies of the Trinity[42] and this, together with the emphasis at this period on the inseparability of the three persons of the Trinity,[43] is probably sufficient to account for the presence of the dove. It is perhaps worth noting, however, that there is at least one early Christian parallel to the scene. The lid of a fifth- or early sixth-century reliquary in the Sancta Sanctorum of Rome is decorated with a cross accompanied by two worshipping angels, the hand of God and a dove with a crown in its beak.[44] The crown held by the dove in early Christian art is a symbol of victory over death and it seems likely that the meaning of the crown in the drawing in the Sherborne Missal is similar.

The details of the Sherborne drawing express ideas about life and healing and victory which would be relevant in many different contexts. However, the fact that the picture is placed opposite the opening words of the canon of the mass suggests that it may have a more specifically eucharistic meaning. Gertrud Schiller has suggested that the engraving on the back of the Lothar Cross, which includes the motif of the dove as the Sherborne drawing does, is a precursor of the throne of grace pictures which became popular in the twelfth century.[45] These pictures show God the Father enthroned and holding a crucifix in front of him; the two figures are linked by the dove of the Holy Spirit. Many representations of the throne of grace are found in missals, on patens or on portable altars and this suggests that their meaning is connected with that of the mass. According to the theology of the Roman church the change from bread and wine to the body and blood of Christ in the mass is brought about by the repetition of Christ's words at the Last Supper; in the Byzantine rite, on the other hand,

[41] Grabar, *Ampoules*, pl. 17
[42] Wormald, 'Late Anglo-Saxon Art', pp. 106–8 and below, p. 175.
[43] See below, p. 155.   [44] *DACL* 3.1, 1126, s.v. 'Chasse', fig. 2697.
[45] Schiller, *Iconography* II, pls. 122–4.

the priest invokes the Holy Spirit to bring about the change in the bread and wine.[46] The western church never accepted this view of the consecration, but there was a widespread belief in the west that the consecrated bread and wine were sanctified by the Holy Spirit. Theologians saw a parallel between the transformation of the bread and wine into Christ's body and blood and the union of the divine and human natures in the person of Christ which took place at the incarnation. Paul the Deacon ended his description of the miraculous mass of St Gregory with the following passage: 'Corpus sibi ex carne semper Virginis, operante sancto Spiritu, fabricavit, panem et vinum aqua mistum, manente propria specie in carnem et sanguinem suum ad catholicam precem ob reparationem nostram Spiritus sui sanctificatione convertit.'[47] Similar passages appear in the writings of Florus of Lyons and Paschasius Radbertus.[48] This belief in the sanctifying role of the Holy Spirit became firmly linked to the celebration of the mass through the prayer *Summe sacerdos* of John of Fécamp, which appears among the private prayers to be recited by the priest before mass from the middle of the eleventh century.[49] Section IX of this prayer contains a passage which is very close to the Byzantine invocation of the Holy Spirit: 'Peto clementiam tuam ut descendat super panem et calicem plenitudo tuae divinitatis. Descendat etiam Domine illa sancti Spiritus tui invisibilis incomprehensibilisque maiestas, sicut quondam in patrum hostiis descendebat, qui et oblationes nostras corpus et sanguinem tuum efficiat.'[50] The basis of this invocation is a passage in the Epistle to the Hebrews[51] in which Christ, the great high priest, is described as offering himself as a perfect sacrifice to God through the Holy

---

[46] *DACL* 5, 142–84, s.v. 'Epiclèse'.

[47] *Sancti Gregorii Magni vita*, xxiii (PL 75, 53): 'He made a body for himself from the flesh of the ever-Virgin, by the operation of the Holy Spirit, and changed bread and wine mixed with water into his flesh and blood by the blessing of his Spirit, while their outward appearance remained the same, at the prayer of the catholic church and for our redemption.'

[48] Florus, *De expositione missae*, 59 (PL 119, 51–2); Paschasius, *De corpore et sanguine Domini*, iii and iv (ed. Paulus, pp. 27, 28 and 30); see above, pp. 22 and 122.

[49] Wilmart, 'L'*Oratio Sancti Ambrosii*', pp. 101–25.

[50] Wilmart, *ibid.*, p. 121: 'I beseech your mercy that the fullness of your divinity should descend on the bread and chalice. May the invisible and incomprehensible majesty of your Holy Spirit, Lord, descend as once it descended on the offerings of the fathers, that it may make our oblations into your body and blood.'

[51] Heb. IX.14.

Spirit, a verse quoted by John of Fécamp in his discussion of the mass in part IV of his *Confessio fidei*.[52] The prayer *Summe sacerdos* was certainly known in England by the end of the eleventh century for it occurs in a psalter-hymnary of this date from St Augustine's Abbey;[53] it could have been known earlier for John visited England in 1054.[54] The Sherborne Missal was written soon after 1061 and could, therefore, have been influenced by John's ideas. The suggestion is plausible for two reasons. First, the inclusion of the dove and of the hand of God in the Sherborne Crucifixion picture implies a wish to emphasize the presence of all three members of the Trinity at Christ's death. John's *Confessio fidei* includes a long discussion of the theology of the Trinity, laying particular stress on the inseparability of the three Persons: Christ's flesh was made by the Trinity even though it belonged only to Christ; the dove at Christ's Baptism was sent by the Trinity even though it belonged to the Spirit; the voice from heaven was sent by the Trinity even though it belonged only to the Father.[55] Secondly, the *Summe sacerdos* itself contains a passage which can be used to explain the female figure in the Sherborne drawing. In section VIII of the prayer the bread and wine of the eucharist are linked to the flesh taken from Mary, who conceived through the Holy Spirit, and to the fountain which flowed from the wound in Christ's side.[56]

Whereas the three pictures discussed so far in this chapter all include triumphal elements the remaining three pictures are concerned with the themes of suffering and compassion. The drawing at the beginning of the Ramsey Psalter (pl. XIV) and the painting grouped with other Passion pictures before the vigil mass of Holy Saturday in the Sacramentary of Robert of Jumièges (pl. XV) are both concerned with the suffering of Mary at her son's death. As was the case with the drawings in the Bury and Tiberius Psalters, they treat the subject differently and for different ends. The most distinctive feature of these two pictures is that they show Mary raising the folds of her cloak to her face as a symbol of grief. The Ramsey Psalter drawing, which dates from the last quarter of the tenth century, shows Christ dead on the cross, his eyes closed and blood flowing from the wounds in his hands, feet and side. There is a board inscribed 'Hic est

[52] *Confessio fidei* IV.iii, ptd under Alcuin (PL 101, 1088).
[53] Rouen, Bibl. Mun., A. 44; Gjerløw, *Adoratio crucis*, p. 145.
[54] Leclercq and Bonnes, *Jean de Fécamp*, p. 14.
[55] *Confessio fidei* III.ix (PL 101, 1059).
[56] Wilmart, *L'Oratio Sancti Ambrosii'*, pp. 120–1.

Nazarenus Iesus rex Iudeorum' over his head but, unusually for an English picture of this date, the hand of God is not present. The manuscript was almost certainly written at Winchester and it has been suggested that the figure of Mary was copied from the mourning figures in the *Dormition* pictures of the Benedictional of Æthelwold and the related Benedictional at Rouen.[57] The figures are similar but there are many parallels in Carolingian art, in particular the figures of Mary in the Crucifixion picture of the Drogo Sacramentary,[58] on the Brunswick Casket and on an engraved rock crystal of the second half of the ninth century.[59] The same iconographic type was in use long before the Carolingian period, in a seventh-century fresco at Santa Maria Antiqua, Rome[60] and in the Crucifixion picture in the Rabbula Gospels. The artist of the Ramsey Psalter was clearly influenced by work in the Rheims style and it is possible that he was copying a Crucifixion picture from Rheims or Metz. If so, he certainly made some alterations for there are no Carolingian parallels to the dancing figure of St John, with his curling scroll, though several later Anglo-Saxon artists seem to have imitated it.[61] The originality of the figure of St John suggests that his meaning is central to the meaning of the picture as a whole. The words which he writes on the scroll come from the end of his Gospel, 'Hic est discipulus ille qui testimonium perhibet',[62] and their purpose is clearly to identify the evangelist as an eye-witness of Christ's death, whose words can be trusted. The idea of an eye-witness account of Christ's death is not unique to the iconography in which Mary is shown hiding her face, for the drawing in the Winchcombe Psalter, which includes a crowned figure of Christ, has the words 'Et ego vidi et testimonium' on the book in which St John is writing (pl. x). The motif is a movable one which can be used to validate different statements about Christ's death.

St John's role in the Ramsey Psalter drawing is concerned with the relationship between picture and audience. The role of Mary, on the other hand, lies within the picture itself though she may also invite imitation by the audience. Whereas the figure of Mary in the drawing in the Sherborne

---

[57] Temple, *Anglo-Saxon Manuscripts*, p. 64.   [58] BN, lat. 9428, 43v.

[59] Schiller, *Iconography* II, pl. 360.

[60] Schiller, *ibid.* II, pl. 328.

[61] See the Ælfwine Prayer-book, the Winchcombe Psalter, the Weingarten Gospels and above, pp. 97–8.

[62] John XXI.24.

Missal (pl. XIIb) directs the attention of the viewer to the wound in Christ's side, the Mary of the Ramsey Psalter drawing is represented as concerned with her own grief at the death of her son.

Mary's grief is not mentioned in the gospels and it was sometimes argued that she was unmoved by Christ's death because she knew that he would rise from the dead. Ambrose, for instance, visualized her standing without weeping by the cross: 'Stantem illam lego, flentem non lego.'[63] Side by side with this view was one based on Simeon's prophecy: 'Simeon blessed them and said to Mary his mother, "You see this child: he is destined for the fall and for the rising of many in Israel, destined to be a sign that is rejected – and a sword will pierce your own soul too – so that the secret thoughts of many may be laid bare."'[64] Mary's sufferings at Christ's death, and their connection with Simeon's prophecy, are mentioned in several late Old English homilies.[65] The theme is not developed to show her prostrated by grief as she is in later medieval literature, though Ælfric maintains that her sufferings were greater than those of other men because her love for Christ was greater.[66] By the end of the eleventh century, however, Anselm portrayed Mary sobbing beneath the cross, with tears streaming down her face.[67] The drawing in the Ramsey Psalter suggests that this more emotional approach to Christ's Passion already existed in the late tenth century even though there is no trace of it in the sermons of the period or in the collections of private prayers preserved from late Anglo-Saxon England. The life of Odilo of Cluny offers a rare early example of the desire to share Mary's compassion for her son. In his sermons Odilo had emphasized Mary's faith: 'Eiusdem Dei et Domini genetrix, ut sanctus evangelista refert, ante crucem stabat, et piis oculis exspectans non pignoris mortem, sed mundi salutem.'[68] On his deathbed, however, it was her compassion at Christ's sufferings which he tried to imitate as he lay watching the crucifix: 'Ita enim suspensis oculis, et lacrymarum imbribus

---

[63] *De obitu Valentiniani consolatio*, xxxix (PL 16, 1371): 'I read that she stood, not that she wept'; see also above, p. 100.

[64] Luke II.34–5.

[65] *CH* I.ix (ed. Thorpe, p. 146); *Early English Homilies*, ed. Warner, pp. 42, 45 and 137.

[66] *CH* I.xxx (ed. Thorpe, p. 444); see above, p. 98.

[67] *Oratio ad Christum* (*Orationes*, ed. Schmitt III, 8); Ward, *Prayers*, pp. 95–6.

[68] *Serm.* vi (PL 142, 1006): 'The mother of the same God and Lord, as the holy evangelist records, stood before the cross with faithful eyes, awaiting, not the death of her child, but the salvation of the world'; cf. *Sermones*, xv (PL 142, 1032); based on Ambrose, *Exp. ev. sec. Luc.*, x.132 (ed. Adriaen, p. 383).

plenis contemplabatur et compatiebatur tui vultus imaginem, quasi iterum te videret crucifigi et mori. Astabat tibi totus suspensus cum Maria matre, pertransiebatque animam illius acerrimae compunctionis gladius.'[69]

The Crucifixion painting in the Sacramentary of Robert of Jumièges (pl. XV) is clearly related to the drawing in the Ramsey Psalter but there are major differences in its iconography and in its setting. As was said earlier,[70] this picture forms part of a short narrative sequence, the other pictures being of the arrest of Christ, the deposition and the three Maries at the tomb. The pictures are based closely on the gospel story. The Crucifixion picture contains none of the motifs used in other Crucifixion pictures of the period to give a triumphal, regal or eucharistic meaning to the scene. It does not even include the hand of God, a detail which is almost universal in late Anglo-Saxon art. Whereas the picture at the *Te igitur* in the Sherborne Missal (pl. XIIb) included several different statements about the significance of Christ's death the painting in the sacramentary concentrates attention on a single point: the grief of Mary and John. Moreover, the figures in the scene are concerned only with their own situation. Christ gazes at his weeping mother; St John holds his right hand to his face as a sign of his sorrow. The picture is conceived quite differently from the superficially similar drawing in the Ramsey Psalter, where the writing figure of St John is intended to establish a relationship between picture and viewer, or from the picture in the Sherborne Missal, where Mary's gesture towards Christ's side is intended for an audience outside the picture and the event it commemorates.[71] The relationship between audience and event is indicated in the sacramentary by the two watching figures in the medallions at the sides of the picture;[72] the painting provides a way to enter into the gospel event and to share the experience of those who were actually there.

The wish to share in the gospel events is taken a stage further in the painting at the beginning of one of four gospel-books which belonged to

---

[69] *De vita et virtutibus S. Odilonis abbatis* I.xiv (PL 142, 910): 'Thus, also, with anxious eyes and with copious showers of tears, he contemplated the image of your face and suffered with you, as if he saw you once more crucified and die. He stood near you with your mother Mary, completely absorbed, and the sword of bitter remorse went through his soul.'

[70] See above, pp. 30 and 88–9.   [71] See above, p. 96.

[72] Cf. above, p. 25.

Judith of Flanders (pl. XVI). The picture shows Christ dead on the cross. Above are the symbols of the sun and moon and the hand of God. Below are Mary and John, the former wiping the blood from Christ's side, the latter writing in a book. The main components of the picture are found elsewhere in late Anglo-Saxon art. The figures of the sun and moon who hide their faces can be paralleled in the drawing in the Winchcombe Psalter, which also shows St John writing in a book (pl. X). The roughly cut tree on which Christ hangs is found in the Crucifixion pictures in the Tiberius and Arundel Psalters (pls. XIII and IX) and in the Sherborne Missal drawing (pl. XIIb). The themes of St John's witness, of the tree of life, of the lament of the created world are well-known. The gesture of Mary, on the other hand, is quite new. Carolingian artists often showed Ecclesia catching the blood from Christ's side in a chalice, a gesture intended to emphasize the preciousness of the blood and also its relationship to the sacraments of which the church was the guardian. Mary's role is quite different. Her movement, which may have developed from pictures such as that in the Sherborne Missal where she points to the wound with one hand, is related to the theme of compassion for Christ's sufferings and is similar in conception to the much later story of Veronica wiping the sweat from Christ's face. As far as I know there is no other example of this motif in western art as early as the eleventh century. There is some evidence, however, that eastern theologians portrayed Mary in this way as early as the ninth century. George of Nicomedea describes Mary kissing Christ's feet and embracing his wounds: 'Osculabatur intemeratos pedes, quasque clavi cicatrices fecissent complexabatur; ac sanguinis decurrentis rivulos hauriens, oculis ac pectori adhibebat.'[73] Another detail which is unparalleled in Anglo-Saxon art is the figure of a woman kneeling below the cross and clasping its foot. Donor figures are, of course, well-known and in one case, at least, a figure of this kind is shown kneeling below the crucifix and grasping it with one hand.[74] The woman in the Weingarten Gospels, however, clasps the cross in a way which goes beyond that of the normal donor figure. A clue to the interpretation of the woman at the foot of the cross is found in the description of the embroidered alb, mentioned in

[73] *Oratio VII* (PG 100, 1470): 'She kissed the undefiled feet and embraced the wounds made by the nails and clasped them to eyes and breast, drinking in the streams of flowing blood.'

[74] The Psalter of Louis the German, Berlin, Staatsbibl., lat. theol. fol. 58, 120r, discussed by Deshman, 'Exalted Servant', p. 389.

chapter 1, on which Edith of Wilton depicted herself in the guise of Mary Magdalen wiping Christ's feet.[75] It seems likely that Judith, too, wished to show herself participating in the gospel story and that the woman at the foot of the crucifix represents both Judith herself and Mary Magdalen.

Most representations of Mary Magdalen date from much later than the Weingarten Gospels and Elźbieta Temple considers it unlikely that she is represented here.[76] Yet Hrabanus Maurus talks of her sorrow beneath the cross[77] and the recollection of her constancy when most of Christ's followers had fled played a part in Cluniac devotion by the first half of the tenth century. Odo of Cluny wrote a sermon celebrating Mary Magdalen's devotion to Christ in which he described how she showed her love especially at his Passion when she saw him arrested, beaten and finally hung on the cross.[78] She remained with Christ, Odo said, because she loved him more than others did. For Odo, Mary, whose sins were many, was contrasted with Eve and linked with Mary, the mother of Christ, so that the sin of Eve was blotted out not, as was usual, through the Mother of God but through Mary Magdalen as well.[79] Mary Magdalen was a potent image of the forgiveness offered by Christ to those who truly loved him. Anselm wrote a prayer to her which was included in the collection of prayers sent to Adelaide in 1071 and which focuses on Christ's compassion for sinners. Three twelfth-century copies of Anselm's prayers and meditations are illustrated with a mixture of narrative scenes and pictures showing a suppliant figure praying at the feet of Christ or a saint and it is thought that the copy of the work sent to Matilda of Tuscany in 1104 probably included illustrations based on Anglo-Saxon models.[80] The Admont manuscript contains a picture of Mary anointing Christ's feet, together with an image of her holding the ointment-jar; most of the figures carry scrolls with gospel

---

[75] See above, p. 24.   [76] Temple, *Anglo-Saxon Manuscripts*, p. 109.

[77] *De vita beatae Mariae Magdalenae*, xxi (PL 112, 1463–5).

[78] *Sermones*, ii (PL 133, 713–21, esp. 714 and 718).

[79] *Ibid*. (PL 133, 721). There is one small piece of artistic evidence which suggests that Odo's view of Mary Magdalen may have influenced the art of the period. An ivory carving of the Crucifixion, s. xi, shows two figures standing below the cross; the woman, who would normally be identified as Mary, mother of Christ, holds an ointment-jar, a motif usually associated with Mary Magdalen; see below, p. 238 (Paris, Musée de Cluny, ivory bookcover).

[80] Pächt, 'St Anselm's Prayers', pp. 68–83.

texts referring to Christ's forgiveness and Mary's faith.[81] The Oxford manuscript shows Mary anointing Christ's head and speaking to Christ in the garden of the Resurrection.[82] Neither manuscript contains a picture of Mary at the cross, but it is possible that there was one for the prayer itself includes a long passage on Mary's grief at Christ's death and at the apparent loss of his dead body which was all that was left to her. 'And can you ask her', Anselm enquires, 'Woman, why are you weeping? Had she not reason to weep? For she had seen with her own eyes – if she could bear to look – what cruel men cruelly did to you.'[83] The Weingarten Gospels are probably earlier than 1071, though not by more than a few years, and it seems likely that Judith, like Anselm, wished to imitate one who loved much because her sins, which were many, had been forgiven.[84]

---

[81] Admont, Stiftsbibl., 289, 83r; Pächt, 'St Anselm's Prayers', pl. 22 (d), inscriptions ptd Buberl, *Illuminierten Handschriften*, p. 37.

[82] Bodleian, Auct. D. 2. 6, 186v, Pächt, 'St Anselm's Prayers', pl. 24(a).

[83] *Oratio ad Sanctam Mariam Magdalenam* (*Orationes*, ed. Schmitt III, 66); Ward, *Prayers*, p. 203.

[84] Luke VII.47.

8

Artistic themes and the thought of the period

The Crucifixion pictures discussed in this book have nearly all been of a non-historical kind, designed to aid the understanding and the will rather than the memory. The understanding of Christ's death which they offer involves four main points. First, his death is not seen as an end in itself: what matters is Christ's passover from death to life.[1] Secondly, there is an emphasis on Christ's two natures: he is presented as God and king, creator of the world and victor over the devil and at the same time as the son of Mary, suffering and dying on the cross.[2] Third, his death is seen within the context of redemption history: it is a recapitulation of God's original creation, a reversal of man's fall.[3] Fourth, the death of Christ is closely linked to the sacraments of the church.[4] Throughout, there is an emphasis on Christ's death as something which belongs to the present rather than to the past and it is this which prompts a response from man, whether in the form of good works or of love and gratitude.

The link between Christ's death and Resurrection, which was so important in late Anglo-Saxon art, was central to the way in which the redemption was understood in the Anglo-Saxon church, as it was in the early years of the Christian church. The historical and narrative commemoration of Christ's Passion which dominated the Holy Week ceremonies in fourth-century Jerusalem and which led to the introduction of similar commemorative services in the Roman rite left intact the earlier emphasis on the redemption as a new Passover.[5] The Roman church celebrated Christ's entry to Jerusalem in the Palm Sunday procession, his institution of the eucharist on Maundy Thursday and his death on the cross on Good

---

[1] See above, pp. 88 and 107–8.   [2] See above, pp. 105–6, 136–7 and 147.
[3] See above, pp. 59, 131 and 148.   [4] See above, ch. 5.
[5] See above, p. 43.

Friday; in the late tenth century English monasteries added further commemorations of Christ's burial and of the visit of the women to the sepulchre on Easter Day.[6] But whereas the Jerusalem church made this reliving of the gospel events the centre of its liturgy, breaking up the Passion narratives into small sections appropriate to the events being commemorated, in the Roman church the Passion story was invariably read as a whole, the four accounts being read on four separate occasions during Holy Week.[7] The reading of St Matthew's account of the Passion on Palm Sunday meant that men recalled Christ's sufferings and death at the same time as his triumphal entry into Jerusalem. The reading of the Passion according to Mark on the Tuesday of Holy Week and of that according to Luke on the following day repeated the account of Christ's supper with his friends, his Betrayal, death and burial so that the congregation relived the last few days of Christ's life three times over. On Maundy Thursday the emphasis became more historical, with the celebration of the Last Supper, to be followed by the memorial of Christ's arrest, trial and death on Good Friday. Even here, however, there was no strict adherence to the chronology of the gospels. Christ's death and Resurrection were seen as two aspects of a single event – God's salvation of man – not as consecutive events in history. When man relived Christ's Passion, seeing him still hanging on the cross, he did so in the knowledge that Christ had already risen from the dead. The church which mourned Christ's death on Good Friday recalled his Resurrection in an antiphon sung during the Veneration of the Cross: 'Crucem tuam adoramus, Domine, et sanctam resurrectionem tuam laudamus et glorificamus; ecce enim propter crucem venit gaudium in universo mundo.'[8] In the same way, the church's celebration of Christ's Resurrection on Easter Day included a reference to his death in the words, 'quem in susceptione mortalitatis Deum maiestatis agnoscimus, et in divinitatis gloria Deum et hominem confitemur, qui mortem nostram moriendo destruxit et vitam resurgendo reparavit'.[9]

The recollection of Christ's Passion in the daily Office followed a similar

---

[6] *Concordia*, iv.46 and v.51–2 (ed. Symons, pp. 44–5 and 49–51).

[7] Jungmann, *Early Liturgy*, p. 261.

[8] *Concordia*, iv.44 (ed. Symons, p. 42): 'We adore your cross, oh Lord, and praise and glorify your holy Resurrection, because through the cross joy came into the whole world.'

[9] *Missal of Robert of Jumièges* (ed. Wilson, p. 102): 'whom we recognize as God of majesty in his taking on of mortality, and confess as God and man in the glory of his divinity, who destroyed our death by dying and restored our life by rising'.

pattern. It had been the practice since the early years of the church to supplement the public prayer of the church with a series of private prayers at midnight and at the third, sixth and ninth hours of the day. It is clear from the accounts of these prayers by early Christian writers that they involved meditation on Christ's Passion. Hippolytus of Rome calls on people to meditate at the third hour on Christ being nailed to the cross, at the sixth hour on the darkness which covered the earth at Christ's death and, at the ninth hour, on the piercing of Christ's side. Prayer at midnight involved the recollection of Christ's second coming, an event closely linked to the memory of his death since it was believed that he would be preceded by the cross on which he had died. Prayer at dawn looked forward to the resurrection of the dead.[10] The subjects for meditation outlined in the *De virginitate* of Athanasius involve the assembling of the cross at the third hour, the raising of Christ on the cross at the sixth, his death at the ninth, the Harrowing of Hell at evening and the Resurrection of Christ at midnight.[11] This practice of sanctifying the day through the memory of Christ's Passion and the thought of the second coming, future resurrection and judgement, was taken up in a more public way in the fourth century when these periods of private prayer developed into the little hours and vigils of the canonical Office. The prayers for the three day hours of Terce, Sext and None in Carolingian prayer-books recall the stages of Christ's Passion[12] and the parallel between Christ's Passion and the prayer of the church is explained in detail in Hrabanus Maurus's *De clericorum institutione*.[13] Parts of Hrabanus's work were translated into Old English and used as introductions to the various hours in the late tenth-century work known as the Benedictine Office. The nature of the meditation which took place can be illustrated from the Office for Sext and for None. The introduction to Sext indicates not only the event being recalled but the response to be made to it:

On midne dæg we sculon God herian forðam to middes dæges Crist wæs on rode aðened and us ealle ða þurh his ðrowunge mid his deorwyrðan blode gebohte of deofles anwealde and of ecan deaðe. And ðy we sculon on ðone timan to Criste beon georne clypigende and hine herigende þæt we mid þam geswytelian þæt we

---

[10] *Apostolic Tradition*, xxxvi, in Dix, *Apostolic Tradition*, pp. 62–7; Jungmann, *Early Liturgy*, pp. 101–3.

[11] Jungmann, *Early Liturgy*, pp. 104–6.

[12] Wilmart, *Precum libelli*, pp. 25–6, 35 and 98.

[13] *De clericorum institutione* II.i–ix (PL 107, 325–9).

gemyndige beon þære myclan mildheortnysse þe he on mancynne geworhte þa ða he let hine sylfne syllan to cwale for mancynnes ðearfe.[14]

The collect sums up this theme in a petition: 'Domine Iesu Christe qui sexta hora pro nobis in cruce ascendisti et Adam de inferno eruisti eumque in paradyso restituisti, te quaesumus ut ab omnibus peccatis nostris eripere nos iubeas et in operibus tuis sanctis semper custodias, Iesu Christe.'[15] The arrangement for None is similar. The introduction reads: 'On non-timan we sculon God herian forðam on þone timan Crist gebæd for ðam þe him deredon and syððan his gast asende; and on ðone timan sculon geleaffulle men hi georne gebiddan and gemunan þæt wundor þæt ða geworden wearð, ða se sylfa for mancyn deað geþolode þe eallum mancynne lifes geuðe.'[16] The collect reads: 'Domine Iesu Christe qui hora nona in crucis patibulo confitentem latronem intra menia paradysi transire iussisti tibi suppliciter confitentes peccata nostra deprecamur deleas et post obitum nostrum paradisi nobis gaudia introire concedas, salvator mundi.'[17] The emphasis in these prayers and meditations is on the reliving of Christ's Passion in a chronological way; the arrangement of the Office as a whole, however, is quite unchronological. The cycle starts with the Night Office, the texts of which look forward to Christ's second coming.[18] The first of the day hours, Lauds, celebrates Christ's Resurrection, which therefore precedes the memorials of his death in the hours of Terce, Sext and None.[19] Vespers is linked to the Last Supper and Compline to Christ's burial.[20] The order in which the hours

[14] *Benedictine Office*, ed. Ure, p. 97: 'At mid-day we must praise God, because at mid-day Christ was stretched on the cross and then, through his suffering, redeemed us all from the power of the devil and from eternal death through his precious blood. And therefore we should eagerly call to Christ at that time and praise him, so that we may show by that that we remember the great mercy he showed mankind when he allowed himself to be given to death for man's need.'

[15] *Ibid.*, p. 97: 'Lord Jesus Christ who ascended the cross for us at the sixth hour, and freed Adam from hell and restored him to paradise, we beg that you will command us to be freed from all our sins and will keep us always in your good works, oh Jesus Christ.'

[16] *Ibid.*, pp. 97–8: 'We must praise God at the ninth hour because at that time Christ prayed for those who injured him and afterwards sent forth his spirit; and at that time believing men should pray eagerly and remember the marvel that came about then, when he who gave life to all men suffered death for mankind.'

[17] *Ibid.*, p. 98: 'Lord Jesus Christ, who at the ninth hour, on the gibbet of the cross, ordered the thief who believed to pass through the walls of paradise, we beg that you will wipe out our sins as we humbly confess you, and will allow us to enter into the joys of paradise after our death, O saviour of the world.'

[18] *Ibid.*, p. 101.   [19] *Ibid.*, p. 82.   [20] *Ibid.*, pp. 98 and 99–100.

are arranged exemplifies three theological points. First, Christ's death is subordinated to his Resurrection. Secondly, the institution of the eucharist which preceded Christ's death historically is shown as dependent on his death. Thirdly, the redemption is presented in relation to the coming resurrection of the dead, not as an event from the past.

The private prayers of the late Anglo-Saxon period, many of which were adapted from the public prayer of the church, reveal a change in emphasis from that of the early Anglo-Saxon period.[21] The prayers of the Book of Nunnaminster and the prayer in the Book of Cerne which was adapted for use in the Good Friday ceremonies of the *Regularis concordia* recalled each detail of Christ's Passion individually;[22] the devotions to the cross and crucifix in eleventh-century manuscripts, on the other hand, tended to focus on theological points. This change is analogous to the difference between the narrative pictures of Ottonian art and the more theological pictures of late Anglo-Saxon art. The most extensive sets of prayers associated with the cross are those in the *Portiforium Wulstani*, in Cotton Tiberius A. iii, in the Ælfwine Prayer-book and in the additions made during the second quarter of the eleventh century to the Vespasian Psalter. The change of emphasis is particularly clear in some of the prayers in the *Portiforium*. The immediacy of Christ's death is brought out by the addition of the words *hodierna die* to one of the prayers borrowed from the *Regularis concordia*.[23] A later prayer links the tearful recollection of Christ hanging on the cross to praise of his Resurrection: 'Salvator mundi qui redemisti me pretioso sanguine tuo pro nobis pendens hodie in cruce, obsecro te salva me peccatorem prostratum adorantem te humiliter et confitentem in cruce lacrimabiliter passionemque tuam recollentem et sanctam resurrectionem tuam laudantem.'[24] What is remembered is the transition from death to life, not the physical details of Christ's death. The significance of that transition is expressed through its relationship to the creation of man and his fall: Christ, who is the tree of life, has overcome the serpent's venom;[25] God, the creator of the world, has condescended to be born of Mary and to

---

[21] See above, pp. 56–9.   [22] See above, pp. 57–8.

[23] *Portiforium* (ed. Hughes II, 21); the prayer begins, *Domine Iesu Christe gloriosissime conditor mundi.*

[24] *Ibid.* (II, 22): 'Saviour of the world who redeemed me with your precious blood, hanging for us today on the cross, I beg you, save me, a sinner, prostrate and humbly adoring you, tearfully confessing you on the cross, recalling your Passion and praising your holy Resurrection.'

[25] *Ibid.* (II, 19); the prayer begins, *Deus cui cuncte.*

be nailed to the cross to save man from death.[26] Man's response is to ask for pity, forgiveness and safe entry to heaven.[27] The tone of the prayers which accompany the drawing of the Crucifixion in the Ælfwine Prayer-book is similar.[28] Although the prayers are to be said in front of different parts of the crucifix they are not related in any way to the wounds in Christ's hands, feet or side. The memory is directed to the person of Christ who is king, son of David, redeemer, master, eternal word of the Father. The cross is praised as having been found worthy to carry Christ, the Redeemer of Israel. The main request of the prayers is that both cross and Christ will free man from his sins and bring him safely to heaven. The theological basis of the appeal is that Christ came to earth to suffer for man, that he, who is true life, defeated death on the cross, so fulfilling the prophecies, that he offered himself as a victim to his Father. The emphasis, then, is on Christ the king and Son of God who freed man by his obedience and death. All is concerned with power, the power of Christ and the power of the cross which derives from him. The themes of the prayers added to the Vespasian Psalter are similar.[29] The cross is praised and venerated because it is the banner of the victorious king and Redeemer, the means by which fallen man was reconciled to God. It is the refuge and help of a shipwrecked world, defending man against the attacks of the devil and leading him into paradise. Christ is adored because he was obedient to death and therefore glorified. He defeated the devil, tore up the accusation against man, bore his sins in his own body. He is the Good Shepherd who will bring all men to heaven as he did the repentant thief.

The way in which Christ's death is recalled in these texts places the theology of the Anglo-Saxon church firmly in the Roman tradition as opposed to the more historical traditions of the Jerusalem church,[30] and provides a parallel to the symbolic, non-narrative Crucifixion pictures which typify late Anglo-Saxon art. It also distinguishes the understanding of the redemption in the late Anglo-Saxon period from that which developed towards the end of the eleventh century under the influence of Anselm. For the Anglo-Saxons the significance of Christ's death was that it defeated death. That is why they constantly linked Christ's death to his Resurrection. The poet of *The Dream of the Rood* completed his reference to

---

[26] *Ibid.* (II, 19 and 21); the prayer begins, *Domine Iesu Christe gloriosissime conditor mundi.*
[27] *Ibid.* (II, 19 and 21), prayer as in previous note.
[28] BL, Cotton Titus D. xxvii, 66r–70r.
[29] BL, Cotton Vespasian A. i, 157v–60v.   [30] See above, p. 163, n. 7.

Christ's death with references to his Resurrection, Ascension and future return as judge.[31] Ælfric talked of Easter as the feast of Christ's passover from death to life and from suffering to glory.[32] Wulfstan described Christ showing his authority over both life and death, freeing man from eternal death and opening the way to eternal life.[33] The author of the Blickling Palm Sunday homily linked the palm branches of the procession – the symbol of victory – with Hosea's prophecy of the killing of death: 'þysne dæg hie nemdon siges dæg; se nama tacnaþ þone sige þe Drihten gesigefæsted wiþstod deofle, ða he mid his deaþe þone ecan deaþ oferswiþde, swa he sylf þurh þone witgan sægde; he cwæþ, "Eala deaþ, ic beo þin deaþ, and ic beo þin bite on helle".'[34] Most importantly, Christ was believed to have saved man by his death and Resurrection, not simply by his death. As Ælfric said in one of his Easter homilies: 'þone timan hi heoldon him to Eastertide seofon dagas mid micclum wurðmynte ðe hi ahredde wurdon wið Pharao, and of ðan earde ferdon; swa we eac cristene men healdað Cristes ærist us to Eastertide þas seofon dagas, for ðan ðe we sind þurh his ðrowunge and æriste alysde.'[35] For Anselm, on the other hand, redemption was brought about by Christ's death.[36]

Prior to the eleventh century the nature of the change in the relationship between man and God which resulted from Christ's death was defined in several different ways. In a passage in the Epistle to the Hebrews the redemption is portrayed as a victory over the devil which freed those who had been imprisoned by him: 'Since all the children share the same blood and flesh, he too shared equally in it, so that by his death he could take away all the power of the devil, who had power over death, and set free all those who had been held in slavery all their lives by the fear of death.'[37] Elsewhere Christ is shown paying a ransom to free man from servitude.

---

[31] *Dream of the Rood* 101–9.

[32] *CH* I.xv (ed. Thorpe, p. 224); *CH* II.xv (ed. Godden, p. 159).

[33] Wulfstan, *Homilies*, nos. vi, vii and xiii (ed. Bethurum, pp. 154, 160 and 227).

[34] *Blickling Homilies*, no. vi (ed. Morris, p. 67): 'They called this day the day of victory; the name denotes the victory by which the victorious Lord withstood the devil when he overcame that eternal death by his death, as he said himself through the prophet. He said, "Oh death, I am your death and I will be your sting in hell"; cf. Hosea XIII.14

[35] *CH* II.xv (ed. Godden, p. 152): 'They kept that time at which they were freed from Pharaoh and left that land as an Easter for seven days, with great honour; so also, we Christians keep Christ's Resurrection as our Easter during these seven days because we are freed by his suffering and Resurrection'; cf. *CH* I.xxii (ed. Thorpe, p. 312).

[36] See below, p. 171.   [37] Heb. II.14–15.

Sometimes man is freed from the bondage of the world or of the law;[38] sometimes the payment is made to God.[39] Whereas in the first view Christ buys off the forces of evil, in the second his action is more in the nature of a propitiatory sacrifice, a view enhanced by the fact that the price paid is invariably Christ's blood. This view is expressed particularly clearly in a passage in the First Epistle to Timothy: 'For there is only one God, and there is only one mediator between God and mankind, himself a man, Christ Jesus, who sacrificed himself as a ransom for them all.'[40] Other passages represent Christ as taking man's place and suffering the punishment rightly due to man: 'He was bearing our faults in his own body on the cross, so that we might die to our faults and live for holiness; through his wounds you have been healed.'[41]

The Anglo-Saxons, like the authors of the epistles, did not limit themselves to any one explanation of the redemption. In the poetry Christ was often portrayed as a heroic figure, warring against the devil. For example, the poet of *Christ and Satan* presented Christ's life and death as a brief sortie by the powerful king of heaven to save man from the devil and bring him back to heaven. Christ is the creative power of God, enthroned in heaven with his Father. Satan covets his throne, rebels against him and seduces his creation, man. Christ becomes man out of pity for his handiwork. He frees the prisoners and conquers death, rising from the dead to return in power to heaven. What matters here is not the details of Christ's death but the fact that he has reigned in heaven from the beginning and that through his death he has allowed man, betrayed by the devil, to go there too. Man's response is one of gratitude that God has led him out of prison and brought him back to heaven. In *The Dream of the Rood* the presentation of Christ's death as a military victory, conveyed through the references to the cross as a standard[42] or a trophy[43] and the allusions to Christ as resting after his great fight,[44] is combined with references to the sufferings of both Christ and his servant, the cross,[45] rather as the manuscript pictures show Christ as both suffering and victorious. This approach was developed by the homilists of the late Anglo-Saxon period who stressed that Christ triumphed through weakness.[46] They continued

---

[38] Gal. I.4 and III.13.   [39] I Tim. II.6.   [40] *Ibid.* II. 5–6.

[41] I Peter II.24.

[42] *Dream of the Rood* 6, *beacen*.

[43] *Ibid.* 15, *wædum geweorðode*; see Raw, 'Dream of the Rood', pp. 241 and 245–6.

[44] *Dream of the Rood* 64–5.   [45] *Ibid.* 46, 52, 59 and 61.   [46] See above, p. 141.

to present the Harrowing of Hell as a military conquest,[47] but in treating Christ's death they emphasized his humility, his love for men and his willingness to suffer for them.[48] The sermons of Wulfstan, in particular, show an awareness of the reality of the incarnation, of Christ's decision to share man's weakness and his willing acceptance of all the hardships which man had to endure.[49] Ælfric is more ambivalent. Sometimes he talks of Christ's death in terms of defeat of the devil, sometimes as a sacrifice to God. His first Palm Sunday homily contains a classic statement of the so-called 'devil's rights' theory, using the traditional image of the devil as a fish, swallowing the bait of Christ's humanity and being caught on the hook of his divinity:

þa getimode ðam reðan deofle swa swa deð þam grædigan fisce, þe gesihð þæt æs, and ne gesihð þone angel ðe on ðam æse sticað; bið þonne grædig þæs æses, and forswylcð þone angel forð mid þam æse. Swa wæs þam deofle: he geseh ða menniscnysse on Criste, and na ða godcundnysse; ða sprytte he þæt Iudeisce folc to his slege, and gefredde ða þone angel Cristes godcundnysse, þurh ða he wæs to deaðe aceocod, and benæmed ealles mancynnes þara ðe on God belyfað.[50]

In a sermon on the Catholic faith Ælfric explains that Christ could have saved man without suffering but he considered that unjust to the devil.[51] In these two passages Christ's human nature is seen as a means of concealing his divinity and tricking the devil into over-reaching himself. But for Ælfric, as for the writers of the New Testament, this was only one of several ways of talking about the redemption. One of his favourite symbols for Christ was the lamb offered to God before the Exodus and thereafter at the Passover feast, a parallel which inevitably leads him to describe Christ's

---

[47] *Heptateuch* (ed. Crawford, p. 414); cf. *Blickling Homilies*, nos. vi and vii (ed. Morris, pp. 67 and 85).

[48] E.g. *CH* I.xv (ed. Thorpe, p. 224); *LS*, no. xvi (ed. Skeat I, 344); Ælfric, *Homilies*, no. xiii (ed. Assmann, p. 152); *CH* I.xx (ed. Thorpe, p. 290).

[49] Wulfstan, *Homilies*, nos. vi and vii (ed. Bethurum, pp. 152–3 and 159–60).

[50] *CH* I.xiv (ed. Thorpe, p. 216): 'Then it happened to the cruel devil as it does to the greedy fish, who sees the bait and does not see the hook concealed in the bait. Then he is greedy for the bait and swallows the hook with the bait. So it was with the devil. He saw the humanity in Christ and not the divinity. Then he urged the Jewish people to kill him, and then he felt the hook of Christ's divinity, through which he was choked to death and deprived of all mankind who believe in God.' Cf. *CH* I.i (*ibid.*, p. 26) and Gregory, *Moralia* XXXIII.ix.17 (ed. Adriaen III, 1687–8).

[51] *CH* I.xx (ed. Thorpe, p. 292).

death as a sacrifice to God.[52] In his commentary on Christ's Baptism he talks of Christ as a sin-offering for the world, linking the lamb sacrificed in Exodus with John's words about Christ: 'Look, there is the Lamb of God that takes away the sin of the world.'[53]

Towards the end of the eleventh century the emphasis on Christ's justice even to the devil was attacked by Anselm of Canterbury. As far as Anselm was concerned, the devil had no rights over man which God needed to respect; he was merely a rebel against God. What mattered to Anselm was God's rights, which he saw as having been damaged by Adam at the fall. In his *Cur Deus homo*, completed in 1098, Anselm rejected the view that God needed to trick the devil. Instead, he explained the necessity of the incarnation to God's scheme of redemption in terms of reparation to God. The situation involved a paradox. Man needed to make amends to God for Adam's sin but was unable to do so since he already owed everything he had to God; the damage could be repaired only by one who owed God nothing, namely God himself. The problem therefore had to be resolved by a God-man who would have both the ability to make amends and the need to do so: 'Necesse est ut de hominibus perficiatur illa superna civitas, nec hoc esse valet, nisi fiat praedicta satisfactio, quam nec potest facere nisi deus nec debet nisi homo: necesse est ut eam faciat deus-homo.'[54] Anselm's argument had in fact been anticipated by Goscelin, who claimed restitution had to be made to God by one who had no sin and could therefore pay the debt he did not owe, in his *Liber confortatorius*, written some sixteen years before the completion of the *Cur Deus homo*.[55] The satisfaction offered by Christ to God was interpreted by Anselm as his death;[56] because of this

---

[52] *CH* I.xxii (*ibid.*, p. 312); *CH* II.xii (ed. Godden, p. 120).

[53] *CH* II.iii (*ibid.*, p. 21); John I.29.

[54] *CDH* II.vi (ed. Schmitt II, 101): 'It is necessary that that heavenly city should be completed by men, but this could not prevail unless the prescribed satisfaction was made, which could not be done except by God, and was not owed except by man. It was necessary that a God-man should do it.'

[55] *Liber confortatorius* (ed. Talbot, p. 52); a similar point is made in a prayer to God the Father published among the meditations of St Augustine, *Meditationum liber unus*, v–viii (PL 40, 904–8), and as the second of the prayers attributed at one time to Anselm (PL 158, 858–65); the prayer sometimes occurs among the works of John of Fécamp, though it is generally agreed that it is not by him; see Wilmart, 'Les méditations sur le Saint-Esprit', p. 420, n. 1; Hurlbut, *Heavenly Jerusalem*, p. vii.5; Leclercq and Bonnes, *Jean de Fécamp*, p. 34.

[56] *Meditatio redemptionis humanae* (ed. Schmitt III, 87–8).

emphasis on Christ's obedience 'unto death', Christ's Resurrection has no part in Anselm's scheme of salvation. For the Anglo-Saxons, however, Christ's whole life was an offering to God;[57] his death was only one part of that offering, to be completed by his Resurrection.[58]

In some respects the passages in late Old English homilies which present Christ's death as a sacrifice, together with the emphasis in the art of the late tenth and early eleventh centuries on Christ's human nature, suggest that the Anselmian view of the redemption was known as early as the beginning of the eleventh century. There are, however, some major differences. For Anselm the crucial thing was Adam's sin against God for which God was obliged, in justice, to demand reparation.[59] Anselm's acute sense of man's responsibility for the evil of sin[60] was quite alien to writers like Ælfric. When the latter talks of man's sin in relation to Christ's death he sees it as something which man suffers rather than as an infinite offence against God. In a long passage on the brazen serpent raised by Moses in the wilderness he compares men's sins to the deadly serpents of the desert and Christ's death on the cross to the image of the serpent which was the antidote to the poison. 'We behealdað Cristes deað', he says,

þæt us se deað ne derige, þe of ðære næddran asprang, seo ðe Adam forspeon. Hwæs deað behealde we? Lifes deað. Hwa is lif buton Crist? Se ðe cwæð, Ic eom ærist and lif, se ðe gelyfð on me, þeah ðe he dead beo, he leofað, and ælc ðæra þe leofað and on me gelyfð, ne swelt he on ecnysse. Crist is lif and swa ðeah he wæs on rode ahangen. He is soð lif, and swa ðeah he wæs dead on ðære menniscnysse, na on godcundnysse. On Cristes deaðe wæs se deað adydd, for ðan þe þæt deade lif acwealde ðone deað, and he wæs fornumen on Cristes lichaman.[61]

Because of this different attitude to sin, Ælfric's attitude to Christ's sufferings is very different from that of Anselm. For Anselm, Christ's

---

[57] Wulfstan, *Homilies*, no. vi (ed. Bethurum, pp. 152–3).   [58] *Ibid.*, p. 154.

[59] *Meditatio redemptionis humanae* (ed. Schmitt III, 86–7).

[60] Aulén, *Christus victor*, pp. 89–90; *CDH* I.xxi (ed. Schmitt II, 88–9).

[61] *CH* II.xiii (ed. Godden, pp. 135–6): 'We behold Christ's death so that death may not harm us, which sprang from the serpent that seduced Adam. Whose death do we behold? Life's death. Who is life except Christ, who said: I am the Resurrection and the life; he who believes in me, though he is dead, yet he lives, and each of those who lives and believes in me shall never die. Christ is life and yet he was hung on the cross. He is true life and yet he died in his humanity, not in his divinity. By Christ's death, death was destroyed, for that dead life killed death and he [i.e. death] was destroyed in Christ's body.' See above, p. 65.

sufferings were essential for the expiation of man's sin.[62] Anglo-Saxon writers, on the other hand, were amazed that Christ submitted to suffering.[63] For them Christ's sufferings were a sign of his love[64] or an example of humility,[65] not a proof of the enormity of man's sin.

The most striking difference between the redemption theology of late Anglo-Saxon England and that of Anselm, however, concerned the relationship between Christ's human and divine natures. In the *Cur Deus homo* and the *Meditatio redemptionis humanae* Christ is seen as essentially human: 'Hominem in cruce pendentem suspendere mortem aeternam genus humanum prementem.'[66] In consequence there is a separation between the Son, who understands what will please his Father, and the Father, who is pleased by what is freely offered by the Son.[67] Of course, Anselm does not deny Christ's divinity but he treats it as a means to an end, the end being to find a representative of the human race who is capable of making amends for Adam's sin.[68] Anglo-Saxon writers, on the other hand, never lost sight of Christ's divinity. Éamonn Ó Carragáin has pointed out in an unpublished lecture that the extracts from *The Dream of the Rood* carved on the Ruthwell Cross refer to Almighty God ascending the gallows of the cross; he gives as a parallel the prayer for Sext in the Antiphonary of Bangor which reads: 'Omnipotens aeternae Deus, qui nobis magnalia fecisti, sexta hora crucem ascendisti et tenebras mundi inluminasti; sic et corda nostra inluminare digneris.'[69] The corresponding passage in the later Vercelli text of the poem describes Christ as 'geong hæleð, þæt wæs God ælmihtig',[70] emphasizing his dual nature rather than his divinity alone,

[62] *Meditatio redemptionis humanae* (ed. Schmitt III, 86 and 89).
[63] Wulfstan, *Homilies*, no. vii (ed. Bethurum, p. 159); Ælfric, *Homilies*, no. xiii (ed. Assmann, p. 152).
[64] Ælfric, *LS* no. xvi (ed. Skeat I, 344); Ælfric, *Homilies*, no. xiii (ed. Assmann, p. 152); *Blickling Homilies*, no. ii (ed. Morris, pp. 15–17 and 23); Wulfstan, *Homilies*, no. xiii (ed. Bethurum, p. 227).
[65] Ælfric, *CH* I.xv (ed. Thorpe, p. 224); *LS*, no. xvi (ed. Skeat I, 344).
[66] *Meditatio redemptionis humanae* (ed. Schmitt III, 84–5): 'A man hanging on the cross lifts the eternal death pressing on the human race.' See also *CDH* II.xi and xviii (ed. Schmitt II, 111–12 and 126).
[67] *Meditatio redemptionis humanae* (ed. Schmitt III, 88).
[68] Aulén, *Christus victor*, p. 87.
[69] *Antiphonary of Bangor* (ed. Warren I, 18v): 'Omnipotent, eternal God, who have done great things for us, you ascended the cross at the sixth hour and illuminated the shadows of the world; deign also to illuminate our hearts.'
[70] *Dream of the Rood* 39.

though in a later passage the poet talks of the God of hosts being stretched out on the cross,[71] suggesting that he still thought of Christ as God rather than as man. The Office collects in the Ælfwine Prayer-book,[72] in the Benedictine Office[73] and in various Carolingian prayer-books[74] address Christ as *Domine Iesu Christe* or *Domine Deus Iesu Christe* with the exception of the collect for Terce in the Benedictine Office which begins *Domine Deus*.[75] Most of the prayers in the eleventh-century manuscripts follow the same practice; they are addressed to God the Father and distinguish between him and his son. The practice of addressing Christ as God does not disappear entirely, however. Many of the prayers in the Book of Nunnaminster address Christ as *Deus* without any further qualification as does the following prayer from the Ælfwine Prayer-book in which it is God himself who suffers for men's sake:

Deus qui voluisti pro redemptione mundi a Iudeis reprobari, a Iuda osculo tradi, vinculis alligari, et agnus innocens ad victimam duci, atque conspectibus Pilati offerri, a falsis quoque testibus accusari, flagellis et obprobriis vexari, et conspui, spinis coronari, colaphis cedi, cruce elevari, atque inter latrones deputari, clavorum quoque aculeis perforari, lancea vulnerari, felle et aceto potari; tu per sanctissimas has poenas tuas ab inferni poenis me libera, et per sanctam crucem tuam salva et custodi, et illuc perduc me miserum peccatorem, quo perduxisti tecum crucifixum latronem, tibi cum Deo Patre et Spiritu Sancto honor, virtus, et gloria, nunc et in omnia secula. Amen.[76]

The drawings and paintings of the Crucifixion in late Anglo-Saxon manuscripts resemble the prayer of the Ælfwine manuscript in depicting Christ as the suffering God rather than the suffering man of Anselm's

---

[71] *Ibid.* 51–2.   [72] BL, Cotton Titus D. xxvi, 45v–46r.

[73] *Benedictine Office*, ed. Ure, pp. 95–8.

[74] Wilmart, *Precum libelli*, pp. 25, 35 and 98.

[75] *Benedictine Office*, ed. Ure, pp. 96–7.

[76] BL, Cotton Titus D. xxvii, 71v–72r: 'Oh God who wished, for the redemption of the world, to be rejected by the Jews, betrayed by the kiss of Judas, bound in chains, led to slaughter like an innocent lamb, brought before the sight of Pilate, accused also by false witnesses, injured by scourges and insults, spat on, crowned with thorns, struck, raised on the cross, assigned a place between thieves, pierced by the points of the nails, wounded by the spear, given gall and vinegar to drink; free me from the punishments of hell through your most holy sufferings, and save and keep me through your holy cross, and lead me, a wretched sinner, where you led with you the crucified thief; to you, with God the Father and the Holy Spirit be honour, power and glory, now and for ever. Amen.'

writings. Two of the drawings of the dead Christ include the 'rex Iudeorum' text[77] and four pictures show the dead Christ wearing a crown, one of the symbols of his divinity.[78] Further evidence of the importance of Christ's divinity for late Anglo-Saxon artists comes from the numerous and varied representations of the Trinity in the art of the period.[79] One of the most important links between the way in which Christ's dual nature is represented in the art and the literature, however, concerns his role as creator of the world. In the art this idea is represented by the motifs of the book, the symbol of the *Logos*, and the sun and moon;[80] in the literature the link between creation and redemption is normally expressed by describing the latter as a recapitulation of God's original creation or as a reversal of Adam's fall.

For Ælfric, Christ's death was a new creation by God rather than an act of reparation by man. Man was created and redeemed by the same God:

God Ælmihtig gesceop man on ðam sixtan dæge, þa ða he gesceafta Scyppende gedihte, and on ðam seofoðan dæge hine sylfne gereste, geendodum weorcum, swa swa he sylf wolde. Eft soðlice se Scyppend, on ðam sixtan dæge, on rode hangiende, his handgeweorc alysde, Adames ofspring, mid his agenum deaðe, and on byrgene siððan anbidiende læg on ðam seofoðan dæge, ðe ge Sæternes hata ð.[81]

The idea is that found in the antiphon for the Good Friday Adoration of the Cross, *Dum fabricator mundi*.[82] Ælfric drew a strict parallel between God's works of creation and re-creation. Man was created on the sixth day and

---

[77] The Ramsey and Tiberius Psalters; see above, pp. 149 and 155–6.

[78] The Winchcombe, Arundel and Tiberius Psalters and the Cambridge Homilies; see above, pp. 134 and 148.

[79] Harley 603; 1r; the Sherborne Pontifical, 5v–6v; the Grimbald Gospels, 114v; the Tiberius Psalter, 126v; Titus D. xxvii, 75v; the Arenberg Gospels, 11v; the Bury Psalter, 88r and 168v–169r; Paris, BN, lat. 6401, 159r; see Wormald, 'Late Anglo-Saxon Art', pp. 106–8.

[80] See above, pp. 105–6, 135–7 and 150.

[81] *CH* II.xiv (ed. Godden, pp. 148–9): 'Almighty God created man on the sixth day when he, the creator, had arranged the creatures, and he rested on the seventh day, his work being finished, as he himself wished. And afterwards, truly, the creator, hanging on the cross on the sixth day, freed his handiwork, Adam's offspring, through his own death, and afterwards lay waiting in the grave on the seventh day, which you call the day of Saturn.' Cf. Augustine, *In Iohannis evangelium tract. cxxiv* XVII.15 (ed. Mayer, pp. 177–8) and Haymo, *Homiliae*, xxxiii and lxv (PL 118, 221 and 381–2); see also Ælfric, *Homilies* (ed. Pope, I, 465–6); *CH* I.i and xx (ed. Thorpe, pp. 24 and 292); *Heptateuch* (ed. Crawford, pp. 22–3).

[82] See above, p. 136.

redeemed on the sixth day; Christ rested from his labours on the sabbath when he lay in the tomb just as God rested from his labours on the seventh day.[83] Ælfric's contemporary, Byrhtferth of Ramsey, carried the idea further: he saw the rest of God on the seventh day as a prefiguration of the rest of Christ on the Jewish sabbath when he lay in the tomb and this in turn was a prefiguration of the seventh day of man's life, the rest of the saints in heaven, to be completed by the eternal sabbath, or eighth day, symbolized by the day on which Christ rose from the tomb.[84]

The idea of reversal is seen in the treatment of the cross as the tree of life, a theme which permeates the liturgy for the feasts of the Invention and Exaltation of the Cross and which became popular in the art about the middle of the eleventh century.[85] The Preface for the feast of the Invention of the Cross talks of Christ's reversal of the evil brought by the tree of knowledge through the cross: 'Qui per passionem crucis mundum redemit, et antiqui arboris amarissimum gustum crucis medicamine indulcavit, mortemque quae per lignum vetitum venerat, per ligni tropheum devicit, ut mirabili suae pietatis dispensatione, qui per ligni gustum a florigera sede discesseramus, per crucis lignum ad paradysi gaudia redeamus.'[86] Because man had been driven out of paradise as the result of eating the fruit of a tree, it was fitting that he should be saved by the fruit of another tree: 'Propter lignum servi facti sumus et per sanctam crucem liberati sumus. Fructus arboris seduxit nos, Filius Dei redemit nos.'[87] The extended verse from Psalm xcv, 'Dicite in gentibus quia dominus regnavit a ligno',[88] used as the *Alleluia* for the feast of the Invention of the Cross,[89] was linked by Hrabanus Maurus to the theme of Adam's tree of death and Christ's tree of

---

[83] Ælfric, *Homilies* (ed. Pope I, 240–1) and *CH* II.xii (ed. Godden, pp. 118–19).

[84] Byrhtferth, *Manual* (ed. Crawford, pp. 214 and 240); cf. Bede, *In Gen.* I.ii.1–3 (ed. Jones, pp. 38–9) and *DTR*, lxxi (ed. Jones, pp. 542–4).

[85] The Winchcombe, Arundel and Tiberius Psalters, the Sherborne Missal and the Weingarten Gospels; see above, pp. 131 and 150.

[86] *Missal of the New Minster* (ed. Turner, p. 92): 'Who redeemed the world through his sufferings on the cross, and sweetened the most bitter taste of the old tree with the medicine of the cross, and conquered the death which came through the forbidden tree by the trophy of the cross so that by the wonderful sharing out of his love we, who by eating from the tree left our flowery seat, may return to the joys of paradise through the wood of the cross.'

[87] *Ibid.* (ed. Turner, pp. 92 and 161): 'We were made slaves through the tree and are freed by the holy cross. The fruit of the tree seduced us, the Son of God redeemed us.'

[88] 'Tell the nations that God has reigned from the tree.' See above, p. 134.

[89] *Missal of the New Minster* (ed. Turner, p. 91).

life.⁹⁰ This text lies behind one of the antiphons for the Friday Office of the cross which celebrates the cross as excelling all other trees: 'Super omnia ligna cedrorum tu sola excelsior in qua vita mundi pependit, in qua Christus triumphavit, et mors mortem superavit alleluia.'⁹¹ These texts probably formed the basis for the passages in the poetry and in the homilies which link the cross to the tree of the Garden of Eden. A passage in *The Dream of the Rood*,⁹² describing how Christ honoured the cross above all other trees, probably derives from the antiphon, *Super omnia ligna cedrorum*, while a passage in Ælfric's second homily for the fifth Sunday in Lent, contrasting Christ's tree of life and Adam's tree of death, is probably based on the text, *Propter lignum*, even though this chant is not normally used in the liturgy for Passion Sunday: 'þurh treow us com deað, þaða Adam geæt þone forbodenan æppel, and ðurh treow us com eft lif and alysednyss, ðaða Crist hangode on rode for ure alysednysse.'⁹³ There is an allusion to this link between the cross and the trees in the Garden of Eden in one of the creation pictures in Junius 11 in the Bodleian Library, where the artist has included a tree with a small cross at its centre in his drawing of paradise.⁹⁴

It is not only the cross which is seen as the tree of life. Ælfric equates Christ himself with the tree of life:

> ðæt we inn moton gaan to ðam upplican Paradise,
> to ðam lifes treowe, ðæt is se leofa Hælend
> ðe ðæt ece life forgifð ðam ðe hine lufiað.⁹⁵

This idea, like the parallel between the trees of Adam and Christ, probably came from the liturgy, from the collect for Vespers of the feast of the Invention of the Cross: 'Deus cui cuncta obediunt creaturae . . . supplices quesumus ineffabilem clementiam tuam, ut quos per lignum sanctae crucis

---

⁹⁰ *Expositio in Paralipomena* II.xvi (PL 109, 359–60).

⁹¹ *Portfiorium* (ed. Hughes II, 59): 'You alone are higher than all the cedar trees, on whom the life of the world hung, on whom Christ triumphed and death defeated death, alleluia.' Cf. the Magnificat antiphon in Titus D.xxvii, 80r–v.

⁹² *Dream of the Rood* 90–4.

⁹³ *CH* II.xiii (ed. Godden, p. 136): 'Death came to us through a tree, when Adam ate the forbidden apple, and afterwards, life and redemption came to us through a tree, when Christ hung on the cross for our redemption.'

⁹⁴ Oxford, Bodleian Library, Junius 11, p. 7.

⁹⁵ *Hexameron* 512–14 (ed. Crawford, pp. 71–2): 'that we may go in to that paradise above, to the tree of life, namely the beloved Saviour, who gives eternal life to those who love him'. Cf. Bede, *In Gen.* I.iii.24 (ed. Jones, pp. 71–2).

filii tui pio cruore es dignatus redimere, tu qui es lignum vitae paradysique reparator, omnibus in te credentibus dira serpentis venena extinguere et per gratiam spiritus sancti poculum salutis infunde.'[96] The identification of Christ with the tree of life depends on a passage in the Apocalypse:[97] 'Those who prove victorious I will feed *from the tree of life set in* God's *paradise.*' Ambrose explains that the passage refers to Christ in the midst of his church, the fruit of the tree being the gift of eternal life.[98] Hrabanus Maurus makes the same point in his commentary on Genesis, but links the passage more specifically to Christ's death through a reference to the repentant thief who was taken into paradise with Christ.[99]

The image of the cross as the tree of life, like the image of Christ's death as a new creation, places the cross at the centre of a redemptive sequence which extends from the original creation to the new creation of the Apocalypse.[100] Christ's death is not something complete in itself: it has to be completed by the Resurrection, first of Christ and then of those he has redeemed. One of the clearest expressions of this theme comes in the poetic meditation, *The Dream of the Rood.* The jewelled cross of the opening vision of the poem, which represents the cross which will announce Christ's return to earth, is also a tree, torn from its roots in the forest. Christ is not only the young hero; he is the king and creator of the world, mourned by his creation.[101] The tree which has co-operated with Christ in his work of redemption becomes a source of healing for men, the tree growing from the river of life in God's new creation.[102]

The Dream of the Rood includes a more striking parallel with late Anglo-Saxon art, however, for it links the honour paid by God to the cross with the honour he paid to his mother.[103] The comparison between the cross and Mary implies a belief in Mary's co-operation with God's plan of redemption

---

96 *Portiforium* (ed. Hughes I, 124): 'God, whom all creatures obey . . . we, whom you deigned to redeem through the wood of the holy cross and through the precious blood of your son, humbly beg your great mercy that you, who are the tree of life and restorer of paradise, will extinguish the dreadful poison of the serpent in all who believe in you and will pour out the cup of salvation through the grace of the Holy Spirit.' The prayer also occurs among the private prayers (*ibid.* II. 19).

97 Apoc. II.7.   98 *In Apocalypsin expositio* (Apoc. II.7) (PL 17, 778–9).

99 *Commentaria in Genesim* I.xii (PL 107, 476–7); cf. Bede, *In Gen.* I.iii.24 (ed. Jones, p. 72).

100 Apoc. XXI.5, XXII.2 and 14.   101 See above, pp. 136–7.

102 Apoc. XXII.1–2; see Raw, '*Dream of the Rood*', p. 244 and n.26.

103 *Dream of the Rood* 90–4.

and in her intercessory powers, comparable to that in the drawings of an orant Mary under the cross.[104] The orant figures of Mary belong to the Crucifixion iconography in which Christ is shown crowned and accompanied by symbols of the sun and moon,[105] suggesting that there might be a link between the theme of Mary's intercession and that of Christ as creator of the world, and this turns out to be the case. Ælfric explores the paradox of Mary's position as mother of her creator in a homily for the Nativity.[106] Christ is presented as the wisdom of God through whom the world was created.[107] He was sent by God out of love to suffer and die and so free man from the devil.[108] He is the descendant of David[109] and king of kings.[110] Mary is compared to the church, the bride of Christ and mother of all Christians.[111] She reverses the sin of Eve, opening the gate of heaven to men.[112] She is the help of all Christians, interceding for man with Christ who is both her son and her creator, true God and true man.[113]

The interest in Mary's role which is so evident in the art of the Anglo-Saxon period, is found too in the *Advent Lyrics*. These poems are based on the antiphons sung at the *Magnificat* in the period immediately before Christmas. They are joyful affairs, celebrating Christ under his Old Testament titles of wisdom, root of Jesse, key of David, daystar, king of the nations, lawgiver and Emmanuel, and praising Mary for the part she played in the redemption by becoming the source of Christ's human nature. Unlike the Latin prayers of the Anglo-Saxon period, the *Advent Lyrics* make no reference to man's guilt. Christ comes to save man from the devil, to free him from prison and lead him back to heaven. The attention given to Mary's role in these poems, their presentation of Christ as the wisdom of God and the creator of the world, the linking of human emotions of doubt and grief with theological truths in the dialogue between Mary and Joseph and, in particular, the clear understanding of the relationship between the incarnation and the redemption are all close to the themes of the Crucifixion pictures of the late Anglo-Saxon period.[114]

The kind of theological analysis which informs the *Advent Lyrics* appears again in the prayers and meditations of Anselm of Canterbury. The title Anselm gave to his work on the existence of God, known as the *Proslogion* –

---

[104] See above, pp. 100–3.   [105] See above, ch. 6.
[106] *CH* II.i (ed. Godden, pp. 3–11).
[107] *Ibid.*, pp. 3 and 5.   [108] *Ibid.*, p. 3.   [109] *Ibid.*, p. 6.   [110] *Ibid.*, p. 7.
[111] *Ibid.*, p. 6.   [112] *Ibid.*, p. 11.   [113] *Ibid.*, pp. 5 and 11.
[114] See above, pp. 98 and 103–7.

Fides quaerens intellectum – sums up Anselm's attitude to prayer. 'I have written the following short work', he says, 'from the point of view of someone trying to raise his mind to the contemplation of God, and seeking to understand what he believes.'[115] The similarities between the weeping Virgin of the Ramsey Psalter Crucifixion picture (pl. XIV), the figure of Mary Magdalen in the Weingarten Gospels (pl. XVI) and passages in Anselm's prayers have already been mentioned,[116] but there are also much wider similarities of thought and argument between Anselm's prayers and meditations and Anglo-Saxon Crucifixion pictures. One of the major differences between Anglo-Saxon Crucifixion pictures and the Latin prayers of the late Anglo-Saxon period is the rarity of references in the prayers to Mary's role in the redemption.[117] The three prayers to Mary, sent by Anselm to Gundolf in 1072, fill this gap. Anselm's devotion to Mary is firmly linked to her position as mother of the Saviour.[118] He begs her to intercede for him on the grounds that she brought into the world the one who would intercede for man.[119] He calls on her as the human mother of God made man to help a human sinner.[120] Mary was not only the mother of the one who gave life to his soul and who redeemed his flesh,[121] but the mother of the creator, giving birth to the one who would recreate the world:[122]

> God who made all things made himself of Mary,
> and thus he refashioned everything he had made.
> He who was able to make all things out of nothing
> refused to remake it by force,
> but first became the Son of Mary.
> So God is the Father of all created things,
> and Mary is the mother of all re-created things.
> God is the Father of all that is established,
> and Mary is the mother of all that is re-established.

---

[115] *Proslogion*, Proemium (ed. Schmitt I, 93–4); Ward, *Prayers*, p. 238.

[116] See above, pp. 157 and 160–1. The closeness of some late Anglo-Saxon prayers to Anselm's writing is discussed by Bestul, 'Continuity of Anglo-Saxon Devotional Traditions'.

[117] See above, p. 66.

[118] *Or.* v (*Orationes*, ed. Schmitt III, 13); Ward, *Prayers*, p. 107.

[119] *Or.* vi (*ibid.*, pp. 15–16); Ward, *ibid.*, pp. 110–11.

[120] *Or.* vi (*ibid.*, p. 16); Ward, *ibid.*, pp. 111–12.

[121] *Or.* vii (*ibid.*, p. 19); Ward, *ibid.*, p. 116.

[122] *Or.* vii (*ibid.*, p. 20); Ward, *ibid.*, p. 118.

For God gave birth to him by whom all things were made
and Mary brought forth him by whom all are saved. [123]

The ideas expressed in this passage are close to those set out by Ælfric in his homily on the Nativity. [124] Elsewhere, however, Anselm's meditative processes are very different from those of the Anglo-Saxon period. In his *Oratio ad Christum* [125] he laments his exile from the presence of the risen Christ and his inability to share in Christ's life on earth except at a distance and through the imagination. The detailed and emotional recall of Christ's sufferings and of Mary's grief in this prayer goes far beyond anything in the art and literature of late Anglo-Saxon England. A comparison with Ælfric's second Palm Sunday homily, [126] which recalls each detail of Christ's Passion separately and in chronological order as Anselm's prayer does, shows how far-reaching the changes were which took place during the eleventh century. Where Anselm saw human suffering which he could enter into, Ælfric saw symbolism. The red robe in which Pilate's soldiers dressed Jesus was a symbol of his death; the crown of thorns symbolized man's sins. [127] Christ was stripped and reclothed as a sign that he would lay down his life and take it up again. [128] The bitter drink was a symbol of the bitterness of death, and the seamless robe a sign of the unity of the church. [129] The two thieves crucified with Christ represented the Jews and the Gentiles. [130] The church was born from Christ's side as Eve was created from that of Adam. [131] The new tomb in which Christ's body was placed resembled Mary's womb. [132]

Late Anglo-Saxon Crucifixion pictures differ from this homily as much as they do from Anselm's prayer to Christ. The difference from Anselm is largely a matter of chronology. The eleventh century was a period of major theological change and this change is reflected in the mixture of suffering and triumphal images of Christ in the art of the period. The difference from Ælfric is related to a difference in function. One of the most striking features of Ælfric's writing is the lavish use he makes of typology. He

---

[123] *Or.* vii (*ibid.*, p. 22); Ward, *ibid.*, pp. 120–21.   [124] See above, p. 179.

[125] *Or.* ii (*Orationes*, ed. Schmitt III, 6–9); Ward, *Prayers*, pp. 93–9.

[126] *CH* II.xiv (ed. Godden, pp. 137–49).   [127] *Ibid.*, p. 144.

[128] *Ibid.*, pp. 144–5.

[129] *Ibid.*, p. 145.   [130] *Ibid.*, p. 146.   [131] *Ibid.*, p. 148.

[132] *Ibid.*, p. 149; most of these details are taken from Haymo, *Homiliae*, lxiv and lxviii (PL 118, 374–7 and 443).

compares Christ's death to the death of Abel[133] and to Abraham's offering of Isaac.[134] The stone which Moses struck to obtain water is a symbol of Christ's side, wounded on the cross;[135] the serpent lifted up in the wilderness signifies Christ raised on the cross.[136] This kind of symbolism was a commonplace of medieval biblical interpretation yet there is virtually no trace of it in Anglo-Saxon art apart from the motif of the tree of life. Even the most common symbol of all – that of the Passover lamb – is used quite differently in the art and in the literature. The design of the lamb among the evangelist symbols which forms the reverse to several crucifixes is essentially a triumphal image, deriving from the description of the throne of God in the Apocalypse.[137] It is a symbol of Christ's sacrificial death, but it relates that death to the glory which sprang from it.[138] The only representation of the Crucifixion from the Anglo-Saxon period which includes the motif of the lamb – that on the portable altar in the Musée de Cluny (pl. VII) – also includes the symbols of the evangelists and therefore links the motif to the Apocalypse scenes rather than to the Exodus.[139] The Passover lamb was one of Ælfric's favourite images for Christ's death but, in contrast to the artists of the time, he invariably focused on the themes of sacrifice and suffering rather than the more triumphal themes of the Apocalypse. Christ was sinless and took away the sins of the world.[140] Christ was unresisting like a lamb.[141] Christ is the new sacrifice typified by the Jewish Passover.[142] Ælfric draws a detailed comparison between the lamb offered in the evening by the Israelites and Christ offered in the evening of the world[143] but, although he makes a brief reference to the second coming at the end of this exposition, he never uses the apocalyptic symbols of the lamb standing on the throne[144] or the lamb on Mount Sion.[145] For him the lamb is always a means of linking Christ's Passion and

---

[133] *CH* II.iv (ed. Godden, p. 33).   [134] *CH* II.iv (*ibid.*, p. 34).

[135] *CH* II.xii (*ibid.*, p. 116).

[136] *CH* II.xiii (*ibid.*, p. 135).   [137] Apoc. IV and V.

[138] Raw, 'Archer' and *'Dream of the Rood'*, p. 243.

[139] See above, pp. 50 and 124.

[140] *CH* I.xxii and xxv (ed. Thorpe, pp. 312 and 358).

[141] *CH* II.i and iii (ed. Godden, pp. 8 and 21); *Old English Letter to Wulfstan* I (ed. Fehr, *Die Hirtenbriefe*, p. 136).

[142] *CH* II.xv (ed. Godden, pp. 151–2); *Latin Letter to Wulfstan* (ed. Fehr, *Die Hirtenbriefe*, pp. 223–4).

[143] *CH* II.xv (ed. Godden, pp. 157–9).   [144] Apoc. V.6–14.

[145] Apoc. XIV.1–5.

its representation in the eucharist with the Old Testament prophecies, just as the tree of life symbolizes the reversal of Adam's fall. The difference is intelligible if, as has been argued in this book, the art is associated with prayer rather than with instruction. Ælfric's use of Old Testament types is related to his teaching role: the parallels between Old and New Testaments are a form of proof.[146] Prayer, on the other hand, is not concerned with proof but with faith, 'the assurance of things hoped for'.[147] It may start from the memory of past events and may contain elements of proof but its focus is eschatological.[148] For a true parallel to the Crucifixion pictures of the late Anglo-Saxon period it is necessary to look at those texts which present Christ's death as something which exists in the present and which has a part in man's hope for the future. This parallel is found in the liturgy and particularly in the mass for, as Ælfric says: 'Æne þrowade Crist ðurh hine sylfne, ac swa ðeah dæghwomlice bið his ðrowung geedniwod ðurh gerynu þæs halgan husles æt ðære halgan mæssan.'[149]

One of the most influential and popular interpretations of the meaning of the mass in the late Anglo-Saxon period was Amalarius of Metz's *Liber officialis*.[150] Whereas other writers focused on the meaning of the words of the mass, especially the words of consecration, which were based on Christ's words at the Last Supper, Amalarius interpreted the actions. For him the mass was a dramatic ritual which re-created the historical events of salvation history. The consecration of the bread and wine was, of course, generally understood as a re-presentation of Christ's actions at the Last Supper and of his offering of himself on the cross, but Amalarius went far beyond this, seeing the whole of the mass as a symbol of Christ's life. Prompted by the actions of the mass those present remembered the events of Christ's life, re-creating them in imagination. Because Christ was believed to be really present in the consecrated bread and wine of the mass this imaginative reconstruction acquired a reality of its own so that the participants felt themselves to be really present not simply at the renewed offering of Christ to his Father on the altar of the church but also at all the events of his life. The early part of the mass, up to the gospel, represented

---

[146] See above, p. 31.   [147] Heb. XI.1 (Revised Standard Version).

[148] See above, p. 38 and Raw, *Old English Poetry*, p. 130.

[149] *CH* II.xv (ed. Godden, p. 156): 'Christ suffered once through himself, but yet his suffering is renewed daily through the mystery of the holy eucharist at the holy mass.'

[150] For a good account of Amalarius's interpretation of the mass see Hardison, *Christian Rite*, pp. 35–79.

Christ's birth and early life, the gospel represented his ministry and the canon his Passion and Resurrection. This drama was framed by the entrance procession and chant, which symbolized the patriarchs and prophets waiting for the Messiah, and by the blessing, which represented the risen Christ blessing his disciples before returning to heaven.[151] The dramatic way in which the action was understood is shown particularly clearly in the interpretation of the canon. The deacons, who stand with bowed heads from the *Te igitur* to the beginning of the communion, play the role of the disciples, 'qui magna tribulatione erant oppressi'.[152] The sub-deacons, who stand facing the celebrant across the altar, represent the holy women who remained with Christ during his sufferings.[153] At the prayer *Supplices te rogamus* Christ commends his soul to God and dies and the sub-deacons raise their heads, 'aspicientes in dilectum sibi corpus, quousque pendet in cruce'.[154] At the beginning of the prayer *Nobis quoque peccatoribus* the celebrant raises his voice and the congregation are invited to recall the centurion plunging the spear into Christ's side.[155] The sense of being really present at the events of the past can be seen vividly at this point in the treatment of the chalice, which is placed to the right of the paten on the altar in order that it can catch the blood from Christ's side.[156] As the prayer of consecration ends the celebrant and the archdeacon wrap the chalice and paten in two cloths and place them on the altar, enacting the parts of Joseph and Nicodemus placing Christ's body in the tomb.[157] The mass reaches its climax at the communion when a particle of the host is placed in the chalice and the congregation relives the Resurrection of Christ.[158]

The main force of Amalarius's interpretation lies in its reliving by clergy and congregation of events from the past, partly through the imagination and partly through playing the roles of characters from the gospel story. It was this which gave it its enormous appeal, particularly to those who could

---

[151] Amalarius, *Liber officialis* III.v.10, III.v.23–4 and III.xxxvi.1 (ed. Hanssens II, 274, 278–9 and 368).

[152] *Ibid.* III.xxiii.3 (II, 330): 'who were weighed down with great suffering'.

[153] *Ibid.* III.xxi.13, III.xxi.15 and III.xxiii.4 (II, 328 and 330).

[154] *Ibid.* III.xxv.7–9 (II, 342–3): 'gazing at his beloved body as long as it hangs on the cross'.

[155] *Ibid.* III.xxvi.4–5 (II, 344–5).

[156] *Ibid.* Proemium 21 and III.xxvi.3–5 (II, 18 and 344–5).

[157] *Ibid.* III.xxvi.9–10 (II, 346).

[158] *Ibid.* III.xxxi.3 (II, 362).

not read or understand the Latin text. But Amalarius also made use of the traditional fourfold method of biblical interpretation, adding anagogical and tropological interpretations to the historical one. The anagogical meaning of the mass appears in the treatment of the blessing where the celebrant turns to the east 'ut se commendet Domini ascensioni'.[159] At this point the eastern part of the church becomes the next world, to which Christ has ascended, in contrast to the altar, the biblical world in which he once lived.[160] The point is emphasized in Amalarius's comment on the dismissal of the congregation by the deacon. As the people reply to his 'Ite missa est' their minds turn to their home in heaven: 'Mens nostra ad illam patriam tendat, quo caput nostrum praecessit, ut ibi simus desiderio, ubi desideratus cunctis gentibus nos exspectat cum suo tropheo.'[161] The tropological or moral sense is seen in the treatment of the altar. It becomes both the stage on which Christ's Passion is re-enacted and also the altar on which the congregation are to offer themselves as an oblation to God, the 'oblatio servitutis nostrae, sed et cunctae familiae tuae' of the words of the mass'.[162]

Amalarius's *Liber officialis* was certainly known in England in the late Anglo-Saxon period and may even have been translated into Old English.[163] Ælfric refers to the work in his *Epistula ad monachos Egneshamnenses directa*[164] and used sections of it in his *Catholic Homilies*.[165] Wulfstan, too, was familiar with it and used it in at least one of his sermons.[166] But although Amalarius's work was clearly known in the reformed monasteries it is not clear how far the approach to the mass embodied in it influenced English practice. Ælfric follows Amalarius in interpreting some parts of the Easter liturgy in a narrative and dramatic way. The Palm Sunday procession recalls Christ's triumphal entry into

---

[159] *Ibid.* III.xxxvi.1 (II, 368): 'to commend himself to the Lord's Ascension'.

[160] See also above, p. 55.

[161] Amalarius, *Liber officialis* III.xxxvi.6 (*ibid.* II, 370): 'Our mind turns to that homeland where our head has preceded us, that we may be there in desire where the desired of all nations awaits us with his trophy.'

[162] *Ibid.* III.xxvi.13 (II, 347).

[163] Gneuss, 'Preliminary List', pp. 9, 14, 27 and 51; Trahern, 'Amalarius', pp. 475–8.

[164] *Epistula*, Prol. (ed. Hallinger, p. 155).

[165] *CH* I.xviii and xxii (ed. Thorpe); *CH* II.iii and II.v (ed. Godden, p. 49); Förster, 'Quellen', pp. 48–9; Fehr, 'Quellen', pp. 378–9.

[166] Wulfstan, *Homilies*, no. viiia (ed. Bethurum, pp. 312–13).

Jerusalem.[167] On Good Friday the altar cloth is stripped from beneath the gospel-book in memory of the division of Christ's garments.[168] On Holy Saturday incense is carried instead of candles at the reading of the gospel in imitation of the women at the tomb.[169] The ceremonies of the burial of the cross on Good Friday and the visit of the women to the tomb, described in the *Regularis concordia* but not in Ælfric's abridgement, are very much in the spirit of Amalarius.[170] Ælfric's interpretation of the mass, on the other hand, differed from that of Amalarius. He accepts the traditional interpretation of the mass as a renewal of Christ's suffering and death yet he makes no attempt to interpret its action in narrative terms, preferring to associate it with Old Testament events, in particular the Passover ceremonies and the sacrifice of the Passover lamb. He also makes a very clear distinction between the human body in which Christ suffered and his sacramental body, present on the altar of the church.[171]

The large Crucifixion groups which were introduced into Anglo-Saxon churches in the middle of the eleventh century[172] would have provided an admirable focus for a liturgical drama of the kind described by Amalarius. The absence of figures other than those of Christ, Mary and John is intelligible in a situation where many of the parts in the drama were played by the clergy and congregation. The deacons, representing the grieving disciples, could take St John as their representative; the sub-deacons, playing the role of the holy women, could use the figure of Mary as a reminder of their role. When they raised their heads at the *Supplices te rogamus* to gaze on the dead Christ who had passed beyond human suffering[173] their imagination would be quickened by the sight of the crucifix. It was unnecessary to show the figures of the soldiers because the centurion's role was taken by the celebrant. The repentant thief, whose role

---

[167] *Epistula*, viii.32 (ed. Hallinger, p. 167); Amalarius, *Liber officialis* I.x.1 (ed. Hanssens II, 58).

[168] *Epistula*, viii.43 (ed. Hallinger, p. 171); this differs from *Liber officialis* I.xiii.13 (ed. Hanssens II, 96), where the action is identified with the flight of the apostles.

[169] *Epistula*, ix.46 (ed. Hallinger, p. 173); Amalarius, *Liber officialis* I.xxxi.8 (ed. Hanssens II, 160).

[170] *Concordia*, iv.46 and v.51 (ed. Symons, pp. 44 and 49–50).

[171] *Old English Letter to Wulfstan* I (ed. Fehr, *Die Hirtenbriefe*, pp. 30–1); *Latin Letter to Wulfstan* II (*ibid.*, pp. 63–4); *Old English Letter to Wulfstan* II (*ibid.*, pp. 182–4) and *CH* II.xv (ed. Godden, p. 154).

[172] See above, pp. 41–2.

[173] Amalarius, *Liber officialis* III.xxv.9 (ed Hanssens II, 342–3).

was so important in the Good Friday liturgy and in the private prayers of the late Anglo-Saxon period with their stress on repentance and forgiveness[174] was irrelevant to Amalarius's understanding of the meaning of the mass where it was Christ's redemptive sacrifice which mattered.

Carolingian writers had maintained that the only true memorial of Christ's Passion was the eucharist;[175] the cross, though superior to other images,[176] was still only an image of Christ's humanity[177] to be left behind in order to adore and follow the risen Christ.[178] For the Anglo-Saxons, however, carvings and paintings, which were closely associated with liturgical celebrations, shared their function of making Christ present. Like the liturgy, art restored the memory by calling to mind the presence of Christ and his saints and by re-creating the gospel events; it aided the understanding both intellectually and experientially by setting out the theological significance of historical events and by allowing man to live through them in imagination; it aided the will by encouraging a response of love, gratitude or repentance. As Ælfric said in a homily for the feast of the Invention of the Cross:

Cristene men sceolon soðlice abugan to gehalgodre rode on ðæs hælendes naman, for ðan ðe we nabbað ða ðe he on ðrowade, ac hire anlicnys bið halig swa ðeah, to ðære we abugað on gebedum symle, to ðam mihtigan drihtne þe for mannum ðrowade, and seo rod is gemynd his mæran þrowunge, halig ðurh hine, ðeah ðe heo on holte weoxe. We hi wurðiað a, for wurðmynte Cristes, se ðe us alysde mid lufe ðurh hi, þæs we him ðanciað, symle on life.[179]

---

[174] See above, pp. 62, 66 and 95.
[175] *LC* II.xxvii (ed. Bastgen, pp. 88–9).
[176] *LC* I.xiii and II.xxviii (*ibid.*, pp. 33 and 89). [177] *LC* II.xv (*ibid.*, p. 75).
[178] *LC* II.xxviii (*ibid.*, p. 91).
[179] *CH* II.xviii (ed. Godden, pp. 175–6): 'Truly, Christian men should bow to the holy cross in the Saviour's name, because we do not possess the cross on which he suffered; nevertheless, its likeness is holy, and we always bow to it when we pray, to the powerful Lord who suffered for men; and that cross is a memorial of his mighty Passion, holy through him even though it grew in a wood. We always honour it, to honour Christ, who lovingly freed us through it; we always thank him for that in this life.' Cf. Amalarius, *Liber officialis* I.xiv.8 and 10 (ed. Hanssens II, 102).

Catalogue and index of works of art

This catalogue contains brief details of drawings, paintings, churches, carvings and other works of art referred to in the text, together with information about reproductions and references to catalogues and other standard works where full details of the items can be found. It is intended as a substitute for footnotes, not as a full catalogue of the works of art. For each entry I give first the origin and date of the work of art (if known), then references to photographs or plates, references to scholarly discussion and, finally, references to discussion in the present book.

AACHEN, CATHEDRAL TREASURY, Gospels of Otto III

Gospel-book

Reichenau, s. x/xi (983–1002)

16r, Otto crowned by the hand of God and surrounded by the four evangelist symbols; reproduced in Schnitzler, *Schatzkammer*, pl. 102, Elbern, *Das erste Jahrtausend* III, pl. 298 and Schramm and Mütherich, *Denkmale*, pl. 103

Kantorowicz, *King's Two Bodies*, pp. 61–78; Schnitzler, *Schatzkammer*, p. 30 (no. 35), pls. VII and 102–7; Elbern, *Das erste Jahrtausend* III, 66 (no. 298), pl. 298; Schramm and Mütherich, *Denkmale*, p. 154 (no. 103), pl. 103

Above, p. 139

AACHEN, CATHEDRAL TREASURY, ivory bookcover

Rhineland, s. xi/xii

Scenes of the Nativity, Baptism and Crucifixion; the latter includes figures of Mary and John, symbols of the sun and moon, a chalice and evangelist symbols; reproduced in Goldschmidt, *Elfenbeinskulpturen* II, pl. xlvii.167

Goldschmidt, *Elfenbeinskulpturen* II, 50 (no. 167), pl. xlvii.167

Above, p. 118

AACHEN, CATHEDRAL TREASURY, Lothar Cross

West German, s. x^2

Jewelled cross with classical cameo on the front; on the back, an engraving of Christ crucified, with a dove encircled in a wreath held in the hand of God above the cross, symbols of sun and moon on the arms of the cross and a serpent at the foot; reproduced in Schiller, *Iconography* II, pl. 395

Schnitzler, *Schatzkammer*, p. 29 (no. 32), pls. I and 90–5; Elbern, *Das erste Jahrtausend* III, 68 (no. 303), pl. 303; Schramm and Mütherich, *Denkmale*, p. 155 (no. 106), pl. 106

Above, pp. 113 and 115

Ælfwine Prayer-book: see LONDON, BRITISH LIBRARY, MS Cotton Titus D. xxvi + xxvii

ADMONT ABBEY, MS 289

Anselm, *Orationes sive meditationes*

Written in the Salzburg diocese, s. xii^{med}, perhaps for Abbess Diemuth of Traunkirchen, and copied from a manuscript sent by Anselm to Matilda of Tuscany in 1104.

83r, Mary Magdalen anointing Christ's feet; reproduced in Pächt, 'Anselm's Prayers and Meditations', pl. 22 (d)

The legends on the scrolls held by the figures are as follows: 'Dimissa sunt ei peccata multa'; 'Fides etenim salvam eam fecit'; 'Ovis abducta revocatur ad eterna gaudia' (See Buberl, *Steiermark*, p. 37)

Buberl, *Steiermark*, pp. 35–8; Pächt, 'Anselm's Prayers and Meditations'

Above, pp. 160–1.

AGRAM, CATHEDRAL TREASURY, ivory bookcover

Rhineland (?), s. xi

Gospel scenes from the Annunciation to the Ascension; the Crucifixion scene includes figures of Mary and John and one flying angel; reproduced in Goldschmidt, *Elfenbeinskulpturen* II, pl. xxi.62

Goldschmidt, *Elfenbeinskulpturen* II, 31–2 (no. 62), pl. xxi.62

Above, p. 117

Alcester Tau: see LONDON, BRITISH MUSEUM, MLA 1903, 3–23, 1

Alfred Jewel: see OXFORD, ASHMOLEAN MUSEUM, 1836.371

Alnmouth Cross: See NEWCASTLE UPON TYNE, MUSEUM OF ANTIQUITIES, no. 1958.8N

Anhalt-Morgan Gospels: see NEW YORK, PIERPONT MORGAN LIBRARY, MS 827

Arenberg Gospels: see NEW YORK, PIERPONT MORGAN LIBRARY, MS 869

Arnulf Ciborium: see MUNICH, SCHATZKAMMER DER RESIDENZ, Arnulf Ciborium

Arundel Psalter: see LONDON, BRITISH LIBRARY, MS Arundel 60

Athelstan Psalter: see LONDON, BRITISH LIBRARY, MS Cotton Galba A. xviii

AYCLIFFE, ST ANDREW, cross-shaft

Northern English, s. x/xi

Crucifixion panel with two soldiers, sun and moon; reproduced in Cramp, *Corpus* I, pl. 7

Cramp, *Corpus* I, 41–3 and pls. 7–8

Above, p. 150

Bamberg Bible: see BAMBERG, STAATSBIBLIOTHEK, Misc. class. Bibl. I {A. I. 5}

Bamberg Sacramentary: see MUNICH, BAYERISCHE STAATSBIBLIOTHEK, Cod. lat. 4456 (Sacramentary of Henry II)

BAMBERG, STAATSBIBLIOTHEK, Misc. class. Bibl. I {A. I. 5} (Bamberg Bible)

Bible

Tours, 834–43

339v, gospel frontispiece, showing the *Agnus Dei* with spear, sponge and chalice, evangelist symbols and representations of the four major prophets; reproduced in Koehler, *Karolingischen Miniaturen* I, pl. I, 56 (b) and Kessler, *Illustrated Bibles*, pl. 47

Koehler, *Karolingischen Miniaturen* I, Pt 1, 209–34 and 389–91, Pt 2, 102–5, pls. I, 55 (d)–58 (n); Kessler, *Illustrated Bibles*, pp. 42–53, pl. 47

Above, pp. 69 and 126

BARTON ON HUMBER, ST PETER

s. x^2

The Anglo-Saxon church consisted of a tower-nave with chancel to the east and baptistry to the west. Excavation within the church has revealed the position of the altar in the eastern porticus with traces of what may have been a screen behind it (see Rodwell and Rodwell, 'St Peter's Church'); a stone slab carved with a man's head above the arch leading from the nave to the chancel may have been a representation of Christ in Majesty (Rodwell and Rodwell, *ibid.*, p. 295, pl. xl, b). There is evidence for a rood-beam across the opening of the arch below this slab (Warwick Rodwell, private communication)

Taylor and Taylor, *Architecture* I, 52–7; Rodwell and Rodwell, 'St Peter's Church'; Rodwell, 'Anglo-Saxon Church Building'

Above, pp. 48 and 51

BAWIT, MONASTERY AND NECROPOLIS

Chapel 42, painting of the Ascension with a figure of Mary holding the Christ Child below; reproduced in Grabar, *Christian Iconography*, pl. 324.

Chapel 51, apse painting of the Ascension with the apostles holding bread and wine; reproduced in Grabar, *ibid.*, pl. 327

Grabar, *Christian Iconography*, pp. 134–5, pls. 324 and 327

Above, pp. 100–1

Benedictional of Archbishop Robert: see ROUEN, BIBLIOTHEQUE MUNICI-PALE, MS Y. 7 [369]

Benedictional of Æthelwold: see LONDON, BRITISH LIBRARY, MS Add. 49598

BERLIN, STAATSBIBLIOTHEK, MS Theol. lat. fol. 58, 120r (Psalter of Louis the German)

German, s. ix^ex; not part of the original manuscript

120r, picture of the Crucifixion with Mary, John, sun, moon and kneeling donor, accompanying a prayer to be said before the cross; the donor grips the stem of the cross with the left hand; reproduced in Goldschmidt, *German Illumination* I, pl. 63

Above, p. 159, n. 74

Bernward Cross: see HILDESHEIM CATHEDRAL, silver crucifix

Bernward Gospels: see HILDESHEIM CATHEDRAL, MS 18

Bernward Sacramentary: see HILDESHEIM CATHEDRAL, MS 19

Bernward Sarcophagus: see HILDESHEIM, ST MICHAEL, Bernward Sarcophagus

BIBURY, ST MARY

s. x/xi

Traces of the supporting figures from a Crucifixion group on the wall above the chancel arch

Taylor and Taylor, *Architecture* I, 63–6; Coatsworth, 'Pre-Conquest Sculptures', p. 188, pl. va

Above, p. 53

BISCHOFSHOFEN, PFARRHOF, processional or altar cross (Rupert Cross)

Processional or altar cross

English, s. viii/ix

Cross decorated with plant scrolls

Karl der Grosse, ed. Braunfels, p. 372 (no. 553), pl. 107; Wilson, 'Bedan Northumbria', pp. 14–16

Above, p. 61

BITTON, ST MARY

s. x/xi

Lower part of crucifix, with a serpent below the feet, on the wall above the chancel arch

Taylor and Taylor, *Architecture* I, 73–6; Coatsworth, 'Pre-Conquest Sculptures', p. 189

Above, pp. 53 and 137

BOBBIO, ABBEY OF ST COLUMBANUS, silver ampullae

Palestinian, s. vi²

Ampulla no. 20, Christ enthroned among angels wiith orant figure of Mary accompanied by John the Baptist and Zechariah, symbolizing the redemption; reproduced in Grabar, *Ampoules*, pl. liii, *Christian Iconography*, pl. 319

Grabar, *Ampoules*, pp. 43–4 and 60–1, pl. liii; Grabar, *Christian Iconography*, pp. 76 and 132–3, pl. 319

Above, p. 101

Book of Cerne: see CAMBRIDGE, UNIVERSITY LIBRARY, MS Ll. 1. 10

Book of Nunnaminster: see LONDON, BRITISH LIBRARY, MS Harley 2965

Bosworth Psalter: see LONDON, BRITISH LIBRARY, MS Add. 37517

BOULOGNE, BIBLIOTHEQUE MUNICIPALE, MS 11 (Boulogne Gospels)

Gospel-book

Saint-Bertin, s. x/xi (990–1007); illustrated by an English artist working on the continent who also illustrated Harley 2904

2r–9v, canon tables; 3v, 4r, 7r and 7v reproduced in Ohlgren, *Catalogue*, pls. 4–7

10r, Christ enthroned, a circlet on his head; reproduced in Dodwell, *Anglo-Saxon Art*, pl. 21

10v, St Matthew, with David, Abraham, Isaac and Jacob; reproduced in Ohlgren, *ibid.*, pl. 8

11r–11v, Christ's ancestors, the Annunciation and Visitation; 11r reproduced in Temple, *Anglo-Saxon Manuscripts*, pl. 147; 11v reprod. *Golden Age*, p. 62 and Ohlgren, *ibid.*, pl. 9

12r, opening of St Matthew's Gospel with the Nativity and annunciation to the shepherds; reproduced in Temple, *ibid.*, pl. 148 and *Golden Age*, p. 63

56r, opening of St Mark's Gospel with Christ enthroned with angels, Mark and Isaiah; reproduced in Temple, *ibid.*, pl. 150

62r, opening of St Luke's Gospel with the annunciation to Zechariah;

107r, portrait of St John, bearded; reproduced in Temple, *ibid.*, pl. 145; a similarly bearded figure of St John, by the same artist, occurs in New York, Pierpont Morgan Library, 827, 98v (Anhalt-Morgan Gospels), reproduced in Temple, *ibid.*, pl. 146

107v, opening of St John's Gospel with Christ adored by angels

Temple, *Anglo-Saxon Manuscripts*, pp. 66–7 (no. 44), pls. 145 and 147–50; *Golden Age*, pp. 60–5 (no. 42); Ohlgren, *Catalogue*, pp. 107–10 (no. 149), pls. 4–10

Above, pp. 84 and 133

BOULOGNE, BIBLIOTHEQUE MUNICIPALE, MS 20 (Odbert Psalter)

Psalter, hymnal

Saint-Bertin, s. x/xi (990–1007)

108r, the betrayal by Judas (Ps. C)

109r, the Crucifixion with the two soldiers, Mary and John, sun and moon; the Maries at the tomb; the Harrowing of Hell (Ps. CI); reproduced in Leroquais, *Psautiers*, pl. xxi

119v, the descent from the cross (Ps. CVI)

Leroquais, *Psautiers* I, 94–101, pls. xv–xxi

Above, pp. 77–8

Boulogne Gospels: see BOULOGNE, BIBLIOTHEQUE MUNICIPALE, MS 11

BRADFORD-ON-AVON, ST LAURENCE, carved angels

Southern English, s. x^2

Carved figures of two flying angels, probably part of a Crucifixion group similar to those in the Arenberg Gospels and the Sherborne Pontifical. The carvings are now above the chancel arch; they have been moved but have probably been replaced in their original position; reproduced in *Golden Age*, p. 130

Taylor and Taylor, *Architecture* I, 86–9; *Golden Age*, p. 130 (no. 135); Coatsworth, 'Pre-Conquest Sculptures', pp. 176–7 and 189, pls. IVa–IVb

Above, pp. 53 and 111

BRADWELL-ON-SEA, ST PETER ON THE WALL

s. vii²

Nave, foundations of apse and north and south porticus, triple arch between nave and apse

Taylor and Taylor, *Architecture* I, 91–3

Above, p. 52

BREAMORE, ST MARY

s. x²

Church with nave, choir, chancel, north and south porticus and western annexe. For a reconstruction of the original plan see Rodwell and Rouse, 'Anglo-Saxon Rood', p. 299, Rodwell, 'Anglo-Saxon Church Building', p. 157

Carving of Christ crucified with Mary and John and symbols of the sun and moon, much mutilated; now over the outside of the south door of the church but not in its original position; possibly originally over the chancel-arch or in a western annexe like the rood at Headbourne Worthy; detailed description in Rodwell and Rouse, 'Anglo-Saxon Rood'; reproduced in Rodwell and Rouse, *ibid.*, pls. xxxvi–xxxix

Taylor and Taylor, *Architecture* I, 94–6; Rodwell and Rouse, 'Anglo-Saxon Rood'; Rodwell, 'Anglo-Saxon Church Building'; Coatsworth, 'Pre-Conquest Sculptures', pp. 169–70 and 189, pl. Ic

Above, pp. 52, 53 and 129

BREEDON-ON-THE-HILL, ST MARY AND ST HARDULPH, carved friezes and figure panels

Midland English, s. viii and ix

Carved friezes with vinescroll, geometric patterns and figures; reproduced in Cramp, 'Mercian Sculpture', pls. 50–54 (b), 55, 57 (a), 58 (a) and (c), 59

Clapham, 'Carved Stones'; Taylor and Taylor, *Architecture* I, 97–8; Cramp, 'Mercian Sculpture', pp. 194–218; Jewell, 'Anglo-Saxon Friezes'

Above, p. 16

BREMEN, STAATSBIBLIOTHEK, MS b. 21 (Pericopes of Henry III)

Gospel-lectionary

Echternach, 1039–43

53r, paintings of the crowning with thorns and carrying of the cross; reproduced in Schiller, *Iconography* II, pl. 240

Boeckler, *Evangelienbuch*, pls. 185–91; Elbern, *Das erste Jahrtausend* III, 72–3 (nos. 330–1), pls. 330–1; Schramm and Mütherich, *Denkmale*, p. 173 (no. 153), pl. 153

Above, p. 8

BRIXWORTH, ALL SAINTS

s. vii^2 to x^2

Church with nave, choir, apsidal chancel, ring crypt and western porch, later raised to a tower. For a diagram of the probable form of the wall between nave and choir see Taylor, *Architecture* III, 793

Taylor and Taylor, *Architecture* I, 108–14; Taylor, *Architecture* III, 793

Above, p. 52

BRUNSWICK, HERZOG ANTON-ULRICH MUSEUM, Brunswick Casket

Ivory casket decorated with scenes from the gospels

Metz, s. ix

Long sides decorated with scenes of the Baptism and Crucifixion, ends with the Annunciation and Nativity; flying angels on the lid; the Crucifixion panel includes the soldiers and Ecclesia as well as John, Mary and other women; the lid on this side includes representations of the chariots of the sun and moon, angels and the hand of God holding a wreath

Goldschmidt, *Elfenbeinskulpturen* I, 52–3 (no. 96), pls. xliv–xlv.96 (a–e)

Above, pp. 94, 105, 117, 119 and 156

BRUSSELS, MUSEUM OF DECORATIVE ARTS, ivory panel from portable altar

s. xi^2

Crucifixion scene with Mary, John and two standing angels; reproduced in Goldschmidt, *Elfenbeinskulpturen* II, pl. xl.139

Goldschmidt, *Elfenbeinskulpturen* II, 43 (no. 139), pl. xl.139

Above, p. 117

BRUSSELS, PRIVATE COLLECTION, ivory panel of the Crucifixion (the Brussels Ivory)

Walrus ivory

Southern English, s. x/xi

Crucifix with Mary, John and crown-carrying angels in an eight-lobed frame

Beckwith, *Ivory Carvings*, p. 121 (no. 17), pl. 38

Above, pp. 111, 112, 119 and 128; pl. IIIa

Bury Psalter: see VATICAN CITY, BIBLIOTECA APOSTOLICA VATICANA, MS Regin. lat. 12

CAMBRIDGE, CORPUS CHRISTI COLLEGE, MS 23 (Cambridge Prudentius)

Prudentius, *Psychomachia*

Christ Church, Canterbury (?), s. x^{ex}; provenance Malmesbury

17v, drawing of a feast; reproduced in Temple, *Anglo-Saxon Manuscripts*, pl. 158

Stettiner, *Prudentius-Handschriften*, pls. 49–66; Ker, *Catalogue*, pp. 42–3 (no. 31); Temple, *Anglo-Saxon Manuscripts*, pp. 69–70 (no. 48), pls. 50 and 155–8; Ohlgren, *Catalogue*, pp. 112–20 (no. 153)

Above, pp. 27 and 112

CAMBRIDGE, CORPUS CHRISTI COLLEGE, MS 41

The Old English Bede; homilies and masses

s. xi^1, given by Leofric (*ob.* 1072) to Exeter

p. 410, initial Ð with Christ on the cross; reproduced in Temple, *Anglo-Saxon Manuscripts*, pl. 261

p. 484, sketch of Christ crucified, overwritten with a homily on the Passion; reproduced in Temple, *ibid.*, pl. 255

Ker, *Catalogue*, pp. 43–5 (no. 32); Grant, *Corpus Christi College 41*; Temple, *Anglo-Saxon Manuscripts*, pp. 98–9 (no. 81), pls. 255, 258 and 261; Ohlgren, *Catalogue*, pp. 201–3 (no. 186).

Above, pp. 83, 91, n. 1, 111, 112, 113, 115 and 119; pl. Va

CAMBRIDGE, CORPUS CHRISTI COLLEGE, MS 183

Bede, prose and verse *Vita S. Cuthberti*

South-west England (Glastonbury?), 934–5; given by Athelstan to the shrine of St Cuthbert at Chester-le-Street

1v, Athelstan presenting the book to St Cuthbert; reproduced in Temple, *Anglo-Saxon Manuscripts*, pl. 29 and *Golden Age*, p. 26

Ker, *Catalogue*, pp. 64–5 (no. 42); Temple, *Anglo-Saxon Manuscripts*, pp. 37–8 (no. 6), pls. 18, 19 and 29; *Golden Age*, pp. 26–7 (no. 6); Keynes, 'King Athelstan's Books', pp. 180–5; Ohlgren, *Catalogue*, pp. 72–3 (no. 84)

Above, p. 133

CAMBRIDGE, CORPUS CHRISTI COLLEGE, MS 286 (St Augustine's Gospels)

Gospel-book

Italian, s. vi

125r, scenes from the Passion story; reproduced in Wormald, *Collected Writings* I, pl. 1

129v, portrait of St Luke with scenes from the life of Christ; reproduced in Wormald, *ibid.*, pl. 2

F. Wormald, *Collected Writings* I, 13–35

Above, pp. 68–9

CAMBRIDGE, CORPUS CHRISTI COLLEGE, MS 391 (Portiforium Wulstani)

Worcester, s. xi²

pp. 581–618, private prayers, including Good Friday prayers (pp. 609–16, ptd Hughes, *Portiforium* II, pp. 18–23) and prayers to the cross for protection (pp. 617–18, ptd *ibid.*, p. 24)

Ker, *Catalogue*, pp. 113–15 (no. 67); Hughes, *Portiforium*; Ohlgren, *Catalogue*, p. 277 (no. 214)

Above, pp. 56–7, 62 and 166–7

CAMBRIDGE, CORPUS CHRISTI COLLEGE, MS 421 (Cambridge Homilies)

Anglo-Saxon homilies

s. xi¹

p. 1, Crucifixion; reproduced in Temple, *Anglo-Saxon Manuscripts*, pl. 254; originally part of the companion manuscript CCCC 419 (see Ker, *Catalogue*, p. 116)

Ker, *Catalogue*, pp. 117–18 (no. 69); Temple, *Anglo-Saxon Manuscripts*, p. 99 (no. 82), pl. 254; Ohlgren, *Catalogue*, pp. 203–4 (no. 187)

Above, pp. 89, 131, 137, 147 and 175, n. 78; pl. XI

CAMBRIDGE, CORPUS CHRISTI COLLEGE, MS 422, pp. 27–586 (Sherborne Missal)

Missal

Winchester, soon after 1060; provenance Sherborne

p. 52, *Vere dignum*, with Christ enthroned between angels; reproduced in Temple, *Anglo-Saxon Manuscripts*, pl. 301

p. 53, *Te igitur*, with Crucifixion; reproduced in Ohlgren, *Catalogue*, pl. 43

Ker, *Catalogue*, pp. 119–21 (no. 70); Temple, *Anglo-Saxon Manuscripts*, p. 121 (no. 104), pls. 300–1; Ohlgren, *Catalogue*, p. 274 (no. 209), pl. 43

Above, pp. 89, 92, 96, 151–5, 156–7 and 158; pl. XIIb

Cambridge Crucifixion Panel: see CAMBRIDGE, FITZWILLIAM MUSEUM, Ivory no. M 24–1938

CAMBRIDGE, FITZWILLIAM MUSEUM, Ivory no. M 24–1938 (Cambridge Crucifixion Panel)

> Walrus ivory
>
> Southern English, s. x/xi
>
> Crucifixion with Mary, John and two flying angels
>
> Beckwith, *Ivory Carvings*, p. 126 (no. 38), pl. 72
>
> Above, pp. 105, n. 74, 111, 112, 119 and 128; pl. 111b

Cambridge Homilies: see CAMBRIDGE, CORPUS CHRISTI COLLEGE, MS 421

CAMBRIDGE, MUSEUM OF ARCHAEOLOGY AND ETHNOLOGY, ivory carving of the Last Judgement

> Walrus ivory
>
> s. x/xi, found at North Elmham, Norfolk
>
> Christ enthroned in a mandorla and accompanied by Mary and Peter; below, a cross held by two flying angels and accompanied by eight standing figures; the inscription on the mandorla is, 'O vos omnes videte manus et pedes meos'
>
> Goldschmidt, *Elfenbeinskulpturen* IV, 9 (no. 2), pl. i.2; Beckwith, *Ivory Carvings*, p. 121 (no. 18), pl. 41
>
> Above, p. 63

CAMBRIDGE, PEMBROKE COLLEGE, MS 301

> Gospel-book
>
> s. xi^{in}
>
> 2v, canon table with female saints; reproduced in Temple, *Anglo-Saxon Manuscripts*, pl. 233
>
> 10v, portrait of St Matthew, with saints in border medallions; reproduced in Temple, *ibid.*, pl. 234 and *Golden Age*, p. 71
>
> Temple, *Anglo-Saxon Manuscripts*, pp. 91–2 (no. 73), pls. 233–6; *Golden Age*, pp. 69 and 71 (no. 53); Ohlgren, *Catalogue*, pp. 193–5 (no. 178)
>
> Above, p. 23

Cambridge Prudentius: see CAMBRIDGE, CORPUS CHRISTI COLLEGE, MS 23

CAMBRIDGE, TRINITY COLLEGE, MS B. 10. 4 (Trinity Gospels)

> Gospel-book

s. xi^in; written by the same scribe as the Sacramentary of Robert of Jumièges

16v, Christ in Majesty; reproduced in Temple, *Anglo-Saxon Manuscripts*, pl. 212 and *Golden Age*, pl. xiii

17v, portrait of St Matthew, with saints in border medallions; reproduced in Temple, *ibid.*, pl. 214

60r, opening of St Mark's Gospel, with saints in border medallions; reproduced in Temple, *ibid.*, pl. 219

Temple, *Anglo-Saxon Manuscripts*, pp. 83–4 (no. 65), pls. 212, 214 and 219; *Golden Age*, p. 68 (no. 49), pl. xiii; Keynes, *Anglo-Saxon Manuscripts*, pp. 31–2; Ohlgren, *Catalogue*, pp. 182–5 (no. 170)

Above, pp. 23, 84, 133 and 140

CAMBRIDGE, TRINITY COLLEGE, MS B. 15. 34

Ælfric, Homilies

Christ Church, Canterbury (?), s. xi^med

1r, Christ as judge; reproduced in Temple, *Anglo-Saxon Manuscripts*, pl. 241 and *Golden Age*, p. 79

Ker, *Catalogue*, pp. 130–2 (no. 86); Temple, *Anglo-Saxon Manuscripts*, p. 92 (no. 74), pl. 241; *Golden Age*, pp. 78–9 (no. 63); Keynes, *Anglo-Saxon Manuscripts*, pp. 33–4; Ohlgren, *Catalogue*, p. 195 (no. 179)

Above, p. 133

CAMBRIDGE, TRINITY COLLEGE, MS B. 16. 3

Hrabanus Maurus, *De laudibus sanctae crucis*

s. x^med

30v, Hrabanus Maurus venerating the cross; reproduced in Temple, *Anglo-Saxon Manuscripts*, pl. 46; there is a similar picture in CUL, Gg, 5. 35, 225r, see Ohlgren, *Catalogue*, pp. 301–3 (no. 224), pl. 50

Temple, *Anglo-Saxon Manuscripts*, pp. 42–3 (no. 14), pls. 45, 46 and 48; Keynes, *Anglo-Saxon Manuscripts*, pp. 10–12; Ohlgren, *Catalogue*, pp. 77–8 (no. 92)

Above, p. 63

CAMBRIDGE, UNIVERSITY LIBRARY, MS Ff. 1. 23 (Winchcombe Psalter)

Roman psalter with Old English gloss

s. xi^med

4v, David with his musicians (Ps. 1); reproduced in Temple, *Anglo-Saxon Manuscripts*, pl. 249

88r, Crucifixion (Ps. LI); reproduced in F. Wormald, *English Drawings*, pl. 21

171r, Christ with angels (Ps. CI); reproduced in Temple, *Anglo-Saxon Manuscripts*, pl. 253

195v, Christ above the beasts (Ps. CIX); reproduced in Ohlgren, *Catalogue*, pl. 30

Ker, *Catalogue*, pp. 11–12 (no. 13); Temple, *Anglo-Saxon Manuscripts*, pp. 97–8 (no. 80), pls. 249–53; *Golden Age*, pp. 78 and 80 (no. 64); Ohlgren, *Catalogue*, pp. 200–1 (no. 185), pl. 30

Above, pp. 23, 32, 36, 58, n. 90, 86, 96, 97, 131, 150, 156, n. 61, 159, 175, n. 78 and 176, n. 85; pl. X

CAMBRIDGE, UNIVERSITY LIBRARY, MS Ll. 1. 10 (Book of Cerne)

Prayers and other religious texts

s. ix[1]

3r–12r, Passion and Resurrection according to Matthew; ptd Kuypers, *Book of Cerne*, pp. 5–23

13r–20v, Passion and Resurrection according to Mark; ptd Kuypers, *ibid.*, pp. 25–40

22r–31r, Passion and Resurrection according to Luke; ptd Kuypers, *ibid.*, pp. 43–61

32r–40r, Passion and Resurrection according to John; ptd Kuypers, *ibid.*, pp. 63–79

57v–59r, prayer *Domine Iesu Christe adoro te*; ptd Kuypers, *ibid.*, pp. 114–17

Kuypers, *Book of Cerne*; Ker, *Catalogue*, pp. 39–40 (no. 27); Alexander, *Insular Manuscripts*, pp. 84–5 (no. 66), pls. 310–15; Ohlgren, *Catalogue*, pp. 58–9 (no. 66)

Above, pp. 56, 57, 59 and 166

CANTERBURY, ST PANCRAS

s. vii[1]

Church with western porch, nave, north and south porticus and eastern apse screened from the nave by a triple arcade

Taylor and Taylor, *Architecture* I, 146–8

Above, p. 52

Charles the Bald's Prayer-book: see MUNICH, SCHATZKAMMER DER RESIDENZ, Prayer-book of Charles the Bald

Charter of New Minster: see LONDON, BRITISH LIBRARY, MS Cotton Vespasian A. viii

Cluny Portable Altar: see PARIS, MUSEE DE CLUNY, CL 11.459

Codex Aureus of St Emmeram: see MUNICH, BAYERISCHE STAATSBIBLIOTHEK, Cod. lat. 14000

Codex Egberti: see TRIER, STADTBIBLIOTHEK, MS 24

COLOGNE CATHEDRAL, Gero Cross

> Cologne, 970–6
>
> Wooden crucifix showing the dead Christ
>
> Elbern, *Das erste Jahrtausend* III, 79 (no. 365), pl. 365; Hausherr, *Der tote Christus*
>
> Above, p. 115

COLOGNE, CATHEDRAL TREASURY, tau cross (Heribert Cross)

> Walrus ivory
>
> Southern English, s. xi^{in}
>
> The ivory head shows Christ on the cross accompanied by Mary, John and symbols of the sun and moon and, on the other side, Christ enthroned with angels; the silver mounts are engraved with figures of the visit to the tomb and the Harrowing of Hell
>
> Goldschmidt, *Elfenbeinskulpturen* IV, 11 (no. 10), pl. ii.10 (a–b); Beckwith, *Ivory Carvings*, p. 124 (no. 30), pls. 80 and 81
>
> Above, pp. 61 and 129

Cologne Tau: see COLOGNE, CATHEDRAL TREASURY, tau cross

Copenhagen Crucifixion Panel: see COPENHAGEN, NATIONALMUSEET, Inv. no. D 13324

COPENHAGEN, NATIONALMUSEET, Inv. no. D 13324 (Copenhagen Crucifixion panel)

> Walrus ivory
>
> Southern English, s. x/xi
>
> Crucifix accompanied by Mary, John and two flying angels in an eight-lobed frame; Mary wears a crown; the beading across the top of Christ's head may also be intended as a crown
>
> Beckwith, *Ivory Carvings*, p. 144 (no. 17a), illustration p. 6
>
> Above, pp. 105, n. 74, 111, 112, 119 and 128; pl. IVa

Cuthbert Coffin: see DURHAM CATHEDRAL, Cuthbert Coffin

Cuthbert Cross: see DURHAM CATHEDRAL, Cuthbert Cross

DAGLINGWORTH, HOLY CROSS

s. x/xi

Carved panels showing the Crucifixion with the two soldiers, Christ enthroned and St Peter; Crucifixion panels described in Coatsworth, 'Pre-Conquest Sculptures', pp. 179 and 193

Taylor and Taylor, *Architecture* I, 187–90; Coatsworth, 'Pre-Conquest Sculptures', pp. 179 and 193, pl. vb

Above, p. 150

Damme Fragments: see MALIBU, CALIFORNIA, J. PAUL GETTY MUSEUM, MS9

DARMSTADT, HESSISCHES LANDESMUSEUM, ivory bookcover

Cologne, s. xi^{med}

Crucifixion scene with Mary, John, Ecclesia, Synagogue, evangelist symbols and chalice; reproduced in Goldschmidt, *Elfenbeinskulpturen* II, pl. xviii.59

Goldschmidt, *Elfenbeinskulpturen* II, 30 (no. 59), pl. xviii.59

Above, p. 118, n. 47

DEERHURST, ST MARY

s. vii–xi

Church with porch, later raised to a tower, nave, choir, north and south porticus and apsidal chancel

Carving of the Virgin and Child over the door from porch to nave, but possibly not in its original position; reproduced but without the head, Rice, *English Art*, pl. 18 (a)

Carving of an angel on the outside of the chancel; reproduced *ibid.*, pl. 8 (b)

Taylor and Taylor, *Architecture* I, 193–209

Above, pp. 18 and 52

Douce Psalter: see OXFORD, BODLEIAN LIBRARY, MS Douce 296

DOVER, ST MARY IN CASTRO

s. x²

Church with nave, choir, chancel and north and south porticus

Taylor and Taylor, *Architecture* I, 214–17

Above, p. 52

Drogo Sacramentary: see PARIS, BIBLIOTHEQUE NATIONALE, MS lat. 9428

DUBLIN, COLLECTION OF MR JOHN HUNT, ivory panel of the Crucifixion

Walrus ivory

Southern English, s. x/xi

Crucifix with four evangelist symbols

Beckwith, *Ivory Carvings*, p. 126 (no. 37), pl. 74

Above, p. 114

Dunstan Classbook: see OXFORD, BODLEIAN LIBRARY, MS Auct. F. 4. 32

DURHAM CATHEDRAL, Cuthbert Coffin

Lindisfarne, 698

Wooden coffin, carved with figures of seven angels, twelve apostles, the Virgin and Child and Christ with the evangelist symbols; reproduced in Battiscombe, *Relics*, pls. IV–XI

Battiscombe, *Relics*, pp. 202–307, pls. IV–XI; Cronyn and Horie, *Coffin*

Above, p. 19

DURHAM CATHEDRAL, Cuthbert Cross

s. vii

Gold and garnet pectoral cross with central shell boss; reproduced in Battiscombe, *Relics*, pls. XV–XVI

Battiscombe, *Relics*, pp. 308–25, pls. XV–XVI, reprinted with revisions, Bruce-Mitford, *Aspects*, pp. 281–302, pls. 94–5

Above, p. 61

DURHAM, CATHEDRAL LIBRARY, MS A. II. 17 (Durham Gospels)

Gospel-book

Lindisfarne (?), s. vii/viii; at Chester-le-Street in s. x

38₃v, Crucifixion picture with robed Christ, accompanied by angels and two soldiers; reproduced in Mynors, *Durham Cathedral Manuscripts*, pl. 3 and Alexander, *Insular Manuscripts*, pl. 202; inscriptions ptd Mynors, *ibid.*, p. 17 and Alexander, *ibid.*, p. 41; the picture follows the end of St Matthew's Gospel

Mynors, *Durham Cathedral Manuscripts*, pp. 15–17, pls. 2–3; Ker, *Catalogue*, p. 144 (no. 105); Werckmeister, 'Three Problems of Tradition', pp. 181–9; Alexander, *Insular Manuscripts*, pp. 40–2 (no. 10), pls. 47 and 202; facsimile: *Durham Gospels*; Ohlgren, *Catalogue*, pp. 9–11 (no. 10)

Above, pp. 108–9

ESSEN, MINSTER TREASURY, ivory bookcover

s. xi^med

Scenes of the Nativity, Crucifixion, Ascension and evangelist symbols; the Crucifixion scene includes Mary, John, Ecclesia, Synagogue, the soldiers, the thieves and the dead rising; above the cross is a jewelled circlet in the hand of God; reproduced in Goldschmidt, *Elfenbeinskulpturen* II, pl. xviii.58

Goldschmidt, *Elfenbeinskulpturen* II, 29–30 (no. 58), pl. xviii.58

Above, p. 134, n. 28

ESSEN, MINSTER TREASURY, Matilda Cross

Essen (?), s.xi^1; the figure of Christ is a replacement, s. xi^2

Jewelled gold cross with figure of the crucified Christ

Schnitzler, *Schatzkammer*, p. 33 (no. 45), pls. 150–3; Elbern, *Das erste Jahrtausend* III, 82 (no. 378), pl. 378

Above, pp. 113 and 114

ESSEN, MINSTER TREASURY, Otto Cross

Rhineland, 973–82

Jewelled gold cross with Christ crucified on the front, a serpent beneath his feet

Schnitzler, *Schatzkammer*, p. 32 (no. 43), pls. 142–5; Elbern, *Das erste Jahrtausend* III, 82 (no. 376), pl. 376

Above, pp. 113 and 114

ESSEN, MINSTER TREASURY, Theophanu Cross

West German, s. xi^med

Jewelled gold reliquary cross

Schnitzler, *Schatzkammer*, p. 33 (no. 46), pls. 154–6; Elbern, *Das erste Jahrtausend* III, 83 (no. 379), pl. 379

Above, p. 113

FLETTON, ST MARGARET, carved friezes and figure panels

s. viii/ix

Standing figures of a saint and an angel framed by arches; busts of saints and angels in friezes; reproduced in Cramp, 'Mercian Sculpture', pl. 56 (a–b)

Clapham, 'Carved Stones', pp. 235–6, pl. xl (1–4); Cramp, 'Mercian Sculpture', pp. 207–11, pl. 56 (a–b)

Above, p. 16

FLORENCE, BIBLIOTECA MEDICEA LAURENZIANA, MS Plutarch i. 56
(Rabbula Gospels)

Gospel-book

Syriac; written at the monastery of St John of Zagba, Mesopotamia, AD 586

Canon tables with figures of Old Testament characters and gospel scenes; full-page miniatures of the Crucifixion, Resurrection, Ascension and Pentecost

3v, the annunciation to Zechariah; Cecchelli, *Rabbula Gospels*, pp. 53–4

4v, the Massacre of the Innocents; *ibid.*, p. 55

5r, the marriage at Cana; *ibid.*, pp. 56–7

13r, the Crucifixion; *ibid.*, pp. 69–71

13v, the Ascension; *ibid.*, pp. 71–2

Facsimile: Cecchelli *et al.*, *Rabbula Gospels*

Above, pp. 68, 69, 70, 100 and 156

FLORENCE, BIBLIOTECA MEDICEA LAURENZIANA, MS Plutarch xvii. 20

Gospel-lectionary

Christ Church, Canterbury, s. xi¹

1r, Christ accompanied by SS Peter and Paul; reproduced in Temple, *Anglo-Saxon Manuscripts*, pl. 232

Temple, *Anglo-Saxon Manuscripts*, p. 88 (no. 69), pl. 232; Ohlgren, *Catalogue*, p. 189 (no. 174)

Above, p. 133, n. 16

FLORENCE, MUSEO NAZIONALE, ivory bookcover

Metz school, s. ix/x

Crucifixion scene with Mary, John, Ecclesia, Synagogue, sun, moon, angels, soldiers and the dead rising; a jewelled circlet in the hand of God above the cross; reproduced in Goldschmidt, *Elfenbeinskulpturen* I, pl. l.114

Goldschmidt, *Elfenbeinskulpturen* I, 58 (no. 114), pl. l.114

Above, p. 134, n. 28

GANNAT, CHURCH OF THE HOLY CROSS, ivory bookcover

Metz school, s. ix/x; on a gospel-book of s. x

Crucifixion scene with Mary, John, Ecclesia, Synagogue, sun, moon, angels, soldiers, serpent and the dead rising; below is a scene of the women at the tomb; reproduced in Goldschmidt, *Elfenbeinskulpturen* I, pl. xxxviii.89

Goldschmidt, *Elfenbeinskulpturen* I, 49–50 (no. 89), pl. xxxviii.89

Above, p. 116, n. 34.

Gellone: see PARIS, BIBLIOTHEQUE NATIONALE, MS lat. 12048 (Sacramentary of Gellone)

Gero Cross: see COLOGNE CATHEDRAL, Gero Cross

GLOUCESTER, ST OSWALD

s. ix^{ex}–x^{ex}

Church with western apse, nave, choir, chancel, north and south porticus; later eastern crypt

Heighway and Bryant, 'St Oswald, Gloucester'

Above, pp. 13, n. 54 and 52

Godescalc Gospels: see PARIS, BIBLIOTHEQUE NATIONALE, Nouvelles acquisitions latines 1203

Godwine Seal: see LONDON, BRITISH MUSEUM, MLA 1881, 4–4, 1, Godwine Seal

Golden Altar of St Ambrose, Milan: see MILAN, SANT'AMBROGIO, Golden Altar

Golden Gospels of Henry III: see MADRID, ESCORIAL, Cod. Vetrinas 17

GOSFORTH, cross

Cumbria, s. x/xi

The Crucifixion scene includes figures of Longinus and a woman holding a horn, possibly Mary Magdalen; reproduced in Bailey and Cramp, *Corpus* II, pl. 304

Bailey, *Viking Age Sculpture*, pp. 125–31, figs. 3, 23 and 60, pl. 32; Bailey and Cramp, *Corpus* II, pp. 100–4, pls. 288–308

Above, p. 150

Gospels of Gundold: see STUTTGART, WURTTEMBERGISCHE LANDESBIBLIOTHEK, Cod. Bibl. 402

Gospels of Otfrid of Weissenburg: see VIENNA, NATIONALBIBLIOTHEK, MS 2687 [Theol. 345]

Gospels of Otto III: see MUNICH, BAYERISCHE STAATSBIBLIOTHEK, Cod. lat. 4453

Gospels of Saint-Médard of Soissons: see PARIS, BIBLIOTHEQUE NATIONALE, MS lat. 8850

Grandval Bible: see LONDON, BRITISH LIBRARY, MS Add. 10546

Grimbald Gospels: see LONDON, BRITISH LIBRARY, MS Add. 34890

HANOVER, KESTNER MUSEUM, MS WM xxi^a 36 (Eadwig Gospels)

Gospel-book

Christ Church, Canterbury, s. xi[1]

147v, bearded figure of St John; reproduced in Temple, *Anglo-Saxon Manuscripts*, pl. 227

Temple, *Anglo-Saxon Manuscripts*, pp. 85–6 (no. 67), pls. 224–9; *Golden Age*, p. 72 (no. 56), pl. xvii; Ohlgren, *Catalogue*, pp. 186–8 (no. 172)

Above, p. 133

HANOVER, NIEDERSACHSISCHES LANDESMUSEUM, left half of ivory diptych

Byzantine, s. x^{med}

Crucifix with angels, labelled 'Michael' and 'Gabriel', Mary and John; deposition

Goldschmidt and Weitzmann, *Elfenbeinskulpturen* II, 37 (no. 40), pl. xvii.40; Elbern, *Das erste Jahrtausend* III, 70–1 (no. 318), pl. 318

Above, p. 117

Harley Gospels: see LONDON, BRITISH LIBRARY, MS Harley 2788

Harley Psalter: see LONDON, BRITISH LIBRARY, MS Harley 603

HEADBOURNE WORTHY, ST SWITHUN

s. x/xi

Carved Crucifixion group with Christ, Mary and John, over the western entrance to the church in an annexe; the carving, which is badly mutilated, seems to be in its original position; reproduced in Coatsworth, 'Pre-Conquest Sculptures', pl. 1d
Taylor and Taylor, *Architecture* I 289–91; Coatsworth, 'Pre-Conquest Sculptures', pp. 170–1 and 190, pl. 1d

Above, p. 53

Hedda Stone: see PETERBOROUGH CATHEDRAL, Hedda Stone

Heinrichsportatile: see MUNICH, SCHATZKAMMER DER RESIDENZ, Heinrichsportatile

Hereford Troper: see LONDON, BRITISH LIBRARY, MS Cotton Caligula A. xiv

Heribert Cross: see COLOGNE, CATHEDRAL TREASURY, tau cross

HILDESHEIM CATHEDRAL, MS 18 (Bernward Gospels)

Gospel-book

Hildesheim, *c.* 1014

16v–17r, Bernward presenting the book to the Virgin Mary; reproduced in Tschan, *Bernward* III, pls. 57–8

18r, the Nativity; the Magi with the star; reproduced *ibid.* III, pl. 59

18v, the calling of Matthew; the meal at Matthew's house; reproduced *ibid.* III, pl. 60

19r, Matthew with his symbol; reproduced *ibid.* III, pl. 61

75r, John the Baptist; Christ with his disciples; reproduced *ibid.* III, pl. 64

75v, Christ and Mary Magdalen in the garden; Peter handing his gospel to Mark; reproduced *ibid.* III, pl. 65

76r, Mark with his symbol; reproduced *ibid.* III, pl. 66

111r, the annunciation to Zechariah; Zechariah struck dumb; reproduced *ibid.* III, pl. 68

111v, the visitation; the naming of John the Baptist; reproduced *ibid.* III, pl. 69

118r, the Last Supper; Judas with the high priests; reproduced *ibid.* III, pl. 70

118v, Luke with his symbol; the Crucifixion with Mary and John, symbols of the sun and moon and of Oceanus and Gaia; reproduced *ibid.* III, pl. 71

174r, Christ holding a medallion with a lamb and accompanied by two seraphs; the nativity with Oceanus and Gaia and Eve taking the apple from the serpent's mouth; reproduced *ibid.* III, pl. 73

174v, the Baptism of Christ; the raising of Lazarus; reproduced *ibid.* III, pl. 74

175r, the entry to Jerusalem; the Crucifixion with John, Mary and Mary Magdalen, the empty tomb to the right; reproduced *ibid.* III, pl. 75

175v, John with his symbol; the Ascension; reproduced *ibid.* III, pl. 76

Tschan, *Bernward* II, 35–54, III, pls. 54–78

Above, pp. 8, 47, 73, 74–5 and 135

HILDESHEIM CATHEDRAL, MS 19 (Bernward Sacramentary)

Sacramentary

Hildesheim, 1014–22

4v, *Te igitur* with Christ on the cross, Mary and John; reproduced in Tschan, *Bernward* III, pl. 45

Tschan, *Bernward* II, 31–5, III, pls. 31–53

Above, p. 81

HILDESHEIM CATHEDRAL, silver crucifix (Bernward Cross)

Hildesheim, 1007–22

Christ hanging dead on the cross, left foot in profile; *Agnus Dei* on the reverse

Tschan, *Bernward* II, 98–111, III, pls. 91–2

Above, p. 115

HILDESHEIM, ST GODEHARD, psalter (St Albans Psalter)

Gallican psalter and other texts

St Albans, s. xii^{in} (1119–23)

pp. 17–55, gospel scenes and scenes of the fall of man; reproduced in Pächt, *St Albans Psalter*, pls. 14–33.

Pächt *et al.*, *St Albans Psalter*; Kauffmann, *Romanesque Manuscripts*, pp. 68–70 (no. 29), pls. 72–4, 76 and 78, fig. 22

Above, pp. 94, n. 14 and 105, n. 75

HILDESHEIM, ST MICHAEL, Bernward Sarcophagus

s. xi^{in}

Gabled sarcophagus decorated with the *Agnus Dei* on one gable and a cross on the other; roof decorated with busts of nine angels; inscription, 'Scio enim quod redemptor meus vivit et in novissimo die de terra surrecturus sum. Et rursum circumdabor pelle mea et in carne mea videbo Deum, Salvatorem meum, quem visurus sum ego ipse et oculi mei conspecturi sunt et non alius. Reposita est hec spes mea in sinu meo' (Job XIX.25–7)

Tschan, *Bernward* I, 205–9, III, pls 260–7

Above, p. 19

Ixworth Cross: see OXFORD, ASHMOLEAN MUSEUM, 1909.453, Ixworth Cross

Judith of Flanders, Gospels: see NEW YORK, PIERPONT MORGAN LIBRARY, MSS 708 and 709

Junius Psalter: see OXFORD, BODLEIAN LIBRARY, MS Junius 27

Lanalet Pontifical: see ROUEN, BIBLIOTHEQUE MUNICIPALE, MS A. 27 [368]

LANGFORD, ST MATTHEW

s. xi^2

Anglo-Saxon tower

Robed figure of Christ crucified, now on east wall of the porch; reproduced in Rice, *English Art*, pl. 17

Carved Crucifixion panel, with Christ, Mary and John, now over the porch door; not in its original position; reproduced in Coatsworth, 'Pre-Conquest Sculptures', pl. IIIa

Taylor and Taylor, *Architecture* I, 367–72; Coatsworth, 'Pre-Conquest Sculptures', pp. 173–5 and 190, pl. IIIa

Above, p. 92

LEIPZIG, STADTBIBLIOTHEK, MS cxc (sacramentary fragment)

s. x

IV, fragment of a sacramentary of s. x stitched into a gospel-book from Reichenau and showing a crucifix with Mary and John; reproduced in Goldschmidt, *German Illumination* I, pl. 84 (a) and Schiller, *Iconography* II, pl. 383

The inscriptions on the frame and background to the painting are: 'Fulgida stella maris pro cunctis posce misellis'; 'Et tu iunge preces cum virgine virgo Iohannes'; 'Annuat hoc agnus mundi pro peste peremptus'; 'In cruce Christe tua confige nocentia cuncta'; 'Stella maris'; 'Virgo Iohannes'

Goldschmidt, *German Illumination* I, pl. 84 (a); Merton, *Buchmalerei*, pp. 83 and 88, pl. xcvii (2)

Above, pp. 81–2 and 102

Leofric Missal: see OXFORD, BODLEIAN LIBRARY, MS Bodley 579

Liber vitae of New Minster: see LONDON, BRITISH LIBRARY, MS Stowe 944

LIMBURG, CATHEDRAL TREASURY, Petrus Staff

Trier, *c.* 980

Staff reliquary decorated with gold reliefs and enamels

Schnitzler, *Schatzkammer*, pp. 24–5 (no. 13), pl. 48; Elbern, *Das erste Jahrtausend* III, 73–4 (nos. 334 and 335), pls. 334–5

Above, p. 114

Lindau Gospels: see NEW YORK, PIERPONT MORGAN LIBRARY, MS 1

LIVERPOOL MUSEUM, Féjerváry Coll., no. 36

Ivory carving of the Crucifixion and the women at the tomb

s. ix[1]; one of a group of ivories possibly associated with the court of Louis the Pious

The Crucifixion scene includes the soldiers, Mary and John and symbols of the sun and moon. The scene of the women at the tomb seems to have been copied from an early Christian ivory, s. iv/v, now at Munich (Lasko, *Ars Sacra*, p. 37)

Goldschmidt, *Elfenbeinskulpturen* I, 68–9 (no. 139), pl. lix.139; Lasko, *Ars Sacra*, p. 37, pl. 31

Above, p. 115

LONDON, BRITISH LIBRARY, MS Add. 10546 (Grandval Bible)

Bible

Tours, 834–43

352v, gospel frontispiece showing Christ in Majesty with evangelist symbols and representations of the four major prophets; reproduced in Koehler, *Karolingischen Miniaturen*, pl. I, 52 and Kessler, *Illustrated Bibles*, pl. 48

Koehler, *Karolingischen Miniaturen*, I, Pt 1, 194–209 and 386–7, Pt 2, 13–27, pls. I, 42–53; facsimile: Duft *et al.*, *Die Bibel von Moutier-Grandval*; Kessler, *Illustrated Bibles*, pp. 36–58, pl. 48

Above, pp. 69 and 70

LONDON, BRITISH LIBRARY, MS Add. 34890 (Grimbald Gospels)

Gospel-book

Christ Church, Canterbury, s. xi¹

114v–115r, opening of St John's Gospel; reproduced in *Golden Age*, pl. xvi

Temple, *Anglo-Saxon Manuscripts*, pp. 86–8 (no. 68), pls. 215 and 218; *Golden Age*, p. 72 (no. 55), pl. xvi; Ohlgren, *Catalogue*, pp. 188–9 (no. 173)

Above, pp. 36–7, 38, 39 and 175, n. 79

LONDON, BRITISH LIBRARY, MS Add. 37517 (Bosworth Psalter)

Roman psalter, hymns and canticles

Canterbury, s. x^{ex}

Decorated initials, 4r, 33r, 64v, 74r, 94v

Ker, *Catalogue*, pp. 161–2 (no. 129); Temple, *Anglo-Saxon Manuscripts*, pp. 48–9 (no. 22), pls. 81–3; *Golden Age*, pp. 55–9 (no. 36), pl. v; Ohlgren, *Catalogue*, p. 86 (no. 110)

Above, p. 23

LONDON, BRITISH LIBRARY, MS Add. 49598 (Benedictional of Æthelwold)

Benedictional

Winchester, 971–84; written by the monk Godeman at the command of Æthelwold and for his personal use

1r–4r, groups of saints, including (4r) St Peter holding a cross and keys

5v, Annunciation

9v, the second coming

24v, the Adoration of the Magi

45v, the entry to Jerusalem

51v, the Maries at the tomb

56v, doubting Thomas

70r, initial with figure of Christ enthroned and wearing a diadem

90v, St Æthelthryth

95v, the martyrdom of St Peter

118v, Æthelwold celebrating mass

Facsimile: Warner and Wilson, *Benedictional*; dedicatory poem trans. F. Wormald, 'Benedictional', pp. 85–6; Temple, *Anglo-Saxon Manuscripts*, pp. 49–53 (no. 23), pls. 85, 86, 88, 90 and 91; *Golden Age*, p. 59 (no. 37), pl. vi; Ohlgren, *Catalogue*, pp. 86–90 (no. 111); Prescott, 'Benedictional of St Æthelwold'

Above, pp. 9, 23, 24, 28–30, 31, 34, 35, 38, 39, 46, 47, 61, 87, 94, 105, 117, 127, 131, 133, 145–6, 147, 149, 152 and 156

LONDON, BRITISH LIBRARY, MS Arundel 60 (Arundel Psalter)

Gallican psalter with Old English gloss

Winchester, New Minster, s. xi^{med}, with later additions

12v, Crucifixion (Ps. I); reproduced in Temple, *Anglo-Saxon Manuscripts*, pl. 312 and *Golden Age*, p. 82

52v, Crucifixion added after the Norman Conquest (Ps. LI); reproduced in Dodwell, *Canterbury School*, pl. 72 (f)

Ker, *Catalogue*, pp. 166–7 (no. 134); Temple, *Anglo-Saxon Manuscripts*, p. 120 (no. 103), pl. 312; *Golden Age*, pp. 82–3 (no. 67); Ohlgren, *Catalogue*, pp. 272–4 (no. 208)

Above, pp. 38, 59, 86, 91, n. 1, 95, 102, n. 61, 105, n. 74, 114, 115, 130, 150, 159, 175, n. 78 and 176, n. 85; pl. IX

LONDON, BRITISH LIBRARY, MS Arundel 155 (Eadwig Psalter)

Roman psalter with Gallican corrections, private prayers

Christ Church, Canterbury, 1012–23

12r, 53r and 93r, decorated initials to Psalms I, LI and CI, the third showing

David and Goliath; reproduced in Temple, *Anglo-Saxon Manuscripts*, pls. 216, 217 and 220

133r, St Benedict with the monks of Canterbury; reproduced in Temple, *ibid.*, pl. 213 and *Golden Age*, pl. xviii

172r–v, prayers to the cross similar to the Good Friday prayers in the *Regularis concordia*

Ker, *Catalogue*, pp. 167–71 (no. 135); Temple, *Anglo-Saxon Manuscripts*, pp. 84–5 (no. 66), pls. 213, 216, 217 and 220; *Golden Age*, pp. 72–4 (no. 57), pl. xviii; Ohlgren, *Catalogue*, pp. 185–6 (no. 171)

Above, pp. 23, 32, 37 and 58

LONDON, BRITISH LIBRARY, MS Cotton Caligula A. xiv (Hereford Troper)

Troper

s. xi^{med}

22r, St Peter rescued from prison; reproduced in Temple, *Anglo-Saxon Manuscripts*, pl. 293 and *Golden Age*, pl. xxi

Temple, *Anglo-Saxon Manuscripts*, pp. 113–15 (no. 97), pls. 293–5; *Golden Age*, p. 86 (no. 71), pl. xxi; Ohlgren, *Catalogue*, pp. 263–5 (no. 202)

Above, p. 35

LONDON, BRITISH LIBRARY, MS Cotton Claudius B. iv (Old English Hexateuch)

Old English translation of parts of the Old Testament

St Augustine, Canterbury, s. xi^{1}

Cycle of Old Testament narrative illustrations

Ker, *Catalogue*, pp. 178–9 (no. 142); facsimile: Dodwell and Clemoes, *Old English Hexateuch*; Temple, *Anglo-Saxon Manuscripts*, pp. 102–4 (no. 86), pls. 265–72; *Golden Age*, p. 153 (no. 157), pl. xxx; Ohlgren, *Catalogue*, pp. 212–48 (no. 191)

Above, pp. 27 and 36

LONDON, BRITISH LIBRARY, MS Cotton Claudius B. v, 132v

Gospel fragment

Court school of Charlemagne, s. viii^{ex}

132v, painting of the annunciation to Zechariah, cut from a Carolingian gospel-book and pasted into the present manuscript; reproduced in Koehler, 'Evangelistary', pl. 13 (a) and *Miniaturen*, pl. ll, 32 (c)

Koehler, 'Evangelistary'; Koehler, *Karolingischen Miniaturen* ll, 47–8, pl. ll, 32 (c)

Above, p. 71

LONDON, BRITISH LIBRARY, MS Cotton Cleopatra C. viii

Prudentius, *Psychomachia*

Christ Church, Canterbury (?), s. x/xi

Numerous narrative illustrations

Stettiner, *Prudentius-Handschriften*, pls. 36, 43–6, 49–50 (13–18), 51–2 (14–18), 53–4 (13–18), 55–6 (14–18), 57–8 (13–18), 59–60 (16–18), 61–2 (13–18) and 63–4 (12–18); Ker, *Catalogue*, p. 185 (no. 145); Temple, *Anglo-Saxon Manuscripts*, pp. 70–1 (no. 49), pls. 159–62; *Golden Age*, pp. 65–6 (no. 45); Ohlgren, *Catalogue*, pp. 120–26 (no. 154)

Above, p. 27

LONDON, BRITISH LIBRARY, MS Cotton Galba A. xiv

Private devotions

Winchester, Nunnaminster (?), s. xi^in

105v–107v, Office collects

E. Bishop, *Liturgica Historica*, pp. 384–91; Ker, *Catalogue*, pp. 198–201 (no. 157); Muir, *Pre-Conquest Prayer-Book*

Above, p. 56

LONDON, BRITISH LIBRARY, MS Cotton Galba A. xviii and OXFORD, BODLEIAN LIBRARY, MS Rawlinson B. 484, 85r (Athelstan Psalter)

Psalter

Winchester, Old Minster, s. x¹

English additions to a continental manuscript of s. ix. The manuscript was owned by the Old Minster, Winchester, during the Middle Ages; later tradition says that it was given to the Old Minster by Athelstan

2v, Christ enthroned with symbols of the Passion; reproduced in Temple, *Anglo-Saxon Manuscripts*, pl. 32

21r, Christ enthroned with symbols of the Passion; reproduced *ibid.*, pl. 33

120v, Ascension (Ps. CI); reproduced *ibid.*, pl. 31

Oxford, Bodleian Library, Rawlinson B. 484, 85r, reproduced *ibid.*, pl. 30, showing the Nativity, originally belonged to this manuscript and was placed before Ps. I; the manuscript probably also included a painting of the Crucifixion at Ps. LI, see *Golden Age*, p. 20 and Wood, 'Æthelstan's Empire', pp. 267–8

Temple, *Anglo-Saxon Manuscripts*, pp. 36–7 (no. 5), pls. 30–3; Wood, 'Æthelstan's Empire', pp. 267–8; *Golden Age*, pp. 20 and 24 (no. 4);

Keynes, 'King Athelstan's Books', pp. 193–6; Ohlgren, *Catalogue*, pp. 70–2 (no. 83)

Above, pp. 14, 23, 38–9, 66, 86–7, 131 and 132

LONDON, BRITISH LIBRARY, MS Cotton Tiberius A. iii

Regularis concordia, 3r–27v; *S. Benedicti regula*, 118r–163v

Christ Church, Canterbury (?), s. xi^{med}

2v, Edgar with Dunstan and Æthelwold; reproduced in Temple, *Anglo-Saxon Manuscripts*, pl. 313 and *Golden Age*, p. 49

114v–115v, Office of the cross; ptd Dewick, *Facsimiles of Horae*, cols. 45–8

117v, St Benedict with the monks of Canterbury; reproduced in Temple, *Anglo-Saxon Manuscripts*, pl. 314

Ker, *Catalogue*, pp. 240–48 (no. 186); Temple, *Anglo-Saxon Manuscripts*, pp. 118–19 (no. 100), pls. 313–14; *Golden Age*, pp. 47 and 49 (no. 28); Ohlgren, *Catalogue*, p. 271 (no. 205)

Above, pp. 56, 62, 64 and 166

LONDON, BRITISH LIBRARY, MS Cotton Tiberius C. vi (Tiberius Psalter)

Gallican psalter with Old English gloss

Winchester, s. xi^{med}

7v, the Creation

8r, David rescuing the lamb from the lion

8v–9r, David and Goliath

9v, the anointing of David

10r, David playing the harp

10v, the Temptation of Christ

11r, the entry to Jerusalem

11v, the washing of the feet

12r, the Betrayal

12v, Christ before Pilate

13r, the Crucifixion

13v, the Maries at the tomb

14r, the Harrowing of Hell

14v, doubting Thomas

15r, the Ascension

15v, Pentecost

18v, Christ holding a cross and accompanied by angels

30v, David with his musicians

114v, Christ above the beasts

126v, the Trinity

All illustrations reproduced in Wormald, 'Eleventh-Century Psalter'

Ker, *Catalogue*, p. 262 (no. 199); F. Wormald, 'Eleventh-Century Psalter'; Temple, *Anglo-Saxon Manuscripts*, pp. 115–17 (no. 98), pls. 297 and 302–11, fig. 37; *Golden Age*, p. 83 (no. 66), pl. xx; Ohlgren, *Catalogue*, pp. 265–70 (no. 203)

Above, pp. 14, 32–4, 35, 36, 46, 59, 60, 61, 87–9, 90, 92, 107, 108, 109, 123, 132, 133, n. 16, 145, 146, 147, 149–51, 153, 155, 159, 175, nn. 77 and 78, 176, n. 85; pl. XIII

LONDON, BRITISH LIBRARY, MS Cotton Titus D. xxvi + xxvii (Ælfwine Prayer-book)

Prayers and other items in Latin and Old English

Winchester, New Minster, 1023–35

Titus D. xxvi, 19v, the monk Ælfwine with St Peter; reproduced in Temple, *Anglo-Saxon Manuscripts*, pl. 243

45v–46r, Office collects

Titus D. xxvii, 57r–64r, Passion according to St John

65v, Crucifixion; reproduced in Temple, *ibid.*, pl. 246

66r–73v, prayers to the cross

75v, the Trinity with Mary; reproduced in Temple, *ibid.*, pl. 245 and *Golden Age*, p. 76

80r–81v, prayers to the cross

New Minster, *Liber Vitae*, ed. Birch, App. D–E, pp. 251–83; Ker, *Catalogue*, pp. 264–6 (no. 202); Temple, *Anglo-Saxon Manuscripts*, pp. 94–5 (no. 77), pls. 243 and 245–6; Kidd, 'Quinity of Winchester'; *Golden Age*, pp. 75–6 (no. 61); Ohlgren, *Catalogue*, pp. 197–8 (no. 182)

Above, pp. 24, 35, 38, 56, 58, 59, 62, 64, 89, 92, 94, 95, 97, 98, 102, n. 61, 106–7, 129–30, 131–3, 138, 148, 152, 156, n. 61, 166, 167, 174, 175, n. 79 and 177, n. 91; pl. VIII

LONDON, BRITISH LIBRARY, MS Cotton Vespasian A. i (Vespasian Psalter)

Psalter

St Augustine, Canterbury, s. viii[1]

30v, David and his musicians, probably originally the frontispiece to the text, opposite the lost *Beatus vir* page (Ps. I); there was at one time an initial at Ps. I showing David and Samuel

31r, initial with David and Jonathan (Ps. XXVI)

53r, initial with David killing the lion (Ps. LII)

155r–160v, prayers to the cross, added to the main part of the manuscript in the 1020s

Ker, *Catalogue*, pp. 266–67 (no. 203); facsimile: Wright, *Vespasian Psalter*; Alexander, *Insular Manuscripts*, pp. 55–6 (no. 29), pls. 143–6; Ohlgren, *Catalogue*, pp. 24–5 (no. 29)

Above, pp. 23, 36, 58, 95, 166 and 167

LONDON, BRITISH LIBRARY, MS Cotton Vespasian A. viii (New Minster Charter)

New Minster Charter

Winchester, New Minster, after 966

2v, Edgar presenting his charter to Christ; reproduced in Temple, *Anglo-Saxon Manuscripts*, pl. 84 and *Golden Age*, pl. iv

Temple, *Anglo-Saxon Manuscripts*, p. 44 (no. 16), pl. 84; *Golden Age*, p. 47 (no. 26), pl. iv; Ohlgren, *Catalogue*, pp. 78–9 (no. 94)

Above, pp. 25, 26, 27, 61, 63 and 133

LONDON, BRITISH LIBRARY, MS Egerton 3763 (Psalter of Arnulph of Milan)

Collection of private prayers and devotions

Northern Italy, s. x/xi

102v, orant figure of Mary; reproduced in Barré, *Prières*, frontispiece

103r–104r, prayers to the Virgin; ptd *ibid.*, pp. 208–9

Turner, 'Prayer-Book'; Barré, *Prières*, pp. 207–9

Above, p. 102

LONDON, BRITISH LIBRARY, MS Harley 76 (Bury Gospels)

Gospel-book

s. xi[in], probably written at Christ Church, Canterbury, but at Bury by s. xi[ex]

6r–12v, canon tables decorated with figures of Christ and saints

6r, standing figure of Christ; reproduced in Ohlgren, *Catalogue*, pl. 26

7v, seated figure of St Peter; reproduced *ibid.*, pl. 27 and *Golden Age*, p. 74

8r, seated figure of St Paul; reproduced *ibid.*, pl. 28 and *Golden Age*, p. 74

8v, Christ accompanied by angels; reproduced in Temple, *Anglo-Saxon Manuscripts*, pl. 230

9r, Mary with two female saints; reproduced in Millar, *English Illuminated Manuscripts*, pl. 21

9v, angel; reproduced in Ohlgren, *Catalogue*, pl. 29

10r, angel; reproduced in Temple, *Anglo-Saxon Manuscripts*, pl. 231

Temple, *Anglo-Saxon Manuscripts*, p. 93 (no. 75), pls. 221, 230 and 231; *Golden Age*, p. 74 (no. 58); Ohlgren, *Catalogue*, pp. 195–7 (no. 180), pls. 26–9

Above, p. 23

LONDON, BRITISH LIBRARY, MS Harley 603 (Harley Psalter)

Psalter

Christ Church, Canterbury, s. xi^{in}, with drawings of various dates of s. xi and xii, partly based on those in the Utrecht Psalter

1r, drawing of the Trinity; reproduced in Temple, *Anglo-Saxon Manuscripts*, pl. 210

12r, drawing of the instruments of the passion; reproduced in Ohlgren, *Catalogue*, pl. 20 and O'Reilly, 'Rough-Hewn Cross', pl. v

Temple, *Anglo-Saxon Manuscripts*, pp. 81–3 (no. 64), pls. 200–7 and 210, fig. 1; Backhouse, 'Making of the Harley Psalter'; *Golden Age*, pp. 74–5 (no. 59), pl. xix; Ohlgren, *Catalogue*, pp. 161–82 (no. 169), pls. 19–25; O'Reilly, 'Rough-Hewn Cross'

Above, pp. 32, 85, 90 and 175, n. 79

LONDON, BRITISH LIBRARY, MS Harley 2788 (Harley Gospels)

Gospel-book

Court school of Charlemagne, s. viii/ix

109r, opening of St Luke's Gospel with a painting of the annunciation to Zechariah; reproduced in Koehler, *Karolingischen Miniaturen*, pl. 11, 59

Koehler, *Karolingischen Miniaturen* 11, 56–69, pls. 11, 42–66

Above, p. 71

LONDON, BRITISH LIBRARY, MS Harley 2904 (Ramsey Psalter)

Gallican psalter

s. x^{ex}, probably written at Winchester for the use of Ramsey Abbey

3v, Crucifixion; reproduced in Temple, *Anglo-Saxon Manuscripts*, pl. 142; the drawing is by an artist who also worked at Fleury and Saint-Bertin and whose work is found in the Boulogne Gospels, the Anhalt-Morgan Gospels, British Library, Harley 2506 and Orleans, Bibliothèque Municipale, 175

Temple, *Anglo-Saxon Manuscripts*, pp. 64–5 (no. 41), pls. 140–2; *Golden Age*, p. 60 (no. 41), pl. ix; Ohlgren, *Catalogue*, pp. 104–5 (no. 146)

Above, pp. 59, 86, 89, 92, 96, 97, 98, 132–3, 151, 155–8, 175, n. 77 and 180; pl. XIV

LONDON, BRITISH LIBRARY, MS Harley 2965 (Book of Nunnaminster)

Private prayers

s. viii/ix, probably belonged to Ealhswith (*ob.* 909), wife of King Alfred

1r–4r, Passion according to Mark, XIV.61–XV.46; ptd Birch, *Ancient Manuscript*, pp. 39–42

4v–10v, Passion according to Luke, XXII.1–XXIII.44; ptd *ibid.*, pp. 43–50

11r–16r, Passion according to John, XVIII.1–XIX.42; ptd *ibid.*, pp. 51–7

19r–32v, prayers on the creation and the life of Christ; ptd *ibid.*, pp. 61–81

Birch, *Ancient Manuscript*; Ker, *Catalogue*, pp. 308–9 (no. 237); Alexander, *Insular Manuscripts*, p. 65 (no. 41), pls. 135 and 137–9; Ohlgren, *Catalogue*, p. 38 (no. 41)

Above, pp. 56, 57, 58, 59, 95, 125, 136, 151, n. 31, 166 and 174.

LONDON, BRITISH LIBRARY, MS Royal 1. D. IX

Gospel-book

s. xi^in Written partly by the same scribe as the Trinity Gospels and the Sacramentary of Robert of Jumièges; at Christ Church, Canterbury by 1016–19

45r, initial page to Mark with saints in medallions in the borders; reproduced in *Golden Age*, pl. xv

111r, initial page to John with saints in medallions in the borders; reproduced in Temple, *Anglo-Saxon Manuscripts*, pl. 222

Ker, *Catalogue*, p. 317 (no. 247); Temple, *Anglo-Saxon Manuscripts*, pp. 88–9 (no. 70), pl. 222; *Golden Age*, p. 69 (no. 52), pl. xv; Ohlgren, *Catalogue*, pp. 189–90 (no. 175)

Above, p. 23

LONDON, BRITISH LIBRARY, MS Royal 1. E. VI (Royal Gospels)

Remains of a bible, though traditionally described as a gospel-book

St Augustine, Canterbury, s. ix

Most of the illustrations have been lost; a full account of their probable subjects is given in Budny, 'Royal 1 E. vi' and Ohlgren, *Catalogue*

Temple, *Anglo-Saxon Manuscripts*, p. 74 (no. 55), pl. 172; Alexander, *Insular Manuscripts*, pp. 58–9 (no. 32), pls. 160–4; Budny, 'Royal 1 E. vi'; Ohlgren, *Catalogue*, pp. 28–30 and 137 (nos. 32 and 160)

Above, p. 83, n. 58

LONDON, BRITISH LIBRARY, MS Royal 1. E. VII (Royal Bible)

Bible

Christ Church, Canterbury, s. x^{ex}, with drawing on 1v added s. xi^{med}

1v, creation picture; reproduced in Temple, *Anglo-Saxon Manuscripts*, pl. 319

Temple, *Anglo-Saxon Manuscripts*, pp. 119–20 (no. 102), pl. 319; Ohlgren, *Catalogue*, p. 272 (no. 207)

Above, p. 35

LONDON, BRITISH LIBRARY, MS Royal 2. A. XX

Prayer-book

s. viii^2

Gospel passages, hymns, canticles and prayers; ptd Kuypers, *Book of Cerne*, pp. 201–25

Kuypers, *Book of Cerne*, pp. 200–25; Ker, *Catalogue*, pp. 317–18 (no. 248); Alexander, *Insular Manuscripts*, pp. 60–1 (no. 35), pl. 133; Ohlgren, *Catalogue*, p. 32 (no. 35)

Above, p. 58

LONDON, BRITISH LIBRARY, MS Stowe 944 (New Minster *Liber vitae*)

New Minster Register

Winchester, New Minster, s. xi^1 (*c.* 1031) with later additions

6r, Cnut and Ælfgifu presenting a cross to the monastery; reproduced in Temple, *Anglo-Saxon Manuscripts*, pl. 244 and *Golden Age*, p. 77

6v–7r, Last Judgement scenes; reproduced in Temple, *ibid.*, pls. 247–8

Birch, *Liber Vitae*; Ker, *Catalogue*, pp. 338–40 (no. 274); Temple, *Anglo-Saxon Manuscripts*, pp. 95–6 (no. 78), pls. 244, 247 and 248; *Golden Age*, pp. 77–8 (no. 62); Ohlgren, *Catalogue*, pp. 198–9 (no. 183)

Above, pp. 25, 26, 27, 35, 47, 61, 63, 106, 113, 133 and 146

LONDON, BRITISH MUSEUM, MLA 1859, 5–12, 1, Wilton Cross

s. vii

Gold and garnet cloisonné pendant cross, containing a coin of Heraclius I and made by the Sutton Hoo workshop

Bruce-Mitford, *Aspects*, pp. 29–31 and 281–302, pl. 96 (d–e)

Above, p. 61

LONDON, BRITISH MUSEUM, MLA 1881, 4–4, 1, Godwine Seal

Walrus ivory

Southern English, s. xi[1]

Seal handle carved with figures of God the Father and the Son seated above the devil

Goldschmidt, *Elfenbeinskulpturen* IV, 19–20 (no. 59), pl. xiv.59 (a–b); Beckwith, *Ivory Carvings*, p. 126 (no. 41), pls. 78–9; *Golden Age*, pp. 113–14 (no. 112)

Above, pp. 147–8

LONDON, BRITISH MUSEUM, MLA 1903, 3–23, 1, Alcester Tau

Walrus ivory tau cross

Southern English, s. xi[in]

The cross-head is decorated with interlace, acanthus and animal ornament enclosing figures of Christ on the cross on one side and Christ above the beasts on the other

Goldschmidt, *Elfenbeinskulpturen* IV, 10 (no. 8), pl. ii.8 (a–c); Beckwith, *Ivory Carvings*, p. 124 (no. 29), pls. 65–6; *Golden Age*, p. 119 (no. 120)

Above, p. 61

LONDON, BRITISH MUSEUM, ivory bookcover

s. xi/xii

Crucifixion scene with Mary, John, sun, moon and chalice; reproduced in Goldschmidt, *Elfenbeinskulpturen* II, pl. xlvi.163

Goldschmidt, *Elfenbeinskulpturen* II, 50 (no. 163), pl. xlvi.163

Above, p. 118, n. 47

LONDON, VICTORIA AND ALBERT MUSEUM, Ivory no. 151–1866

Ivory panel

Rhineland, s. xi/xii

Crucifixion scene with Mary, John and two flying angels; reproduced in Goldschmidt, *Elfenbeinskulpturen* II, pl. xlvi.161

Goldschmidt, *Elfenbeinskulpturen* II, 49 (no. 161), pl. xlvi.161

Above, p. 117, n. 37

LONDON, VICTORIA AND ALBERT MUSEUM, Ivory no. 250–1867

Ivory bookcover

Metz school, s. ix/x

Crucifixion scene with Mary, John, Ecclesia, Synagogue, Oceanus and Gaia, sun, moon, angels, serpent, soldiers and the dead rising; reproduced in Goldschmidt, *Elfenbeinskulpturen* I, pl. xxxvi.85

Goldschmidt, *Elfenbeinskulpturen* I, 47–8 (no. 85), pl. xxxvi.85

Above, p. 116, n. 34

LONDON, VICTORIA AND ALBERT MUSEUM, Ivory no. 251–1867

Ivory cover of a gospel-book

Metz school, s. ix/x

Crucifixion scene with Mary, John, Ecclesia, Synagogue, Oceanus and Gaia, sun, moon, angels, serpent, soldiers and the dead rising; reproduced in Goldschmidt, *Elfenbeinskulpturen* I, pl. xxvii.88

Goldschmidt, *Elfenbeinskulpturen* I, 49 (no. 88), pl. xxxvii.88

Above, p. 116, n.34

LONDON, VICTORIA AND ALBERT MUSEUM, Ivory no. 254–1867

Ivory panel

Southern English (?), s. x^2

Ascension scene with orant figure of Mary; reproduced in Beckwith, *Ivory Carvings*, pls. 50 and 52

Goldschmidt, *Elfenbeinskulpturen* I, 36–7 (no. 70), pl. xxviii.70; Beckwith, *Ivory Carvings*, p. 122 (no. 22), pls. 50 and 52

Above, p. 131, n. 6

LONDON, VICTORIA AND ALBERT MUSEUM, Ivory no. 268–1867 (St Lawrence Box)

Walrus ivory box with scenes thought to be connected with a miracle of St Lawrence

English, s. x/xi

Goldschmidt, *Elfenbeinskulpturen* IV, 22–3 (no. 73), pl. xviii.73 (a–d); Beckwith, *Ivory Carvings*, pp. 121–2 (no. 19), pls. 25 and 42–5; Heslop, 'Walrus Ivory Pyx'; *Golden Age*, p. 116 (no. 116)

Above, pp. 47 and 52

LONDON, VICTORIA AND ALBERT MUSEUM, Ivory no. A 6–1966, ivory reliquary cross

Southern English, s. xi[1]

Walrus ivory box carved with foliage designs, an archer and, on the reverse, the Lamb among the evangelist symbols

Raw, 'Archer'; Beckwith, *Ivory Carvings*, p. 128 (no. 45), pls. 99–102; *Golden Age*, pp. 122–3 (no. 125)

Above, p. 61

LONDON, VICTORIA AND ALBERT MUSEUM, Department of Metalwork no. M 7943–1862, reliquary crucifix (Victoria and Albert Crucifix)

s. x[ex]

Walrus ivory figure mounted on gold filigree and enamel cross on a cedarwood core. The ivory figure is English but parts of the mount may be German; see *Golden Age*, pp. 117–18

Goldschmidt, *Elfenbeinskulpturen* IV, 9 (no. 3), pl. i.3; Beckwith, *Ivory Carvings*, p. 122 (no. 20), frontispiece and pl. 47; *Golden Age*, pp. 117–18 (no. 118), pl. xxvi

Above, pp. 61, 111, 112, 113–15, 128 and 129; pl. ivb

LONDON, VICTORIA AND ALBERT MUSEUM, Ivory no. A 10–1921, ivory reliquary or pectoral cross

Walrus ivory

English (?), s. x/xi

Christ standing on the cross and accompanied by evangelist symbols

Goldschmidt, *Elfenbeinskulpturen* IV, 19 (no. 54), pl. xiv.54 (a–b); Beckwith, *Ivory Carvings*, pp. 124–5 (no. 32), pl. 68

Above, p. 114

Lothar Cross: see AACHEN, CATHEDRAL TREASURY, Lothar Cross

MADRID, ESCORIAL, Cod. Vetrinas 17 (Golden Gospels of Henry III)

Gospel-book

Echternach, 1043–6

Numerous narrative illustrations, identified by inscriptions; reproduced in Boeckler, *Evangelienbuch*

2v, Christ enthroned, evangelist symbols peering over unrolled scrolls in border medallions; reproduced in Boeckler, *ibid.*, pl. 6 and Goldschmidt, *German Illumination* II, pl. 57

Boeckler, *Evangelienbuch*; Schramm and Mütherich, *Denkmale*, p. 173 (no. 154), pl. 154

Above, pp. 8 and 114

MALIBU, CALIFORNIA, J. PAUL GETTY MUSEUM, MS 9 (Damme Fragments)

Southern English, s. x/xi

Two leaves from a gospel-lectionary, with paintings of the Gadarene swine and Peter with the tribute money; formerly at the Musée van Maerlant, Damme; reproduced in Temple, *Anglo-Saxon Manuscripts*, pls. 173–6

Temple, *Anglo-Saxon Manuscripts*, pp. 72–3 (no. 53), pls. 173–6; Ohlgren, *Catalogue*, pp. 136–7 (no. 158)

Above, pp. 27 and 83

Matilda Cross: see ESSEN, MINSTER TREASURY, Matilda Cross

Metz Gospels: see PARIS, BIBLIOTHEQUE NATIONALE, MS lat. 9388

Metz Coronation Sacramentary: see PARIS, BIBLIOTHEQUE NATIONALE, MS lat. 1141

MILAN, SANT'AMBROGIO, golden altar (Golden Altar of St Ambrose)

Rheims (?), c. 870

Golden altar with scenes from the gospels: similar to the Pala d'Oro at Aachen Cathedral (Schnitzler, *Schatzkammer*, pp. 28–9 (no. 31), pls. 71–89) with a scene of Christ in Majesty at the centre and gospel scenes around

Elbern, *Der karolingische Goldaltar*

Above, pp. 8, 50 and 122

Mont Saint-Michel Sacramentary: see NEW YORK, PIERPONT MORGAN LIBRARY, MS 641

MONZA, ST JOHN, silver ampullae (Monza Ampullae)

Palestinian, s. vi^2

Ampullae nos. 1, 2, 10 and 11 are decorated with Ascension scenes with an orant figure of Mary; reproduced in Grabar, *Ampoules*, pls. iii, v, xvii and xix

The Ascension scene on no. 10 includes the *dextera Dei* and a dove, possibly to represent a link between the Ascension and Pentecost; reproduced in Grabar, *ibid.*, pl. xvii

Grabar, *Ampoules*, pp. 16–20 and 26–7, pls. iii, v, xvii and xix

Above, pp. 100 and 153

MUNICH, BAYERISCHE STAATSBIBLIOTHEK, Clm. 4452 (Gospels of Henry II)

Gospel-lectionary

Reichenau, s. xi^{in} (1007 or 1012)

2r, Henry crowned by Christ; reproduced in Heer, *Holy Roman Empire*, pl. 26

Bookcover of s. xi, with metal and enamel frame surrounding an ivory of the Crucifixion, s. ix; reproduced in Lasko, *Ars Sacra*, frontispiece and Schramm and Mütherich, *Denkmale*, pl. 110. The ivory may originally have decorated the cover of the Codex Aureus of St Emmeram (Munich, Bayerische Staatsbibl., Cod. lat. 14000), see Lasko, *ibid.*, pp. 36 and 265, n. 17

Schramm and Mütherich, *Denkmale*, pp. 156–7 (no. 110), pl. 110

Above, pp. 114 and 140

MUNICH, BAYERISCHE STAATSBIBLIOTHEK, Clm. 4453 (Gospels of Otto III)

Gospel-book

Trier (?), Reichenau (?), s. x^{ex} (after 997)

248v, Crucifixion, deposition, burial

For a discussion of the place of origin see Dodwell and Turner, *Reichenau Reconsidered*, pp. 27–30

Facsimile: Dressler, Mütherich and Beumann, *Das Evangeliar Ottos III*

Above, pp. 72–3 and 93

MUNICH, BAYERISCHE STAATSBIBLIOTHEK, Clm. 4456 (Sacramentary of Henry II)

Sacramentary

Regensburg, 1002–1014; given to Bamberg by Emperor Henry II

11r, Henry crowned by Christ; reproduced in Heer, *Holy Roman Empire*, pl. 11 and Swarzenski, *Regensburger Buchmalerei*, pl. VIII.19

15r, Crucifixion; reproduced in Swarzenski, *ibid.*, pl. VII.18

15v, the Maries at the tomb and the Resurrection; reproduced in Swarzenski, *ibid.*, pl. IX.21; Swarzenski, p. 67, says that there is no parallel to the use of this scene at the *Te igitur*

16r, *Te igitur*; reproduced in Swarzenski, *ibid.*, pl. X.24

G. Swarzenski, *Regensburger Buchmalerei*, pp. 63–87, pls. V.14, VI.16 and VII.17–XI.27; Schramm and Mütherich, *Denkmale*, p. 157 (no. 111), pl. 111

Above, pp. 82 and 140

MUNICH, BAYERISCHE STAATSBIBLIOTHEK, Clm. 10077 (Verdun Sacramentary)

s. x²; written for the abbey of Corvey at either Fulda or Corvey

12r, *Te igitur* with crucifix, Mary and John; reproduced in Goldschmidt, *German Illumination* II, pl. 111

Above, p. 81

MUNICH, BAYERISCHE STAATSBIBLIOTHEK, Clm. 13601 (Uta Gospels)

Gospel-book

Regensburg, 1002–1025

1v, the hand of God; reproduced in Swarzenski, *Regensburger Buchmalerei*, pl. XII.28

2r, Uta with the Virgin and Child; reproduced in Swarzenski, *ibid.*, pl. XII.29

3v, Crucifixion with Ecclesia, Synagogue, Vita, Mors, and border medallions with figures and gospel scenes; reproduced in Swarzenski, *ibid.*, pl. XIII.30; for the inscriptions on the painting see Swarzenski, pp. 94–7

4r, Erhard saying mass; reproduced in Swarzenski, *ibid.*, pl. XIII.31

The borders of the evangelist portraits of Mark (41v), Luke (59v) and John (89v) contain small figure scenes relating to the events in these gospels (see Swarzenski, *ibid.*, pp. 100–4); their function is similar to that of the groups of pictures in the Bernward gospel-book

G. Swarzenski, *Regensburger Buchmalerei*, pp. 88–122, pls. XII.28–XVIII.47

Above, pp. 8, 47, 73, 74, 101, n. 54, 136 and 139

MUNICH, BAYERISCHE STAATSBIBLIOTHEK, Clm. 14000 (Codex Aureus of St Emmeram)

Gospel-book

Court school of Charles the Bald, 870

5v, painting of Charles the Bald; reproduced in Koehler and Mütherich, *Karolingischen Miniaturen*, pl. V, 46

6r, the Adoration of the Lamb; reproduced in Koehler and Mütherich, *ibid.*, pl. V, 47

11r, canon tables with a representation of the fountain of life; reproduced in Koehler and Mütherich, *ibid.*, pl. V, 54

Gold covers decorated with narrative scenes surrounding a figure of Christ; reproduced in Lasko, *Ars Sacra*, pl. 55

Koehler and Mütherich, *Karolingischen Miniaturen* V, 175–98, pls. V, 45–70

Above, pp. 8, 21, 26 and 47

MUNICH, SCHATZKAMMER DER RESIDENZ, Arnulf Ciborium

Portable altar

s. ix²; given by Arnulf of Carinthia to the Abbey of St Emmeram between 887 and 896, probably in 893

The ciborium of the altar is decorated with gospel scenes in relief; reproduced in Schramm and Mütherich, *Denkmale*, pl. 61

Schramm and Mütherich, *Denkmale*, p. 139 (no. 61), pl. 61; Lasko, *Ars Sacra*, pp. 64–5

Above, p. 47

MUNICH, SCHATZKAMMER DER RESIDENZ, Heinrichsportatile

Portable altar and reliquary

West German, 1014–24

The front has a cross-shaped cavity for a relic of the cross, surrounded by engraved figures of the evangelists; the reverse shows the *Agnus Dei* with angels, Melchisedech and Aaron and, below this, the sacrifice of Isaac; reproduced in Lasko, *Ars Sacra*, pls. 128–9 and Schramm and Mütherich, *Denkmale*, pl. 134

Elbern, *Das erste Jahrtausend* III, 68–9 (nos. 306–7), pls. 306–7; Schramm and Mütherich, *Denkmale*, p. 164 (no. 134), pl. 134

Above, p. 50

MUNICH, SCHATZKAMMER DER RESIDENZ, Prayer-book of Charles the Bald

Prayer-book

Court school of Charles the Bald, 846–69

38v–39r, Charles kneeling before the crucified Christ; reproduced in Schramm and Mütherich, *Denkmale*, pl. 43 and Koehler and Mütherich, *Karolingischen Miniaturen*, pl. v, 1 (b)

39v–43r, the Good Friday prayers and Office collects

Schramm and Mütherich, *Denkmale*, pp. 130–31 (no. 43), pl. 43; Koehler and Mütherich, *Karolingischen Miniaturen*, v, 75–87, pls. v, 1–3; Deshman, 'Exalted Servant'

Above, pp. 63–4

MUNSTER, ST MAURICE, Erpho Cross

s. xi^ex (1085–97)

Jewelled gold cross, with Christ crucified accompanied by angels

Elbern, *Das erste Jahrtausend* III, 85–6 (no. 395), pl. 395

Above, pp. 113 and 118

Musée de Cluny: see PARIS, MUSEE DE CLUNY

NANCY CATHEDRAL, gospels (St Gauzelin Gospels)

Gospel-book

Tours, s. ix[1] (*c.* 830)

3v, frontispiece with Lamb, spear, sponge and chalice, evangelist symbols, seraphs and figures of the four major prophets; reproduced in Koehler, *Karolingischen Miniaturen*, pl. 1, 35 (c) and Kessler, *Illustrated Bibles*, pl. 64

Koehler, *Karolingischen Miniaturen* I, Pt 1, 179–86, Pt 2, 94–6, pls. 1, 35–9; Kessler, *Illustrated Bibles*, pp. 42–53, pls. 64 and 73

Above, pp. 69–70 and 126

NETHER WALLOP, ST ANDREW, wall-painting

Southern English, s. x/xi

Painting of flying angels supporting a mandorla above the chancel-arch; probably part of a scene comparable to the upper part of the painting in Edgar's charter for the New Minster

Gem and Tudor-Craig, 'Wall-Painting at Nether Wallop'

Above, pp. 13 and 16

NEWCASTLE UPON TYNE, MUSEUM OF ANTIQUITIES, no. 1958.8N (Alnmouth Cross)

Cross-shaft

Northern English, s. ix/x

Crucifixion panel with 2 soldiers, 2 other figures, sun and moon; reproduced in Cramp, *Corpus* I, pl. 156

Cramp, *Corpus* I, 161–2, pls. 156–7

Above, p. 150

New Minster Charter: see LONDON, BRITISH LIBRARY, MS Cotton Vespasian A. viii

New Minster *Liber vitae*: see LONDON, BRITISH LIBRARY, MS Stowe 944

New Minster, Winchester, fragment of wall-painting. See WINCHESTER CITY MUSEUM

NEW YORK, PIERPONT MORGAN LIBRARY, MS 1 (Lindau Gospels)

Bookcover

Court school of Charles the Bald, s. ix[2] (840–77), on a St Gallen manuscript of s. ix[2]

Front cover of gold and jewels with relief of the Crucifixion with Mary and John, sun, moon and flying angels

H. Swarzenski, *Monuments*, pl. 11 (22–3); Needham, *Bookbindings*, pp. 27–9 (no. 6), frontispiece

Above, p. 116

NEW YORK, PIERPONT MORGAN LIBRARY, MS 333 (Odbert Gospels)

Gospel-book

Saint-Bertin, s. x/xi (986–1008)

51r, opening of St Luke's Gospel with scenes of the annunciation to Zechariah and the Nativity

85r, opening of St John's Gospel with scenes of the Crucifixion, the Harrowing of Hell, the Maries at the tomb and the Ascension; reproduced in H. Swarzenski, *Monuments*, pl. 69 (161)

Above, pp. 73–4 and 126, n. 92

NEW YORK, PIERPONT MORGAN LIBRARY, MS 641 (Mont Saint-Michel Sacramentary)

Sacramentary

Mont Saint-Michel, s. xi^{med}

155v, Heraclius returning the relics of the cross to Jerusalem; reproduced in Alexander, *Norman Illumination*, pl. 44; the picture may be related to a visit by Abbot Radulfus to Jerusalem, *c.* 1058 (Alexander, *ibid.*, p. 172)

Alexander, *Norman Illumination*, pp. 127–72, 228 and 240–2, pls. 31–6 and 38–46

Above, p. 143, n. 87

NEW YORK, PIERPONT MORGAN LIBRARY, MS 708 (Judith Gospels)

Gospel-book

s. xi^{med}

Belonged to Judith of Flanders (*c.* 1028–94)

Gold and gilt silver bookcover with figures of Christ enthroned between two seraphs and Crucifixion with Mary and John; reproduced in Needham, *Bookbindings*, pl. xxi and Ohlgren, *Catalogue*, pl. 34

Temple, *Anglo-Saxon Manuscripts*, pp. 109–11 (no. 94), pl. 286; Needham, *Bookbindings*, pp. 33–5 (no. 8), pl. xxi; Ohlgren, *Catalogue*, pp. 259–60 (no. 199), pls. 34–7

Above, p. 58

NEW YORK, PIERPONT MORGAN LIBRARY, MS 709 (Weingarten Gospels)

Gospel-book

s. xi^{med}

Belonged to Judith of Flanders (*c.* 1028–94)

1v, Crucifixion with figures of Mary, John and Judith/Mary Magdalen; reproduced in Temple, *Anglo-Saxon Manuscripts*, pl. 289 and Ohlgren, *Catalogue*, pl. 1

Temple, *Anglo-Saxon Manuscripts*, pp. 108–9 (no. 93), pls. 285 and 289; Ohlgren, *Catalogue*, pp. 257–9 (no. 198), pls. 1 and 31–3

Above, pp. 24, 38, 59, 63, 83, 84, 85, 89, 92, 96, 97, 105, n. 74, 123, 129, 156, n. 61, 158–61, 176, n. 85 and 180; pl. XVI

NEW YORK, PIERPONT MORGAN LIBRARY, MS 827 (Anhalt-Morgan Gospels)

Gospel-book

Saint-Bertin, s. x/xi, with evangelist portraits by an English artist who also worked on the Ramsey Psalter and the Boulogne Gospels

98v, bearded figure of St John; reproduced in Temple, *Anglo-Saxon Manuscripts*, pl. 146

Temple, *Anglo-Saxon Manuscripts*, pp. 67–8 (no. 45), pl. 146; Ohlgren, *Catalogue*, pp. 110–11 (no. 150)

Above, p. 133

NEW YORK, PIERPONT MORGAN LIBRARY, MS 869 (Arenberg Gospels)

Gospel-book

Christ Church, Canterbury, s. x^{ex}

9v, Crucifixion; reproduced in Temple, *Anglo-Saxon Manuscripts*, pl. 171

10r–13v, decorated canon tables; 11v and 13v reproduced in Temple, *ibid.*, pls. 167 and 168; 10r, 10v, 11r, 12r, 12v and 13r reproduced in Ohlgren, *Catalogue*, pls. 11–16

17v, 57v, 83v and 126v, evangelist portraits; 17v and 83v reproduced in Temple, *ibid.*, pls. 169 and 170; 57v and 126v reproduced in Ohlgren, *ibid.*, pls. 17–18; 126v reproduced in *Golden Age*, pl. xi

Rosenthal, 'Arenberg Gospels'; Temple, *Anglo-Saxon Manuscripts*, pp. 74–5 (no. 56), pls. 167–71; *Golden Age*, p. 68 (no. 47), pl. xi; Ohlgren, *Catalogue*, pp. 137–40 (no. 161), pls. 11–18

Above, pp. 53, 84–5, 86, 88, 90, 92, 94, 105, 106, 111, 112, 113, 114, 115, 116, 117, 118, 119, 120, 123, 124, 126, 128, 152 and 175, n. 79; pl. II

Odbert Gospels: see NEW YORK, PIERPONT MORGAN LIBRARY, MS 333

Odbert Psalter: see BOULOGNE, BIBLIOTHEQUE MUNICIPALE, MS 20

Old English Hexateuch: see LONDON, BRITISH LIBRARY, MS Cotton Claudius B. iv

Otto Cross: see ESSEN, MINSTER TREASURY, Otto Cross

OXFORD, ASHMOLEAN MUSEUM, 1836.371, Alfred Jewel

English, s. ix^{ex}

Gold and enamel ornament, originally attached to a rod; the enamel figure, holding two flowers, may be a personification of sight

Bakka, 'Alfred Jewel'; Hinton, *Catalogue*, pp. 29–48 (no. 23), pls. x (23a)–xi (23i); *Golden Age*, pp. 33–4 (no. 13), pl. i

Above, p. 114

OXFORD, ASHMOLEAN MUSEUM, 1909.453, Ixworth Cross

s. vii

Gold and garnet cloisonné pendant cross

Bruce-Mitford, *Aspects*, pp. 281–302, pl. 5 (a)

Above, p. 61

OXFORD, BODLEIAN LIBRARY, MS Auct. D. 2. 6, 156r–200v

Anselm, *Orationes sive meditationes*

English, s. xii^{med}

186v, Mary Magdalen anointing Christ's head and speaking to him in the garden; reproduced in Pächt, 'Anselm's Prayers and Meditations', pl. 24 (a)

Pächt, 'Anselm's Prayers and Meditations'; Kauffmann, *Romanesque Manuscripts*, pp. 103–4 (no. 75), pls. 208–10

Above, p. 161

OXFORD, BODLEIAN LIBRARY, MS Auct. F. 4. 32 (Dunstan Classbook)

Composite volume

Glastonbury, s. ix to xi^2; parts 1 and 3–4 were apparently at Glastonbury during Dunstan's abbacy (*c.* 940–56); the drawing on 1r (s. x^{med}) is said to have been done by Dunstan himself

1r, drawing of Dunstan at the feet of Christ; reproduced in Temple, *Anglo-Saxon Manuscripts*, pl. 41 and *Golden Age*, p. 53

Ker, *Catalogue*, p. 355 (no. 297); facsimile: Hunt, *Dunstan's Classbook*;

Temple, *Anglo-Saxon Manuscripts*, p. 41 (no. 11), pl. 41; Higgitt, 'Glastonbury, Dunstan, Monasticism and Manuscripts'; *Golden Age*, pp. 51 and 53 (no. 31); Ohlgren, *Catalogue*, p. 76 (no. 89)

Above, pp. 24 and 149

OXFORD, BODLEIAN LIBRARY, MS Bodley 579 (Leofric Missal)

Sacramentary

Northern France, s. ix/x; English additions of s. x^{med} and x^2; given by Leofric (1046–72) to Exeter

49r, diagram of paschal hand; reproduced in Warren, *Leofric Missal*, p. 43 and Temple, *Anglo-Saxon Manuscripts*, pl. 54

49v, figure of Vita; reproduced in Warren, *ibid.*, p. 44 and Temple, *ibid.*, pl. 55

50r, figure of Mors; reproduced in Warren, *ibid.*, p. 45 and Temple, *ibid.*, pl. 56

Warren, *Leofric Missal*; Ker, *Catalogue*, pp. 378–9 (no. 315); Temple, *Anglo-Saxon Manuscripts*, pp. 44–5 (no. 17), pls. 53–6; Ohlgren, *Catalogue*, pp. 79–80 (no. 95)

Above, p. 35

OXFORD, BODLEIAN LIBRARY, MS Douce 176

Ivory bookcover with gospel scenes

Court school of Charlemagne, s. viii/ix, on a manuscript of s. ix^{in} attributed to Chelles

Central scene of Christ above the beasts, surrounded by scenes of the prophecy of Isaiah, the Annunciation, Nativity, Adoration of the Magi, Massacre of the Innocents, Baptism, marriage at Cana, stilling of the storm and four healings

Goldschmidt, *Elfenbeinskulpturen* I, 10–11 (no. 5), pl. iii.5

Above, p. 8

OXFORD, BODLEIAN LIBRARY, MS Douce 296 (Douce Psalter)

Psalter

Crowland (?), s. xi^1

40r, Christ above the beasts (Ps. LI); reproduced in Temple, *Anglo-Saxon Manuscripts*, pl. 259 and *Golden Age*, p. 84

Temple, *Anglo-Saxon Manuscripts*, pp. 96–7 (no. 79), pls. 259–60; *Golden Age*, pp. 83–4 (no. 68); Ohlgren, *Catalogue*, pp. 199–200 (no. 184)

Above, p. 32

OXFORD, BODLEIAN LIBRARY. MS Junius 11 (Cædmon Manuscript)

Old English paraphrase of parts of Genesis, Exodus and Daniel, together with a New Testament poem known as *Christ and Satan*

Christ Church, Canterbury (?), s. xi^{in}

Numerous narrative illustrations

Facsimile: Gollancz, *Cædmon Manuscript*; Ker, *Catalogue*, pp. 406–8 (no. 334); Raw, 'Illustrations in Junius 11'; Temple, *Anglo-Saxon Manuscripts*, pp. 76–8 (no. 58), pls. 189–96; *Golden Age*, pp. 151–2 (no. 154); Ohlgren, *Catalogue*, pp. 141–8 (no. 163)

Above, pp. 27 and 177

OXFORD, BODLEIAN LIBRARY, MS Junius 27 (Junius Psalter)

Roman psalter with Old English gloss

Winchester, s. x^1

Decorated initials with birds, dragons and foliage

118r, initial D with a representation of David fighting the lion; reproduced in Temple, *Anglo-Saxon Manuscripts*, pl. 26

Ker, *Catalogue*, pp. 408–9 (no. 335); Temple, *Anglo-Saxon Manuscripts*, pp. 38–9 (no. 7), pls. 1, 20–24 and 26; Ohlgren, *Catalogue*, pp. 73–4 (no. 85)

Above, p. 23

PARIS, BIBLIOTHEQUE NATIONALE, MS lat. 1 (Vivian Bible)

Bible

Tours, 845–6

215v, psalter illustration showing David with his musicians and personifications of the four cardinal virtues; reproduced in Koehler, *Karolingischen Miniaturen*, pl. 1, 72 and Kessler, *Illustrated Bibles*, pl. 140

330v, gospel frontispiece showing Christ in Majesty with the evangelist symbols and representations of the evangelists and the four major prophets; reproduced in Koehler, *ibid.*, pl. 1, 73 and Kessler, *ibid.*, pl. 49

423r, presentation scene showing Charles the Bald receiving the bible; reproduced in Koehler, *ibid.*, pl. 1, 76 and Kessler, *ibid.*, pl. 196

Koehler, *Karolingischen Miniaturen* 1, Pt 1, 250–5 and 396–401, Pt 2, 27–65, pls. 1, 68–89; Kessler, *Illustrated Bibles*, pp. 36–58, 96–110 and 125–38

Above, pp. 26, 69 and 70

PARIS, BIBLIOTHEQUE NATIONALE, MS lat. 257 (Gospels of Francis II)

Gospel-book

Saint-Amand, s. ix²

12v, Crucifixion with the two soldiers; reproduced in Hubert *et al.*, *Carolingian Art*, pl. 152

Mütherich and Gaehde, *Carolingian Painting* (no. xv), pls. 30–1

Above, pp. 150 and 151

PARIS, BIBLIOTHEQUE NATIONALE, MS lat. 943 (Sherborne Pontifical)

Pontifical

Canterbury (?), s. x/xi; at Sherborne by s. xi ⁱⁿ

4v, Crucifixion; reproduced in Temple, *Anglo-Saxon Manuscripts*, pl. 134; 5v–6v, Holy Trinity; reproduced in Temple, *ibid.*, pls. 135–7

Leroquais, *Pontificaux* II, 6–10 (no. 93); Ker, *Catalogue*, pp. 437–9 (no. 364); Temple, *Anglo-Saxon Manuscripts*, pp. 60–1 (no. 35), pls. 134–8; Rosenthal, 'Three Drawings'; *Golden Age*, pp. 55 and 57 (no. 34); Ohlgren, *Catalogue*, pp. 100–1 (no. 140)

Above, pp. 53, 92, 94, 111, 112, 113, 114, 115, 116, 117, 118, 119, 123, 124, 126, 127–8, 133 and 175, n. 79; pl. I

PARIS, BIBLIOTHEQUE NATIONALE, MS lat. 1141 (Metz Coronation Sacramentary)

Fragment of a sacramentary

Court school of Charles the Bald, *c.* 869

2v, king crowned by the hand of God and accompanied by two archbishops

5r, Christ in Majesty accompanied by angels (*Vere dignum*)

5v, heavenly choirs

6r, Christ with seraphs, Oceanus and Gaia (*Sanctus*)

6v, *Te igitur* with crucifix

Leroquais, *Sacramentaires* I, 35–6 (no. 13); Koehler and Mütherich, *Karolingischen Miniaturen* V, 165–74, pls. 41–4; facsimile: Mütherich, *Sakramentar von Metz*

Above, pp. 80, 133, 135, 137 and 139–40

PARIS, BIBLIOTHEQUE NATIONALE, MS lat. 6401

Boethius, *De consolatione philosophiae* and other works

Fleury, s. xᵉˣ, with illustrations by an English artist

159r, initial with the Trinity; reproduced in F. Wormald, *Collected Writings*, pl. 84

Temple, *Anglo-Saxon Manuscripts*, p. 59 (no. 32), pls. 94–5; *Golden Age*, pp. 64 and 65 (no. 44); Ohlgren, *Catalogue*, p. 99 (no. 137)

Above, p. 175, n. 79

PARIS, BIBLIOTHEQUE NATIONALE, MS lat. 8850 (Gospels of Saint-Médard of Soissons)

Gospel-book

Court school of Charlemagne, s. ix^in; presented to Saint-Médard of Soissons by Louis the Pious in 827

1v, the Adoration of the Lamb; reproduced in Koehler, *Karolingischen Miniaturen*, pl. II, 67

6v, the fountain of life; reproduced *ibid.*, pl. II, 68

10v, Canon 5, with a picture of Christ as Emmanuel; reproduced *ibid.*, pl. II, 76

11r, Canons 6, 7 and 8, with a picture of the fountain of life; reproduced *ibid.*, pl. II, 77

82r, opening of St Mark's Gospel with the Baptism of Christ; reproduced *ibid.*, pl. II, 84

123v, St Luke with the annunciation to Zechariah; reproduced *ibid.*, pl. II, 85

124r, opening of St Luke's Gospel with the Annunciation and Visitation; reproduced *ibid.*, pl. II, 86

180v, St John with the marriage at Cana; reproduced *ibid.*, pl. II, 87

181r, opening of St John's Gospel with the woman of Samaria; reproduced *ibid.*, pl. II, 88

Koehler, *Karolingischen Miniaturen* II, 70–82, pls. II, 67–93

Above, pp. 22, 71 and 126

PARIS, BIBLIOTHEQUE NATIONALE, MS lat. 9388 (Metz Gospels)

Gospel-book

Metz, s. ix^med

19r, the Annunciation; reproduced in Koehler, *Karolingischen Miniaturen*, pl. III, 71 (a)

19v, the Nativity; reproduced *ibid.*, pl. III, 71 (b)

102r, the birth of John the Baptist; reproduced *ibid.*, pl. III, 74 (a)

103r, the journey to Bethlehem; reproduced *ibid.*, pl. III, 74 (b)

Koehler, *Karolingischen Miniaturen* III, 134–42, pls. III, 66–75

Above, p. 71

PARIS, BIBLIOTHEQUE NATIONALE, MS lat. 9428 (Drogo Sacramentary)

Sacramentary

Metz, 850–5

Decorated with historiated initials

14v, 15r and 15v, *Vere dignum, Sanctus* and *Te igitur*; reproduced in Koehler, *Karolingischen Miniaturen*, pls. III, 78 (a)–79 (a)

23v, annunciation to the shepherds; reproduced *ibid.*, pl. III, 80 (c)

24v, Nativity scenes; reproduced *ibid.*, pl. III, 81 (a)

34v, scenes of the Magi; reproduced *ibid.*, pl. III, 82 (c)

43v, Crucifixion; reproduced *ibid.*, pl. III, 83 (c)

46v, 51v and 87v, initials with mass scenes; reproduced *ibid.*, pls. III, 83(e), 84 (b) and 90(a)

Leroquais, *Sacramentaires* I, 16–18 (no. 6); Koehler, *Karolingischen Miniaturen* III, 143–62, pls. III, 76–91; cover reproduced in Hubert *et al.*, *Carolingian Art*, pls. 214–15; facsimile: Koehler and Mütherich, *Drogo-Sakramentar*; Unterkircher, *Ikonographie*

Above, pp. 52, 78–80, 94, 134 and 156

PARIS, BIBLIOTHEQUE NATIONALE, MS lat. 9436

Missal

Ivory figures on bookcover

Liuthard group, s. ix, mounted on the cover of a missal from Saint-Denis, s. xi

The figures of Mary and John are mounted below an engraved cross from which the figure of Christ has been lost

Goldschmidt, *Elfenbeinskulpturen* II, 60–61 (no. 194), fig. 40, pl. lxx.194

Above, p. 59

PARIS, BIBLIOTHEQUE NATIONALE, MS lat. 9453

Ivory cover of a gospel-book from Metz

Metz school, s. ix/x, on a manuscript of s. x

Crucifixion scene with Mary, John, Ecclesia, Synagogue, sun, moon, angels, serpent and the dead rising; below, a scene of the women at the tomb; reproduced in Goldschmidt, *Elfenbeinskulpturen* I, pl. xxxvi.86

Goldschmidt, *Elfenbeinskulpturen* I, 48 (no. 86), pl. xxxvi.86

Above, p. 116, n. 34

PARIS, BIBLIOTHEQUE NATIONALE, MS lat. 12048 (Sacramentary of Gellone)

Sacramentary

Meaux (?), s. viii^{ex}

76v, painting of the discovery of the cross; reproduced in Dumas, *Liber*, fig. 59

143v, painting of the Crucifixion at the *Te igitur*; reproduced *ibid.*, fig. 99

Leroquais, *Sacramentaires* I, 1–8 (no. 2); Teyssèdre, *Sacramentaire de Gellone*; Baldwin, 'Gellone'; *Liber sacramentorum Gellonensis*, ed. Dumas, with colour reproductions of all illuminated folios

Above, pp. 80 and 116

PARIS, BIBLIOTHEQUE NATIONALE, Nouvelles acquisitions latines 1203 (Godescalc Gospels)

Gospel-lectionary

Court school of Charlemagne, 781–3

1r–2v, evangelist pictures; reproduced in Koehler, *Karolingischen Miniaturen*, pls. II, 1 (b)–3 (a)

3r, Christ enthroned; reproduced *ibid.*, pl. II, 3 (b)

3v, fountain of life; reproduced *ibid.*, pl. II, 4 (a)

Koehler, *Karolingischen Miniaturen* II, 22–28, pls. II, 1–12

Above, pp. 22, 70 and 126

PARIS, MUSEE DE CLUNY, ivory bookcover

Cologne (?), s. xi^1

Crucifixion scene with fully robed Christ, Mary, John, sun, moon and chalice; scenes of the women at the tomb, the Ascension and Christ in Majesty; the figure of Mary in the Crucifixion scene holds an ointment-jar and it is therefore possible that the figure represents Mary Magdalen rather than the mother of Christ; reproduced in Goldschmidt, *Elfenbeinskulpturen* II, pl. xv.48

Goldschmidt, *Elfenbeinskulpturen* II, 27 (no. 48), pl. xv.48

Above, pp. 118, n. 47 and 160, n. 79

PARIS, MUSEE DE CLUNY, CL 11.459, portable altar

Southern English, s. xi^1

The altar slab is framed with incised silver sheets decorated with figures of Christ on the cross, Mary, John, Gabriel, Raphael, the *Agnus Dei* and the evangelist symbols; reproduced in Okasha and O'Reilly, 'Anglo-Saxon Portable Altar', pl. 15 (a–c) and *Golden Age*, p. 93

Okasha and O'Reilly, 'Anglo-Saxon Portable Altar'; *Golden Age*, pp. 92–3 (no. 76)

Above, pp. 38, 50, 111, 123–6 and 182; pl. VII

PENRITH, cross ('Giant's Thumb')

Northern English, s. x^1

Representation of the Crucifixion with the two soldiers; reproduced in Bailey, *Viking Age Sculpture*, fig. 9, and Bailey and Cramp, *Corpus* II, pl. 484

Bailey, *Viking Age Sculpture*, pp. 78 and 152; Bailey and Cramp, *Corpus* II, 135–6, pls. 484–8

Above, p. 150

Pericopes of Henry III: see BREMEN, STAATSBIBLIOTHEK, MS b. 21

PETERBOROUGH CATHEDRAL, Hedda Stone

s. viii/ix

Stone shrine decorated with standing figures of Christ, Mary and ten apostles, framed by arches

Cramp, 'Mercian Sculpture', p. 210, pl. 57 (c)

Above, p. 16

Petrus Staff: see LIMBURG, CATHEDRAL TREASURY, Petrus Staff

Portiforium Wulstani: see CAMBRIDGE, CORPUS CHRISTI COLLEGE, MS 391

Prayer-book of Charles the Bald: see MUNICH, SCHATZKAMMER DER RESIDENZ, Prayer-book of Charles the Bald

Prudentius, *Psychomachia*: see CAMBRIDGE, CORPUS CHRISTI COLLEGE, MS 23 and LONDON, BRITISH LIBRARY, MS Cotton Cleopatra C. viii

Rabbula Gospels: see FLORENCE, BIBLIOTECA MEDICEA LAURENZIANA, MS Plutarch i. 56

Ramsey Psalter: see LONDON, BRITISH LIBRARY, MS Harley 2904

RAUNDS, pre-Conquest church

s. ix/x

Two-celled church with altar foundation and post-holes for ciborium to the west of the chancel-arch; plan in Parsons, '*Sacrarium*', p. 106

Boddington and Cadman, 'Raunds', pp. 107–8; Parsons, '*Sacrarium*', p. 106

Above, p. 52

RAVENNA, MAUSOLEUM OF GALLA PLACIDIA

s. v^{med}

Mosaic of Christ as the Good Shepherd; reproduced in Bovini, *Ravenna Mosaics*, pl. 2

Bovini, *Ravenna Mosaics*, pp. 7–13, pls. 1–5

Above, p. 42

RAVENNA, SANT'APOLLINARE IN CLASSE

s. vi¹ (535–49)

Apse mosaic showing St Apollinaris below a jewelled cross accompanied by three lambs, symbolizing the transfiguration; reproduced in Bovini, *Ravenna Mosaics*, pls. 44–5

Grabar, *Byzantium*, pls. 148, 151 and 153; Bovini, *Ravenna Mosaics*, pp. 49–55, pls. 44–6

Above, pp. 42 and 50

RAVENNA, SANT'APOLLINARE NUOVO

493–526, with mosaics of various dates

Mosaics showing processions of saints and martyrs, s. vi^{med}; reproduced in Bovini, *Ravenna Mosaics*, pls. 20–2 and 26

Bovini, *Ravenna Mosaics*, pp. 26–38, pls. 20–7

Above, p. 42

RAVENNA, SAN VITALE

521–47

Apse mosaic showing Christ with angels, St Vitalis and Bishop Ecclesius; reproduced in Grabar, *Byzantium*, pls. 147 and 150

Mosaics of Justinian and Theodora; reproduced in Grabar, *Byzantium*, pls. 170–3 and Bovini, *Ravenna Mosaics*, pls. 28 and 33

Bovini, *Ravenna Mosaics*, pp. 39–48, pls. 28–43

Above, p. 42

RECULVER, ST MARY

s. vii²–viii

Church with nave, apse and flanking porticus; the altar foundation is placed to the west of the triple arcade dividing nave from apse

Taylor and Taylor, *Architecture* II, 503–9

Above, p. 52

Regularis concordia: see LONDON, BRITISH LIBRARY, MS Cotton Tiberius A. iii

REICHENAU, SANKT GEORG, OBERZELL, wall-paintings

s. x^ex

Figures of apostles and abbots; scenes of the Gadarene swine, the healing of the man with dropsy, the stilling of the storm, the healing of the man blind from birth, the healing of the leper, the raising of the widow's son, the raising of Jairus's daughter, the raising of Lazarus, all on the walls of the nave; a crucifix accompanied by a saint on the east wall of the crypt

Martin, *Reichenau-Oberzell*

Above, p. 7

REPTON, ST WYSTAN

s. vii–xi

Chancel with crypt below, choir and porticus

Taylor and Taylor, *Architecture* II, 510–16

Above, p. 52

RHEIMS, BIBLIOTHEQUE MUNICIPALE, MS 9

Gospel-book

s.xi^med (*c.* 1062); given to Rheims by Ælfgar, earl of Mercia, in memory of his son Burchard who was buried there

18r–22v, canon tables

23r, 60r, 88r, 128r, evangelist portraits; 88r reproduced in Temple, *Anglo-Saxon Manuscripts*, pl. 299

Temple, *Anglo-Saxon Manuscripts*, pp. 121–2 (no. 105), pl. 299; Ohlgren, *Catalogue*, pp. 274–5 (no. 210)

Above, p. 58

Robert of Jumièges, Sacramentary: see ROUEN, BIBLIOTHEQUE MUNICIPALE, MS Y. 6 [274]

ROME, SAN PAOLO FUORI LE MURA, bible (San Callisto Bible)

Bible

Court school of Charles the Bald, Rheims (?), *c.* 870

170v, David and his musicians, with an inscription linking them with Christ and the evangelists; reproduced in Kessler, *Illustrated Bibles*, pl. 141

259v, Christ enthroned among the evangelists, their symbols and the four major prophets; reproduced in Kessler, *ibid.*, pl. 50

Gaehde, 'Turonian Sources', 'Early Christian Picture Cycle' and 'Pictorial Sources'; Mütherich and Gaehde, *Carolingian Painting*, xix, pls. 42–5

Above, pp. 36, 69 and 70

ROME, SANTA PRASSEDE

s. ix[1]

Mosaic on the triumphal arch showing the heavenly Jerusalem; reproduced in Oakeshott, *Mosaics of Rome*, pl. 121

Mâle, *Churches*, pp. 87–91, pls. 51–4; Oakeshott, *Mosaics of Rome*, pp. 204–12, pls. 121, 123–7, v, xix, xxi and xxii

Above, p. 17

ROME, SANTA PUDENZIANA

s. iv[2]

Apse mosaic showing Christ teaching the apostles, the buildings of Constantinian Jerusalem behind; reproduced in Grabar, *Byzantium*, pl. 145

Oakeshott, *Mosaics of Rome*, pp. 65–7, pls. 6 and 42–5

Above, p. 50

ROMSEY ABBEY, HAMPSHIRE

Crucifix in cloisters, s. xi[in]

Large stone crucifix with the hand of God above the cross; the figure of Christ was probably originally crowned. The carving is dated by Coatsworth to s. x. It is not in its original position; reproduced in Coatsworth, 'Pre-Conquest Sculptures', pl. 1b

Crucifixion panel over altar, s. xi[in]

Christ is accompanied by figures of Mary and John and the two soldiers; there are the busts of two angels above the arms of the cross; foliage sprouts from the stem of the cross. The carving is not in its original position; reproduced in Coatsworth, *ibid.*, pl. 1a

Coatsworth, 'Pre-Conquest Sculptures', pp. 167–9 and 191–2, pls. 1a–1b

Above, pp. 58, 118, 129, 150 and 151

ROSSANO CATHEDRAL, Gospels

Greek gospel-book

s. vi[1]

Fifteen full-page illustrations of gospel scenes related to the liturgy of Holy Week together with figures of Old Testament prophets; all reproduced in Muñoz, *Il codice purpureo* and Santoro, *Il codice purpureo*

Muñoz, *Il codice purpureo di Rossano*; Santoro, *Il codice purpureo di Rossano*

Above, pp. 68, 69 and 70

ROUEN, BIBLIOTHEQUE MUNICIPALE, MS A. 27 [368] (Lanalet Pontifical)

Pontifical and benedictional

English, s. xi[in]

1v, bishop and acolyte; reproduced in Temple, *Anglo-Saxon Manuscripts*, pl. 256

2v, bishop consecrating a church; reproduced in Rice, *English Art*, pl. 70 (a)

Leroquais, *Pontificaux* II, 287–300 (no. 188); Ker, *Catalogue*, pp. 447–8 (no. 374); Temple, *Anglo-Saxon Manuscripts*, p. 106 (no. 90), pl. 256; Ohlgren, *Catalogue*, pp. 255–6 (no. 195)

Above, p. 127

ROUEN, BIBLIOTHEQUE MUNICIPALE, MS A. 292 [26]

Collection of biblical, patristic and computistical material Northern France, s. ix[med]; at Jumièges in s. xi

48r, drawing of Christ on the cross by an English artist on a folio added to the original, s. x; the devotional texts which accompany the drawing and which were added at various dates s. x to s. xii have not previously been identified:

1 At foot of cross and partly erased by it: 'Alleluia. Beati qui persecu[tionem patiuntur pr]opter iustitiam quoniam ipsorum est reg[num]'; dated by Hartzell to s. x

2 At the top of the page:
   Arce crucis domini summa prudentia sistit
Hrabanus, *De laudibus sanctae crucis* I.vi: PL 107, 174; s. x[2]

3 On the cross-bar of the cross:
   Dextra dei summi cuncta creavit Iesus;
   Christus laxavit e sanguine debita mundi
Hrabanus, *ibid.*, I.i: PL 107, 154; s. x[2]

4 Below Christ's right arm:
   Undique quadratum
   Se pignus co'hsmo [= cosmo ?] dominus, dum solvit in orbem

s. x^2 (I am indebted to Michael Lapidge for help with this item)

5 Below 4:

In cruce quadrifida cr

6 To the left of Christ's head:

Dulcis amice vides, pro te quos porto dolores:

Hic pro te fixus toto sum corpore tensus,

Nil pro me patior, immeritus crucior.

Crimina quippe tua sunt mea supplicia.

[Ut tu non pereas, has mortis profero penas]

Amodo non moreris vivere si mihi vis

Quantumcumque potes non cesses reddere grates,

Nam meus iste dolor est tuus altus honor.

Walther, *Initia*, p. 242 (no. 4803); s. xi/xii, not previously found before s. xii.

7 Below the arms of the cross:

Rex obit haec plorat carus gemit impius orat

Walther, *ibid.*, p. 407 (no. 8051) and p. 876 (no. 16748); s. xii

(I am grateful to Andrew Watson for help with the dating of these hands)

Hartzell, 'New English Drawings'; Ohlgren, *Catalogue*, pp. 303–4 (no. 226)

Above, pp. 83, 111, 112, 119 and 124; pl. vb

ROUEN, BIBLIOTHEQUE MUNICIPALE, MS Y. 6 [274] (Sacramentary of Robert of Jumièges)

Sacramentary

s. xi[1]; written by the same scribe as the Trinity Gospels and BL, Royal 1 D. IX; given by Robert of Jumièges to Jumièges while he was bishop of London, 1044–51

32v–33r, Nativity scenes

36v–37r, Epiphany scenes

71r, the Betrayal

71v, the Crucifixion, with adoring figures in border medallions

72r, the deposition, with adoring figures in border medallions

72v, the Maries at the tomb

81v, the Ascension

84v, Pentecost

132v, St Peter

158v, Adoration of the Lamb, with adoring figures in border medallions

164v, St Andrew

Ptd and all pictures reproduced in *The Missal of Robert of Jumièges*, ed. Wilson; Leroquais, *Sacramentaires* I, 99 (no. 40); Ker, *Catalogue*, p. 449 (no. 377); Temple, *Anglo-Saxon Manuscripts*, pp. 89–91 (no. 72), pls. 237–40; *Golden Age*, p. 69 (no. 50), pl. xiv; Ohlgren, *Catalogue*, pp. 190–92 (no. 177)

Above, pp. 24–5, 30–1, 33, 34, 35, 47, 59, 60, 83, 88, 89, 90, 94, 96, 117, 131, 151, 152, 155 and 158; pl. xv

ROUEN, BIBLIOTHEQUE MUNICIPALE, MS Y. 7 [369] (Benedictional of Archbishop Robert)

Pontifical

Winchester, New Minster, s. x^{ex}; possibly made for Æthelgar, abbot of New Minster and later bishop of Selsey and archbishop of Canterbury

The paintings of the women at the tomb, Pentecost and the death of the Virgin on 21v, 29v and 54v are very close to those in the Benedictional of Æthelwold

Leroquais, *Pontificaux* II, 300–5 (no. 189); Temple, *Anglo-Saxon Manuscripts*, pp. 53–4 (no. 24), pls. 87 and 89; *Golden Age*, p. 60 (no. 40), pl. viii; Ohlgren, *Catalogue*, pp. 90–1 (no. 112)

Above, pp. 94, 133, 152 and 156

Royal Bible: see LONDON, BRITISH LIBRARY, MS Royal 1. E. VII

Royal Gospels: see LONDON, BRITISH LIBRARY, MS Royal 1. E. VI

Rupert Cross: see BISCHOFSHOFEN, PFARRHOF, processional or altar cross (Rupert Cross)

RUTHWELL CROSS

Northumbria, s. viii^{med}

Carved with gospel scenes and other figures. The overall scheme has been interpreted in many different ways, though most involve instruction in biblical and theological ideas

Saxl, 'Ruthwell Cross'; Cramp, *Early Northumbrian Sculpture*; Cramp, 'Evangelist Symbols'; Henderson, 'John the Baptist Panel'; O'Carragáin, 'Ruthwell Crucifixion Poem'

Above, pp. 12 and 20

St Albans Psalter: see HILDESHEIM, ST GODEHARD, psalter

St Augustine's Gospels: see CAMBRIDGE, CORPUS CHRISTI COLLEGE, MS 286

ST GALLEN, STIFTSBIBLIOTHEK, MS 51 (St Gallen Gospels)

Gospel-book

s. viii²; probably made in Ireland and taken to St Gallen

pp. 266–7, paintings of the Crucifixion and Last Judgement; reproduced in Alexander, *Insular Manuscripts*, pls. 203 and 206

Alexander, *Insular Manuscripts*, pp. 66–7 (no. 44), pls. 200, 201 and 203–8; Ohlgren, *Catalogue*, pp. 40–1 (no. 44)

Above, pp. 108, 109 and 151

St Gauzelin Gospels: see NANCY CATHEDRAL, gospels

St Lawrence Box: see LONDON, VICTORIA AND ALBERT MUSEUM, Ivory no. 268–1867

Sacramentary of Gellone: see PARIS, BIBLIOTHEQUE NATIONALE, MS lat. 12048

Sacramentary of Henry II: see MUNICH, BAYERISCHE STAATSBIBLIOTHEK, Clm. 4456

Sacramentary of Mont Saint-Michel: see NEW YORK, PIERPONT MORGAN LIBRARY, MS 641

Sacramentary of Robert of Jumièges: see ROUEN, BIBLIOTHEQUE MUNICI-PALE, MS Y. 6 [274]

SAINT-OMER, MUSEE SANDELIN, Ivory no. 2822 (Saint-Omer Ivories)

Southern English, s. x/xi

Figures of Mary and John from a Crucifixion group, probably from a bookcover

Goldschmidt, *Elfenbeinskulpturen* IV, 9 (nos. 4 and 5), pl. i.4–5; Beckwith, *Ivory Carvings*, p. 123 (no. 25), pls. 57–8; *Golden Age*, pp. 118–19 (no. 119), pl. xxvii

Above, pp. 59, 111, 112 and 151; pl. VI

San Callisto Bible: see ROME, SAN PAOLO FUORI LE MURA, bible

SANDBACH, cross-shaft

s. ix

Cross-shaft, one panel showing Christ on the cross accompanied by the evangelist symbols

Echternach, s. xi^{med}

3v, Christ crowning Henry and Agnes; border with evangelist symbols peering over unrolled scrolls; reproduced in Goldschmidt, *German Illumination* II, pl. 63

Schramm and Mütherich, *Denkmale*, p. 174 (no. 155), pl. 155

Above, p. 114

Uta Gospels: see MUNICH, BAYERISCHE STAATSBIBLIOTHEK, Cod. lat. 13601

UTRECHT, UNIVERSITEITSBIBLIOTHEK, MS 32 (Utrecht Psalter)

Psalter

Hautvillers, s. ix¹; at Canterbury by *c.* 1000

12r, symbols of the Passion (Ps. XXI)

51v, Crucifixion with soldiers (Ps. LXXXVIII)

64v, God the Father and God the Son seated above their enemies (Ps. CIX)

67r, Crucifixion with chalice (Ps. CXV)

85v, Crucifixion with thieves and soldiers (Canticle of Habbakuk)

89v, the Trinity with Mary (*Gloria*)

90r, the Trinity with Mary; Crucifixion with soldiers, Mary and John (Apostles' Creed)

Facsimile: De Wald, *Utrecht Psalter* and van der Horst, *Utrecht-Psalter*

Above, pp. 32, 76–7, 85, 93–4, 105, 115, 119, 120, 131–2 and 134

VATICAN CITY, BIBLIOTECA APOSTOLICA VATICANA, MS Ottobon. lat. 74 (Gospels of Henry II)

Gospel-book

Regensburg, s. xi (*c.* 1014)

193v, Henry II seated in front of a medallion cross, wearing a crown and stole; reproduced in Schramm and Mütherich, *Denkmale*, pl. 141

G. Swarzenski, *Die Regensburger Buchmalerei*, pp. 123–32, pls. XIX.48–XXI.53; Schramm and Mütherich, *Denkmale*, p. 167 (no. 141), pl. 141

Above, p. 139, n. 60

VATICAN CITY, BIBLIOTECA APOSTOLICA VATICANA, MS Regin. lat. 12 (Bury Psalter)

Gallican psalter

Christ Church, Canterbury (?), s. xi¹, provenance Bury

35r, Crucifixion (Ps. XXI)

62r, painting of Ecclesia; reproduced in Temple, *Anglo-Saxon Manuscripts*, pl. 262

Harris, 'Bury St Edmunds Psalter'; Temple, *Anglo-Saxon Manuscripts*, pp. 100–2 (no. 84), pls. 262–4, fig. 26; Ohlgren, *Catalogue*, pp. 205–11 (no. 189)

Above, pp. 25, 32–3, 36, 85, 90, 92, 123, 129, 137, 147–9 and 175, n. 79; pl. XIIa

VATICAN, MUSEO CRISTIANO, ivory diptych (Rambona Diptych)

Italian, s. ix^{ex}

Crucifixion scene with Mary, John, classical figures of sun and moon, Romulus and Remus with the wolf; reproduced in Goldschmidt, *Elfen-beinskulpturen* I, pl. lxxxiv. 181 (a)

Goldschmidt, *Elfenbeinskulpturen* I, 86–7 (no. 181), pl. lxxxiv. 181 (a–b)

Above, p. 132, n. 11

Verdun Sacramentary: see MUNICH, BAYERISCHE STAATSBIBLIOTHEK, Cod. lat. 10077

Vespasian Psalter: see LONDON, BRITISH LIBRARY, MS Cotton Vespasian A. i

Victoria and Albert Crucifix: see LONDON, VICTORIA AND ALBERT MUSEUM, Department of Metalwork, no. M 7943–1862

VIENNA, NATIONALBIBLIOTHEK, MS 2687 [Theol. 345] (Gospels of Otfrid of Weissenburg)

Gospel-book

s. ix², possibly an autograph copy

153v, Crucifixion with Mary, John, sun and moon, a chalice at the foot of the cross; reproduced in Hermann, *Frühmittelalterlichen Handschriften*, fig. xxx

Hermann, *Frühmittelalterlichen Handschriften*, pp. 126–31, figs. 90–1, xxix and xxx

Above, pp. 116 and 118

Vivian Bible: see PARIS, BIBLIOTHEQUE NATIONALE, MS lat. 1

Weingarten Gospels: see NEW YORK, PIERPONT MORGAN LIBRARY, MS 709

Wilton Cross: see LONDON, BRITISH MUSEUM, MLA 1859, 5–12, 1, Wilton Cross

Winchcombe Psalter: see CAMBRIDGE, UNIVERSITY LIBRARY, MS Ff. 1. 23

WINCHESTER, CITY MUSEUM, fragment of wall-painting

Southern English, s. ix^{ex}

Discovered during excavation of the New Minster, built into the foundations of the south wall. The painting is usually identified as part of a picture of the heavenly choirs, similar to those in the Athelstan Psalter, but the gesture of the figure to the right suggests that it is more probably from a picture of the washing of the feet similar to that in the Tiberius Psalter, 11v; reproduced in *Golden Age*, p. 44

Golden Age, p. 44 (no. 25)

Above, p. 14

Winchester, New Minster *Liber vitae*: see LONDON, BRITISH LIBRARY, MS Stowe 944

WINCHESTER, OLD MINSTER, fragments of wall-painting

Fragments of painted plaster recovered during excavation of the Old Minster, 1962–9

s. x^2

Gem and Tudor-Craig, 'Wall-Painting at Nether Wallop', App. 11, pp. 135–6

Above, p. 15

WINCHESTER, ST MARY, TANNER ST

s. x^1 to xi^2

Two-celled church with apse and with supports for what was probably a rood-beam across the chancel-arch; excavated in 1971

Biddle, 'Tenth and Final Interim Report: Part II', p. 312 and fig. 15

Above, p. 51

WIRKSWORTH, Carved Grave-slab

Midland English, s. viii

Carved grave-slab with representations of the Annunciation, washing of the feet, Ascension, burial of Mary, the apocalyptic Lamb and other scenes, not conclusively identified; reproduced in Kendrick, *Anglo-Saxon Art*, pl. lxvii (2)

Kurth, 'Wirksworth Slab'; Cockerton, 'Wirksworth Slab'

Above, p. 19

WOOTTON WAWEN, ST PETER

s. xi[1]

Central tower with arches leading to nave, chancel, north and south porticus

Taylor and Taylor, *Architecture* II, 685–8

Above, p. 53

ZURICH, PRIVATE COLLECTION, ivory Crucifixion panel

German, s. ix/x

Crucifix with Mary, John, sun and moon, chalice at the foot of the cross and two standing angels above

Goldschmidt, *Elfenbeinskulpturen* IV, 60 (no. 308), pl. lxxix.308

Above, p. 116

Bibliography

Aachen. *Karl der Grosse, Werk und Wirkung*, ed. W. Braunfels (Aachen, 1965)

Abbo. *Passio S. Edmundi. See* Winterbottom

Ademar. *Historiarum libri tres*: PL 141, 19–80

Adriaen, M. *See* Ambrose, Cassiodorus, Gregory the Great *and* Jerome

Advent Lyrics. *The Advent Lyrics of the Exeter Book*, ed. J. J. Campbell (Princeton, 1959)

See also Burlin

Ælfric. *The Homilies of the Anglo-Saxon Church*, ed. B. Thorpe, 2 vols. (London, 1844–6)

'Excerpta ex institutionibus monasticis Æthelwoldi episcopi Wintoniensis compilata in usum fratrum Egneshamnensium per Ælfricum abbatem', ed. M. Bateson, in G. W. Kitchin, *Compotus Rolls of the Obedientiaries of St Swithun's Priory, Winchester*, Hampshire Record Society (Winchester, 1892), pp. 171–98 (App. VII)

Exameron Anglice, or The Old English Hexameron, ed. S. J. Crawford, Bibliothek der angelsächsischen Prosa 10 (Hamburg, 1921)

The Old English Version of the Heptateuch, Ælfric's Treatise on the Old and New Testament and his Preface to Genesis, ed. S. J. Crawford, EETS os 160 (1922, repr. with additions by N. R. Ker, 1969). See also under Hexateuch for a facsimile of the manuscript

Angelsächsische Homilien und Heiligenleben, ed. B. Assmann, Bibliothek der angelsächsischen Prosa 3 (Kassel, 1889), reissued with introduction by P. Clemoes (Darmstadt, 1964)

Die Hirtenbriefe Ælfrics in altenglischer und lateinischer Fassung, ed. B. Fehr, Bibliothek der angelsächsischen Prosa 9 (Hamburg, 1914), reissued with supplement by P. Clemoes (Darmstadt, 1966)

Ælfric's Lives of Saints, ed. W. W. Skeat, EETS os 76, 82, 94 and 114 (1881–1900)

Homilies of Ælfric: A Supplementary Collection, ed. J. C. Pope, EETS os 259–60 (1967–8)

Ælfric's Catholic Homilies, the Second Series, ed. M. Godden, EETS ss 5 (1979)

Epistula ad monachos Egneshamnenses directa, ed. K. Hallinger, CCM 7.3 (1984), 149–85

Vita S. Æthelwoldi. See Winterbottom

Æthelwold, Benedictional. *See* Benedictional

Æthelwold, lives by Ælfric and Wulfstan. *See* Winterbottom

Æthelwulf. *De abbatibus*, ed. A. Campbell (Oxford, 1967)

Ailred of Rievaulx. *Sermones de tempore et de sanctis*: PL 195, 209–360

Sermones inediti B. Aelredi abbatis Rievallensis, ed. C. H. Talbot (Rome, 1952)

La vie de recluse, la prière pastorale, ed. C. Dumont, Sources chrétiennes 76 (Paris, 1961)

Liber de speculo caritatis, ed. C. H. Talbot, CCCMed 1 (1971), 3–161

De institutione inclusarum, ed. C. H. Talbot, CCCMed 1 (1971), 637–82

Albers, B., 'Les "Consuetudines Sigiberti Abbatis" dans Clm. 14765', *RB* 20 (1903), 420–33

See also Cluny

Alcuin. *Alcuin: The Bishops, Kings and Saints of York*, ed. P. Godman (Oxford, 1982).

Aldhelm. *De virginitate*, ed. R. Ehwald, MGH, Auct. antiq. 15 (Berlin, 1914–19), 226–323 (prose), 350–471 (verse)

Aldhelm: The Prose Works, trans. M. Lapidge and M. Herren (Cambridge, 1979)

Alexander, J. J. G., *Norman Illumination at Mont St Michel 966–1100* (Oxford, 1970)

Insular Manuscripts, 6th to the 9th Century, A Survey of Manuscripts Illuminated in the British Isles 1 (London, 1978)

'Scribes as Artists: The Arabesque Initial in Twelfth-Century English Manuscripts', in *Medieval Scribes, Manuscripts and Libraries: Essays Presented to N. R. Ker*, ed. M. B. Parkes and A. G. Watson (London, 1978), pp. 87–116

See also under York Gospels

Amalarius. *Amalarii episcopi opera liturgica omnia*, ed. J. M. Hanssens, Studi e testi 138–40 (Vatican City, 1948–50)

Ambrose. *De institutione virginis et S. Mariae virginitate perpetua ad Eusebium, liber unus*: PL 16, 305–34

De obitu Valentiniani consolatio: PL 16, 1357–84

Expositio super septem visiones libri Apocalypsis: PL 17, 765–970

Expositio evangelii secundum Lucam, ed. M. Adriaen, CCSL 14 (1957), 1–400

Andrieu, M., 'L' *Ordo Romanus antiquus* et le *Liber de divinis officiis* du Pseudo-Alcuin', *Revue des sciences religieuses* 5 (1925), 642–50

Bibliography

Anglo-Saxon Chronicle. *Two Saxon Chronicles, Parallel*, ed. C. Plummer, 2 vols. (Oxford, 1892–9)

Anglo-Saxon Poetic Records, ed. G. P. Krapp and E. V. K. Dobbie, 6 vols. (New York, 1931–42).

Anselm, archbishop of Canterbury. *Proslogion*, in *S. Anselmi Cantuariensis archiepiscopi opera omnia*, ed. F. S. Schmitt, 6 vols. (Edinburgh, 1946–61) I, 89–122

   Cur Deus homo, ed. F. S. Schmitt, *ibid.* II, 37–133

   Orationes sive meditationes, ed. F. S. Schmitt, *ibid.* III, 3–91, and trans. B. Ward, *The Prayers and Meditations of St Anselm* (Harmondsworth, 1973)

Antiphonary of Bangor. *The Antiphonary of Bangor: An Early Irish Manuscript in the Ambrosian Library at Milan*, ed. F. E. Warren, 2 vols., HBS 4 and 10 (1893–5)

Antiphons. *Corpus antiphonalium officii*, ed. R.-J. Hesbert, 6 vols., Rerum ecclesiasticarum documenta, Series maior, Fontes 7–12 (Rome, 1963–79)

Armi, C. E. and E. B. Smith, 'The Choir Screen of Cluny III', *Art Bulletin* 66 (1984), 556–73

Arnold, T. *See* Henry of Huntingdon

Assmann, B. *See* Ælfric

Audradus Modicus. *Liber de fonte vitae*, ed. L. Traube, MGH, PLAC 3 (Berlin, 1896), 73–84

Augustine of Hippo. *Sermones*: PL 38 and 39

   In Iohannis evangelium tractatus cxxiv, ed. A. Mayer, CCSL 36 (1954)

   Enarrationes in Psalmos, ed. E. Dekkers and J. Fraipont, 3 vols., CCSL 38, 39 and 40 (1956)

   De Trinitate libri XV, ed. W. J. Mountain, 2 vols., CCSL 50 and 50A (1968)

Aulén, G., *Christus Victor: An Historical Study of the Three Main Types of the Idea of the Atonement*, trans. A. G. Hebert, repr. with new foreword (London, 1970)

Backhouse, J., 'Reichenau Illumination: Facts and Fictions', *Burlington Magazine* 109 (1967), 98–100

   'The Making of the Harley Psalter', *British Library Journal* 10 (1984), 97–113

   See also Golden Age

Bailey, R. N., *The Durham Cassiodorus*, Jarrow Lecture (1978)

   Viking Age Sculpture in Northern England (London, 1980)

Bailey, R. N. and R. Cramp, *Corpus of Anglo-Saxon Stone Sculpture, II: Cumberland, Westmorland and Lancashire North-of-the-Sands* (Oxford, 1988)

Bakka, E., 'The Alfred Jewel and Sight', *AntJ* 46 (1966), 277–82

Baldwin, C. R., 'The Scriptorium of the Sacramentary of Gellone', *Scriptorium* 25 (1971), 3–17

Bandmann, G., 'Früh- und hochmittelalterliche Altaranordnung als Darstellung', in *Das erste Jahrtausend* I, ed. V. H. Elbern (Dusseldorf, 1962), 371–411

Bangor. *See* Antiphonary of Bangor

Banks, R. A., 'Some Anglo-Saxon Prayers from British Museum MS Cotton Galba
    A. xiv', *N&Q* 210 (1965), 207–13

Barasch, M., *Gestures of Despair in Medieval and Early Renaissance Art* (New York,
    1976)

Barker, N. *See* York Gospels

Barlow, F., *The English Church 1000–1066*, 2nd ed. (London, 1979)

Barr, B. *See* York Gospels

Barré, H., 'Marie et l'église du Vénérable Bède à Saint Albert le Grand', *Etudes
    Mariales* 9 (1951), 59–143

    'La lettre du Pseudo-Jérôme sur l'assomption est-elle antérieure à Paschase
    Radbert?' *RB* 68 (1958), 203–25

    'La maternité spirituelle de Marie dans la pensée médiévale', *Etudes Mariales* 16
    (1959), 87–118

    'L' homiliaire carolingien de Mondsee', *RB* 71 (1961), 71–107

    'L'apport marial de l'orient à l'occident de Saint Ambroise à Saint Anselme',
    Etudes Mariales 19 (1962), 27–89

    Prières anciennes de l'occident à la Mère du Sauveur des origines à Saint Anselme (Paris,
    1963)

Bastgen, H. See *Libri Carolini*

Bateson, M., 'Rules for Monks and Secular Canons after the Revival under King
    Edgar', *EHR* 9 (1894), 690–708

See also Ælfric

Battiscombe, C. F., ed., *The Relics of Saint Cuthbert* (Oxford, 1956)

Baumstark, A., 'Der Crucifixus mit dem königlichen Diadem auf einem
    modernen mesopotamischen Silberdeckel', *Römische Quartalschaft für christ-
    liche Altertumskunde und für Kirchengeschichte* 24 (1910), 30–50

    Comparative Liturgy, trans. F. L. Cross (London, 1958)

Beckwith, J., *Ivory Carvings in Early Medieval England* (London, 1972)

Bede. *Historia abbatum*: *Venerabilis Baedae opera historica*, ed. C. Plummer, 2 vols.
    (Oxford, 1896) I, 364–87

    Historia ecclesiastica gentis Anglorum: *Bede's Ecclesiastical History of the English
    People*, ed. B. Colgrave and R. A. B. Mynors (Oxford, 1969)

    Homiliae: PL 94, 9–268

    Homeliae evangelii, ed. D. Hurst, CCSL 122 (1955), 1–378

    In Lucam evangelium expositio, ed. D. Hurst, CCSL 120 (1960), 5–425

    Libri quattuor in principium Genesis, ed. C. W. Jones, CCSL 118A (1967)

    De templo, ed. D. Hurst, CCSL 119A (1969), 141–234

    De temporum ratione liber, ed. C. W. Jones, CCSL 123B (1977)

Beissel, S., *Des hl. Bernward Evangelienbuch im Dome zu Hildesheim* (Hildesheim,
    1891)

Bibliography

Geschichte der Evangelienbücher in der ersten Hälfte des Mittelalters, Stimmen aus Maria-Laach, Ergänzungsheft 92–3 (Freiburg im Breisgau, 1906)

Entstehung der Perikopen des römischen Messbuches: Zur Geschichte der Evangelienbücher in der ersten Hälfte des Mittelalters, Stimmen aus Maria-Laach, Ergänzungsheft 96 (Freiburg im Breisgau, 1907)

Benedictine Office. *The Benedictine Office: An Old English Text*, ed. J. M. Ure (Edinburgh, 1957)

Benedictine Rule. *Benedicti regula*, ed. R. Hanslik, CSEL 75 (1960)

Benedictional. *The Benedictional of Archbishop Robert*, ed. H. A. Wilson, HBS 24 (1903)

The Benedictional of Saint Æthelwold Bishop of Winchester 963–984, ed. G. F. Warner and H. A. Wilson, Roxburghe Club (Oxford, 1910)

Berger, R., *Die Darstellung des thronenden Christus in der romanischen Kunst*, Tübinger Forschungen zur Archäologie und Kunstgeschichte 5 (Reutlingen, 1926)

Beskow, P., *Rex gloriae. The Kingship of Christ in the Early Church*, trans. E. J. Sharpe (Stockholm, 1962)

Bestul, T. H., 'St Anselm and the Continuity of Anglo-Saxon Devotional Traditions', *Annuale mediaevale* 18 (1977), 20–41

'British Library, MS Arundel 60, and the Anselmian Apocrypha', *Scriptorium* 35 (1981), 271–5

'Continental Sources of Anglo-Saxon Devotional Writing', in *Sources of Anglo-Saxon Culture*, ed. P. E. Szarmach (Kalamazoo, 1986), pp. 103–26

Bethurum, D., 'Episcopal Magnificence in the Eleventh Century', in *Studies in Old English Literature in Honor of Arthur G. Brodeur*, ed. S. B. Greenfield (Eugene, Oregon, 1963), pp. 162–70

See also Wulfstan of Worcester

Beumann, H. *See* Gospels of Otto III

Bharatha Iyer, K., ed., *Art and Thought. Issued in Honour of Dr Ananda K. Coomaraswamy on the Occasion of his 70th Birthday* (London, 1947)

Biddle, M., 'Excavations at Winchester 1965: Fourth Interim Report', *AntJ* 46 (1966), 308–32

'Excavations at Winchester, 1970: Ninth Interim Report', *AntJ* 52 (1972), 93–131

'Excavations at Winchester, 1971: Tenth and Final Interim Report: Part II', *AntJ* 55 (1975), 295–337

'*Felix urbs Winthonia*: Winchester in the Age of Monastic Reform', in *Tenth-Century Studies*, ed. D. Parsons (Chichester, 1975), pp. 123–40

'Archaeology, Architecture, and the Cult of Saints in Anglo-Saxon England', in *The Anglo-Saxon Church*, ed. L. A. S. Butler and R. K. Morris (London, 1986), pp. 1–31

Birch, W. de G., ed., *Cartularium Saxonicum*, 3 vols. (London, 1885–93)
  See also Book of Nunnaminster *and* New Minster

Bishop, E., *Liturgica Historica: Papers on the Liturgy and Religious Life of the Western Church* (Oxford, 1918)

Bishop, T. A. M., *English Caroline Minuscule* (Oxford, 1971)

Blake, E. O. *See* Ely

Blickling Homilies. *The Blickling Homilies of the Tenth Century*, ed. R. Morris, EETS os 58, 63 and 73 (1874–80)

Boddington, A. and G. Cadman, 'Raunds: An Interim Report on Excavations 1977–1980', in *Anglo-Saxon Studies in Archaeology and History* 2, BAR 92 (1981), 103–22

Boeckler, A., *Das goldene Evangelienbuch Heinrichs III* (Berlin, 1933)

Boinet, A., *La miniature carolingienne, ses origines, son développement* (Paris, 1913)

Bond, F. B. and B. Camm, *Roodscreens and Roodlofts*, 2 vols. (London, 1909)

Book of Cerne. *The Prayer Book of Aedeluald the Bishop Commonly Called The Book of Cerne*, ed. A. B. Kuypers (Cambridge, 1902)

Book of Nunnaminster. *An Ancient Manuscript of the Eighth or Ninth Century Formerly Belonging to St Mary's Abbey, or Nunnaminster, Winchester*, ed. W. de G. Birch, Hampshire Record Society (London, 1889)

Bornscheuer, L., *Miseriae Regum: Untersuchungen zum Krisen- und Todesgedanken in den herrschaftstheologischen Vorstellungen der ottonisch-salischen Zeit*, Arbeiten zur Frühmittelalterforschung, Schriftenreihe des Instituts für Frühmittelalterforschung der Universität Münster 4 (Berlin, 1968)

Bovini, G., *Ravenna Mosaics*, trans. G. Scaglia (Oxford, 1978)

Braunfels, W., ed., *Karl der Grosse*, 5 vols. (Dusseldorf, 1965–8)
  Die Welt der Karolinger und ihre Kunst (Munich, 1968)
  See also Aachen

Brou, L., ed., *The Psalter Collects from V–VIth Century Sources*, HBS 83 (1949)

Brown, P., *The Cult of the Saints, its Rise and Function in Latin Christianity* (Chicago, 1981)

Brown, T. J. *See* Durham *and* Lindisfarne Gospels

Bruce-Mitford, R. L. S., *The Art of the Codex Amiatinus*, Jarrow Lecture (1967)
  'The Gold Cross from Thurnham, Kent', *AntJ* 47 (1967), 290–91
  Aspects of Anglo-Saxon Archaeology: Sutton Hoo and other Discoveries (London, 1974)
  See also Lindisfarne Gospels

Bruyne, D. de, *Préfaces de la Bible Latine* (Namur, 1920)

Bruyne, E. de, *Etudes d'esthétique médiévale*, 3 vols. (Bruges, 1946)
  The Esthetics of the Middle Ages, trans E. B. Hennessy (New York, 1969)

Buberl, P., *Die illuminierten Handschriften in Steiermark* I, Beschreibendes Verzeichnis der illuminierten Handschriften in Oesterreich IV.1 (Leipzig, 1911)

Budny, M. O., 'British Library MS Royal 1 E.vi. The Anatomy of an Anglo-Saxon

Bible Fragment' (unpubl. PhD dissertation, 3 vols., London Univ., 1985)

Bullough, D., 'Burial, Community and Belief in the Early Medieval West', in *Ideal and Reality in Frankish and Anglo-Saxon Society*, ed. P. Wormald, D. Bullough and R. Collins (Oxford, 1983), pp. 177–201

Burlin, R. B., *The Old English Advent. A Typological Commentary* (New Haven, Conn., 1968)

Butler, H. E. *See* Jocelin of Brakelond

Butler, L. A. S. and R. K. Morris, eds., *The Anglo-Saxon Church: Papers on History, Architecture and Archaeology in Honour of Dr H. M. Taylor*, CBA Research Report 60 (London, 1986)

Byrhtferth. *Byrhtferth's Manual (A.D. 1011)*, ed. S. J. Crawford, EETS os 177 (1929)

Vita S. Oswaldi. See Oswald

Bzdyl, D. G., 'The Sources of Ælfric's Prayers in Cambridge University Library MS Gg. 3. 28', *N&Q* 222 (1977), 98–102

Cabaniss, J. A., *Amalarius of Metz* (Amsterdam, 1954)

Caesarius of Arles. *Sancti Caesarii Arelatensis sermones*, ed. G. Morin, 2 vols., CCSL 103–4 (1953)

Calkins, R. G., *Illuminated Books of the Middle Ages* (London, 1983)

Campbell, A. *See* Æthelwulf, Emma *and* Frithegod

Campbell, J. J., 'Prayers from MS Arundel 155', *Anglia* 81 (1963), 82–117
See also Advent Lyrics

Campbell, J., ed., *The Anglo-Saxons* (Oxford, 1982)

Capelle, B., 'Regnavit a ligno', in his *Travaux liturgiques de doctrine et d'histoire* III (Louvain, 1967), 211–14
'Les épîtres sapientiales des fêtes de la Vierge', in his *Travaux liturgiques de doctrine et d'histoire* III (Louvain, 1967), 316–22

Cassiodorus. *Expositio psalmorum*, ed. M. Adriaen, 2 vols., CCSL 97–8 (1958)

Cecchelli, C. *See* Rabbula Gospels

Cerne. *See* Book of Cerne

Chambers, R. W. *See* Exeter Book

Chaney, W. A., *The Cult of Kingship in Anglo-Saxon England: The Transition from Paganism to Christianity* (Manchester, 1970)

Charlemagne. *See* Aachen

Chase, C. L., '"Christ III", "The Dream of the Rood", and Early Christian Passion Piety', *Viator* 11 (1980), 11–33

Chevalier, U., *Repertorium hymnologicum. Catalogue des chants, hymnes, proses, séquences, tropes en usage dans l'église latine depuis les origines jusqu'à nos jours*, 6 vols. (Louvain, 1892–1920)

Christ and Satan, an Old English Poem, ed. M. D. Clubb (New Haven, Conn., 1925)
See also Sleeth

Clapham, A. W., 'The Carved Stones at Breedon-on-the-Hill, Leicestershire, and their position in the History of English Art', *Archaeologia* 77 (1927), 219–40
English Romanesque Architecture before the Conquest (Oxford, 1930)
See also Peers *and* Graham

Clayton, M., 'An Examination of the Cult of the Virgin Mary in Anglo-Saxon England, with Special Reference to the Vernacular Texts' (unpubl. DPhil dissertation, Oxford Univ., 1983); rev. ed. forthcoming as *The Cult of the Virgin Mary in Anglo-Saxon England*, Cambridge Studies in Anglo-Saxon England 2
'Feasts of the Virgin in the Liturgy of the Anglo-Saxon Church', *ASE* 13 (1984), 209–33
'Ælfric and *Cogitis me*', *N&Q* 231 (1986), 148–9

Clédat, J., *Nouvelles recherches à Baouît, Haute-Egypte, Campagnes 1903–4*, Comptes rendus des séances de l'Académie des inscriptions et belles-lettres (1904)
Le monastère et la nécropole de Baouît, 2 vols., Mémoires de l'Institut français d'archéologie orientale du Caire 12 and 39 (Cairo, 1904–16)

Clemoes, P., 'Language in Context: *Her* in the 890 *Anglo-Saxon Chronicle*', *Leeds Studies in English*, ns 16 (1985), 27–36
See also Ælfric, Hexateuch *and* Lapidge and Gneuss

Clemoes, P., and K. Hughes, ed., *England before the Conquest. Studies in Primary Sources presented to Dorothy Whitelock* (Cambridge, 1971)

Clubb, M. D. See *Christ and Satan*

Cluny. *Antiquiores consuetudines Cluniacensis monasterii collectore Udalrico monacho Benedictino*: PL 149, 655–778
Consuetudines Farfenses, ed. B. Albers, Consuetudines Monasticae 1 (Stuttgart, 1900)
Consuetudines Cluniacenses antiquiores, ed. B. Albers, Consuetudines Monasticae 2 (Monte Cassino, 1905)
Consuetudines Cluniacensium antiquiores cum redactionibus derivatis, ed. K. Hallinger, CCM 7.2 (1983)
Liber Tramitis aevi Odilonis Abbatis, ed. P. Dinter, CCM 10 (1980)
See also Hallinger

Coatsworth, E., 'Two Examples of the Crucifixion at Hexham', in *Saint Wilfrid at Hexham*, ed. D. P. Kirby (Newcastle upon Tyne, 1974), pp. 180–4
'Late Pre-Conquest Sculptures with the Crucifixion South of the Humber', in *Bishop Æthelwold: His Career and Influence*, ed. B. A. E. Yorke (Woodbridge, 1988), pp. 161–93
See also Durham

Cockerton, R. W. P., 'The Wirksworth Slab', *Journal of the Derbyshire Archaeological and Natural History Society* 82 (1962), 1–20

Codex Egberti. *Codex Egberti der Stadtbibliothek Trier*, ed. H. Schiel, 2 vols. (Basel, 1960)

Colgrave, B. *See* Bede *and* Eddius

Conant, K. J., 'The Original Buildings at the Holy Sepulchre in Jerusalem',
    Speculum 31 (1956), 1–48

'Cluny II and St Bénigne at Dijon', *Archaeologia* 99 (1965), 179–94

Cluny, les églises et la maison du chef d'ordre, Mediaeval Academy of America
    Publications 77 (Cambridge, Mass., 1968)

Cook, A. S. *See* Cynewulf

Coüasnon, C., *The Church of the Holy Sepulchre in Jerusalem*, trans. J.-P. B. and
    C. Ross (London, 1974)

Cramp, R., *Early Northumbrian Sculpture*, Jarrow Lecture (1965)

The Monastic Arts of Northumbria, Arts Council (London, 1967)

'Early Northumbrian Sculpture at Hexham', in *Saint Wilfrid at Hexham*, ed.
    D. P. Kirby (Newcastle upon Tyne, 1974), pp. 115–40

'Anglo-Saxon Sculpture of the Reform Period', in *Tenth-Century Studies*, ed.
    D. Parsons (Chichester, 1975), pp. 184–99

'Schools of Mercian Sculpture', in *Mercian Studies*, ed. A. Dornier (Leicester,
    1977), pp. 191–233

'The Evangelist Symbols and their Parallels in Anglo-Saxon Sculpture', BAR 46
    (1978), 118–30

Corpus of Anglo-Saxon Stone Sculpture, 1.1–2: County Durham and Northumberland
    (Oxford, 1984)

See also Bailey

Crawford, S. J. *See* Ælfric *and* Byrhtferth

Cronyn, J. M. and C. V. Horie, *St Cuthbert's Coffin, the History, Technology and
    Conservation* (Durham, 1985)

Customaries. *Consuetudinum saeculi X/XI/XII monumenta non-Cluniacensia*, ed.
    K. Hallinger, CCM 7.3 (1984)

See also Ælfric *and* Cluny

Cynewulf. *The Christ of Cynewulf: A Poem in Three Parts*, ed. A. S. Cook (Boston,
    1900)

D'Alverny, M.-T., 'Le symbolisme de la sagesse et le Christ de Saint Dunstan',
    Bodleian Library Record 5 (1954–6), 232–44

Dekkers, E. *See* Augustine of Hippo

Deonna, W., 'Le crucifix de la vallée de Saas (Valais): Sol et Luna, histoire d'un
    thème iconographique', *Revue de l'histoire des religions* 132 (1947), 5–47 and
    133 (1948), 49–102

Deshman, R., 'Anglo-Saxon Art after Alfred', *Art Bulletin* 56 (1974),
    176–200

'*Christus rex et magi reges*: Kingship and Christology in Ottonian and Anglo-
    Saxon Art', *Frühmittelalterliche Studien* 10 (1976), 367–405

'The Exalted Servant: The Ruler Theology of the Prayerbook of Charles the
    Bald', *Viator* 11 (1980), 385–417

'The Imagery of the Living Ecclesia and the English Monastic Reform', in *Sources of Anglo-Saxon Culture*, ed. P. E. Szarmach (Kalamazoo, 1986), pp. 261–82

De Wald, E. T. *See* Utrecht Psalter

Dewick, E. S., ed. *Facsimiles of Horae de beata Maria Virgine from English MSS of the Eleventh Century*, HBS 21 (1902)

Dicta Einsidlensia, ed. K. Hallinger, CCM 7.3 (1984), 187–256

Dinter, P. *See* Cluny

Dix, G., *The Shape of the Liturgy* (London, 1945)

    The Treatise on the Apostolic Tradition of St Hippolytus of Rome, Bishop and Martyr, reissued with corrections (London, 1968)

Dodwell, C. R., *The Canterbury School of Illumination 1066–1200* (Cambridge, 1954)

    Painting in Europe 800 to 1200 (Harmondsworth, 1971)

    'Losses of Anglo-Saxon Art in the Middle Ages', *Bull. of the John Rylands Library* 56 (1973–4), 74–92

    Anglo-Saxon Art: A New Perspective (Manchester, 1982)

    See also Hexateuch, St Albans Psalter *and* Theophilus

Dodwell, C. R. and D. H. Turner, *Reichenau Reconsidered: A Reassessment of the Place of Reichenau in Ottonian Art*, Warburg Institute Surveys 2 (London, 1965)

Dolley, M., 'The Nummular Brooch from Sulgrave', in *England before the Conquest: Studies in Primary Sources presented to Dorothy Whitelock*, ed. P. Clemoes and K. Hughes (Cambridge, 1971), pp. 333–49

Dornier, A., ed., *Mercian Studies* (Leicester, 1977)

Dressler, F. *See* Gospels of Otto III

Drogo Sacramentary. *Drogo-Sakramentar. MS lat. 9428, Bibliothèque Nationale, Paris. Vollständige Faksimile-Ausgabe im Originalformat*, ed. W. Koehler and F. Mütherich (Graz, 1974)

    See also Unterkircher

Dümmler, E. *See* Ermoldus Nigellus

Dufrenne, S., *Les illustrations du Psautier d'Utrecht: sources et apport carolingien* (Paris, 1979)

Duft, J. *See* Grandval Bible

Dugdale, W., *Monasticon Anglicanum*, ed. J. Caley, H. Ellis and B. Bandinel, 6 vols. (London, 1817–30)

Dumas, A. *See* Gellone

Dumont, C. *See* Ailred

Dunstan. *Saint Dunstan's Classbook from Glastonbury: Codex Biblioth. Bodleianae Oxon. Auct. F. 4. 32*, ed. R. W. Hunt, Umbrae Codicum Occidentalium 4 (Amsterdam, 1961)

Durham. *Rituale Ecclesiae Dunelmensis. The Durham Collectar*, ed. A. H. Thompson
and U. Lindelöf, Surtees Society 140 (London, 1927)
*The Durham Ritual: A Southern English Collectar of the Tenth Century with
Northumbrian Additions*, ed. T. J. Brown, F. Wormald, A. S. C. Ross and
E. G. Stanley, EEMF 16 (1969)
*The Durham Gospels Together with Fragments of a Gospel Book in Uncial (Durham,
Cathedral Library, MS A II. 17)*, ed. C. D. Verey, T. J. Brown and E.
Coatsworth, EEMF 20 (1980)
Earle, J. *See* Anglo-Saxon Chronicle
Early English Homilies from the Twelfth-Century MS Vesp. D.xiv, ed. R. D.-N.
Warner, EETS os 152 (1917)
Eddius. *The Life of Bishop Wilfrid by Eddius Stephanus*, ed. B. Colgrave (Cambridge,
1927)
Edith of Wilton. *See* Goscelin
Edmund, life by Abbo. *See* Winterbottom
Egeria. See *Itinerarium Egeriae*
Ehwald, R. *See* Aldhelm
Elbern, V. H., *Der karolingische Goldaltar von Mailand* (Bonn, 1952)
'Der fränkische Reliquienkasten und Tragaltar von Werden', in *Das erste
Jahrtausend* I (Dusseldorf, 1962), 436–70
'Der eucharistische Kelch im frühen Mittelalter', *Zeitschrift des deutschen Vereins
für Kunstwissenschaft* 17 (1963), 1–76 and 117–88
Elbern, V. H., ed., *Das erste Jahrtausend: Kultur und Kunst im werdenden Abendland
an Rhein und Ruhr*, 3 vols. (Dusseldorf, 1962–4)
Ellard, G., *Master Alcuin, Liturgist. A Partner of our Piety* (Chicago, 1956)
Elsen, A. E., *Purposes of Art: An Introduction to the History and Appreciation of Art*,
3rd ed. (New York, 1972)
Ely. *Liber Eliensis*, ed. E. O. Blake, Camden Society 3rd ser. 92 (1962)
Emma. *Encomium Emmae reginae*, ed. A. Campbell, Camden Society 3rd ser. 72
(1949)
Epistola ad Paulam et Eustochium. See Paschasius Radbertus
Epitaphium Sanctae Paulae. See Jerome
Ermoldus Nigellus. *In honorem Hludowici Christianissimi Caesaris Augusti Ermoldi
Nigelli exulis elegiaci carminis*, ed. E. Dümmler, MGH, PLAC 2 (Berlin,
1884), 5–79
Evans, G. R., 'Mens devota: The Literary Community of the Devotional Works of
John of Fécamp and St Anselm', *MÆ* 43 (1974), 105–15
Evans, J., *Monastic Life at Cluny 910–1157* (London, 1931)
Cluniac Art of the Romanesque Period (Cambridge, 1950)
Exeter Book. *The Exeter Book of Old English Poetry*, ed. R. W. Chambers, M. Förster
and R. Flower (London, 1933)

Farrell, R. T., ed., *Bede and Anglo-Saxon England. Papers in Honour of the 1300th Anniversary of the Birth of Bede, given at Cornell University in 1973 and 1974*, BAR 46 (1978)

Fehr, B., 'Uber einige Quellen zu Ælfrics *Homiliae Catholicae*', *Archiv* 130 (1913), 378–81
See also Ælfric

Fernie, E., *The Architecture of the Anglo-Saxons* (London, 1983)

Finberg, H. P. R., *The Early Charters of Wessex* (Leicester, 1964)

Fleming, J. V., '*The Dream of the Rood* and Anglo-Saxon Monasticism', *Traditio* 22 (1966), 43–72

Flower, R. *See* Exeter Book

Förster, M., 'Uber die Quellen von Ælfrics exegetischen *Homiliae Catholicae*', *Anglia* 16 (1894), 1–6

'Zur Geschichte des Reliquienkultus in Altengland', *Sitzungsberichte der Bayerischen Akademie der Wissenschaften, philosophisch-historische Abteilung* 8 (1943)
See also Exeter Book *and* Vercelli Homilies

Fraipont, J. *See* Augustine of Hippo

Franceschini, E. See *Itinerarium Egeriae*

Freeman, A., 'Theodulf of Orléans and the *Libri Carolini*', *Speculum* 32 (1957), 663–705

'Further Studies in the *Libri Carolini*', *Speculum* 40 (1965), 203–89

'Carolingian Orthodoxy and the Fate of the *Libri Carolini*', *Viator* 16 (1985), 65–108

Frere, W. H. *See* Winchester

Friend, A. M., 'Carolingian Art in the Abbey of St Denis', *Art Studies* 1 (1923), 67–75

Frithegod. *Frithegodi monachi breviloquium vitae beati Wilfredi et Wulfstani cantoris narratio metrica de Sancto Swithuno*, ed. A. Campbell (Zürich, 1950)

Frolow, A., *La relique de la vraie croix. Recherches sur le développement d'un culte*, Archives de l'orient chrétien 7 (Paris, 1961)

Fulda. *Annales Fuldenses, sive Annales regni Francorum orientalis*, ed. G. H. Pertz, MGH, Script. Germ. 7 (Hanover, 1891)

Gaehde, J. E., 'The Turonian Sources of the Bible of San Paolo fuori le Mura in Rome', *Frühmittelalterliche Studien* 5 (1971), 359–400

'Carolingian Interpretations of an Early Christian Picture Cycle to the Octateuch in the Bible of San Paolo fuori le Mura in Rome', *Frühmittelalterliche Studien* 8 (1974), 351–84

'The Pictorial Sources of the Illustrations to the Books of Kings, Proverbs, Judith and Maccabees in the Carolingian Bible of San Paolo fuori le Mura in Rome', *Frühmittelalterliche Studien* 9 (1975), 359–89
See also Mütherich

Gatch, M. McC., *Preaching and Theology in Anglo-Saxon England: Ælfric and Wulfstan* (Toronto, 1977)

Gellone. *Liber sacramentorum Gellonensis*, ed. A. Dumas, CCSL 159–159A (1981) *See also* Teyssèdre

Gem, R. D. H., 'The Anglo-Saxon Cathedral Church at Canterbury: A Further Contribution', *ArchJ* 127 (1970), 196–201

'A Recession in English Architecture during the Early Eleventh Century, and its Effect on the Development of the Romanesque Style', *JBAA* 38 (1975), 28–49

'Towards an Iconography of Anglo-Saxon Architecture', *JWCI* 46 (1983), 1–18

Gem, R. D. H. and L. Keen, 'Late Anglo-Saxon Finds from the Site of St Edmund's Abbey', *Proc. of the Suffolk Inst. Arch.* 35 (1981), 1–30

Gem, R. D. H. and P. Tudor-Craig, 'A "Winchester School" Wall-Painting at Nether Wallop, Hampshire', *ASE* 9 (1981), 115–36

George of Nicomedea. *Oratio* viii. *In S. Mariam assistentem cruci*: PG 100, 1457–90

Gervase of Canterbury. *Chronica*, in W. Stubbs, ed., *The Historical Works of Gervase of Canterbury*, RS 73, 2 vols. (1879)

Gilson, E., *Introduction à l'étude de Saint Augustin*, 2nd ed., Etudes de philosophie médiévale 11 (Paris, 1943)

The Christian Philosophy of Saint Augustine, trans. L. E. M. Lynch (London, 1961)

Gjerløw, L., *Adoratio crucis. The Regularis concordia and the Decreta Lanfranci* (Oslo, 1961)

Glastonbury. *The Early History of Glastonbury. An Edition, Translation and Study of William of Malmesbury's De antiquitate Glastonie ecclesie*, ed. J. Scott (Woodbridge, 1981)

Gneuss, H., *Hymnar und Hymnen im englischen Mittelalter. Studien zur Uberlieferung, Glossierung und Ubersetzung lateinischer Hymnen in England* (Tübingen, 1968)

'A Preliminary List of Manuscripts Written or Owned in England up to 1100', *ASE* 9 (1981), 1–60

See also Lapidge

Godden, M. R., 'The Development of Ælfric's Second Series of *Catholic Homilies*', *ES* 54 (1973), 209–16

See also Ælfric

Godman, P., *Poetry of the Carolingian Renaissance* (London, 1985)

See also Alcuin

Golden Age. *The Golden Age of Anglo-Saxon Art 966–1066*, ed. J. Backhouse, D. H. Turner and L. Webster (London, 1984)

Goldschmidt, A., *Die Elfenbeinskulpturen aus der Zeit der karolingischen und sächsischen Kaiser, VIII–XI Jahrhundert*, and *Die Elfenbeinskulpturen aus der romanischen Zeit, XI–XIII Jahrhundert*, 4 vols., Denkmäler der deutschen Kunst (Berlin, 1914–26)

German Illumination, 2 vols. (Florence, 1928)

Goldschmidt, A. and K. Weitzmann, *Die byzantinischen Elfenbeinskulpturen des X–XIII Jahrhunderts*, 2 vols. (Berlin, 1930–34)

Gollancz, I., ed., *The Cædmon Manuscript of Anglo-Saxon Biblical Poetry, Junius XI in the Bodleian Library* (Oxford, 1927)

Goscelin. *De Sancta Editha virgine et abbatissa*: A. Wilmart, 'La légende de Ste Edith en prose et vers par le moine Goscelin', *AB* 56 (1938), 5–101 and 265–307

   Liber confortatorius: C. H. Talbot, 'The Liber confortatorius of Goscelin of Saint Bertin', *Studia Anselmiana* 37 (1955), 1–117

Gospels of Otto III. *Das Evangeliar Ottos III, Clm 4453 der Bayerischen Staatsbibliothek München*, ed. F. Dressler, F. Mütherich and H. Beumann, 2 vols. (Frankfurt, 1978)

Gougaud, L., 'Muta praedicatio', *RB* 42 (1930), 168–71

   'Etude sur les "Ordines commendationis animae"', *EL* 49 (1935), 3–27

Grabar, A., *Les peintures de l'Evangeliaire de Sinope, Bibliothèque Nationale, Suppl. gr. 1286* (Paris, 1948)

   Ampoules de Terre Sainte (Monza-Bobbio) (Paris, 1958)

   Byzantium from the Death of Theodosius to the Rise of Islam, trans. S. Gilbert and J. Emmons (London, 1966)

   The Beginnings of Christian Art 200–395, trans. S. Gilbert and J. Emmons (London, 1967)

   Christian Iconography: A Study of its Origins, trans. T. Grabar (London, 1969)

Graef, H., *Mary: A History of Doctrine and Devotion*, 2 vols. (London, 1963–5)

Graham, R. and A. W. Clapham, 'The Monastery of Cluny, 910–1155', *Archaeologia* 80 (1930), 143–78

Grandval Bible. *Die Bibel von Moutier-Grandval, British Museum Add. MS 10546*, with introduction by J. Duft, B. Fischer, A. Bruckner, E. J. Beer, A. A. Schmid and E. Irblich (Bern, 1971)

Grant, R. J. S., *Cambridge, Corpus Christi College 41: The Loricas and the Missal* (Amsterdam, 1979)

Green, A. R. and P. M., *Saxon Architecture and Sculpture in Hampshire* (Winchester, 1951)

Greene, B. da C. and M. P. Harrsen, *The Pierpont Morgan Library: Exhibition of Illuminated Manuscripts Held at the New York Public Library* (New York, 1934)

Grégoire, R., *Les homéliaires du moyen âge: inventaire et analyse des manuscrits*, Rerum ecclesiasticarum documenta, Series Maior, Fontes 6 (Rome, 1966)

Gregory the Great. *Homiliae .xl. in evangelia:* PL 76, 1075–1312

   Dialogi, ed. U. Moricca (Rome, 1924)

Letter to Serenus of Marseilles: MGH, Epist. 2.1 (Gregorii I Registri L. x–xiv), ed.
L. M. Hartmann (Berlin, 1895), 269–72

Homiliae in Hiezechihelem prophetam, ed. M. Adriaen, CCSL 142 (1971)

Moralia in Iob, ed. M. Adriaen, 3 vols., CCSL 143–143B (1979–85).

Grodecki, L., F. Mutherich, J. Taralon and F. Wormald, *Le siècle de l'an mil*
(Paris, 1973)

Grube, E., 'Majestas und Crucifix: zum Motiv des Suppedaneums', *Zeitschrift für
Kunstgeschichte* 20 (1957), 268–87

Hallinger, K., *Gorze-Kluny. Studien zu den monastischen Lebensformen und Gegensätzen
im Hochmittelalter*, 2 vols., *Studia Anselmiana* 22–3 (1950) and 24–5 (1951)

Initia consuetudinis Benedictinae. Consuetudines saeculi octavi et noni, CCM 1 (1963)

'The Spiritual Life of Cluny in the Early Days', in *Cluniac Monasticism in the
Central Middle Ages*, ed. N. Hunt (London, 1971), pp. 29–55

See also Ælfric, Cluny, Customaries and *Dicta Einsidlensia*

Hamilton, N. E. S. A. *See* William of Malmesbury

Hanslik, R. *See* Benedictine Rule

Hanssens, J. M. *See* Amalarius

Hardison, O. B., *Christian Rite and Christian Drama in the Middle Ages: Essays on the
Origin and Early History of Modern Drama* (Baltimore, 1965)

Hariulf, *Chronicon Centulense*: PL 174, 1212–366

Harmer, F. E., *Anglo-Saxon Writs* (Manchester, 1952)

Harris, R. M., 'The Marginal Drawings of the Bury St Edmunds Psalter (Rome,
Vatican Library, MS Reg. lat. 12)' (unpubl. PhD dissertation, Princeton
Univ., 1960)

Harrsen, M., 'The Countess Judith of Flanders and the Library of Weingarten
Abbey', *Papers of the Bibliographical Society of America* 24 (1930), 1–13

Hartmann, L. M. *See* Gregory the Great

Hartzell, K. D., 'Some New English Drawings of the Tenth Century', *Acta* 6
(1982 for 1979), 83–93

Haseloff, A., *Codex purpureus Rossanensis. Die Miniaturen der griechischen Evangelien-
Handschrift in Rossano* (Berlin and Leipzig, 1898)

Hasler, R., 'Zu zwei Darstellungen aus der ältesten Kopie des Utrecht-Psalters',
Zeitschrift für Kunstgeschichte 44 (1981), 317–39

Haussherr, R., 'Das Imervardkreuz und der Volto-Santo-Typ', *Zeitschrift für
Kunstwissenschaft* 16 (1962), 129–70

Der tote Christus am Kreuz. Zur Ikonographie des Gerokreuzes (Bonn, 1963)

Hautecoeur, L., 'Le soleil et la lune dans les crucifixions', *Revue archéologique*, 5th
ser., 14 (1921), 13–32

Haymo of Auxerre. *Homiliae*: PL 118, 11–804

Heer, F., *The Holy Roman Empire*, trans. J. Sondheimer (London, 1968)

Heighway, C. and R. Bryant, 'A Reconstruction of the Tenth-Century Church of

St Oswald, Gloucester', in *The Anglo-Saxon Church*, ed. L. A. S. Butler and R. K. Morris (London, 1986), pp. 188–95

Heimann, A., 'A Twelfth-Century Manuscript from Winchcombe and its Illustrations: Dublin, Trinity College, MS 53', *JWCI* 28 (1965), 86–109

'Three Illustrations from the Bury St Edmunds Psalter and their Prototypes', *JWCI* 29 (1966), 39–59

Heitz, C., 'Architecture et liturgie processionnelle à l'époque préromane', *Revue de l'art* 24 (1974), 30–47

L'architecture religieuse carolingienne: les formes et leurs fonctions (Paris, 1980)

'The Iconography of Architectural Form', in *The Anglo-Saxon Church*, ed. L. A. S. Butler and R. K. Morris (London, 1986), pp. 90–100

Henderson, G., *Bede and the Visual Arts*, Jarrow Lecture (1980)

'The John the Baptist Panel on the Ruthwell Cross', *Gesta* 24 (1985), 3–12

From Durrow to Kells. The Insular Gospel-Books 650–800 (London, 1987)

Henry of Huntingdon. *Historia Anglorum*, ed. T. Arnold, RS 74 (1879)

Henry Knighton. *Chronicon*, ed. J. R. Lumby, 2 vols., RS 92 (1889–95)

Hermann, H. J., *Die frühmittelalterlichen Handschriften des Abendlandes*, Beschreibendes Verzeichnis der illuminierten Handschriften in Oesterreich 8 (Leipzig, 1923)

Herren, M. *See* Aldhelm

Hesbert, R.-J., *Le problème de la transfixion du Christ dans les traditions* (Paris, 1940). *See also* Antiphons

Heslop, T. A., 'A Walrus Ivory Pyx and the *Visitatio sepulchri*', *JWCI* 44 (1981), 157–60

Hexateuch. *The Old English Illustrated Hexateuch (British Museum Cotton Claudius B. iv)*, ed. C. R. Dodwell and P. Clemoes, EEMF 18 (1974)

For an edition of the text see under Ælfric

Higden. *Polychronicon*, ed. J. R. Lumby, 9 vols., RS 41 (1865–86)

Higgitt, J., 'Glastonbury, Dunstan, Monasticism and Manuscripts', *Art History* 2 (1979), 275–90

Higgitt, J., ed., *Early Medieval Sculpture in Britain and Ireland*, BAR 152 (1986)

Hilberg, I. *See* Jerome

Hinks, R., *Carolingian Art: A Study of Early Medieval Painting and Sculpture in Western Europe* (Michigan, 1962)

Hinton, D. A., *A Catalogue of the Anglo-Saxon Ornamental Metalwork, 700–1100 in the Department of Antiquities, Ashmolean Museum* (Oxford, 1974)

Hoffmann, W. *See* Stuttgart Psalter

Homburger, O., *Die Anfänge der Malschule von Winchester im X. Jahrhundert* (Leipzig, 1912)

'L'art carolingien de Metz et l'"école de Winchester"', in *Essais en l'honneur de*

Jean Porcher: Etudes sur les manuscrits à peintures, ed. O. Pächt (Paris, 1963), pp. 35–46

Hope, W. H. St J., 'Durham Abbey', *Proceedings of the Society of Antiquaries* 22 (1907–9), 416–24

'Quire Screens in English Churches with Special Reference to the Twelfth-Century Quire Screen formerly in the Cathedral Church of Ely', *Archaeologia* 68 (1917), 43–110

Horn, W. and E. Born, *The Plan of St Gall: A Study of the Architecture and Economy of, and Life in, a Paradigmatic Carolingian Monastery*, 3 vols. (Berkeley, 1979)

Horst, K. van der. *See* Utrecht Psalter

Hourlier, J., *Saint Odilon abbé de Cluny*, Bibliothèque de la Revue d'histoire ecclésiastique 40 (Louvain, 1964)

Hrabanus Maurus. *De laudibus sanctae crucis*: PL 107, 133–294

De clericorum institutione: PL 107, 297–420

Commentariorum in Genesim libri quatuor: PL 107, 439–670

Commentariorum in Matthaeum libri octo: PL 107, 727–1156

Expositio in Paralipomena: PL 109, 279–540

Homiliae de festis praecipuis: PL 110, 9–134

De vita beatae Mariae Magdalenae: PL 112, 1431–1508

Hubert, J., *Arts et vie sociale de la fin du monde antique au moyen âge: études d'archéologie et d'histoire*, Mémoires et documents publiés par la Société de l'école des chartes 24 (Geneva, 1977)

Hubert, J., J. Porcher and W. F. Volbach, *Europe in the Dark Ages*, trans. S. Gilbert and J. Emmons (London, 1969)

Carolingian Art, trans. J. Emmons, S. Gilbert and R. Allen (London, 1970)

Hughes, A. *See* Wulfstan II of Worcester

Hunt, E. D., *Holy Land Pilgrimage in the Later Roman Empire* AD 312–460 (Oxford, 1982)

Hunt, N., *Cluny under Saint Hugh, 1049–1109* (London, 1967)

Hunt, N., ed., *Cluniac Monasticism in the Central Middle Ages* (London, 1971)

Hunt, R. W. *See* Dunstan

Hurlbut, S. A., *The Picture of the Heavenly Jerusalem in the Writings of Johannes of Fécamp, 'De contemplativa vita' and in the Elizabethan Hymns* (Washington, D.C., 1943)

Hurst, D. *See* Bede *and* Jerome

Huygens, R. B. C., 'Le moine Idung et ses deux ouvrages: "Argumentum super quatuor questionibus" et "Dialogus duorum monachorum"', *Studi medievali* 3rd ser. 13 (1972), 291–470

Isidore. *Isidori Hispalensis episcopi Etymologiarum sive originum libri xx*, ed. W. M. Lindsay, 2 vols., Scriptorum classicorum bibliotheca Oxoniensis (Oxford, 1911)

Itinerarium Egeriae, ed. E. Franceschini and R. Weber, CCSL 175 (1965), 35–90

James, M. R., 'On the Abbey of S. Edmund at Bury: II, The Church', *Cambridge Antiquarian Society* 28 (1895), 115–212

'Pictor in Carmine', *Archaeologia* 94 (1951), 141–66

James, M. R., trans., *The Apocryphal New Testament*, corrected version (Oxford, 1953)

Jerome. *Adversus Jovinianum libri duo*: PL 23, 211–338

Epistola cviii *(Epitaphium Sanctae Paulae)*, ed. I. Hilberg, CSEL 55 (1912), 306–51

Tractatus sive homiliae in psalmos, ed. G. Morin, CCSL 78 (1958), 3–446

Commentariorum in Matheum libri iv, ed. D. Hurst and M. Adriaen, CCSL 77 (1969)

Epistula adversus Rufinum, ed. P. Lardet, CCSL 79 (1982), 73–116

Jewell, R. H. I., 'The Anglo-Saxon Friezes at Breedon-on-the-Hill, Leicestershire', *Archaeologia* 108 (1986), 95–115

Jocelin of Brakelond. *Cronica: The Chronicle of Jocelin of Brakelond Concerning the Acts of Samson, Abbot of the Monastery of St Edmund*, ed. H. E. Butler (London, 1949)

John of Fécamp. *Confessio fidei*: PL 101, 1027–98

Confessio theologica. See Leclercq and Bonnes

Summe sacerdos: A. Wilmart, *Auteurs spirituels et textes dévots* (Paris, 1932), pp. 101–25

Prayer to God the Father [probably not by John of Fécamp]. Ptd under *Sancti Anselmi orationes*, no. ii, in PL 158, 858–65 and Augustine, *Meditationum liber unus*, chs. v–viii, in PL 40, 904–8

John, E., 'The Sources of the English Monastic Reformation: A Comment', *RB* 70 (1960), 197–203

Orbis Britanniae and Other Studies (Leicester, 1966)

'The World of Abbot Ælfric', in *Ideal and Reality in Frankish and Anglo-Saxon Society*, ed. P. Wormald, D. Bullough and R. Collins (Oxford, 1983), pp. 300–16

Jones, C. W. *See* Bede

Jungmann, J. A., *The Mass of the Roman Rite, its Origins and Development*, trans. F. A. Brunner and rev. C. K. Riepe (London, 1959)

The Early Liturgy to the Time of Gregory the Great, trans. F. A. Brunner (London, 1960)

Kahsnitz, R., *Der Werdener Psalter in Berlin, MS theol. lat. fol. 358: Eine Untersuchung zu Problemen mittelalterlicher Psalterillustration* (Dusseldorf, 1979)

Das goldene Evangelienbuch von Echternach. Eine Prunkhandschrift des 11 Jahrhunderts (Frankfurt am Main, 1982)

Kantorowicz, E. H., 'Ivories and Litanies', *JWCI* 5 (1942), 56–81

Bibliography

'The Quinity of Winchester', *Art Bulletin* 29 (1947), 73–85

The King's Two Bodies: A Study in Mediaeval Political Theology (Princeton, 1957)

Laudes Regiae: A Study in Liturgical Acclamations and Mediaeval Ruler Worship, University of California Publications in History 33, (Berkeley, 1946)

Kauffmann, C. M., *Romanesque Manuscripts 1066–1190*, A Survey of Manuscripts Illuminated in the British Isles 3 (London, 1975)

Kendrick, T. D., *Anglo-Saxon Art to A.D. 900* (London, 1938)

Late Saxon and Viking Art (London, 1949)

See also Lindisfarne Gospels

Ker, N. R., *Catalogue of Manuscripts Containing Anglo-Saxon* (Oxford, 1957)

Kessler, H. L., *The Illustrated Bibles from Tours*, Studies in Manuscript Illumination 7 (Princeton, 1977)

Keynes, S., *Anglo-Saxon Manuscripts and Other Items of Related Interest in the Library of Trinity College, Cambridge* (Cambridge, 1985)

'King Athelstan's Books', in *Learning and Literature in Anglo-Saxon England*, ed. M. Lapidge and H. Gneuss (Cambridge, 1985), pp. 143–201

See also York Gospels

Kidd, J. A., 'The Quinity of Winchester Reconsidered', *Studies in Iconography* 7–8 (1981–2), 21–33

Kirby, D. P., ed., *Saint Wilfrid at Hexham* (Newcastle, 1974)

'Bede, Eddius Stephanus and the "Life of Wilfrid" ', *EHR* 98 (1983), 101–14

Kitzinger, E., 'The Cult of Images in the Age before Iconoclasm', *Dumbarton Oaks Papers* 8 (1954), 83–150

'Christian Imagery: Growth and Impact', in *Age of Spirituality*, ed. K. Weitzmann (New York, 1980), pp. 141–63

Kjølbye-Biddle, B., 'The Seventh-Century Minster at Winchester Interpreted', in *The Anglo-Saxon Church*, ed. L. A. S. Butler and R. K. Morris (London, 1986), pp. 196–209

Klukas, A. W., 'The Architectural Implications of the *Decreta Lanfranci*', *Anglo-Norman Studies* 6 (1984), 136–71

'Liturgy and Architecture: Deerhurst Priory as an Expression of the *Regularis concordia*', *Viator* 15 (1984), 81–106

Koehler, T., 'Les principales interprétations traditionnelles de Jean xix. 25–27 pendant les douze premiers siècles', *Etudes Mariales* 16 (1959), 119–55

Koehler, W. R. W., *Die karolingischen Miniaturen im Auftrage des deutschen Vereins für Kunstwissenschaft* I–III (Berlin, 1930–60)

'An Illustrated Evangelistary of the Ada School and its Model', *JWCI* 15 (1952), 48–66

See also Drogo Sacramentary

Koehler, W. R. W. and F. Mütherich, *Die karolingischen Miniaturen im Auftrage des deutschen Vereins für Kunstwissenschaft* IV–V (Berlin, 1971–82)

Krapp, G. P. and E. V. K. Dobbie *See* Anglo-Saxon Poetic Records

Krautheimer, R., 'Introduction to an "Iconography of Mediaeval Architecture" ', *JWCI* 5 (1942), 1–33

Kurth, B., 'The Iconography of the Wirksworth Slab', *Burlington Magazine* 86 (1945), 114–21

Kuypers, A. B. *See* Book of Cerne

Lambot, D. C., 'L'homélie du Pseudo-Jérôme sur l'assomption et l'évangile de la nativité de Marie d'après une lettre inédite d'Hincmar', *RB* 46 (1934), 265–82

Lapidge, M., *The Cult of St Swithun*, Winchester Studies 4.2 (Oxford, forthcoming)

See also Aldhelm

Lapidge, M. and H. Gneuss, ed., *Learning and Literature in Anglo-Saxon England. Studies presented to Peter Clemoes on the Occasion of his Sixty-Fifth Birthday* (Cambridge, 1985)

Lardet, P. *See* Jerome

Lasko, P., *Ars Sacra 800–1200* (Harmondsworth, 1972)

Leclercq, J., 'Ecrits spirituels de l'école de Jean de Fécamp', *Studia Anselmiana* 20 (*Analecta Monastica* I (1948), 91–114)

'Les collections de sermons de Nicolas de Clairvaux', *RB* 66 (1956), 269–302

L'idée de la royauté du Christ au moyen âge, Unam sanctam 32 (Paris, 1959)

The Love of Learning and the Desire for God, a Study of Monastic Culture, 2nd ed., trans. C. Misrahi (New York, 1974)

'La réforme bénédictine anglaise du Xe siècle vue du continent', *Studia Monastica* 24 (1982), 105–25

'*Otium monasticum* as a Context for Artistic Creativity', in *Monasticism and the Arts*, ed. T. G. Verdon (Syracuse, 1984), pp. 63–80

Leclercq, J. and J.-P. Bonnes, *Un maître de la vie spirituelle au XIe siècle: Jean de Fécamp*, Etudes de théologie et d'histoire de la spiritualité 9 (Paris, 1946)

Leclercq, J., F. Vandenbroucke, and L. Bouyer, *A History of Christian Spirituality* II, *The Spirituality of the Middle Ages* (London, 1968)

Leechdoms. *Kleinere angelsächsische Denkmäler I*, ed. G. Leonhardi, Bibliothek der angelsächsischen Prosa 6 (Hamburg, 1905), 1–109

Legg, J. W. *See* Sarum Missal

Lehmann, E., 'Die Anordnung der Altäre in der karolingischen Klosterkirche zu Centula', in *Karl der Grosse* III, *Karolingische Kunst*, ed. W. Braunfels and H. Schnitzler (Dusseldorf, 1966), 374–83

Lehmann-Brockhaus, O., ed., *Schriftquellen zur Kunstgeschichte des 11. und 12. Jahrhunderts für Deutschland, Lothringen und Italien*, 2 vols. (Berlin, 1938)

Lateinische Schriftquellen zur Kunst in England, Wales und Schottland vom Jahre 901 bis zum Jahre 1307, 5 vols. (Munich, 1955–60)

Leo, F. *See* Venantius Fortunatus

Leofric Missal. *The Leofric Missal as Used in the Cathedral of Exeter during the Episcopate of its First Bishop* AD *1050–1072*, ed. F. E. Warren (Oxford, 1883)

Leonhardi, G. *See* Leechdoms

Leroquais, V., *Les sacramentaires et les missels manuscrits des bibliothèques publiques de France*, 4 vols. (Paris, 1924)

   Les pontificaux manuscrits des bibliothèques publiques de France, 3 vols. (Paris, 1937)

   Les psautiers manuscrits latins des bibliothèques publiques de France, 3 vols. (Macon, 1940–41)

Liber Eliensis. *See* Ely

Liber Tramitis. *See* Cluny

Liber vitae. *See* New Minster

Libri Carolini sive Caroli Magni Capitulare de imaginibus, ed. H. Bastgen, MGH, Concilia II, Suppl. (Hanover, 1924)

Liebermann, F., ed., *Die Gesetze der Angelsachsen*, 3 vols. (Aalen, 1903–16)

Lindelöf, U. *See* Durham

Lindisfarne Gospels. *Evangeliorum quattuor codex Lindisfarnensis*, ed. T. D. Kendrick, T. J. Brown, R. L. S. Bruce-Mitford, H. Roosen-Runge, A. S. C. Ross, E. G. Stanley and A. E. Werner, 2 vols. (Olten and Lausanne, 1956–60)

Lindsay, W. M. *See* Isidore

Loerke, W., ' "Real Presence" in Early Christian Art', in *Monasticism and the Arts*, ed. T. G. Verdon (Syracuse, 1984), pp. 29–51

Longhurst, M. H., 'Two Ivory Reliefs at South Kensington', *Burlington Magazine* 46 (1925), 93–4

   English Ivories (London, 1926)

Loomis, D. B., '*Regnum* and *sacerdotium* in the Early Eleventh Century', in *England before the Conquest: Studies in Primary Sources presented to Dorothy Whitelock*, ed. P. Clemoes and K. Hughes (Cambridge, 1971), pp. 129–45

Lucchesi, J. *See* Peter Damian

Lumby, J. R. *See* Henry Knighton *and* Higden

McGurk, P. *See* York Gospels

McKenzie, D. A., *Otfrid von Weissenburg: Narrator or Commentator?*, Stanford University Publ., in Lang. and Lit., 6.3 (Stanford, 1946)

Madden, F. *See* Matthew Paris

Mahuet, J. de, 'Essai sur la part de l'orient dans l'iconographie mariale de l'occident', *Etudes Mariales* 19 (1962), 145–83

Mâle, E., *The Early Churches of Rome*, trans. D. Buxton (London, 1960)

Martin, K., *Die ottonischen Wandbilder der St Georgskirche Reichenau-Oberzell*, 2nd ed. (Sigmaringen, 1975)

Bibliography

Martindale, A., 'The Romanesque Church of S. Bénigne at Dijon and MS 591 in the Bibliothèque Municipale', *JBAA* 3rd ser. 25 (1962), 21–55

Maspero, J., *Fouilles exécutées a Baouît*, Mémoires de l'Institut français d'archéologie orientale du Caire 59 (Cairo, 1931–43)

Matthew Paris, *Historia minor*, ed. F. Madden, 3 vols., RS 44 (1866–9)

Mayer, A. *See* Augustine of Hippo

Mayor, J. E. B. *See* Richard of Cirencester

Merton, A., *Die Buchmalerei in St Gallen vom neunten bis zum elften Jahrhundert* (Leipzig, 1912)

Metz Coronation Sacramentary. *Sakramentar von Metz Fragment, MS lat. 1141, Bibl. Nat. Paris. Vollständige Faksimile-Ausgabe*, ed. F. Mütherich (Graz, 1972)

Metz, P., *The Golden Gospels of Echternach, Codex Aureus Epternacensis* (London, 1957)

Meyvaert, P., 'Bede and the Church Paintings at Wearmouth-Jarrow', *ASE* 8 (1979), 63–77

Millar, E. G., *English Illuminated Manuscripts from the Xth to the XIIIth Century* (Paris, 1926)

Millet, G., *Recherches sur l'iconographie de l'évangile aux XIVe, XVe et XVIe siècles d'après les monuments de Mistra, de la Macédoine et du Mont-Athos* (Paris, 1916)

Missal. *See* Leofric Missal, New Minster *and* Robert of Jumièges

Mitchell, H. P., 'Flotsam of Later Anglo-Saxon Art I', *Burlington Magazine* 42 (1923), 63–72, 2 plates

'English or German? A Pre-Conquest Gold Cross', *Burlington Magazine* 47, (1925), 324–30, 2 plates

Moricca, U. *See* Gregory the Great

Morin, G. *See* Caesarius of Arles *and* Jerome

Morris, R. *See* Blickling Homilies

Morris, R., 'Alcuin, York, and the *alma sophia*', in *The Anglo-Saxon Church*, ed. L. A. S. Butler and R. K. Morris (London, 1986), pp. 80–9

Morrish, J. J., 'An Examination of Literacy and Learning in England in the Ninth Century' (unpubl. DPhil dissertation, Oxford Univ., 1982)

Mountain, W. J. *See* Augustine of Hippo

Mütherich, F. *See* Drogo Sacramentary, Gospels of Otto III, Grodecki, Koehler, Metz Coronation Sacramentary, Munich *and* Schramm

Mütherich, F. and J. E. Gaehde, *Carolingian Painting* (London, 1977)

Muir, B. J., ed., *A Pre-Conquest English Prayer-Book (BL MSS Cotton Galba A. xiv and Nero A. ii (ff. 3–13))*, HBS 103 (1988)

Munich, Zentralinstitut für Kunstgeschichte. *Mittelalterliche Schatzverzeichnisse I. Von der Zeit Karls des Grossen bis zur Mitte des 13. Jahrhunderts*, ed. B. Bischoff and F. Mütherich (Munich, 1967)

Muñoz, A., *Il codice purpureo di Rossano e il frammento Sinopense* (Rome, 1907)

Mynors, R. A. B., *Durham Cathedral Manuscripts to the End of the Twelfth Century* (Oxford, 1939)

See also Bede

Needham, P., *Twelve Centuries of Bookbindings, 400–1600* (New York, 1979)

Nees, L., 'Image and Text: Excerpts from Jerome's *De Trinitate* and the *Maiestas Domini* Miniatures of the Gundohinus Gospels', *Viator* 18 (1987), 1–21

New Minster. *Liber Vitae: Register and Martyrology of New Minster and Hyde Abbey, Winchester*, ed. W. de G. Birch, Hampshire Record Society (London, 1892)

The Missal of the New Minster Winchester (Le Havre, Bibliothèque municipale MS 330), ed. D. H. Turner, HBS 93 (1962)

Niver, C., 'The Psalter in the British Museum, Harley 2904', in *Medieval Studies in Memory of A. Kingsley Porter*, ed. W. R. W. Koehler, 2 vols. (Cambridge, Mass., 1939), pp. 667–87

Nordenfalk, C., 'The Apostolic Canon Tables', in *Essais en l'honneur de Jean Porcher. Etudes sur les manuscrits à peintures*, ed. O. Pächt (Paris, 1963), pp. 17–34

Oakeshott, W., *The Mosaics of Rome from the Third to the Fourteenth Centuries* (London, 1967)

Ó Carragáin, É., '*Vidi aquam*: The Liturgical Background to *The Dream of the Rood* 20a: "swætan on þa swiðran healfe"', *N&Q* 228 (1983), 8–15

'The Ruthwell Crucifixion Poem in its Iconographic and Liturgical Context', *Peritia* (forthcoming)

Odilo of Cluny, *Sermones*: PL 142, 991–1036

Epitaphium Adalheidae imperatricis, ed. G. H. Pertz, MGH, Script. fol. 4 (Hanover, 1841), 637–45

Odo of Cluny, *Collationes*: PL 133, 517–638

Sermones: PL 133, 709–52

Ogilvy, J. D. A., *Books Known to the English, 597–1066* (Cambridge, Mass., 1967)

Ohlgren, T. H., *Insular and Anglo-Saxon Illuminated Manuscripts: An Iconographic Catalogue c. AD 625 to 1100* (New York, 1986)

Okasha, E. and J. O'Reilly, 'An Anglo-Saxon Portable Altar: Inscription and Iconography', *JWCI* 47 (1984), 32–51

Old English Hexateuch. *See* Hexateuch

Oppenheimer, F., *The Legend of the Ste Ampoule* (London, 1953)

O'Reilly, J., 'The Rough-Hewn Cross in Anglo-Saxon Art', in *Ireland and Insular Art AD 500–1200*, ed. M. Ryan (Dublin, 1987), pp. 153–8

See also Okasha

Oswald. *Vita S. Oswaldi archiepiscopi Eboracensis*, in *Historians of the Church of York*, ed. J. Raine, 3 vols., RS (1879–94), I, 399–475

Otto III. *See* Gospels of Otto III

Ouspensky, L., and V. Lossky, *The Meaning of Icons*, trans. G. E. H. Palmer and
  E. Kedloubovsky (New York, 1982)
Pächt, O., 'The Illustrations of St Anselm's Prayers and Meditations', *JWCI*
  19 (1956), 68–83
  The Rise of Pictorial Narrative in Twelfth-Century England (Oxford, 1962)
  See also Porcher *and* St Albans Psalter
Park, D., 'The "Lewes Group" of Wall Paintings in Sussex', *Anglo-Norman Studies*
  6 (1984), 200–37
Parsons, D., ed., *Tenth-Century Studies: Essays in Commemoration of the Millennium of
  the Council of Winchester and the Regularis Concordia* (Chichester, 1975)
  '*Sacrarium*: Ablution Drains in Early Medieval Churches', in *The Anglo-Saxon
  Church*, ed. L. A. S. Butler and R. K. Morris (London, 1986), pp. 105–20
Paschasius Radbertus. *Epistola ad Paulam et Eustochium*: PL 30, 122–42
  De corpore et sanguine Domini, ed. B. Paulus, CCCMed 16 (1969), 1–131
  Epistola ad Fredugardum, ed. B. Paulus, CCCMed 16 (1969), 145–73
  Expositio in Mattheo libri xii, ed. B. Paulus, 3 vols., CCCMed 56–56B (1984)
Paul the Deacon. *Sancti Gregorii Magni vita*: PL 75, 41–60
  Homiliarius: PL 95, 1159–584
Paulus, B. *See* Paschasius Radbertus
Peers, C. R. and A. W. Clapham, 'St Augustine's Abbey Church, Canterbury,
  Before the Norman Conquest', *Archaeologia* 77 (1927), 201–18
Pertz, G. H. *See* Fulda *and* Odilo
Peter Damian. *Sancti Petri Damiani sermones*, ed. J. Lucchesi, CCCMed 57
  (1983)
Peterson, E., *The Angels and the Liturgy: The Status and Significance of the Holy Angels
  in Worship*, trans. R. Walls (London, 1964)
Planchart, A. E., *The Repertory of Tropes at Winchester*, 2 vols. (Princeton, 1977)
Plummer, C. *See* Anglo-Saxon Chronicle *and* Bede
Pope, J. C. *See* Ælfric
Porcher, J. *Essais en l'honneur de Jean Porcher. Etudes sur les manuscrits à peintures*, ed.
  O. Pächt (Paris, 1963)
  See also Hubert
Portiforium Wulstani. See Wulfstan II of Worcester
Prescott, A., 'The Text of the Benedictional of Æthelwold', in *Bishop Æthelwold:
  His Career and Influence*, ed. B. A. E. Yorke (Woodbridge, 1988),
  pp. 119–47
Prudentius, *Psychomachia. See* Stettiner
Quirk, R. N., 'Winchester Cathedral in the Tenth Century', *ArchJ* 114 (1957),
  28–68
  'Winchester New Minster and its Tenth-Century Tower', *JBAA* 3rd ser. 24
  (1961), 16–54

Rabbula Gospels. *The Rabbula Gospels. Facsimile Edition of the Miniatures of the Syriac Manuscript, Plut. 1. 56 in the Medicaean-Laurentian Library*, ed. C. Cecchelli, G. Furlani and M. Salmi (Olten and Lausanne, 1959)

Raine, J. *See* Oswald

Ramsey. *Historia Ramesiensis*, ed. W. D. Macray, RS 83 (1886)

Raw, B., 'The Archer, the Eagle and the Lamb', *JWCI* 30 (1967), 391–4
 '*The Dream of the Rood* and its Connections with Early Christian Art', *MÆ* 39 (1970), 239–56
 'The Probable Derivation of Most of the Illustrations in Junius 11 from an Illustrated Old Saxon *Genesis*', *ASE* 5 (1976), 133–48
 The Art and Background of Old English Poetry (London, 1978)

Regularis concordia Anglicae nationis monachorum sanctimonialiumque ed. T. Symons (London, 1953)

Reil, J., *Die frühchristlichen Darstellungen der Kreuzigung Christi*, Studien über christliche Denkmäler 2 (Leipzig, 1904)
 Die altchristlichen Bildzyklen des Lebens Jesu, Studien über christliche Denkmäler 10 (Leipzig, 1910)
 Christus am Kreuz in der Bildkunst der Karolingerzeit, Studien über christliche Denkmäler 21 (Leipzig, 1930)

Rhetorica ad Herennium, ed. H. Caplan (London, 1954)

Rice, D. T., *English Art 871–1100*, Oxford History of English Art 2 (Oxford, 1952)

Rice, D. T., ed., *The Dark Ages. The Making of European Civilization* (London, 1965)

Richard of Cirencester. *Speculum historiale*, ed. J. E. B. Mayor, 2 vols., RS (1863–9)

Robert of Jumièges. *The Missal of Robert of Jumièges*, ed. H. A. Wilson, HBS 11 (1896)

Robertson, A. J., ed., *Anglo-Saxon Charters*, 2nd ed. (Cambridge, 1956)

Rodwell, W., 'Anglo-Saxon Church Building: Aspects of Design and Construction', in *The Anglo-Saxon Church*, ed. L. A. S. Butler and R. K. Morris (London, 1986), pp. 156–75

Rodwell, W., and K. Rodwell, 'St Peter's Church, Barton-upon-Humber: Excavation and Structural Study, 1978–81', *AntJ* 62 (1982), 283–315

Rodwell, W., and E. C. Rouse, 'The Anglo-Saxon Rood and other Features in the South Porch of St Mary's Church, Breamore, Hampshire', *AntJ* 64 (1984), 298–325

Rollason, D., 'The Shrines of Saints in Later Anglo-Saxon England: Distribution and Significance', in *The Anglo-Saxon Church*, ed. L. A. S. Butler and R. K. Morris (London, 1986), pp. 32–43

Roosen-Runge, H. *See* Lindisfarne Gospels

Rosenthal, J. E., 'The Historiated Canon Tables of the Arenberg Gospels', (unpubl. PhD dissertation, Columbia Univ., 1974)

'Three Drawings in an Anglo-Saxon Pontifical: Anthropomorphic Trinity or Threefold Christ?', *Art Bulletin* 63 (1981), 547–62

Ross, A. S. C. *See* Durham *and* Lindisfarne Gospels

Ross, M. C., 'An Eleventh-Century English Bookcover', *Art Bulletin* 22 (1940), 83–5

Rossano Gospels. *Il codice purpureo di Rossano*, ed. C. Santoro (Rome, 1974)

See also Haseloff *and* Muñoz

Rouse, E. C., 'Late Saxon Painted Wall Plaster', *ArchJ* 139 (1982), 350–4

See also Rodwell

Sacramentary of Gellone. *See* Gellone

Sacramentary of Robert of Jumièges. *See* Robert of Jumièges

St Albans Psalter. *The St Albans Psalter (Albani Psalter)*, ed. O. Pächt, C. R. Dodwell and F. Wormald (London, 1960)

Salaville, S., *An Introduction to the Study of Eastern Liturgies*, trans. J. M. T. Barton (London, 1938)

Santoro, C. *See* Rossano Gospels

Sarum Missal. *The Sarum Missal, edited from Three Early Manuscripts*, ed. J. W. Legg (Oxford, 1916)

Saxl, F., 'The Ruthwell Cross', *JWCI* 6 (1943), 1–19

Schapiro, M., 'The Image of the Disappearing Christ: The Ascension in English Art around the Year 1000', *Gazette des Beaux-Arts*, 6th ser., 23 (1943), 135–52

'On the Aesthetic Attitude in Romanesque Art', in *Art and Thought*, ed. K. Bharatha Iyer (London, 1947), pp. 130–50

Schiel, H. *See* Codex Egberti

Schiller, G., *Iconography of Christian Art*, 2 vols., trans. J. Seligmann (London, 1971–2)

Schlosser, J. von, *Schriftquellen zur Geschichte der karolingischen Kunst*, Quellenschriften für Kunstgeschichte und Kunsttechnik des Mittelalters und der Neuzeit, Neue Folge 4 (Vienna, 1892)

Schmitt, F. S. *See* Anselm

Schnitzler, H., *Rheinische Schatzkammer* (Dusseldorf, 1957)

Schramm, P. E., *A History of the English Coronation*, trans. L. G. W. Legg (Oxford, 1937)

Herrschaftszeichen und Staatssymbolik. Beiträge zu ihrer Geschichte von dritten bis zum sechzehnten Jahrhundert, Schriften der Monumenta Germaniae historica 13, 3 vols. (Stuttgart, 1954–6)

Kaiser, Könige und Päpste, 4 vols. (Stuttgart, 1968–71)

Schramm, P. E. and F. Mütherich, *Denkmale der deutschen Könige und Kaiser. Ein*

Beitrag zur Herrschergeschichte von Karl dem Grossen bis Friedrich II (Munich, 1962)

Schuster, I., 'L'abbaye de Farfa et sa restauration au XIe siècle sous Hugues 1', *RB* 24 (1907), 374–402

Scott, J. *See* Glastonbury

Shepherd, M. H., 'Christology: A Central Problem of Early Christian Theology and Art', in *Age of Spirituality*, ed. K. Weitzmann (New York, 1980), pp. 101–20

Shorr, D. C., 'The Mourning Virgin and St John', *Art Bulletin* 22 (1940), 61–9

Silverman, M. J., 'Ælfric's Designation of the King as "Cristes sylfes speligend"', *RES* 35 (1984), 332–4

Sisam, C. and K., eds., *The Salisbury Psalter, edited from Salisbury Cathedral MS 150*, EETS os 242 (1959)

Skeat, W. W. *See* Ælfric

Sleeth, C. R., *Studies in Christ and Satan* (Toronto, 1982)

Smalley, B., *The Study of the Bible in the Middle Ages*, 3rd ed. (Oxford, 1983)

Smetana, C. L., 'Ælfric and the Early Medieval Homiliary', *Traditio* 15 (1959), 163–204

'Ælfric and the Homiliary of Haymo of Halberstadt', *Traditio* 17 (1961), 457–69

Stanley, E. G. *See* Durham *and* Lindisfarne Gospels

Steenbock, F., 'Kreuzförmige Typen frühmittelalterlicher Prachteinbände', in *Das erste Jahrtausend* I, ed. V. Elbern (Dusseldorf, 1962), 495–513

Stettiner, R., *Die illustrierten Prudentius-Handschriften* (Berlin, 1905)

Storms, G., *Anglo-Saxon Magic* (Hague, 1948)

Stubbs, W. *See* Gervase of Canterbury

Stuttgart Psalter. *Der Stuttgarter Bilderpsalter, Bibl. fol. 23, Württembergische Landesbibliothek Stuttgart*, ed. W. Hoffman *et al.*, 2 vols. (Stuttgart, 1965–8)

Suntrup, R., '*Te igitur*-Initialen und Kanonbilder in mittelalterlichen Sakramentarhandschriften', in *Text und Bild: Aspekte des Zusammenwirkens zweier Künste in Mittelalter und früher Neuzeit*, ed. C. Meier and U. Ruberg (Wiesbaden, 1980), pp. 278–382

Swarzenski, G., *Die Regensburger Buchmalerei des X. und XI. Jahrhunderts* (Leipzig, 1901)

Swarzenski, H., 'The Anhalt-Morgan Gospels', *Art Bulletin* 31 (1949), 77–83

Monuments of Romanesque Art: The Art of Church Treasures in North-Western Europe (London, 1954)

Swithun. *See* Frithegod *and* Lapidge

Symons, T. See *Regularis concordia*

Szarmach, P. E., ed., *Sources of Anglo-Saxon Culture*, Studies in Medieval Culture 20 (Kalamazoo, 1986)

See also Vercelli Homilies

Szövérffy, J., ' "Crux fidelis": Prolegomena to a History of the Holy Cross Hymns', *Traditio* 22 (1966), 1–41

Talbot, C. H. *See* Ailred *and* Goscelin

Taralon, J. *See* Grodecki

Taylor, H. M., 'Reculver Reconsidered', *ArchJ* 125 (1968), 291–6
  'The Anglo-Saxon Cathedral Church at Canterbury', *ArchJ* 126 (1969), 101–30
  'Tenth-Century Church Building in England and on the Continent', in *Tenth-Century Studies*, ed. D. Parsons (Chichester, 1975), pp. 141–68
  Anglo-Saxon Architecture III (Cambridge, 1978)
  See also L. A. S. Butler and R. K. Morris

Taylor, H. M. and J. Taylor, *Anglo-Saxon Architecture*, 2 vols. (Cambridge, 1965)
  'Architectural Sculpture in Pre-Norman England', *JBAA* 29 (1966), 3–51

Temple, E., *Anglo-Saxon Manuscripts 900–1066*, A Survey of Manuscripts Illuminated in the British Isles 2 (London, 1976)

Teyssèdre, B., *Le sacramentaire de Gellone et la figure humaine dans les manuscrits francs du VIIIe siècle* (Toulouse, 1959)

Theophilus. *De diversis artibus*, ed. C. R. Dodwell (London, 1961)

Thoby, P., *Le crucifix des origines au Concile de Trente*, 2 vols. (Nantes, 1959–63)

Thompson, A. H. *See* Durham

Thorpe, B., ed., *Ancient Laws and Institutes of England*, 2 vols. (London, 1840)
  See also Ælfric

Trahern, J. B., 'Amalarius *Be becnum*: A Fragment of the *Liber officialis* in Old English', *Anglia* 91 (1973), 475–8

Traube, L. *See* Audradus Modicus

Tschan, F. J., *Saint Bernward of Hildesheim*, 3 vols., Publications in Mediaeval Studies, University of Notre Dame 6, 12 and 13 (Notre Dame, Indiana, 1942–52)

Tselos, D., 'English Manuscript Illustration and the Utrecht Psalter', *Art Bulletin* 41 (1959), 137–49

Turner, D. H., 'The Prayer-Book of Archbishop Arnulph II of Milan', *RB* 70 (1960), 360–92
  See also Golden Age *and* New Minster

Tyrer, J. W., *Historical Survey of Holy Week, its Services and Ceremonial*, Alcuin Club Collections 29 (Oxford, 1932)

Ulrich. *See* Cluny

Underwood, P. A., 'The Fountain of Life in Manuscripts of the Gospels', *Dumbarton Oaks Papers* 5 (1950), 41–138

Unterkircher, F., *Zur Ikonographie und Liturgie des Drogo-Sakramentars* (Graz, 1977)

Ure, J. M. *See* Benedictine Office

Bibliography

Utrecht Psalter. *The Illustrations of the Utrecht Psalter*, ed. E. T. de Wald (Princeton, 1933)

Utrecht-Psalter: Vollständige Faksimile-Ausgabe im Originalformat der Handschrift 32 aus dem Besitz der Bibliothek der Rijksuniversiteit te Utrecht, ed. K. van der Horst and J. H. A. Engelbregt, 2 vols. (Graz, 1984)

Vallance, A., *Greater English Church Screens, Being Great Roods, Screenwork and Rood-Lofts in Cathedral, Monastic and Collegiate Churches in England and Wales* (London, 1947)

van Engen, J., 'Theophilus Presbyter and Rupert of Deutz: The Manual Arts and Benedictine Theology', *Viator* 11 (1980), 147–63

Venantius Fortunatus. *In laudem Sanctae Mariae virginis et matris Domini*, ed. F. Leo, MGH, Auct. antiq. 4.1 (Berlin, 1881), 371–80

Vexilla regis, ed. F. Leo, MGH, Auct. antiq. 4.1 (Berlin, 1881), 34–5

Vercelli Homilies. *Die Vercelli-Homilien i–viii*, ed. M. Förster, Bibliothek der angelsächsischen Prosa 12 (Hamburg, 1932)

Vercelli Homilies ix–xxiii, ed. P. E. Szarmach (Toronto, 1981)

Verdon, T. G., ed., *Monasticism and the Arts* (Syracuse, 1984)

Verey, C. D. *See* Durham

Vespasian Psalter. *The Vespasian Psalter (British Museum Cotton Vespasian A. i)*, ed. D. H. Wright, EEMF 14 (1967)

Vikan, G., 'Byzantine Art as a Mirror of its Public', *Apollo* 118 (1983), 164–7

Volbach, W. F. *See* Hubert

Walker, R. M., 'Illustrations to the Priscillian Prologues in the Gospel Manuscripts of the Carolingian Ada School', *Art Bulletin* 30 (1948), 1–10

Walther, H., *Carmina medii aevi posterioris latina* 1.1, *Initia carminum ac versuum medii aevi posterioris Latinorum* (Göttingen, 1969)

Ward, B. *See* Anselm

Warner, G. F. *See* Benedictional

Warner, R. D.-N. See *Early English Homilies*

Warren, F. E. *See* Antiphonary of Bangor *and* Leofric Missal

Way, A., 'The Gifts of Æthelwold, Bishop of Winchester (A.D. 963–984), to the Monastery of Peterborough', *ArchJ* 20 (1863), 355–66

Webb, D. M., 'The Holy Face of Lucca', *Anglo-Norman Studies* 9 (1987), 227–37

Weber, R. See *Itinerarium Egeriae*

Webster, L. *See* Golden Age

Weitzmann, K., '*Loca sancta* and the Representational Arts of Palestine', *Dumbarton Oaks Papers* 28 (1974), 31–55

Weitzmann, K., ed., *Age of Spirituality: A Symposium* (New York, 1980)

Werckmeister, O. K., 'Three Problems of Tradition in Pre-Carolingian Figure-Style. From Visigothic to Insular Illumination', *Proceedings of the Royal Irish Academy* 63 (1962–4), 167–89, pls. 21–34

Werner, A. E. *See* Lindisfarne Gospels

Whitelock, D., ed., *Anglo-Saxon Wills* (Cambridge, 1930)

'Scandinavian Personal Names in the Liber Vitae of Thorney Abbey', *Saga-Book of the Viking Society* 12 (1940), 127–53

See also P. Clemoes and K. Hughes

Wickham, G. W. G., 'The Romanesque Style in Medieval Drama', in *Tenth-Century Studies*, ed. D. Parsons (Chichester, 1975), pp. 115–22

Wieland, G. R., 'The Glossed Manuscript: Classbook or Library Book?', *ASE* 14 (1985), 153–73

Wilfrid. *See* Eddius *and* Frithegod

William of Malmesbury. *Gesta pontificum Anglorum*, ed. N. E. S. A. Hamilton, RS (1870)

See also Glastonbury

Willis, R., *Architectural History of some English Cathedrals, a Collection of Papers [in facs.]* Delivered *1842–63* (Chicheley, 1972–3)

Wilmart, A., 'Le receuil des poèmes et des prières de saint Pierre Damien', *RB* 41 (1929), 342–57

'The Prayers of the Bury Psalter', *Downside Review* 48 (1930), 198–216

Auteurs spirituels et textes dévots du moyen âge latin: études d'histoire littéraire (Paris, 1932)

'L'*Oratio Sancti Ambrosii* du missel romain', in *Auteurs spirituels*, pp. 101–25

'Les prières de saint Pierre Damien pour l'adoration de la croix', in *Auteurs spirituels*, pp. 138–146

'Les méditations sur le Saint-Esprit attribuées à saint Augustin', in *Auteurs spirituels*, pp. 415–56

'La prière *O intemerata*', in *Auteurs spirituels*, pp. 474–504

'Prières médiévales pour l'adoration de la croix', *EL* 46 (1932), 22–65

'Cinq textes de prière composés par Anselme de Lucques pour la Comtesse Mathilde', *Revue d'ascétique et de mystique* 19 (1938), 23–72

Precum libelli quattuor aevi Karolini (Rome, 1940)

See also Goscelin

Wilson, D. M., 'Tenth-Century Metalwork', in *Tenth-Century Studies*, ed. D. Parsons (Chichester, 1975), pp. 200–7

'The Art and Archaeology of Bedan Northumbria', in *Bede and Anglo-Saxon England. Papers in Honour of the 1300th Anniversary of the Birth of Bede, Given at Cornell University in 1973 and 1974*, ed. R. T. Farrell, BAR 46 (1978), 1–22

The Anglo-Saxons, 3rd ed. (Harmondsworth, 1981)

Wilson, H. A. *See* Benedictional *and* Robert of Jumièges

Winchester. *The Winchester Troper from MSS of the Xth and XIth Centuries*, ed. W. H. Frere, HBS 8 (1894)

See also New Minster

Winterbottom, M., ed., *Three Lives of English Saints*, Toronto Medieval Latin Texts 1 (Toronto, 1972)

Wood, M., 'The Making of King Æthelstan's Empire: An English Charlemagne?', in *Ideal and Reality in Frankish and Anglo-Saxon Society*, ed. P. Wormald, D. Bullough and R. Collins (Oxford, 1983), pp. 250–72

Woolf, R., *The English Religious Lyric in the Middle Ages* (Oxford, 1968)

Wormald, F., *English Drawings of the Tenth and Eleventh Centuries* (London, 1952)

Collected Writings, I: Studies in Medieval Art from the Sixth to the Twelfth Centuries, ed. J. J. G. Alexander, T. J. Brown and J. Gibbs (Oxford, 1984)

'The Miniatures in the Gospels of St Augustine, Corpus Christi College Cambridge, MS 286', in *Collected Writings*, pp. 13–35

'The "Winchester School" before St Æthelwold', in *Collected Writings*, pp. 76–84

'The Benedictional of St Ethelwold', in *Collected Writings*, pp. 85–100

'An English Eleventh-Century Psalter with Pictures', in *Collected Writings*, pp. 123–37

'Late Anglo-Saxon Art: Some Questions and Suggestions', in *Collected Writings*, pp. 105–10

'A Fragment of a Tenth-Century English Gospel Lectionary', in *Collected Writings*, pp. 101–4

'Anniversary Address 20 April 1967', *AntJ* 47 (1967), 159–65

See also Durham, Grodecki *and* St Albans Psalter

Wormald, P., D. Bullough and R. Collins, ed., *Ideal and Reality in Frankish and Anglo-Saxon Society: Studies presented to J. M. Wallace-Hadrill* (Oxford, 1983)

Wright, D. H. *See* Vespasian Psalter

Wulfstan of Winchester. *See* Frithegod, Lapidge *and* Winterbottom

Wulfstan of Worcester. *The Homilies of Wulfstan*, ed. D. Bethurum (Oxford, 1957)

Wulfstan II of Worcester. *The Portiforium of Saint Wulstan (Corpus Christi College, Cambridge, MS 391)*, ed. A. Hughes, 2 vols., HBS 89–90 (1958–60)

Yates, R., *An Illustration of the Monastic History and Antiquities of the Town and Abbey of St Edmund's Bury* (London, 1805)

York Gospels. *The York Gospels. A Facsimile with Introductory Essays by J. Alexander, P. McGurk, S. Keynes and B. Barr*, ed. N. Barker, Roxburghe Club (London, 1987)

Yorke, B. A. E., ed., *Bishop Æthelwold: His Career and Influence* (Woodbridge, 1988)

Zarnecki, G., '1066 and Architectural Sculpture', *PBA* 52 (1966), 87–104 and pls. i–xxiv

Index

For references to specific carvings, churches, manuscripts and other works of art see Catalogue and index to works of art

Index

portrait with episcopal cross, 61
Æthelric, abbot of Crowland
  gifts to Crowland, 11
Æthelwold, St, bishop of Winchester
  Abingdon retable, 17, 24; gifts to
    Abingdon, 8–9, 11; gifts to
    Peterborough, 63; gives treasure of
    Winchester to the poor, 9;
    represented celebrating mass, 46
altars
  dedications, 21; items placed on, 47–8;
    linked with Christ's death, 50, 55;
    and Resurrection, 14, 47, 48; and
    tomb, 22, 46, 82; of the cross,
    44–6, 48, 51; with representations of
    Christ in Majesty, 48–9; and
    Crucifixion groups, 49–50
Amalarius of Metz
  altars and Christ's tomb, 82; David and
    Louis the Pious, 140; Joseph and
    Nicodemus, 184; knowledge of, in
    England, 185–6; Liber officialis,
    183–6; Veneration of the Cross, 55,
    64
Ambrose, St
  Christ's words from the cross, 95–6;
    imitation of John, 100; John as
    witness to Christ's will, 98–9; Mary
    and Isaiah's prophecy, 28–9; Mary as
    symbol of faith, 100, 157; Mary's
    virginity, 99; prayer before a crucifix,
    100; tree of life, 178
angels
  adoring Christ, 123; at the Crucifixion,
    120–1; at the mass, 122; carved at
    Deerhurst, 18; holding crowns or
    sceptres, 29, 112, 128, 147; holding
    a mass-bread, 123; in Liber vitae, 26;
    in pictures of the baptism and second
    coming, 29, 147; names of, 121,
    124–6; on altars, 50; on Bernward
    Sarcophagus, 19; on Cuthbert coffin,
    19; round the cross, 94, 111,
    116–18, 119, 120–23
annunciation to the shepherds

site of, mentioned by Ælfric, 31
Anselm, St, archbishop of Canterbury
  Cur Deus homo, 171, 173; Mary's grief,
    157, 181; Mary Magdalen, 160–61;
    Mary mother of the creator, 180–1;
    Meditatio redemptionis humanae, 173;
    Oratio ad Christum, 181; prayers sent
    to Adelaide, 160; and to Matilda of
    Tuscany, 160; prayers to Mary (sent
    to Gundolf), 180–81; Proslogion,
    179–80; redemption theology,
    171–2, 173, 174–5
Anselm of Lucca
  prayer for Matilda of Tuscany, 102
antiphons and other chants
  in Sarum Missal, 138; to the cross, at
    Lauds and Vespers, 40; Ave rex noster,
    138; Christus vincit, 140; Crucem
    tuam, 163; Dicite in gentibus, 176;
    Dum fabricator mundi, 175; Gloria
    laus, 138, 140; Ingredere benedicte
    Domine, 16; Propter lignum, 176; Salve
    rex, 138; Super omnia ligna cedrorum,
    177
Antiphonary of Bangor, 173
apostles
  at Reichenau, 7; at Wearmouth, 13; on
    Abingdon retable, 17, 24; on
    Cuthbert Coffin, 19; on Waltham
    altar, 17; on Wilton alb, 24
art
  analogous to the Holy Places and relics,
    31; and to the liturgy, 187; as an aid
    to prayer and meditation, 12, 23–5,
    38–9, 59–60; as a form of proof, 7,
    31; as metaphor, 4; commemorative,
    25; comments on, by Ælfric, 15; and
    Bede, 12–13; and Libri Carolini,
    5–8, 13, 39, 187; early Christian, 4,
    42–3; for display, 8–12, 23; and
    instruction, 4–7, 14, 15, 27; and
    protection, 18–20; human detail in,
    31; iconic and symbolic, 12, 20–23;
    making past events present, 24–5,
    30–1, 158, 187; narrative, 27;